D1581177

De

Edited by Guy Lodge and Katie Schmuecker with Adam Coutts

Contents

Institute for Public Policy Research

About ippr

The Institute for Public Policy Research is the UK's leading progressive think tank, producing cutting-edge research and innovative policy ideas for a just, democratic and sustainable world. Since 1988, we have been at the forefront of progressive debate and policymaking in the UK. Through our independent research and analysis we define new agendas for change and provide practical solutions to challenges across the full range of public policy issues. With offices in both London and Newcastle, we ensure our outlook is as broad-based as possible, while our Global Change programme extends our partnerships and influence beyond the UK, giving us a truly world-class reputation for high quality research.

About the contributors

John Adams is a consultant and was a Special Adviser at the Welsh Office during the 1997 Referendum and the passage of the 1998 Government of Wales Act.

Pete Alcock is professor of social policy and administration at the University of Birmingham and director of the ESRC Third Sector Research Centre.

David Bell is professor of economics in the School of Management, University of Stirling and Budget Adviser to the Finance Committee, Scottish Parliament

Adam Coutts is co-editor of *Options for Britain*.

Dalia Ben-Galim is a senior research fellow at ippr.

Derek Birrell is professor of social administration and policy at the University of Ulster.

John Curtice is professor of politics at the University of Strathclyde, deputy director of CREST, and director of the Social Statistics Laboratory, University of Strathclyde.

Scott L. Greer is assistant professor, University of Michigan School of Public Health and a senior research fellow at LSE Health.

Charlie Jeffery is professor of politics at the University of Edinburgh.

Ewart Keep is deputy director of SKOPE Research Centre, Cardiff School of Social Sciences, Cardiff University.

Guy Lodge is an associate director of ippr and a visiting fellow in the Department of Politics and International Relations at the University of Oxford.

James McCormick is the Joseph Rowntree Foundation's Scotland Adviser.

Eleanor McDowell is co-founder of McCormick-McDowell research partnership. She was previously a lecturer in the School of Law and Social Sciences at Glasgow Calendonian University.

Rick Muir is a senior research fellow at ippr.

Emma Norris is a researcher at the RSA.

Richard Parry is a reader in social policy at the University of Edinburgh.

Jonathan Payne is a senior researcher at SKOPE Research Centre, Cardiff School of Social Sciences, Cardiff University.

Gareth Rees is an associate director of SKOPE Research Centre, Cardiff School of Social Sciences, Cardiff University.

Katie Schmuecker is a senior research fellow at ippr north.

Alan Trench is an Hon. Fellow, School of Social and Political Studies, University of Edinburgh and author of the 'Devolution Matters' blog.

Steve Wilcox is professor of housing policy at York University.

Acknowledgements

The editors would like to thank all those who have contributed to the ideas contained in this book, through the project conferences and informal discussions. In particular we would like to thank all the authors who have contributed to the book. A special thanks are also due to the members of our Project Advisory Group: Fiona Armstrong, Bobby Clulow, Angela Evans, David Guy, Professor Charlie Jeffery, Professor Jim Gallagher, James McEldownie, Barry McEvoy and Lisa Williams.

We would like to thank all those who participated in the conferences that informed and shaped this project, including: John Adams, Rachel Arrundale, Professor David Bell, Sir Michael Bichard, Professor Alistair Cole, Professor John Curtice, Dr Jennifer Dixon, Professor Jim Gallagher, Neil Gibson, Gary Gillespie, Dr Scott Greer, Gareth Hall, David Halpern, Professor Charlie Jeffery, Henry Johnston, Richard Johnston, Professor Michael Keating, Professor Ewart Keep, Iain McWhirter, Andy Milne, Dr Rick Muir, Carey Oppenheim, Richard Parry, Professor Lindsay Paterson, Emyr Roberts, Professor Jon Shaw, John Simpson, Paul Steeples, Jason Strelitz, Mike Sullivan, Alan Trench, Professor Steve Wilcox and Professor Gareth Williams.

The editors would also like to thank Dafydd Tristan, Giles Wilkes and Malcolm Dean for kindly agreeing to review specific aspects of the book.

We would like to acknowledge the help and support of Holly Andrew, Ed Cox, Tim Finch, Georgina Kyriacou, Joe Millar, Suzanne Roy, Joanne Thomas and Lisa Williams.

Finally ippr and ippr north gratefully acknowledge the generous financial support for this project from ESRC Knowledge Transfer, the Welsh Assembly Government and the Office of the First Minister and Deputy First Minister in Northern Ireland. Without their willingness to invest in and contribute to original and independent research, this project could not have been undertaken. The findings of our research, however, do not necessarily represent the views of our funding partners.

1. Preface

Guy Lodge, Katie Schmuecker and Adam Coutts

This is the third volume in the series which analyses the impact devolution has had on public policy across the UK in the first full decade of devolution. The two earlier volumes, *Devolution in Practice* and *Devolution in Practice 2006,* were published in 2002 and 2005 respectively[1].

The approach adopted in this volume is similar to that in previous editions. Leading academic and policy experts have been asked to address the following key questions in their specialist area:

- What policy approach has each devolved administration adopted?
- Has policy diverged, and if so why?
- What can we learn from the different approaches taken by the devolved nations?
- What impact have different approaches adopted across the nations had on policy outcomes?

Contributors to the project were asked to present papers to an expert audience at four major conferences held across the UK in 2009. The first conference, *Devolution and life chances*, was held in February 2009 in London. The second, *Devolution, communities and regeneration*, took place in Cardiff in May. The third, *Devolution in a downturn: responding to the recession*, was held in Belfast in June. The final conference, *Devolution, governance and delivery: does difference matter?*, was held in Edinburgh in October. At each conference a panel of practitioners, made up of senior officials from the devolved administrations and relevant Whitehall departments, responded to the papers presented by the policy experts. We are very grateful to all those who participated in these conferences.

The conferences also allowed us to cover some policy areas that are not explicitly captured in the final book. For instance we do not have chapters here on transport policy or education policy but both were important themes of the conferences. All the presentations are available from the ippr website.

Devolution in Practice 2010 is divided into four parts.

- **Part 1: Devolution and social citizenship** looks at the impact policy divergence is having on accounts of social citizenship and how the devolution settlement needs to be reformed to respond to this dynamic. It locates this analysis in the radically transformed political context in which devolution now operates. The UK is now made up of four distinct centres of political power, each governed by different political parties.

1. Both are available to order from www.ippr.org/publicationsandreports

- **Part 2: Devolution in a downturn** looks at how the recession has affected the devolved administrations and how they have responded to the first major economic downturn in the history of devolution. It also covers approaches to economic development and skills policy.
- **Part 3: Public services and social policy** covers a number of major policy areas.
- Finally, **Part 4: Devolution and delivery**, covers the different approaches the devolved administrations have pioneered in terms of public administration and delivery.

2. The devolution paradox

Charlie Jeffery, Guy Lodge and Katie Schmuecker

Devolution remains one of the most radical and important set of reforms undertaken by the 1997 Labour government. The creation of the Northern Ireland Assembly, Scottish Parliament and National Assembly for Wales amounted to a decentralisation of power unlikely to be overturned by any future UK government. Devolution had multiple rationales. On the one hand it was an expression of Scottish and Welsh identity, creating elected institutions to embody the difference of those nations and to recognise them formally as components of the UK's multi-national state. On the other it was a sort of insurance policy, providing protection against rule by a Westminster government with little mandate in those nations. In Northern Ireland the narrative was one of building a sustainable peace through locally accountable, cross-community institutions.

What was less central to the devolution debates of a decade ago was the likelihood that creating new centres of political decision-making with significant powers would allow territorially distinctive policy agendas to emerge, and result in variations in policy outcomes from one part of the UK to the next. Indeed, the fact that devolved governments might want to do things differently than had been the case at Westminster appeared to surprise and annoy the UK Government, with Paddy Ashdown's diaries noting an exasperated Tony Blair telling him, 'you can't have Scotland doing something different from the rest of Britain' with regard to tuition fees (Ashdown 2001: 446). Similarly, Henry McLeish, Scottish First Minister from 2000–1, recalls how difficult the discussions with UK government were (and the 'pit language' used) when the then Scottish Executive resolved to introduce free personal care in Scotland (McLeish 2004: 142).

But the emergence of distinctive devolved policies did not surprise anyone with knowledge of how devolved or federal systems of government operate elsewhere. Managing policy differences and associated resource distribution issues across territories is simply everyday politics in devolved and federal states, and as the contributions to this book demonstrate, policy variation is increasingly evident across the UK. This is not a new phenomenon as such – there were policy differences prior to the creation of the devolved administrations – but it is more visible now as a result of direct election.

This book has been written against a backdrop of considerable political and economic change. Devolution was born in benign times: the same party was in power or leading a coalition in all parts of Great Britain (the party political system has always differed in Northern Ireland), and was able to take advantage of a sustained period of economic growth and rising public spending. The conditions for the next 10 years, however, could not be more different.

In 2007 the nationalist parties entered government for the first time, in coalition with Labour in Wales and as a minority government in Scotland. This put different parties in power in different parts of the UK for the first time since devolution, and increased the likelihood of policy divergence. The establishment of a Conservative–Liberal Democrat coalition government in Westminster following the 2010 general election has transformed this situation further still.

This political upheaval has mirrored a rapid transformation in the economic sphere (see David Bell in this volume). In 2008 the UK entered its worst recession in decades, heralding the prospect of deep cuts to public spending, a development that is likely to put questions about resource allocation high on the public and political agenda.

Making these cuts will fall to the coalition government. But with only 23 of its 342 MPs coming from Scotland and Wales the new government is likely to face serious questions about its 'mandate' to govern all parts of the UK. This will be particularly acute for the Conservatives – the leading coalition partner – who have only one MP in Scotland. Indeed the 2010 general election underlines the extent to which the UK is divided electorally: with Conservative support largely confined to England (or more accurately to the South of England and the Midlands) and Labour dominant in Scotland and Wales. Political imbalances in the make-up of the UK government at Westminster and its representation across the nations are likely to test the devolution settlement in the coming years, particularly in an era of significant spending cuts.

This edition of *Devolution in Practice* also comes amid a vigorous debate about the further evolution of the institutional arrangements for devolution. The All-Wales Convention reported in November 2009 with a recommendation that a referendum be held on the transfer of full legislative powers to the National Assembly for Wales, with the National Assembly resolving in February 2010 to begin the process of calling the referendum. The coalition agreement signed by the Conservative and Liberal Democrat parties commits the Government to holding a referendum, though they have yet to specify when this will take place. In June 2009 the Calman Commission on Scottish Devolution recommended a modest set of changes to the Scottish Parliament's legislative powers and a substantial – if controversial – measure of fiscal autonomy. The new Westminster coalition government has also said that it will implement the Calman proposals. In the same month that Calman was published the Scottish Government published its own White Paper – *Choosing Scotland's Future* – which argued for two alternatives to the status quo: independence, the Scottish National party's historic aim; or 'devolution-max', the full devolution of legislative and tax-raising powers in domestic matters. In February 2010 the Scottish Government launched a consultation on a draft referendum bill, with the intention of holding a referendum in November 2010. In Northern Ireland – in its characteristic stop-start way – agreement was finally reached in February 2010 about the devolution of powers in policing and justice first envisaged over a decade ago.

In England, there are some signs that the hitherto subterranean debate on English identity and governance is now gathering momentum, although it is far from clear where it will end up (Kenny and Lodge forthcoming). The overwhelming strength of the Conservative party in England – it now holds 297 of the 533 English seats – means that there is less pressure to address the so-called West Lothian Question (a reference to the anomaly created by devolution which allows non-English MPs to vote on matters only affecting England). Indeed, given the weak mandate of the coalition government outside of England, David Cameron is going to need to tread carefully in the way he handles relations with the devolved nations. He is pushing a 'respect' agenda, which purports to achieve greater dialogue and openness between the Westminster and devolved parliaments. He also appears to have rowed back on measures that might provoke tension with the devolved nations. The party's policy of introducing a version of 'English votes on English laws' (which would restrict the voting rights of non-English MPs at Westminster) has been kicked into the long grass with the establishment of a commission to consider the West Lothian question, and Cameron has also offered a short-term deferral of spending cuts in Scotland and Wales. However, while he will be anxious to appeal to Scottish and Welsh sensitivities so as not to undermine the union, Cameron is also going to come under serious pressure from the growing English nationalist wing of the Conservative Party to address English grievances with the devolution settlement. Conservative MPs tend to think that England has suffered as a result of asymmetric devolution and that the devolved nations are too generously funded (Kenny and Lodge forthcoming).

What we clearly do not have is the 'settled will' that some felt the initial devolution reforms would realise. It is not yet clear which directions the devolution debates in the different parts of the UK will take in the coming years. Much will depend on the attitude of the new coalition government – and the response from the devolved nations – to questions of further-reaching devolution, the issue of how to govern England, and the meaning of 'union' in the post-devolution era. But the general tendency has so far been a centrifugal one: each part of the UK is the locus of a largely compartmentalised, even insular debate about the appropriate structures for governing that part of the UK and there are still no effective mechanisms for systematic coordination across jurisdictions, whether as means of conflict resolution or of identifying common purpose.

The consequence is a gradual differentiation of how policy is made in each part of the UK, and of the outcomes experienced by citizens. As this book demonstrates, there do exist some powerful forces for convergence, such as the UK's common market, the generally shared set of values and policy preferences, the sheer weight of current policy commitments and the impact of policy overspills (see also Schmuecker and Adams 2005, Keating 2002). But devolution has also unleashed countervailing forces that allow for significant divergence, resulting in a growing number of policy differences opening up across the UK. There are of course the headline divergences, such as different approaches to tuition fees, prescription charges and in Scotland, free personal care for the elderly (see Birrell in this volume). Beyond these well known cases, this book identifies a number of other areas of divergence, for example in the approach to criminal justice policy (see Muir), social housing (see Wilcox), adult skills policy (see Keep), approaches to managing healthcare and defining its priorities (see Greer) and the different approaches to public administration and delivery (see Parry and Alcock). Such differences are to be welcomed: they demonstrate that devolution is working.

This chapter provides a context for exploring and understanding these instances and consequences of policy variation. It does so by considering the idea of shared 'social citizenship' and its meaning – or meanings – in a devolved UK. Ideas about social citizenship are at heart ideas about the territorial scale at which citizens express solidarity with one another. Most ideas of this nature have focused on the scale of the postwar state; devolution opens up the scope to express and secure solidarity on smaller – and multiple – scales. We explore the possibilities of a 'rescaling' of social citizenship by focusing on what the UK's citizens think. The scale and content of shared citizenship may depend on how the public view territorial policy variation between different parts of the same state. We set out below – and offer some explanations for – a 'devolution paradox' in public opinion. Citizens appear to want devolved institutions to have more powers yet they appear also to be uncomfortable with territorial policy variation. We conclude by considering some of the difficult issues that policymakers might need to confront in addressing this devolution paradox.

What kind of union?

Does it matter if one part of the UK has free personal care for the elderly while the others do not? Or that a prescription has to be paid for in England but not in Wales? Or that a patient may spend less time waiting for a hospital appointment in England than in other parts of the UK? The answer is: it might, but that depends on the wider set of beliefs about community and solidarity that citizens might have. It depends in particular on understandings of 'union' in the UK – and what role and purpose is attached to union after devolution. Some understandings of union propose that there should be some limits to (or in certain cases no) variations in policy outcomes by territory, with commonality giving meaning to an overarching sense of British community. Others propose that policy should vary from one part of the UK to the next in line with the differences in preferences that Scottish, Welsh or Northern Irish communities have, as expressed through devolved democratic processes. The current devolution settlement treads something of a middle line, with core welfare entitlements reserved to the UK level, and therefore held in common, while other areas – most notably public services – are devolved with few legal constraints.

The idea of emphasising shared entitlements and rights for all citizens has been central to the debate that Gordon Brown has sought to promote over the last decade on 'Britishness', by highlighting the values and interests that might bind all UK citizens in common cause. For Brown, these values are embodied in the institutions that underpin the union, citing the BBC and NHS, to which all have equal access regardless of geography or income (Jeffery 2009b). In practice, however, the appeal to these particular UK institutions is complicated by the fact that the *British* National Health Service (if there ever was such a thing) has now been superseded by four NHSs and the BBC is characterised more by four national conversations than by one (Fraser 2008).

The Calman Commission came to similar conclusions regarding the importance of emphasising some shared UK-wide entitlements and rights. Its first report was pointedly titled 'the future of Scottish devolution *within the union*' (our emphasis). In that report the Commission highlighted the dimension of 'social union', asking 'how uniform or integrated a welfare state the UK should be, and just how much of a common social citizenship should be shared across the UK' (Commission on Scottish Devolution 2009: 35). Its answer was clear in its final report: 'The Scottish Parliament and the UK Parliament should confirm that each agrees to the elements of the common social rights that make up the social union and also the responsibilities that go with them' (ibid: 64).

The notion of a 'social' union is a novel one in the UK which has attracted novel criticism. Michael Keating calls it a form of 'neo-unionism' (Keating 2009: 130-2). Traditional unionism opposed devolution, but accepted difference among the component parts of the UK. Neo-unionists by contrast, according to Keating, are pro devolution, but seek to limit differences between the different parts of the UK by establishing commitments or regulations for common policy standards. This conception would seem something of a caricature, since it is difficult to find any serious political actor arguing in favour of imposing common standards in devolved policy areas. Nonetheless it does raise important questions for unionists, in particular about the appropriate balance between UK-wide and devolved accounts of citizenship and social rights.

As Keating notes, the 'neo-unionism' of Brown and Calman has seized on the terminology associated with T.H. Marshall's conception of 'social citizenship' (Marshall 1950 [1992]). Marshall – whose most influential work on this subject was written in the late 1940s, in the period when the postwar UK welfare state was established – identified different and inter-related components of citizenship. First came civil rights, which emerged in the 18th century; these then became a platform for the achievement of political rights (most notably the extension of the suffrage) in the 19th and 20th centuries; and these then became the platform for the establishment of social rights in the form of the welfare state after World War II.

Marshall understood citizenship rights as 'national'. Though he was curiously ambiguous on what the 'nation' was (he appeared at times to focus solely on England and to ignore the rest of the UK), his work was fundamental to a tradition of postwar writing on the welfare state – in the UK and in comparative analysis – and has underpinned widespread and powerful normative assumptions that welfare *should* be delivered on the same terms to all citizens across the whole of the state territory. If it is not, if devolution undermines common statewide standards, then it 'threatens the Welfare State', marking the end of 'the belief that a benign government at Westminster can secure the distribution of benefits and burdens on the basis not of geography but of need' (Bogdanor 2001: 153-4). There may even be, as US and Canadian scholars have put it, a risk of a 'race to the bottom' as devolved regions compete on (lowering) welfare standards (for example, Peterson 1995, Harrison 2006).

So, *'obviously'*, according to Dietmar Braun, 'social policy and health policy are areas which *need* a high degree of standardisation and harmonisation' (Braun 2000: 15, our emphasis). Elsewhere Keith Banting and Richard Corbett (2002: 19) tugged the heartstrings to ask the rhetorical question: 'Does a sick baby in one region have access to the same level of care on similar terms and conditions as a sick baby in another region of the same country?' We are left in no doubt as to what our answer should be. Strikingly, the Calman Commission echoed the very point, minus the sick baby, in its arguments for common, UK-wide social rights: 'It does not matter whether an individual who is ill is in Caithness or Cornwall: he or she has free access to health care when and where they need it, supported by the UK taxpayer' (Commission on Scottish Devolution 2008: 36). Of course it should be noted that beyond a commitment to free access to health care, this does not preclude health *policy* varying between Caithness and Cornwall.

Although it may be 'obvious' to some that the state should do the same things for its citizens no matter where they live, it is clearly not so to others. McEwen and Henderson (2005), Beland and Lecours (2007) and others (c.f. Jeffery 2006) have identified attempts in devolved nations and regions in the UK, Belgium, Canada and elsewhere to enlist social policy to agendas of maximising sub-state autonomy, in some cases including independent statehood. A distinctive social policy agenda can become part of a 'nation-building' project – 'welfare nationalism' – at territorial scales smaller than the state, just as it did at the statewide scale in Marshall's understanding: for Marshall social rights secured the inclusion of disadvantaged social classes into a 'national' citizenship. For welfare nationalists – a category that can encompass both supporters of independence and of fuller autonomy within the state – a distinctive agenda on social rights may be a vital underpinning of distinctive territorial community within (and in some cases against) the state.

Mooney *et al* (2006: 492), for example, point to the scope devolution has created for the renegotiation of welfare arrangements in Scotland and Wales and the questions this raises about 'the nature of UK citizenship – and of citizenship in the devolved nations'. And Simeon (2003: 232), reflecting on post-devolution innovations in social policy, noted that the devolved administrations understood the 'appropriate boundaries of social citizenship ... more broadly than London'. Indeed, the tendency in Scotland and Wales since devolution has been to restore some of the universalist principles that (perhaps mythically) evoke the original premises of the postwar welfare state. It may well be argued that universal entitlements to long-term care, free university tuition or prescriptions are questionable subsidies for the middle classes but they are clearly not evidence of a 'race to the bottom'.

Such a distinctive, universalist approach may, however, provide evidence of a rescaling of the territorial community at which citizens seek to express solidarity with one another. Nations and regions within the state may be perceived as a better locus for guaranteeing social rights than the state as a whole. There is some evidence to suggest that Scottish support for devolution in the run-up to the 1997 referendum was based on a desire of Scots to insulate themselves from UK-level governments that did not share Scottish traditions of social solidarity (McEwen and Henderson 2005). There is a similar pattern in Quebec in Canada of seeking to contract out from the social policy jurisdiction of a central government no longer trusted to deliver traditional understandings of social rights. In other places the perceived problem is not the centre, but other devolved regions, typically where economically stronger regions – such as Flanders, or Bavaria, or parts of northern Italy – resent 'their' tax revenues being transferred to other regions in the interests of guaranteeing common, statewide social rights (Jeffery 2006). In each case a smaller scale of 'solidarity community' is presented as more in the interests of the devolved region than a statewide one.

This is certainly the kind of case made by the Scottish Government in its 2009 White Paper, which argues that there are 'traditional Scottish values' – by implication not British ones – 'of striving for a fairer and more inclusive society, combining equality of opportunity to thrive and excel, with support for those in need' (Scottish Government 2009: 59), and that maximising Scottish autonomy is the way to guarantee their expression. Significantly, even the Scottish Government can envisage these 'traditional Scottish values' being achieved within UK 'union', even if it would prefer independence. But this would be a union in which social rights would, and in the Scottish Government view *should*, vary from place to place in the UK.

A milder form of the same argument – presented amid much rhetorical flourish, but in the end with little substance – was Rhodri Morgan's imagery of 'clear red water' between what he saw as 'traditional' Labour values in Wales and the pro-market policies in the public services promoted by 'new' Labour under Tony Blair (Jeffery 2006). The thrust is the same: to challenge understandings that social rights have to be the same everywhere and to argue instead that they may and should differ where values differ, even with the same state.

To put this another way, even if social citizenship was something that was guaranteed in uniform ways across the whole state territory, there is no reason that it should continue to be. One of the key insights of Marshall's seminal work on social citizenship was that different kinds of citizenship rights interacted with one another to produce shifts in the content of citizenship. Devolution entails the recalibration of political rights: the establishment of rights of political participation in devolved democratic processes. If the establishment of statewide political rights in the 19th and 20th centuries became a platform for statewide social rights after World War II, should it surprise us that devolved political rights become a platform for arguments that (at least some) social rights are something to be achieved at devolved scales? Equally, it should not surprise us that while significant political rights also reside at the UK level, arguments will continue to be made for (at least some) social rights to be achieved at the UK-wide level. Social citizenship in Marshall's terms might well, in other words, be multi-levelled.

Neo-unionism and welfare nationalism offer important, and polarising, perspectives on how to conceive social citizenship in a devolved UK, but in practice neither of these positions adequately reflects mainstream public opinion. Indeed the shortcomings of both of these positions are exposed by the complexities and paradoxes of public attitudes towards devolution and social citizenship, which we explore in the next section.

Unravelling the devolution paradox

Whether or not territorial policy variation matters is, then, a moot point. The debate on policy variation is inherently normative, based on deep-seated beliefs about different scales of community, and reflected in seemingly irreconcilable claims that follow from those beliefs about the right constitutional architecture. In that sense we cannot say there is a right or a wrong answer to the question 'does variation matter?' What we can do is explore public opinion to identify what resonance these different claims have among those in whose name they are made: the UK's citizens.

The UK has, relatively speaking, very good data on post-devolution public attitudes through the findings of the British Social Attitudes Survey and related surveys in Scotland, Wales and Northern Ireland,[1] with more recent international public attitudes work placing our knowledge of Scotland and Wales in a comparative context.[2] But what they reveal is a contradiction. On the one hand, people consistently claim to want greater devolution and the power to take more decisions in devolved settings. Table 2.1 shows that clear majorities of the Scots and Welsh think their devolved administrations rather than the UK government should make 'most of the important decisions' on the NHS, schools and welfare benefits (that is, the heartland issues of Marshallian social citizenship), while on defence the preference flips to the UK government.

At a more general level, surveys have also shown repeatedly that while the Scots, the Welsh and Northern Irish think the UK government does have most influence over the way their territory is run, majorities think that the devolved administrations should

---

1. The Scottish Social Attitudes Survey, the Wales Life and Times Survey, and the Northern Ireland Life and Times Survey.

2. The Citizenship after the Nation-State (CANS) survey, coordinated from the University of Edinburgh was fielded as a common, translated questionnaire in 14 European regions in five states in spring 2009. See www.institute-of-governance.org/major_projects/citizen_after_the_nation_state. Unfortunately the CANS data does not cover England or Northern Ireland.

Table 2.1: Who should make the most important decisions for Wales/Scotland (2007)

	Scottish Parliament/Welsh Assembly Government (%)	UK Government (%)
Scotland		
NHS	63	25
Schools	63	14
Welfare benefits	63	18
Defence and foreign affairs	34	58
Wales		
NHS	61	26
Schools	56	18
Welfare benefits	58	22
Defence and foreign affairs	21	72

have the most influence (for example, Jeffery 2009a, Curtice and Seyd 2009). Data from the new Citizenship after the Nation-State (or CANS) survey, which measured attitudes across 14 European regions[3], shows that respondents in all but one region thought that the regional level of government should have more influence than it currently does. As Table 2.2 shows, Scotland and Wales are strongly of this view, showing the biggest gap between those who think the devolved administrations should have most influence and those who think it does.

In similar vein Table 2.3 reports responses from the CANS survey on constitutional options on a five-point scale ranging from no regional government to independence, ranking them by the total of those whose preferences is to move beyond the current status quo, either with more regional powers or with independence. Again Scotland and Wales are towards the top of the table among a small group – also including Catalonia, Brittany and Galicia – with more than 50 per cent of respondents arguing for more powers than the regional level currently has. However it is important to note that while Scotland and Wales (along with Catalonia and Bavaria) display the strongest support for independence, in each case at least twice as many people support more powers than independence.

On the other hand, and despite wanting more powers and influence for their devolved administrations, it is less clear that people want this to lead – as it logically ought – to differences in policy outcomes. Table 2.4 reports on a broadly phrased question fielded across Great Britain, with variations in Wales and Scotland in 2003, showing

3 We use 'region' in this context as shorthand, but acknowledge that some of these 'regions' would be better described as 'nations'.

Table 2.2. Which is correct in your opinion? Regional government <u>does</u> have most influence or regional government <u>should</u> have most influence?

	a) Regional should (%)	b) Regional does (%)	a) – b)
Scotland	73	38	35
Wales	70	40	30
Catalonia	79	58	21
Brittany	76	58	18
Salzburg	89	73	16
Upper Austria	82	67	15
Vienna	79	65	14
Alsace	75	61	14
Thuringia	76	63	13
Lower Saxony	73	60	13
Galicia	65	54	11
Ile de France	66	53	9
Bavaria	75	67	8
Castilla la Mancha	55	58	-3

Table 2.3: Level of support for different constitutional options (%)

	a) No reg. government	b) Fewer powers	c) Status quo	d) More powers	e) Indep'ce	d) + e)
Catalonia	2	7	15	51	21	72
Scotland	7	4	28	39	20	59
Brittany	1	2	31	52	5	57
Wales	9	6	28	42	14	56
Galicia	5	8	26	51	3	54
Alsace	1	2	42	41	6	47
Bavaria	3	8	41	29	15	44
Thuringia	9	13	28	39	5	44
Salzburg	3	7	45	42	2	44
Upp. Austria	3	5	47	41	2	43
C. la Mancha	7	10	37	40	1	41
Ile de France	3	3	35	38	0	38
Lower Sax	6	13	40	30	4	34
Vienna	5	12	51	27	2	29

that the English are most in favour of policy uniformity, but also that majorities in Wales and Scotland are too, even in areas like tuition fees (Scotland) and prescriptions (Wales), where different devolved policies have been introduced. The 2009 CANS survey has added further nuance to our understanding of this preference for uniformity. It showed that with one exception (juvenile crime in Catalonia) majorities of respondents in all regions felt that a series of policy issues – alongside juvenile crime, unemployment benefits, tuition fees and long-term care – should be dealt with uniformly across the whole of the state concerned rather than being a matter for each region to decide itself.

Table 2.4. Attitudes towards territorial policy variation in Britain, 2003 (%)

	Should be the same in every part of Britain	Should be allowed to vary
England		
Standards for services such as health, schools, roads and police	66	33
Scotland		
Standards for services such as health, schools, roads and police	59	40
Level of unemployment benefit	56	42
University tuition fees	56	40
Wales		
Standards for services such as health, schools, roads and police	55	44
Level of unemployment benefit	57	41
University tuition fees	58	40
Cost of NHS prescriptions	63	37

Sources: Data collated by John Curtice from British and Scottish Social Attitudes Survey 2003; Wales Life and Times survey 2003

The CANS survey also showed that majorities in all 14 regions surveyed favoured a role for central government in evening out economic disparities (Table 2.5). Unsurprisingly, those regions with enduring economic weaknesses – including Wales – are most in favour of government intervention. But Scotland – which is close to the UK average on key economic indicators – and even places like Bavaria and Salzburg which are net contributors to inter-regional transfers effected by central governments – also favour a role for central government in evening out economic differences.

The above discussion has revealed what the CANS team has labelled the 'devolution paradox': an apparent contradiction between the desire for greater powers for

Table 2.5: Responses to question: 'Should central governments step in to even out economic differences between regions?' (%)

	Yes they should	No they should not
Castilla la Mancha	90.3	5.8
Brittany	85.4	8.0
Galicia	84.4	9.2
Ile de France	84.1	12.5
Wales	81.1	17.3
Thuringia	80.8	15.6
Alsace	77.8	16.2
Vienna	77.7	20.5
Lower Saxony	75.1	20.6
Scotland	71.4	25.2
Salzburg	71.0	28.4
Catalonia	70.8	26.2
Upper Austria	67.6	30.8
Bavaria	57.8	38.4

devolved government – implying a greater likelihood that the policies delivered by devolved governments will vary from place to place – and the desire for uniformity of policy outcomes. It is not yet clear how to interpret this paradox. It may be that while people want more decisions to be made at the devolved level, the fear that other people might 'do better' under such a system results in people opting for uniformity. It may be that they understand 'uniformity' as to be delivered at the standard of the policy that applies in their jurisdiction. But it may also be that other factors intervene to lend greater weight to one aspect of the devolution paradox so that it outweighs the other. Two such factors appear possible.

The first concerns community: whether people give priority to Scottish, or Welsh (or Catalan, or Bavarian) community over that at the statewide scale. One route into this question is to explore how citizens balance senses of sub-state identity (Scottish, Welsh and so on) over statewide (British) identity. There is now a very substantial time series for Scotland, Wales and England on the so-called 'Moreno' question, which shows that the Scots have the strongest sense of exclusively or predominantly sub-state (Scottish) identity, the Welsh less so but there is still a substantial sub-state Welsh identity, and the English the least, although even here a significant minority identify themselves as predominantly or exclusively English (Table 2.6).

Table 2.6: Trends in Moreno National Identity 1992–2007 (%)

	1992	1997	1999	2000	2001	2003	2005	2006	2007
Scotland									
Scottish not British	19	23	32	37	36	31	32	33	37
More Scottish than British	40	38	35	31	30	34	32	32	30
Equally Scottish and British	33	27	22	21	24	22	22	21	28
More British than Scottish	3	4	3	3	3	4	4	4	5
British not Scottish	3	4	4	4	3	4	5	5	6
Wales									
Welsh not British	n/a	17	17	n/a	24	21	n/a	n/a	24
More Welsh than British	n/a	26	19	n/a	23	27	n/a	n/a	20
Equally Welsh and British	n/a	34	37	n/a	28	29	n/a	n/a	32
More British than Welsh	n/a	10	8	n/a	11	8	n/a	n/a	9
British not Welsh	n/a	12	14	n/a	11	9	n/a	n/a	9
England									
English not British	n/a	7	17	19	17	17	n/a	n/a	19
More English than British	n/a	17	15	14	13	19	n/a	n/a	14
Equally English and British	n/a	45	37	34	42	31	n/a	n/a	31
More British than English	n/a	14	11	14	9	13	n/a	n/a	14
British not English	n/a	9	14	12	11	10	n/a	n/a	12

Table 2.7. Identity using the Moreno scale

	Just 'region'	Region > state	Equal	State > region	Just state
Scotland	19	41	26	4	7
Catalonia	16	29	37	6	6
Wales	11	29	33	10	15
Upper Austria	10	16	38	11	22
Bavaria	9	19	36	11	19
Thuringia	9	18	44	9	17
Salzburg	9	17	50	9	10
Vienna	7	14	38	15	19
Galicia	6	25	57	6	4
Lower Saxony	6	11	34	15	27
Brittany	2	23	50	15	9
Castilla la Mancha	2	4	52	18	20
Alsace	1	17	42	20	15
Ile de France	1	7	30	42	12

Note: To use Scotland as an example, those selecting 'just region' identify themselves only as Scottish and not at all British; those selecting region>state identify themselves as more Scottish than British; those selecting equal identify themselves as equally Scottish and British and so on.

Table 2.8. Percentage 'very' attached to region/state

	a) % region	b) % state	a) – b)
Scotland	80	43	37
Wales	69	49	20
Catalonia	55	25	30
Brittany	65	49	16
Thuringia	57	42	15
Galicia	58	44	14
Bavaria	53	42	9
Alsace	60	60	0
Vienna	52	61	-9
Salzburg	52	64	-12
Upper Austria	51	62	-11
Lower Saxony	36	51	-15
Castilla la Mancha	33	52	-19
Ile de France	26	53	-27

The CANS dataset again helps put the Scottish and Welsh findings into a fuller context. It shows that Scotland has the strongest exclusively 'regional' (and the strongest predominantly 'regional') identity, followed by Catalonia then Wales, with other regions having a substantially less strong sense of regional identity (Table 2.7). The CANS questionnaire also asked how 'attached' respondents felt to Scotland (or Catalonia, and so on) as compared to the UK (or Spain, and so on). Once again Scotland and Wales, split by Catalonia, top the table. Table 2.8 shows the percentage of those who professed 'very strong' attachment to the state concerned, subtracted from those who professed 'very strong' attachment to the 'region'. There appears to be an especially powerful, distinctive sense of community in Scotland and Wales when compared with other European regions. This powerful sense of community may be an important factor which 'weighs' on the side of the demand for devolution and the acceptance of growing policy variation.

A second factor that may lend greater weight to one aspect of the devolution paradox is the way that territorial political debates are 'compartmentalised' in each part of the UK. This sense of compartmentalisation has become evident in research on devolved elections. The common denominator of most research on devolved elections has been to test the assumption that these would be 'second order' elections, that is reflections of and responses to the issues and personalities that drive voting behaviour in the more important, 'first order' UK elections (Hough and Jeffery 2006). Though it is clear that 'first order' issues do play a role – for example controversies over the Iraq War, or Tony Blair's increasingly unpopularity in the mid-2000s – UK-level issues certainly have no systematic impact on devolved election processes, and are often marginal to them. In their modelling of voting behaviour in the 2003 Scottish and Welsh devolved elections Wyn Jones and Scully (2006: 129) found that:

> Voters in Scotland and Wales can, and often do, make different electoral choices for devolved elections from Westminster ones … they are often guided by factors specific to Scotland and Wales when making such choices … Significant numbers of voters in Wales and Scotland appear to recognise Westminster and devolved levels as distinct political arenas, to evaluate parties differently for those respective arenas, and to vote accordingly.

Johns et al's (2007) rather different approach to analysing the 2007 devolved election in Scotland confirms broadly the same point. They applied a 'valence' model of voting to that election, using a public attitudes survey to explore how far questions of performance, competence and leadership of the leading parties in Scotland dealing with Scottish issues shaped voting behaviour. They found that these valence variables, focused on the Scottish context, were important determinants of how Scots voted, with the SNP holding leads over Labour on issue competence, leadership and campaigning. UK-level factors by contrast were subordinate in explaining the election outcome (or, to put it another way, UK factors were second order; the devolved election was in this instance a first order contest)

These accounts of devolved elections confirm a sense that devolved politics has become increasingly self-contained, focused, as Bromley *et al* (2003) put it, on 'Scottish answers to Scottish questions'. This is further evidenced by the patterns of media content across the UK, with its component parts increasingly consuming media that is tailored to their national context, and hearing little about one another's national conversations. This is strikingly illustrated in Scotland, where British 'national' newspapers 'put a kilt' on, producing Scottish editions with different news coverage and comment, enabling them to strip this content out of their English editions (Fraser 2008).

So even if people dislike cross-jurisdictional policy variation, there appears to be a tendency to reframe politics, through the lens of the democratic process, at smaller, distinctive devolved scales. The possibility that emerges from this is that statewide social citizenship may be eroded by default, as policy changes introduced by devolved institutions accumulate, as these are judged in compartmentalised, jurisdiction-specific terms, and in the absence of political structures which facilitate UK-wide thinking and comparison. Greer for example concludes that devolution, for such reasons, has 'already had an impact on the meaning and rights associated with citizenship in the UK' (2007: 159). Jeffery echoes the point, arguing that social citizenship has become less UK-wide and increasingly 'territorialised' (2006: 90).

Dealing with multi-level social citizenship

What, if anything, might be the policy response to the emergence of a multi-levelled social citizenship? Clearly one response would be to do nothing and let the flowers of diversity bloom. However, there do exist countervailing forces, not least an ongoing attachment to a sense of community at a UK-wide scale and an ongoing sense of UK-wide solidarity. While Scotland and Wales both display strong attachment to and identification with Scottishness and Welshness, there is still a strong identification with Britishness too. As Table 2.6 above shows, Britishness still features to varying degrees in the identity of 69 per cent of people in Wales and 70 per cent of people in Scotland. Moreover, data from the British Social Attitudes survey, comparing Scottish and English opinion, on the question of who benefits most from the union, reveal that a significant proportion of Scots still believe that their interests are well served (see Curtice *et al* 2010).

The data from the CANS survey in Table 2.5 also suggest a continuing preference for the pooling of risk through central government action to limit inter-regional economic disparities. Citizens see a role for the UK level as a guarantor of some degree of equity and solidarity. The challenge remains how to balance this equity with the greater diversity that results from devolution.

These features of the devolution paradox trace the outline of a policymaker's dilemma. Support for devolution is high but its introduction has changed the context of social citizenship rights. If social citizenship rights were ever provided uniformly at statewide scales, there are now multiple scales for realising social citizenship.[4] Devolution has overlaid these differences with the transparency brought about by democratic election, making them more visible to those that choose to look. This is the messy world of 21st century social citizenship rights and it is a world where more rather than less difference within the UK looks likely.

There are a number of key factors that are likely to shape this debate over the next decade:

- **Politics:** Differences in party competition between the UK and devolved electoral arenas will continue to produce governments with divergent party political composition. Different parties with different political traditions and beliefs will inevitably chart different policy courses. Furthermore, the relative strengths of the parties in different parts of Britain are likely to become a salient feature of devolved politics with the arrival of a coalition government that lacks significant support in Scotland and Wales. Controversy is most likely to arise when the Conservative–Liberal Democrat administration starts implementing unpopular spending cuts in those territories where their legitimacy to do so will be called into question. This may serve to accelerate the rescaling of political community, with the smaller territorial unit being seen as offering insurance against an unpopular government, leading to vociferous demands for greater powers and greater policy difference. This may result in the chipping away of UK-level social rights, as demands for powers extend to policy realms such as benefits.

- **Time:** The compartmentalised nature of the political system opens up the prospect of a steady accumulation of incremental policy changes. While each change alone might be minor, collectively they may achieve such a critical mass that they emerge unpredictably as politically salient.

- **Devolved finance:** Greater divergence, especially in a context of public spending cuts, is likely to provoke a debate about whether the distribution of resources across the nations is fair. A number of recent inquiries into the future of devolved finance have all called for the reform of the Barnett Formula, which is used to determine the size of the block grants available to the devolved administrations (Commission on Scottish Devolution 2009, Independent Commission on Funding and Finance for Wales 2009, House of Lords 2009, House of Commons Justice Select Committee 2009, McLean *et al* 2008). Furthermore, public awareness is growing of the inequities of the Barnett formula, which is not a needs-based formula. Data from the British Social Attitudes Surveys shows the proportion of people in England who think Scotland gets 'more than its fair share' of public spending has doubled from 20 to 40 per cent in the last decade (Curtice in this volume). It does not take much imagination to foresee these issues rising up the political agenda as the squeeze on public spending begins to be felt around the country.

---

4. It should be noted that EU membership also means that UK citizens' social rights are also expressed at the European level, which adds another important dimension to this debate.

- **England:** The other unpredictable dynamic force that is likely to shape these debates concerns attitudes in England. There are some tentative signs of the emergence of a distinct political community within England (Kenny and Lodge forthcoming). English identity has become more salient in recent years, though it is has not yet eclipsed a sense of allegiance to Britain (Kenny and Lodge 2009), and it is certainly the case that English public opinion has become increasingly aware of – and irritated by – the West Lothian anomaly and the allocation of public money across the UK. However, it is not yet clear whether these shifts in English public opinion will result in demands for political reform for England. Should a politically mobilised sense of Englishness emerge which demands political rights, be it at a national or local level, such pressures might pave the way for even greater divergence in social citizenship.

What is clear is that the UK and its constituent nations will continually have to adapt and respond to the reality of devolved politics. The response needs to reflect the multiple sites of social citizenship that have arisen since the advent of devolution, balancing the desire for greater diversity, and hence a growing appetite to express social citizenship at the devolved level, with a continuing role for the UK government – at least while there remains support for the union. Even if support for UK social citizenship recedes, there remains a need for a more mature debate on these issues. The Scottish debate on further-reaching devolution (in both unionist and nationalist variants) often ignores the continuing interdependencies that Scotland will have with the rest of the UK whatever its constitutional future, and the 'spillovers' from UK-level decisions that impact on Scotland.

The current devolution settlement is clearly not well equipped to deal with the messy reality of multi-level social citizenship rights. We set out here a number of areas where the current arrangements for devolution are at best contested, if not deeply criticised, and a different approach is needed.

- **Reforming finance:** The devolution settlement needs a financial settlement that is more suited to multi-level social citizenship. Devolved spending is currently funded almost entirely by an unrestricted block grant; there are few revenue-raising powers. The size of the grant is set by the Barnett formula, which employs a combination of change to levels of spending in England and relative population size to adjust a historical baseline of territorial spending outside of England. This funding arrangement is no longer suitable to meet the needs of the devolved nations. It is true that Barnett has helped deliver generous funding settlements to the devolved nations (especially Scotland and Northern Ireland) but the model has serious drawbacks. Since their grants are determined by spending decisions made in England by the government in Westminster, over which they exercise little influence, the devolved administrations cannot control the size of their budgets (though they are free to spend the block grant as they see fit). This did not matter when spending was rising but now it is set to be cut this inability to influence the size of their budgets and being at the mercy of decisions made in England is likely to cause more controversy.

One way of moving beyond the problems of the Barnett formula is to increase the revenue-raising powers available to the devolved administrations. Such change would respond to what is now more or less a consensus position in political debate in Scotland – that for reasons of autonomy and accountability the Scottish Parliament should raise at least a substantial proportion of the money it spends on devolved matters. Fuller fiscal autonomy is likely also to help with the question of managing difference, as a source of some tension in recent years has been a perception, often stoked by the English redtops, that Scotland enjoys greater social entitlements as a result of an over-generous transfer of money from England. Clearly one element of this debate has to be greater public awareness that English frustrations at the perceived better deal in Scotland should be targeted at politicians in Westminster, and the policy choices they make for England. Nonetheless, if a greater proportion of devolved spending were funded from taxes raised by devolved institutions, it may help to take the sting out of some of these arguments.

In most views – the big exception being the SNP – greater tax raising powers should go hand in hand with some level of fiscal equalisation through a needs-based formula in order to ensure equity and deliver the UK-wide aspect to social citizenship. Indeed such an arrangement perfectly reflects the contours of public opinion outlined above: great fiscal powers will strengthen the scope of the devolved nations to act more autonomously, while a grant aimed at fiscal equalisation would ensure that concerns about preserving union-wide equity are met. A number of federal states, most notably Germany and Australia, have constructed mechanisms for distributing financial resources to ensure that all areas have sufficient funding in principle to deliver services of equivalent (not necessarily uniform) standards. The commitment to fiscal equalisation is rather stronger in Wales, which by most calculations would benefit from inter-jurisdictional transfers, than Scotland, which would not. This debate is less open and advanced in Northern Ireland, but a position similar to that in Wales might be expected. In other words there should be no assumption that a single system applicable equally to Scotland, Wales and Northern Ireland would be appropriate.

• Articulating social citizenship rights: The UK devolution settlement contains limited opportunities for articulating and communicating which social citizenship rights are shared and guaranteed at a UK-wide scale and which at devolved scales. A laissez-faire approach is taken to intergovernmental coordination (see Trench in this volume), resulting in a lack of clarity over where the balance between equity and diversity currently lies.

Other countries have sought to achieve such an articulation of shared citizenship while still allowing for difference, in various ways. For example, Canada and Belgium have experimented with intergovernmental agreements, to set out the social rights of all citizens in an overarching social contract or charter of rights. In practice this approach has run into difficulty as a result of becoming mired in the politics of nationalism. Nevertheless, in the UK there is scope for agreements on specific issues and principles on a less formal, ad hoc basis, rather than as part of an overarching framework or grand gesture. A recent example would be the cross-government agreement to enshrine the target to abolish child poverty by 2020 in law, where each devolved government has backed a Legislative Consent Motion in support of the Bill, which requires each administration to produce a child poverty strategy.

Such an approach can work well where the interests of the governing parties across the UK align, and will come down to the ability of elected politicians to make the case for agreements and negotiate their content. Rather than uniformity, it is likely that different agreements will be reached between different parts of the UK. This kind of approach seems to chime with David Cameron's 'respect' agenda.

- **Intergovernmental relations and policy learning:** The UK's laissez-faire approach also restricts capacity for the systematic sharing of perspectives and learning, and where relevant, the identification of priorities that are to be shared and others that are to be pursued separately across the UK and devolved jurisdictions. There is widespread support for more systematic inter-governmental relations. Major enquiries by both Commons and Lords Select Committees (Lords 2002, Commons 2009) recommended this, as did the Calman Commission. So too, strikingly, has the SNP since coming to power in 2007. Obviously enough, the purpose behind advocacy of fuller intergovernmental relations differs among these actors. The SNP wants more formal relationships so it has a clear route for asserting distinctive Scottish interests, for example in EU matters, through the UK level of government. The House of Commons Justice Committee by contrast was more concerned with coordination across jurisdictions in a UK-wide interest. There is also a role for such inter-governmental mechanisms in managing conflicts over the content of social citizenship as and when they arise.

Despite diverse motivations, there is clearly a sense across different streams of opinion that the UK's jurisdictions need a more structured way of working either in cooperation with, or autonomously of one another. And again it may be that some parts of the UK are more focused on cooperation than autonomy; the purposes of inter-governmental relations may vary from place to place.

Inter-governmental relations are also important in the context of policy learning. Policy divergence provides space for policy innovation and learning, which can result in pushing up standards overall. There have been some examples of this over the last decade: all parts of the UK have adopted the Welsh innovation of creating the post of Children's Commissioner; while the greater scrutiny enabled by democratic devolution resulted in pressure for improvement on hospital waiting times in Wales (Schmuecker and Adams 2005; see Birrell in this volume). Harnessing the creativity released by devolution more systematically will bring benefits to all parts of the UK, and the UK Commission for Employment and Skills may be a good model of how this can work within a particular policy field (see Keep in this volume).

The proposals we have set out here suggest some ways in which the UK can adapt to the new reality of multi-level social citizenship, but ultimately an adjustment to the territorial constitution is likely to be required. The arrangements for this are clearly still in flux. They are untidy and asymmetrical. Why? Because they represent the latest ways in which distinctive unions of the Scots, the Welsh and (now the Northern) Irish have been adapted and accommodated. At one level there might appear to be a convergence of Northern Ireland (following the devolution of policing and justice powers) and Wales (in the light of the anticipated referendum on full legislative powers) on a Scottish model of extensive devolution of domestic policy functions. But the trajectory of the Scottish debate is headed into a grey area marked out by new terminologies of 'devolution-max' and 'independence-lite' that suggest a different, looser quality of relationship with the rest of the UK. The Northern Ireland arrangements – should they ever work entirely as foreseen in 1998 – blur traditional understandings of state sovereignty across the UK–Irish border. Only Wales appears to be on a trajectory that looks more like a conventional devolved region.

But perhaps the biggest contribution to the UK's untidiness is England. England is more than five times as big as Scotland, Wales and Northern Ireland combined in terms of population and GDP. England is a highly centralised, unitary sub-state that has probably been the location, through the actions of the UK government, of more territorial policy innovation than the three devolved administrations combined. Curiously it has no set of institutions that provide systematically for the government of its territory. The government of England is bound up – perhaps irreversibly – with the government of the UK as a whole, with Westminster and Whitehall combining and often confusing the territorial scales of their responsibilities. England is the oddest one out of the UK's territories. It is England much more than the semi-detached Scots or Northern Irish that renders some kind of broadly uniform, federal territorial constitutional arrangements for the UK implausible.

The UK is made up of a series of ambivalent and distinctive relationships between the constituent nations. Many aspects of those relationships involve shared values and interests. Others do not. And they all vary according to place: Wales's relationship with England is different to that which exists between Scotland and England, and Northern Ireland's are different again. Wales is keen on fiscal equalisation; Scotland is not. Northern Ireland has distinctive powers in the field of social security but aligns its policies with those of the UK government acting for England, Scotland and Wales. Many in Scotland – in Labour and the Liberal Democrats as well as the SNP – would rather Scotland were not part of a single social security system, a single social citizenship (though none of them have credibly explained how they would pay for it). The political class in England appears to favour market-based approaches in public services, a view largely rejected by Scottish and Welsh elites.

What the appropriate constitutional relationship for capturing this diversity might be is presently unclear: perhaps something like confederation, with contracted relationships between different states; certainly something different for each part of the UK. What we do know is that it now falls to the Conservative–Liberal Democrat coalition to run and manage this eclectic and decentralised union. In many respects this task will be made more difficult by the fact that the coalition lacks a strong mandate outside of England (particularly the Conservative component). It will have to show that it is sensitive to Scottish, Welsh and Northern Irish interests and differences – and show willingness to accommodate them within the union. Paradoxically, however, the very fact that electoral and parliamentary arithmetics will force the coalition to adopt a negotiated approach to governing the UK – working with the nations on a case by case basis – might help ensure that it succeeds in working with the devolved nations in an effective way.

References

Ashdown P (2001) *The Ashdown Diaries: 1997-1999,* vol 2, London: Allen Lane

Banting K and Corbett R (2002) *Health Policy and Federalism: A comparative perspective* Kingston: McGill-Queens University

Béland D and Lecours A (2008) *Nationalism and Social Policy: The Politics of Territorial Solidarity* Oxford: OUP

Bogdanor V (2001) *Devolution in the United Kingdom* Oxford: OUP

Braun D (2000) *Public Policy and Federalism* Aldershot: Ashgate

Bromley C et al (2003) *Devolution – Scottish Answers to Scottish Questions?* Edinburgh: Edinburgh University Press

Commission on Scottish Devolution (2009) *Serving Scotland Better: Scotland and the United Kingdom in the 21st Century, Final Report,* Edinburgh: Commission on Scottish Devolution

Curtice J, Ormston R and Reid S (2010) 'Ready for the Next Step? Nationalist Government and Attitudes towards Independence in Scotland', paper presented to the PSA Territorial Politics conference, Oxford

Curtice J and Seyd B (2009) 'Devolution and the Union' in Curtice J and Seyd B (eds) *Has Devolution Worked?* Manchester: Manchester University Press

Fraser D (2008) *Nation Speaking unto Nation: Does the media create cultural distance between England and Scotland?* London: ippr: www.ippr.org.uk/publicationsandreports/publication.asp?id=607

McEwen N and Henderson A (2005) 'Do shared values underpin national identity?: National identity and value consensus in Canada and the UK', *National Identities* 7.2

Harrison K (2006) (ed) *Racing to the Bottom? Provincial interdependence in the Canadian federation* Vancouver: UBC Press

House of Lords Select Committee on the Barnett Formula (2009) *The Barnett Formula* London: TSO: www.publications.parliament.uk/pa/ld200809/ldselect/ldbarnett/139/139.pdf

House of Commons Justice Select Committee (2009) *Devolution a Decade On: Fifth report of session 2008-09* London: TSO Hough D and Jeffery C (eds) (2006) *Devolution and Electoral Politics* Manchester: Manchester University Press

Independent Commission on Funding and Finance for Wales [Holtham Commission] (2009) *Funding devolved government in Wales: Barnett & beyond?* Cardiff: Independent Commission on Funding and Finance for Wales: http://wales.gov.uk/docs/icffw/report/090708barnettfullen.pdf

Jeffery C (2005) 'Devolution and Divergence: Public attitudes and institutional logics' in Adams J and Schmuecker K (eds) *Devolution in Practice 2006: Public policy differences within the UK* 10-28, London: ippr

Jeffery C (2009a) 'Devolution, Public Attitudes and Social Citizenship' in Greer SL (ed) *Devolution and Social Citizenship in the UK* Bristol: Policy Presspp73-95

Jeffery C (2009b) 'Devolution, Britishness and the Future of the Union' *Political Quarterly* 78 (1) pp112-121

Johns R *et al* (2007) 'The Holyrood Elections 2007: Explaining the Results', Scottish Election Study Paper: www.scottishelectionstudy.org.uk/paperspubs.htm

Keating M (2002) 'Devolution and public policy in the UK: Divergence or convergence?' in Adams J and Robinson P (eds.) *Devolution in Practice: Public policy differences within the UK* pp3-21, London: ippr

Keating M (2009) *The Independence of Scotland. Self-Government and the Shifting Politics of Union*, Oxford: Oxford University Press

Kenny M and Lodge G (2009) *More than one English question*, London: ippr

Kenny M and Lodge G (2010) *The English Question: the view from Westminster* London: ippr

Kenny M and Guy Lodge (forthcoming) *English Questions* London: ippr

Marshall T [1950] (1992) 'Citizenship and Social Class' in Marshall T and Bottomore T (eds) *Citizenship and Social Class*, London: Pluto Press, pp. 3-51

McLean I, Lodge G and Schmuecker K (2008) *Fair Shares? Barnett and the politics of public expenditure,* London: ippr

McLeish H (2004) *Scotland First: Truth and Consequences* Edinburgh: Mainstream Publishing

Mooney G, Scott G and Williams C (2006) 'Introduction: Rethinking Social Policy through Devolution', *Critical Social Policy* 26.3, pp. 483-97

Peterson P (1995) *The price of federalism* Washington: Brooking Institution Press

Scottish Government (2009) *Your Scotland Your Voice: A national conversation* Edinburgh: Scottish Government

Schmuecker K and Adams J (2006) in Adams J and Schmuecker K (eds) *Devolution in Practice: Public policy differences within the UK* London: ippr

Simeon R (2003) 'Free Personal Care: Policy Divergence and Social Citizenship' in Hazell R (ed) *State of the Nations: The Third Year of Devolution in the UK* Exeter: Imprint Academic

Wyn Jones R and Scully R (2006) 'Devolution and Electoral Politics in Wales and Scotland,' *Publius: The Journal of Federalism* 36.1, pp. 115-34

3. Policy divergence: recognising difference or generating resentment?

John Curtice

As is made clear throughout this book, the devolution settlement has created plenty of opportunities for policy divergence across the UK. So far as the delivery of public services is concerned, such divergence has emerged in two main areas. The first is in how services are delivered. In England the UK Government has pursued a policy of public service reform characterised by giving users of public services 'choice' in how they access such services, using various forms of private provision to deliver some services, and developing quasi-market mechanisms that encourage competition between and among state and private providers. In contrast, such mechanisms have been downplayed and sometimes even been explicitly rejected elsewhere in the UK.

The second main area of difference has been in charging for certain public services. Scotland, Wales and Northern Ireland have all moved in the direction of abolishing prescription charges. Scotland and Wales have also both taken steps to reduce or eliminate university tuition fees, while in addition Scotland has introduced 'free' personal care for older people. None of these policies, however, has so far been introduced in England.

For advocates of devolution, such divergence is to be welcomed. One of the aims of devolution was to make it possible for public policy to match the public's needs and aspirations more closely. If the geography of Scotland, the values upheld by the people of Wales, or the community division in Northern Ireland meant that the needs and/or aspirations of the people there were different from those that pertained in England, then public policy in those parts of the UK could be adapted accordingly. The result should be more effective public policy and perhaps even a strengthening of support for continued membership of the United Kingdom.

But for others such variation is a source of concern. As discussed elsewhere in this book, nowadays citizenship is widely regarded as not just simply being about political rights, such as the right to vote or the right to free speech. It also involves social rights, such as access to education or health, together with an acceptance that a society has an obligation to pool certain risks, such as ill health or unemployment. And just as notions of 'one person, one vote' imply that all citizens should have equal access to political rights, so ideas of social citizenship may be thought to imply a right of equal access to the social rights afforded by the state. Such equality might be thought to be undermined if some people can choose which hospital they attend, while others cannot, or if some have to pay for their prescriptions, while others in the same personal material situation do not.

This could lead to resentment. Those who have to pay for a service may feel resentful that fellow citizens living elsewhere can enjoy the same service for free. Those who cannot exercise some choice in respect of how they access a service may feel hard-done-by as compared with those who can. Indeed, it is not uncommon for territorial variation in the provision of public services to be referred to disparagingly as a 'postcode lottery'.

If such resentment festers for any length of time it might well undermine the acceptance of a common obligation to share risk. This danger might be thought to be particularly acute if those parts of the country that seem to have a better deal are also ones that benefit from monetary transfers, as is often argued to be the case so far as Scotland, Wales and Northern Ireland are concerned. If they can apparently afford largesse that England cannot, then perhaps the feeling might grow that they should finance their public services out of their own resources. If that happens then it is hard to see how devolution might be expected to strengthen the bonds that help keep the United Kingdom together.

In this chapter we examine the force of these two particular arguments. First, we consider the premise upon which the advocates of devolution base their argument, by examining whether or not the differences of approach to the delivery of public services and charging for the use of certain services reflect differences in public attitudes across the UK. Are people in England, for example, keener on choice and less unhappy about paying for their prescriptions than people are elsewhere in the UK? Second, we examine the possibility that policy divergence, and the financial settlement that currently underpins devolution in the UK, might be a source of resentment. Are people willing to accept that public services and welfare benefits vary across the UK? Or are they inclined to feel resentful when one part of the UK appears to have a better deal than another?

Data

Our evidence comes from a set of social attitudes surveys that are conducted regularly across Britain as a whole, and in Scotland and Northern Ireland in particular. In 2007 these three surveys, the British Social Attitudes survey, the Scottish Social Attitudes survey, and the Northern Ireland Life and Times survey all fielded the same set of questions on attitudes towards public services, while these same questions were also included on a specially commissioned, similarly conducted survey in Wales.[1]

1. The questions were fielded on two of four versions of the British Social Attitudes questionnaire, and were answered by 2,022 respondents, of whom 1,735 were resident in England (response rate, 52%). The 2007 Scottish Social Attitudes survey interviewed 1,508 respondents (response rate, 56%), the Northern Ireland Life and Times survey interviewed 1,179 respondents (response rate, 60%), and the specially commissioned survey in Wales, 884 respondents (response rate, 54%). All four surveys were based on a clustered random sample. Interviews were conducted face to face together with a self completion questionnaire. The data are weighted to take account of known unequal selection probabilities and patterns of non-response, and further weighted to reflect the current age and gender profile of the relevant population.

This collaboration, which means that we can systematically compare attitudes in England (by looking at respondents to the British survey living in England), Scotland, Wales and Northern Ireland, provides much of the material on which the first part of this chapter is based. At the same time, these surveys have variously collaborated since 1999 in asking questions about how devolution is thought to be operating and how it should operate.[2] It is this latter collaboration that provides the basis for most of the discussion in the second part of this chapter.

Different policies, different preferences?

In this section we examine first of all whether variations across the UK in policy in respect of public service delivery reflect differences in public preferences. We then consider whether the same can be said of co-payment.

Delivering public services

We begin by examining whether or not our two key differences in the approach that has been adopted to the provision of public services across the UK are a reflection of differences in public opinion across the UK. Table 3.1 summarises the answers that were received in 2007 when respondents to the four social attitudes surveys were asked about how much 'choice' they felt people should have when using various public services. The table focuses on three possible subjects of choice – of a secondary school for a child, of a hospital when in need of inpatient treatment, and of the provider of personal care for an older person. In each case the possible answers were 'none', 'a little', 'quite a lot' and 'a great deal'; the table shows the proportion in each part of the UK who answered 'a great deal'.

Table 3.1. Attitudes across the UK towards choice

	% favouring a great deal of choice of over…		
	Secondary school	Hospital	Who provides care
England	32	26	30
Scotland	27	32	35
Wales	35	40	41
N. Ireland	29	36	39

Sources: British Social Attitudes 2007, Scottish Social Attitudes 2007, Wales Life and Times 2007, Northern Ireland Life and Times 2007

In each case and in all parts of the UK only a minority said there should be a 'great deal' of choice. That does not mean that choice is unpopular; in each case the most popular response was 'quite a lot', with the result that two-thirds or more said either

2. The design and sample sizes for years other than 2007 are similar to those detailed for 2007 in footnote 1, except that the number of number of versions of the British Social Attitudes questionnaire on which the questions were asked varied from year to year.

a 'great deal' or 'quite a lot'. Rather, it simply means that enthusiasm for choice is not unbridled.

What is of most interest to us is whether or not attitudes towards choice vary across the UK, and in particular if people in England are more enthusiastic than those living elsewhere. The answer is apparently 'No'. In fact, in each case it is Wales which is marginally the most enthusiastic about choice. Meanwhile, so far as both choice of hospital or who provides someone with care are concerned, people in England actually prove to be the least enthusiastic about choice. It is very difficult on this evidence to argue that the variation in the promotion of choice across the UK that has emerged since the advent of devolution can be regarded as a demonstration of the ability of devolution to deliver a closer fit between public policy and the varying contours of public opinion.

But what about what some regard as the more controversial feature of the way in which public service reform has been implemented in England – the use of private providers to provide public services? Of course not all private providers are the same. Some, such as the organisations behind most Independent Health Treatment Centres, are private companies. Others, such as some of the organisations that have become involved in running City Academies, are charitable organisations. One reason why people might object to private companies becoming involved in delivering public services is that they have objections to the idea of companies being able to make a profit out of people's needs. For this reason at least we might anticipate greater antipathy towards private companies running public services than there is towards charitable organisations doing so. We thus look at attitudes towards the two types of organisation separately.

First, Table 3.2 shows attitudes in all four parts of the UK towards private companies running or providing three key services: state schools, NHS hospitals, and personal care. It shows that there is indeed considerable antipathy towards the idea of using private providers, and especially to their involvement in running state schools or NHS hospitals. The scale of that opposition is rather less in England than elsewhere, and to that extent at least the greater use there of private companies to run services mirrors a difference from the rest of the UK in the pitch of public opinion. However, even in England over half oppose private companies running schools and hospitals, while even in the case of personal care, the balance of opinion between supporters and opponents clearly favours the former. So while it might be argued that devolution may have enabled Scotland, Wales and Northern Ireland largely to avoid implementing a policy approach that is apparently rather unpopular in those nations, it seems that if public policy were reflecting majority opinion then much the same approach towards the use of private companies would be being used throughout the UK.

However, as we anticipated, the picture is rather different when we look at the possibility of charities running and providing public services. Public opinion

Table 3.2. Attitudes across the UK towards private companies providing public services across the UK

	Private companies …					
	Running state schools		Running NHS hospitals		Providing personal care	
	Support (%)	Oppose (%)	Support (%)	Oppose (%)	Support (%)	Oppose (%)
England	20	53	23	55	31	43
Scotland	12	65	17	67	28	51
Wales	14	64	18	64	29	49
N. Ireland	14	55	17	58	27	49

Sources: British Social Attitudes 2007, Scottish Social Attitudes 2007, Wales Life and Times 2007, Northern Ireland Life and Times 2007

everywhere is more sympathetic to this idea than it is to private companies running services. As a result, throughout the UK the balance of opinion is in favour of charities providing personal care, an area where a mixed economy of provision has long been commonplace. More importantly, however, opinion in England is more or less evenly divided in its attitude towards charities running schools or hospitals, whereas elsewhere in the UK the balance of opinion is still clearly opposed. This evidence hardly suggests that people in England have been clamouring for a more mixed pattern of public service provision. But it does suggest that the divergence of policy across the UK in the use of non-state providers might reasonably be regarded as an exaggerated reflection of difference of outlook between England and the rest of the UK, rather than a complete distortion.

Table 3.3. Attitudes across the UK towards charities running public services

	Charities…					
	Running state schools		Running NHS hospitals		Providing personal care	
	Support (%)	Oppose (%)	Support (%)	Oppose (%)	Support (%)	Oppose (%)
England	36	34	36	36	53	17
Scotland	24	49	27	48	41	31
Wales	27	44	29	46	46	31
N. Ireland	27	44	28	43	47	31

Sources: British Social Attitudes, 2007, Scottish Social Attitudes, 2007, Wales Life and Times, 2007, Northern Ireland Life and Times, 2007

Co-payment

So it seems that the policy differences towards the delivery of public services (see for instance Birrell, this volume) that have emerged since the advent of devolution are rather greater than the differences in public opinion across the UK. It would appear difficult, at least so far as this area of public policy is concerned, to argue straightforwardly that devolution has facilitated a better fit between public policy and public preferences across the UK. But what of the second key area where policy in respect of public services has diverged: in the charges that are made for certain services? Do the differences that have emerged in respect of university tuition fees, personal care and prescription charges reflect differences in public attitudes in different parts of the UK?

The social attitudes surveys asked rather different questions about each of these topics, so we should look at their wording in some detail. On prescription charges, respondents were simply asked whether they agreed or disagreed that:

> *Nobody should have to pay prescription charges for medicine they need, even if they can afford to do so*

Given how the item was worded, designed to avoid expressions of unthinking opposition to prescription charges, in Table 3.4 those who support prescription charges are those who said that they *disagreed* with this statement, while the opponents are those who *agreed*. Meanwhile, in the case of university tuition fees, respondents were first of all introduced to the subject via the following statement:

> *I'm now going to ask you what you think about university or college students or their families paying towards the costs of their tuition, either while they are studying or after they have finished. Which of the views on this card comes closest to what you think about that?*

Three possible views were summarised on the card:

> *All students or their families should pay towards the costs of their tuition*

> *Some students or their families should pay towards the costs of their tuition, depending on their circumstances*

> *No students or their families should pay towards the costs of their tuition*

In Table 3.4 opponents of tuition fees are those who chose the last option, while supporters are those who gave either of the first two responses.

Finally, in the case of charging for personal care, respondents were asked:

> *Thinking about an older person who needs regular help with looking after themselves, which of these statements comes closest to what you believe about who should pay for this help?*

> *The government should pay, no matter how much money the person has*

The person should pay, no matter how much money he/she has

Who pays should depend on how much money the person has

Those who gave the first response are regarded as opposed to charges for personal care, while those who indicated support for either the second or the third option are regarded as being in favour.

Table 3.4. Attitudes across the UK towards charging for public services

	Prescription charges		University tuition fees		Personal care	
	Support (%)	Oppose (%)	Support (%)	Oppose (%)	Support (%)	Oppose (%)
England	49	38	74	25	58	41
Scotland	41	46	69	30	44	55
Wales	29	62	68	31	51	47
N. Ireland	44	43	66	32	40	58

Sources: British Social Attitudes, 2007, Scottish Social Attitudes, 2007, Wales Life and Times, 2007, Northern Ireland Life and Times, 2007

The table does uncover some evidence of a divergence in public opinion that is consistent with differences in public policy. The public in Wales, where prescription charges were abolished first, are clearly opposed to their imposition. The balance of opinion is no less than two to one against. In contrast, in England, where no major reduction in prescription charges has been proposed, the balance of opinion is somewhat in the other direction. Of course the decision to abolish prescription charges in Wales may itself have influenced public opinion there, thereby perhaps widening any initial difference of opinion between Wales and England that may have existed. But at least it can be argued that on this issue the difference in current policy matches a current difference in public opinion.

But what about Scotland and Northern Ireland, where prescription charges are now also gradually being eliminated? Here we discover that public opinion is more or less evenly divided on both sides of the argument. So the slower implementation of the abolition of charges in those two parts of the UK certainly mirrors what appears to be a less pressing demand than in Wales, while the fact that the policy is being pursued at all is consistent with a greater level of opposition to charges than is evident in England. Equally, however, it is far from clear that the decision to abolish prescription charges in Scotland and Northern Ireland means that public policy there is now more in tune with majority public opinion than it had been previously.

There is some evidence that the distinctive policy in Scotland of providing older people with free personal care also reflects a somewhat different public mood. On balance public opinion in Scotland appears to be opposed to charging for personal care, while in England the balance is in the opposite direction. However, it seems that the public in Northern Ireland are at least as keen as their counterparts in Scotland for charges for personal care to be eliminated, yet no such move has been proposed there. On the other hand, perhaps the proposal put forward by the Welsh Assembly Government in July 2009 to cap but not abolish charges for personal care represents a reasonable compromise, given that public opinion in Wales appears to be more or less evenly balanced on the issue.

However, when it comes to attitudes towards university tuition fees, it seems that the distinctive policies pursued in Scotland and Wales do not reflect a different public mood at all. Nowhere in the UK do as many as a third oppose the idea of charging at least some students for the cost of their tuition. Moreover, opinion varies relatively little from one part of the country to another; England simply seems just a little more content with tuition fees than the rest of the UK does. On this subject, then, it is far from clear that the policy difference that has emerged reflects differences of public outlook in different parts of the UK.

So it seems that on the matter of charging for public services, the claim can plausibly be made that devolution has sometimes enabled public policy to match variations in public opinion across the UK more closely. But the record is only a patchy one. In the case of prescription charges and, to some degree at least, personal care, variations in current public policy do apparently mirror differences in the balance of opinion. On the other hand it is far from clear why university tuition fees should have become a totemic policy difference in Scotland and Wales, for on that subject at least public opinion is apparently little different from that in the rest of the UK.

A source of resentment?

Devolution was introduced in Scotland and Wales in response to the feeling that people there wanted greater say and control over their own domestic affairs, while it was reintroduced in Northern Ireland as part of the attempt to secure a political settlement designed to bring an end to 30 years of civil strife in the province. Indeed, it is quite clear from the evidence presented in Table 3.5 that a majority of people in those three parts of the UK feel that their devolved institutions should have most influence over what happens in their part of the country. Only distinct minorities in each case believe that the UK Government at Westminster should be the dominant force locally.

The extent of the demand for local autonomy was further underlined in 2007 when respondents in Scotland and Wales were asked who should make most of the decisions about particular policy areas. As Table 3.6 shows, in Scotland not only did nearly two-thirds say that the Scottish Parliament should make most of the decisions about schools and the NHS, areas for which responsibility is already devolved, but the same proportion said the same about welfare benefits, control of which rests with the UK Government in Westminster. In Wales, too, 58 per cent said that decisions about welfare benefits should be made by the Welsh Assembly, little

Table 3.5. Opinions across the UK on which tier of government ought to have most influence in their part of the UK, 1999–2007

	1999 (%)	2001 (%)	2003 (%)	2007 (%)
England				
English Parliament or Regional Assemblies	-	21	25	-
UK Government at Westminster	-	54	48	-
Scotland				
Scottish Parliament	74	74	66	71
UK Government at Westminster	13	14	20	14
Wales				
Welsh Assembly	59	54	54	72
UK Government at Westminster	24	25	27	17
Northern Ireland				
N. Ireland Assembly	-	65	50	69
UK Government at Westminster	-	17	18	11

Note: Other possible answers – local councils, European Union, and (in N. Ireland in 2007) the Irish government – not shown.
Sources: British Social Attitudes, 2001 and 2003, Scottish Social Attitudes, 1999–2007, Welsh Assembly Election Study, 1999, Wales Life and Times, 2001–2007, Northern Ireland Life and Times, 2001–7

different from the equivalent proportions for schools (56 per cent) and the NHS (61 per cent). Only when it came to defence and foreign affairs did a majority draw the line at giving primary responsibility to the devolved institutions.

It might therefore be thought that, in Wales and Scotland at least, people are tolerant of the inevitable corollary of devolved decentralised decision-making – policy difference. Yet this is not necessarily the case (for more on the 'devolution paradox see Jeffery et al, this volume). In 2003 people in Scotland and Wales were asked if the level of unemployment benefit should be the same everywhere in the UK or if their devolved institutions should be able to increase or lower it. Much the same question was also asked about tuition fees. In both cases and in both parts of the UK, the majority response was that they should be the same throughout the UK. On unemployment benefit this was the response given by 56 per cent in Scotland

Table 3.6. Opinions in Scotland and Wales over the institutions that should make important decisions about health, schools, welfare, and defence/foreign affairs

Which institution should make important decisions about...	Scotland		Wales	
	Scottish Parliament	UK Government at Westminster	Welsh Assembly	UK Government at Westminster
	%	%	%	%
Health service	63	25	61	26
Schools	62	13	56	18
Welfare benefits	63	18	58	22
Defence and foreign affairs	33	58	21	71

Note: Other possible answers – local councils and the European Union – not shown.
Sources: Scottish Social Attitudes, 2007, Wales Life and Times, 2007

and 57 per cent in Wales, while the equivalent figures for tuition fees were 58 per cent and 56 per cent respectively. Even though people in Scotland and Wales apparently want their devolved institutions to be making most domestic policy decisions for their part of the UK, this does not mean they will necessarily be tolerant of policy differences that seemingly put them at a disadvantage.

The mood in England is, it seems, very different from that in the rest of the UK. For as Table 3.5 also shows, when people there have been asked who should have most of the decisions for their part of the UK, only around a quarter have named one of the two kinds of devolved bodies that have been proposed – regional assemblies or a new English parliament. In contrast around a half said that the UK Government should make most decisions. Equally, when in 2003 people in England were asked who should make most of the decisions about welfare benefits, as many as 65 per cent said the UK Government. In Scotland and Wales the equivalent figures at the same time were just 24 and 39 per cent.

Unsurprisingly, therefore, people in England appear also to be even less tolerant of policy difference than their counterparts in Scotland and Wales. In 2003 they, along with people in Scotland and Wales, were asked a question that had first been asked as part of research undertaken in 1970 for the Royal Commission on the Constitution. It read as follows:

> *Thinking about things like the health service, schools, the roads, the police and so on, in general do you think it is better that the standards for such services be...*
>
> *the same in every part of Britain,*
>
> *or do you think each region should be allowed to set its own standards?*

Even in Scotland (59 per cent) and Wales (55 per cent) a majority said that standards should be the same in every part of Britain. But in England no fewer than 66 per cent gave that response, twice as many as said that each region should be allowed to set its own standards. On this evidence there certainly seems little reason to believe that people in England would be tolerant of policy difference that put them at a disadvantage.

Meanwhile, as we have already noted, public spending per head in England is lower than elsewhere in the UK. This would appear to give people plenty of reason for resentment. The British Social Attitudes survey has regularly monitored whether or not people in England are unhappy with this disparity by asking them whether they felt that Scotland secures more than, less than, or more or less its fair share of government spending. Table 3.7 shows that up to and including 2003 only around a quarter said that Scotland secured more than its fair share. But more recently that figure has increased, reaching 40 per cent or so in the two most recent readings taken in 2008 and 2009.

Table 3.7. Attitudes in England towards the financial relationship between England and Scotland, 2000–8

	2000	2001	2002	2003	2007	2008	2009
Compared with other parts of the UK, Scotland's share of government spending is…	%	%	%	%	%	%	%
… much more than its fair share	8	9	9	9	16	21	18
… a little more than its fair share	13	15	15	13	16	20	22
… pretty much its fair share	42	44	44	45	38	33	30
a little less than its fair share	10	8	8	8	6	3	4
… much less than its fair share	1	1	1	1	1	*	*
Don't know	25	23	22	25	22	23	25

Source: British Social Attitudes 2000–9

Policy difference would appear, then, to have the potential to offend people's sensibilities. But we should be careful of presuming that policy difference will necessarily generate resentment. One plausible explanation for why, until recently at least, there was so little discontent in England about the territorial distribution of public expenditure across the UK was that the difference in spending per head was not particularly salient to most people. Note that nearly a quarter say they do not know whether Scotland's share is fair or not. Equally, one reason why discontent may now be becoming more common is that elite level debate about the current financial arrangements behind devolution may finally be beginning to percolate through to the wider public. In short, policy difference is only likely to become a subject of dispute if political or other elites successfully start to arouse public interest.

Equally, even when policy difference is the source of some discontent, it does not necessarily follow that it gives rise to strain on public support for maintenance of the Union. In Table 3.8 we show how people in England respond when asked how they think Scotland should be governed. It shows that consistently no more than around one in five would like Scotland to leave the Union. There is no sign that the recent increase in discontent with Scotland's share of public spending has served to boost that proportion. At most it might have helped to undermine some of the support for Scottish devolution, though this is seemingly still by far the most popular option in England for how Scotland should be governed.

Table 3.8. Attitudes in England towards how Scotland should be governed, 1997–2007

Scotland should …	1997	1999	2000	2001	2002	2003	2007
	%	%	%	%	%	%	%
…be independent, separate from UK and EU or separate from UK but part of EU	14	21	19	19	19	17	19
…remain part of UK, with its own elected parliament which has some taxation powers	38	44	44	53	41	50	36
…remain part of UK, with its own elected parliament which has no taxation powers	17	13	8	7	11	8	12
…remain part of UK, without an elected parliament	23	14	17	11	15	13	18

Source: British Social Attitudes 1997 2009

Conclusion

Devolution has seemingly had some success in ensuring that differences in public opinion are reflected in differences of public policy across the UK. Perhaps the two clearest examples are the abolition of prescription charges in Wales and free personal care in Scotland. But in some cases, such as tuition fees, differences have emerged that appear to have little resonance in public opinion, or, as in the use of private companies or charities to help deliver public services, would appear to exaggerate such differences of outlook that exist (not least because on this issue the policy of the UK Government appears rather out of step with opinion in England). Even in the case of prescription charges and personal care we cannot be sure that the distinctive patterns of opinion in Wales and Scotland are not a consequence of the distinctive public policies that have been pursued there rather than a precursor. Other research certainly suggests that these are not issues on which attitudes are firmly rooted in people's social position and thus may be particularly open to persuasion[3]. Devolution's success at providing a better fit between public policy and public opinion can thus only be regarded as a limited one.

Meanwhile, policy difference seemingly has the potential to generate resentment. Even though people outside England are inclined to the view that most of the decisions about domestic policy in their part of the UK should be taken by their devolved institutions rather than by the UK Government, this does not necessarily mean that they are ready to embrace different levels or regimes of social provision. England itself embraces neither devolution for itself, nor the principle that public policy might vary. However, policy difference only seems likely to cause resentment if and when it becomes salient in the eyes of the public. And of that at least it seems there is, perhaps fortunately for devolution, no guarantee.

Acknowledgements
Collection of the data on attitudes towards public services across the UK was funded by the Economic and Social Research Council (ESRC) as part of its Public Services Research Programme. Collection of the data on attitudes towards devolution was funded by various grants from the ESRC (including as part of its Devolution and Constitutional Change Research Programme) and the Leverhulme Trust (including as part of its Nations and Regions Research Programme) as well as by the National Centre for Social Research from its own resources. None of these bodies is responsible for the opinions expressed here.

---

3. See J Curtice and S Patrikios, 'The Devolution Debate about Co-Payment: Reflection or Reality?' Paper presented at the Annual Meeting of the American Political Science Association. Toronto, 3-6 September 2009

4. Intergovernmental relations and social citizenship: opportunities Labour missed

Alan Trench

This chapter is about devolution and 'social citizenship', and what might be done – or might have been done – about it. Its starting point is that devolution is one institutional way of solving certain constitutional problems about the relationship of the various parts of UK to each other and to the whole. Devolution therefore eschews two sets of simple solutions to that issue – a single government from Westminster, as before 1999, and separate statehood (independence) for some or all of those parts from the UK. It is about reconciling self-rule for some purposes with shared rule for others. Devolution offers many benefits – on one level, by keeping the UK together, but more importantly by offering the ability to shape different futures and paths for the various parts of the UK while also sharing commonalities in other areas. However, it also prompts a number of questions, including the broad one of what the relations are between the whole and the various parts, and the narrower ones of what interactions there should be between the various levels of government, and how their interactions are managed.

This chapter will argue that devolution, and the policy variations that should result from it, call for the active engagement of all the various governments involved, and that each of them can benefit from that sort of engagement. The failure to do so does not just result in poorer policy, but also in wider political threats to the Union. This chapter discusses possible ways of doing that, and so help realise the benefits devolution has to offer to the UK in both constitutional and policy terms. However, some of these are inconsistent with the constitutional framework of devolution, while others are politically unworkable at this point in the development of devolved government. Others still are unlikely to be attractive to an incoming Conservative UK Government.

The upshot is a negative one: in practical terms, it is hard to see what sorts of steps could now be taken by a Labour government that wishes to consolidate a decentralised social-democratic Union for the longer term. It could have done so in the early 2000s, but did not. It is hard to avoid concluding that Labour has missed a huge set of opportunities over the last decade.

How devolution changed social citizenship

Devolution wrought many changes in the way the UK works, although the full impact of these is only now becoming clear. On one hand, it was a way of establishing democratic self-government in Scotland and Wales. It was also a way of bridging the communal divide in Northern Ireland and ending the democratic deficit associated with direct rule. The first purpose of devolution was therefore political, as a way of restoring legitimacy to government within and across the Union. On the other hand, it had significant effects on the functions of the UK state, and particularly of the welfare state. The architects of devolution probably did not consider that at all, and to the extent that they did, appear to have concluded that the effect of this change would be limited, because devolved functions were only distributive ones like health or education, not redistributive ones like social security. But the division of powers did not actually do this; it created scope for very considerable policy divergence, with few legal or policy restraints on how the devolved administrations used their powers. While there is debate about the extent of policy divergence in various sectors (discussed elsewhere in this book), the constraints on such divergence are largely political, though the financial system is also important.

Is that a problem? Many would say that it is not, arguing that policy divergence was a natural and logical consequence of devolution, if not its chief goal. Expecting policies to remain the same across the UK, with only limited variations in administration and delivery, was simply impracticable after the late 1990s. However, for those concerned with the United Kingdom as a whole, there is an issue. The question of what happened to UK-wide social citizenship is discussed elsewhere in this book (and see also Greer 2009). The point is not the substantive policy differences but who makes decisions about those and whom they regard as part of the community with whom they share their social citizenship. If social citizenship in Scotland has become distinctively 'Scottish', not UK-wide, part of the cement that has bound the Union has ceased to hold. Individual citizens are increasingly unclear about what they have in common with other citizens in other parts of the UK, whose experiences of the state are very different. That will not matter to nationalists (whether inside or outside the SNP); it will matter to those concerned with maintaining the Union as well as securing self-government for Scotland, Wales or Northern Ireland.

However, this is not to suggest that the devolved administrations have the powers to develop a distinct 'Scottish' welfare state (if not Welsh or Northern Irish ones). Three particular sets of factors inhibit it:

1. *The fact that a number of key functions are not devolved.* Of these, social security is notable (but not alone). This means that a large part of the welfare state is outside the scope of devolved competence altogether. It also means that the Scottish scope for distinct action is much more limited, due to the many interactions between devolved and non-devolved policies. Devolved policy has to take account of UK policy (much less often the other way round). Perhaps the clearest example

of this is the row that erupted between the Scottish and UK Governments when the former attempted to replace the council tax with a local income tax but was thwarted when the UK Government indicated that it would not allow the Scottish Government to continue to receive £300 million or so per year to support council tax benefit if there were no council tax. This can be a potent source of intergovernmental disagreement and friction which serves no useful purpose for anyone. From a devolved point of view, it is simply a constraint on autonomy, made worse by the fact that all parties in Scotland considered that they did have autonomy over these matters. It may enable the UK Government to frustrate devolved policies of which it disapproves, but such devolved policymaking is supposed to be the point of devolution, and this sort of vetoing does nothing to increase support for the UK level of government and its policies.

2. The proximity, size and scale of England. This creates serious pressure on Scotland to maintain a substantial degree of parity with what happens in England. Border issues are all the more serious for Wales, given the length and porosity of the England-Wales border. Thus, in 2006 more than 19,000 patients resident in England were registered with a GP in Wales and nearly 14,000 patients resident in Wales were registered with a GP in England – while about 7,000 more Welsh patients are treated in English hospitals than vice versa (Greer and Trench 2008, House of Commons 2008).

3. The financial system. One less-noticed effect of the block grant and formula system, underpinned by the Barnett formula, is that it assumes that public services in Scotland, Wales and Northern Ireland will be substantially similar in scale and scope to those in England. England is the reference point for the block grant, and it is changes in spending in England that determine changes in the grant to the devolved administrations. The system breaks down if devolved policy departs very far from what happens in England, which becomes a *de facto* norm. Higher education is an area where it has. Universities in England can be better funded than in Scotland because the UK Government found a source of revenue (in deferred variable fees) that does not trigger a Barnett consequential. That English policy choice, not followed by Scotland, in turn puts further pressure on the Scottish Government to ensure Scottish universities are adequately funded, whether by finding revenue from the block grant or using other sources of revenue (which are unattractive for political reasons). Furthermore, if spending decisions for England result in cuts, those cuts will feed through directly to the devolved administrations too.

The problem is that all these factors lie within the control of the UK level, and are beyond the control of the devolved administrations. This is not surprising given the size of England and its even greater importance as an electoral battleground over the last few years (when the key areas to win votes have been the suburbs of the larger cities, particularly London). The devolved administrations are affected by those policy choices that are driven by English concerns, but have little influence over them.

There are three ways that this sort of defect might be challenged. One is through mechanisms within the UK Parliament. These failed to deliver during the 1980s and 1990s, which is why devolution was needed in the first place. A second is within the UK Government. These mechanisms have not been very effective since 1999, however. The Secretaries of State for Scotland, Wales and Northern Ireland have had limited impact on such decisions, possibly managing to help tweak certain detailed aspects, but not the general policy goal or structure. Neither does Whitehall's structure help reduce the likelihood of this: the UK Government is both the government for the UK as a whole and the only government for England, and most departments in Whitehall have functions crossing the boundary between devolved and non-devolved matters. One exception is the Department for Work and Pensions, which has different problems in dealing with devolution questions – rooted in the fact that it is so used to dealing with Whitehall departments that form part of the same government that it failed to work out how to make sure the devolved administrations agreed with the objectives of the Welfare Reform Bill for getting jobless people back to work. These involved initiatives both for those with disabling illnesses claiming incapacity benefit, and those out of the labour market for so long that their skills had ossified. While the Scottish Government was willing to support many of these policies, there were still a good many issues to resolve – and the Welsh Assembly Government was much less sympathetic to both the objectives of the UK Government and the means by which it was pursuing them.

A common way of describing Scotland's relations with England has been to liken it to being in bed with an elephant. When it comes to social policy even in devolved areas, that is true in double measure. The UK Government does what it wants for its own reasons but with profound, possibly even devastating, effects on devolved functions and devolved government. That things were able to work as well as they did between 1999 and 2007 (when Labour dominated all three British governments) was not simply due, as many journalists suggested, to an absence of disagreement within the Labour Party, but to a more generally supportive climate in which governments mostly sought not to embarrass one another and with a huge amount of civil service work going into making sure they did not do so. It is telling that the occasions when there were problems were much more frequent when the UK Government did something detrimental to devolved concerns without prior warning, not vice versa.[1] Given the fundamental asymmetry of this system, none of this is surprising.

The third possible way the devolved parts of the UK might influence UK Government decisions that affect devolved policies is by intergovernmental (and perhaps interparliamentary) mechanisms. These are discussed in more detail in the rest of this chapter.

---

1. One reason was that the devolved administrations complied more fully with the underlying principle of 'no surprises' much better than the UK did. Another was that such policies as free NHS prescriptions in Wales or long-term care for the elderly in Scotland cause no more than limited and short-term embarrassment, while the difficulties caused by (say) the English approach to funding higher education are more fundamental and long-lasting.

The political implications of devolution finance

The way the Barnett formula allocates finance (and indeed the way funding is allocated within England, which is outside the formula) means that a sense that the UK is a community assuring equity in public services to all its citizens has been eroded over the last decade or so. Scotland has been a significant beneficiary here, with the connivance of the UK Government. During the early years of devolution, a major objective of the Labour/Liberal Democrat coalitions was to keep the issue off the UK-wide political agenda – in which they succeeded to such an extent that it remains impossible, from official statistics, to say how large Scotland's 'Barnett bonus' is.[2]

The perception in Scotland has been that Scotland is entitled to more generous funding than other parts of the UK – either because of higher but unspecified 'needs', or in order to justify the Union in Scotland, or for other reasons. Work for the Lords Select Committee on the Barnett Formula suggests that the present level of public spending in Scotland is hard to relate to current levels of most factors of need (House of Lords 2009, particularly Chapter 7; this is also the implication of Independent Commission on Funding and Finance for Wales 2009b). This difference in funding is seen in England as being the reason why policy in Scotland, Wales and Northern Ireland is different – and even if this is wrong, the idea has entered public discussion, and is hard to shake off. Moreover, the political problem is that the issue of the Barnett formula has plainly entered political debate in England, particularly southern England, and will not go away (see Curtice, this volume).

There is a further political issue: the rationale for a grant like Barnett is that it allows for policy divergence (which it does, but to a more limited extent than first thought), that it secures support for the Union in Scotland (which it does not, as it is taken for granted), while the English do not notice (they now clearly do). This suggests that the present system emphatically does not work. However, changing it is another matter.

The UK is not alone in facing these sorts of problems. They are common to all federal and decentralised states. In some – such as Germany or Australia – there is a strong commitment to state-wide equity (a uniform approach to social citizenship in the terms used above). These come with detailed systems of fiscal and resource equalisation, and (in Germany's case) a constitutional commitment to state-wide equality in public service provision.

Multinational systems – such as Canada, Spain or Belgium – are different. In those systems, the locus of welfare – which government is responsible for what – is a highly

---

2. It is evident that public spending in Scotland is around 18 per cent higher per head than the UK average, and 20 per cent higher than the average in England (HM Treasury 2009a, Table 9.2). Numerous papers, including work by ippr, have shown an overall inequity in the general distribution of public spending across the UK, especially when correlated to relative needs (McLean *et al* 2008, also House of Lords 2009). However, these figures do not pay regard to the division of powers between the two levels of government – what is important for the system of devolution finance is not just whether Scotland, in general, receives 'more than it should', but whether Scotland receives more for similar functions. The Holtham Commission in Wales is to be commended for seeking to redress this, by using English criteria rather than some external norm to assess how well Wales is funded in comparison to England (Independent Commission on Funding and Finance for Wales 2009a).

contested matter, and the effect of equalisation systems is limited (Obinger *et al* 2005). Moreover, many state or regional governments are concerned that equalisation systems lead to centralisation through the back-door. As a result, strong opposition means that equalisation is confined to addressing the most marked differences in fiscal capacity between states or regions (Shah 2007).

Is Calman the answer?

As noted above, some will see no problem with the present, ad hoc way of managing social policy after devolution. This may be either because they are only concerned with one part of the UK and not with the whole, or because they are willing to accept a constrained measure of devolved autonomy and the fact that this may be interfered with more or less at random by the UK level. Others will be happy to leave things as they are. The problem with this approach – for those who want to retain a United Kingdom – is that it leaves too much to chance. It assumes that problems will not arise, that if they do they will not be serious problems, and that even if they are serious they will not have significant constitutional ramifications.

The Calman Commission's solution was to talk of a social union, but never to define that clearly, let alone consider what sort of division of powers would be needed to deliver it (Commission on Scottish Devolution 2009). For Calman, the 'social union' was the status quo. Given the political differences within the Commission (and between the three unionist parties), this is not surprising, but it means that the Commission's final report fails to reconsider the logic of the present division of powers. In essence it says 'this is what happened in 1997, largely following what the Scottish Constitutional Convention recommended, and in order to make that work you need a limited measure of fiscal responsibility'. In addition, there should be an increased use of intergovernmental coordination to iron out problems in the relationship between devolved and UK-level policies.

Understood in these terms, it is hard for any party that claims to support devolution (as all three unionist parties do) to reject, or fail to act on, the Commission's recommendations. It is therefore little wonder that the UK Government has largely accepted the Calman recommendations, though with some significant restrictions – or that the key principles appear also to be supported by the Conservative Party leadership (Scotland Office 2009, Osborne 2009, Cameron 2010). However, merely implementing Calman is not enough to make devolution work on a UK-wide level, for two reasons. One is its failure to analyse what sort of structure there should be for devolution. The other is that it addressed only the Scotland–UK relationship; it took no account of the implications of devolved government in Wales and Northern Ireland, or the complexities that come with dealing with England. Tackling these issues for all the UK requires a more far-reaching approach.

How should the welfare state for a devolved United Kingdom be restructured?

Finding ways of restructuring the welfare state is not easy. One idea that is sometimes canvassed would involve an explicit attempt to establish the welfare state as a UK-wide system, with generally defined rights for all citizens that can be varied (upwards but not downwards) by particular governments. The minimum entitlement might be a legal right for all UK residents to have free treatment on the NHS for a range of conditions. It would be open to particular governments to decide how to apply that. Thus, the UK-wide standard could provide for only one cycle of IVF treatment being available for couples with fertility problems, with the woman aged between 28 and 35. Then particular governments might decide whether and how to extend that. However, there are serious problems with this approach. One is the impact that whatever was done in England would have on such rights. The effect of the financial system and the size of England (and England's prominence in the media) would mean that English practice would *de facto* become the norm, whatever the formal standard was. The effect would be to limit the scope for variation in policy.

A second problem is legal: implementing this would imply a use of some sort of 'framework law', setting out the 'UK' standards. Framework laws of this sort would be new to the British legal system and would present considerable challenges to officials and government lawyers, whether of intellectual approach and policy formulation or of drafting technique. Experience with framework laws when they have been used elsewhere is that either they are meaninglessly general, or become so prescriptive as to allow no room for manoeuvre at all (witness the development of European Community/Union directives, as well as German experience). Most damaging of all, though, is that this involves putting toothpaste back into the tube. It is not what was done in 1997–9, and (at least in Scotland) would not have commanded cross-party support for the referendum campaign if it had been proposed then. It is probably not desirable, but even if it were it is impracticable.

A more effective approach might involve a number of techniques, each of them often used in other decentralised or federal systems.

First, intergovernmental agreements and declarations can be used to set out general rights and expectations for citizens. Thus, one could have a political declaration that the NHS was to provide universal care for UK residents, free at the point of use. This would not be enforceable legally, and would not spell out what 'universal care' meant. That would be left to the political domain. While this does have a patchy track-record around the world, most vividly illustrated by Canadian experiences with the Social Union Framework Agreement, by setting out rights in a general way it creates political commitments to deliver them, and leaves it to political factors to determine what that means at any particular time or in any specific circumstance. It therefore ensures that there is a high degree of flexibility in the policy process.

In the UK this approach has scarcely been used. The only occasion when it has concerned the principles of the NHS, in an April 2008 declaration on the proposed NHS constitution. However, only the three devolved health ministers took part in that, with the Scottish, Welsh and Northern Ireland administrations committing themselves to an NHS that 'provides a universal and comprehensive service with equal access for all, free at the point of use and based on clinical need rather than the ability to pay' (Scottish Government 2008). The UK Government was not even at the table, though subsequently it sought to emphasise its own commitment by saying that 'The core principles of the National Health Service apply across the UK'. It also emphasised the importance of ensuring 'that a common framework of NHS principles for all UK citizens is maintained ... [to] strengthen a truly National Health Service' (Department of Health 2009: 1, 4). However, that 'common framework' has never been explicitly or publicly agreed by all four governments or legislatures. We therefore have two overlapping but not intersecting sets of political commitments to those general principles.

To make this approach work properly, it would need to have been adopted by a UK Labour Government in the early days of devolution, and then used consistently to underpin a range of UK-wide policies. That would have helped all involved to become accustomed to this as a tool of government. Even so, the challenges are considerable – nationalist parties in government could be expected to resist the Union-building or Union-reinforcing aspect of it (the three-government declaration on the NHS is carefully worded to address this point). Making it work would probably involve the UK Government putting some money on the table to create an incentive – that is the common approach in federal systems. It is also unlikely to be attractive to an incoming Conservative government. This therefore also has to be regarded as an opportunity whose time has now passed, whatever merits it might have had in principle.

Beyond this, it would also be desirable to make more use of written, published intergovernmental agreements about important matters of policy, when matters have been resolved between governments. At present, it this happens, it is in private, mainly in minutes of meetings or inter-ministerial correspondence. The public (and elected legislatures) do not know what agreements have been reached on their behalf, or what the terms are that their governments have agreed to. This material is seldom if ever published voluntarily, and is exempt from disclosure under the Freedom of Information Act 2000. Not only are there problems of transparency and accountability, but greater care and formality in recording such agreements would probably do no harm within government – and publication would greatly improve the transparency of the conduct of government business as well.

Second, one could reshape the scope of devolved competences, so that points of potential interaction (and therefore friction) are reduced. As most distributive aspects of welfare are already devolved, this would mean looking at redistributive ones. In particular, it would mean reviewing the number and scope of welfare benefits, and both funding and permitting devolved administrations to provide benefits as well as (and in some cases perhaps instead of) the UK Government. Clearly the major redistributive benefits – jobseekers' allowances and old age pensions – cannot easily be devolved. There would also be major questions about devolving incapacity benefit/employment and support allowance.

However, there is no reason why all other benefits need to be provided by the UK Government, even if the funds that pay for them are from UK Government sources and so are redistributive in territorial terms. The worst political problems have arisen with smaller benefits in financial terms, such as attendance allowance or council tax benefits, which target groups of people with specific problems and which interact directly with devolved services. The same considerations apply to housing benefit. Such benefits could be decentralised, with funding for them becoming part of an extended block grant, and delivery (including setting levels of benefit and criteria for entitlement) being a devolved matter. To the extent standards are needed, they can be either a condition of the grant, or left to political factors in each part of the UK to determine. That would avoid intergovernmental disputes that serve little purpose, certainly as far as the UK Government is concerned. Other targeted benefits are often now delivered through tax credits, however, so pose greater problems if they were to be devolved – though in principle that has considerable attractions if it were practicable.

This approach was deliberately eschewed by the Calman Commission in Scotland, though there is good reason to think that it would accord with the stated preferences of voters (an argument developed in Trench 2009b). This would not be a simple 'concession to nationalism' (though it might appeal to many nationalist voters); it would enable unionist parties to make clear what the Union did and did not do, and take credit for that – while avoiding unproductive disputes. It is possible to have both more 'Scottishness' or 'Welshness', and more unionism – this is not a zero-sum game. Rethinking the division of powers is an important part of achieving that.

While this remains a more practicable approach, it depends on a UK Government being committed to this vision of a decentralised social-democratic Union. It is now much too late for Labour to deliver such a vision, and the social policy aspect is unlikely to attract the Tories. However, other features of this approach – in particular, disentangling the responsibilities of each level of government to minimise their interaction – may have greater appeal. There may therefore be some scope to develop this approach in the coming years.

Third, it would be possible to make greater use of more formal mechanisms of intergovernmental coordination – a more serious attempt, through intergovernmental machinery, to manage differences where these exist, respecting each government's policy autonomy, and to ensure policies mesh with each other when possible. Such approaches are far from straightforward. In the best of circumstances, they call for a considerable investment of time and effort on the part of ministers as well as officials, and for their willingness, particularly at the UK end, to exercise self-restraint and accept that such coordination, and finding space within the UK framework for the expression of Scottish and Welsh distinctiveness, is what comes with running a complex, decentralised, multi-national state like the UK. If such meetings and processes are a substitute for thinking hard about which government should do what (which is essentially the position of the Calman Commission), they will probably not work. Agreement is unlikely to materialise simply because governments meet each other, while the practice of having meetings for the sake of having meetings is clearly undesirable. If such meetings and processes are used simply by the UK Government to tell devolved governments what it plans to do, or especially if they are used to suborn devolved governments into implementing UK policies, they will fail in that broader objective too.

Improving intergovernmental coordination poses sufficient difficulties that Labour in office eschewed this, abandoning even the plenary Joint Ministerial Committee (JMC) for more than five-and-a-half years. The one significant attempt to use the JMC framework for social policy matters foundered. This involved a meeting of the JMC (Poverty) in September 2002, which set out an ambitious policy agenda and planned at least two further meetings for 2003 which never took place. Its failure appears to have been because of devolved resistance to an attempt to impose Brownite social policy goals on them, without any incentive such as extra funding to join in.

Use of the JMC framework has undergone something of a revival since 2007, with the plenary JMC meeting more or less annually, and meetings of a new JMC (Domestic) to address some policy spillovers and interactions in areas such as the marine environment, welfare reform and finance. Those have been steps in the right direction, though most of the business discussed has arisen from failures in the UK Government to think about devolved constitutional responsibilities and policy goals at an early stage. Despite those problems, it was sufficiently attractive (as the least bad of the options on offer) for the Calman Commission to place considerable weight on it – probably excessive weight. Improved coordination can serve symbolic purposes which may be attractive to the Conservatives in government, and will fit well with the 'respect' agenda towards Scotland that David Cameron has spoken of repeatedly. Using this as a means to improve the overall coherence of social policy is unlikely to be attractive to Conservatives, however, and again Labour left it too late to use this way of achieving its strategic objectives between the 2007 and 2010 elections.

Finally, a more effective approach to intergovernmental finance is needed. In fact, of all the steps needed this is the most significant, but also politically the most problematic – as it involves many losers but few winners (and the losers will notice their losses much more than the winners will notice their gains).

Fixing finance

The present financial system is running out of supporters. It delivers neither fairness nor autonomy, and fails by most other criteria (such as transparency), too. While the system may be generous in the grant it provides to Scotland (creating good reasons for Scottish unionist politicians to want to minimise debate about it), it is nothing like as kind to Wales. While Scotland remains in the Union, the Scottish Government would prefer to retain all tax revenues generated in Scotland, remitting only an amount to Westminster to cover the costs of common services (Scottish Government 2009). Many parts of England resent it too (see Curtice, this volume), even though funding decisions for England are made wholly by the UK Government and are not subject to the Barnett Formula arrangements.

Little wonder that all the recent inquiries – the Holtham Commission (Independent Commission on Funding and Finance for Wales 2009a), the Commons Justice Committee (House of Commons 2009), the Lords Select Committee on the Barnett Formula (House of Lords 2009), and even the Calman Commission – agreed that any grant should be calculated according to the relative need of the various recipient administrations.

It is possible to sketch out the main elements of a reformed financial system that is designed to support a more decentralised social union:

1. A grant, calculated according to relative need of the varying parts of the UK, for the functions for which they are responsible. Such a grant needs to serve the interests of equity, not equality. It cannot be absolutely fair, and setting absolute fairness as a criterion that a new grant needs to satisfy will ensure no change, whatever comes about. That in turn will fuel the multiple senses of grievance that already exist.

The model suggested by the Lords Committee and the Holtham Commission is for a 'top down' grant, calculated according to a small number of general indicators rather than the detailed, bottom-up costing of demands for specific services used on the last occasion such an exercise was carried out, in the Needs Assessment of the late 1970s (HM Treasury 1979). The particular indicators used would need to be determined at the time the assessment was carried out, and no doubt would be the source of a good deal of wrangling. There should be only a few of them, and they should relate to factors (demographic, for example) that are outside the control of the devolved administrations to minimise the possibility of governments making policies designed to increase their grants (in other words, to avoid rent-seeking).

2. Institutional mechanisms that would ensure that the decisions on technical matters were put in the hands of those with technical expertise. This would probably mean an independent expert advisory commission. As politicians would both design the remit for such a commission and formally adopt its recommendations, this would not displace political responsibility for matters of political importance – but it would disentangle matters for expert judgement and matters for political judgement. This would entail removing the powers to make such decisions from HM Treasury, where they reside at present. A system that allows the Treasury to be judge and jury (and often gaoler) in its own cause, in the way the present one does, fails any standard of openness or fairness.

3. Institutional arrangements to improve transparency both about decision-making and in data, and to disentangle spending (and decisions about spending) in England from those that relate to the UK level. At present England is the reference point, in different ways and to different degrees, for all calculations relating to the block grant. That is inconsistent with ensuring that grants for the devolved institutions are stable and predictable and puts them on the same footing as the UK Government.

4. A degree of fiscal autonomy, at least along the lines recommended by Calman and at least for Scotland. Calman's suggestion is that the grant be reduced on a proportionate basis to create room for the devolution of 10 'tax points' on all rates of income tax. It is worth bearing in mind that that recommendation was rooted in a limited understanding of how devolution should work. The 10 points the Commission recommended be devolved were, in their view, necessary to bring an adequate degree of fiscal accountability to the present arrangements, not to transform the way devolution works more generally. (There is a further issue about whether such fiscal autonomy should apply only for Scotland, or for other places as well. The Holtham Commission is presently considering if it would be appropriate for Wales. If it were applied to Wales or Northern Ireland, some sort of system of fiscal equalisation would be needed, though it would probably be a technically simple one.)

There are two big political problems with realising this sort of system. First, it means accepting that redistribution from richer parts of the UK to poorer ones is part of the UK's financial system, and that that is part of what the Union is for: a zone of mutual social solidarity. This will be highly contentious, particularly initially, because there will be more losers (or at least places that see themselves as losing) involved than winners. Moreover, the losers will lose more than the winners will gain. It is, however, the only way to do what is necessary to keep the UK together (financial redistribution of some sort), and get some sort of political dividend for doing so. Labour, the party naturally sharing such an outlook, has ducked the opportunities it had to do so. The appeal of such an approach to the Conservatives is likely to be much less.

The second problem is the timing of any changes. Changes to the financing arrangements of federal and decentralised systems are always highly contentious and fractious. Usually, central or federal governments try to introduce them over a number of years when economies and tax revenues are buoyant, so that any 'losers' lose over the longer term, not immediately. Various sorts of 'hold-harmless' provisions are common, to cushion the impact and ensure that no government suffers a nominal reduction in their funding, and that any reduced entitlements are introduced over several years.

The worst time to make such changes is when public spending is tight and everyone is fighting to protect their share of a shrinking cake. However, that is exactly the position the UK will find itself in: the looming constraints on public spending will make the next few years a tough time for everyone, and there will simply be no money available to make life easier when introducing a new system.

Indeed, the rationale for making changes may well be to reduce the share of overall public spending that flows to the devolved parts of the UK, particularly Scotland and maybe Northern Ireland. The only upsides will be the removal of various grievances for the longer term, and the creation of a firmer foundation for arguments about cross-territorial equity. The case for letting matters lie is a persuasive one for many elected politicians, whose thoughts seldom stray beyond the next election (for an example, see the evidence of the Secretaries of State for Scotland, Wales and Northern Ireland to the Lords Barnett Formula Committee: House of Lords 2009, 246-59).

All this is a considerable distance away from what the Labour UK Government has committed itself to (Scotland Office 2009, HM Treasury 2009b). This can be described as 'Calman-minus': a limited measure of fiscal autonomy, on earned income tax and some minor taxes, for Scotland only, based on estimates of revenue, not actual tax income, and subject to extensive control by HM Treasury. There is to be no needs-related review of the block grant, and no new impartial body to carry out such an assessment or monitor the system more generally. The system will therefore remain centralised and opaque, even if Labour is returned to office. While the Conservative position is still unclear (Osborne 2009, Cameron 2010), the general thrust appears to be in a similar direction. Although that may redress some immediate political grievances, it will not address the underlying issues.

Conclusion

A different approach to intergovernmental relations could have helped to cement a UK-wide conception of social citizenship in place, in the post-devolution UK. Such an approach would undermine neither devolved autonomy nor UK unity, but would help produce a UK in which the benefits of union were coupled with those of self-government in a way that the general public could comprehend. There are undoubtedly considerable political difficulties with putting such a system in place, and those difficulties have persuaded politicians since 1999 not to even try making them. In retrospect, that will look like a huge missed opportunity. Not only would they have made a devolved, social-democratic UK work well, but they would have locked in commitments to social democracy in ways that would be hard to unpick.

Any incoming Conservative Government would be unlikely to share such commitments – and only a majority UK Government would have the political capital to expend on such a venture. For Conservatives the ways of keeping the UK together would likely be very different, relying on a combination of legal powers and bilateral deals that would not underpin shared characteristics of the UK. It may be less concerned about uniformity and UK-wide consistency, and willing to do bilateral deals to increase the degree of variation in the UK's constitutional geometry. However, it would also want to emphasise the primacy of the UK level and the subordinate status of the devolved administrations, as well as eliminate English subsidies to Scotland. The sort of social union that the UK may have in five years' time would, as a result, be very different from the sort that was possible in 1999, and that in turn may undermine broader institutional features that help underpin the Union.

References

Cameron D (2010) 'The real choice in British Politics'. Speech at Scottish Conservative and Unionist Party Conference, Perth, 12 February: www.scottishconservatives.com/news/speeches/224

Commission on Scottish Devolution (2009) *Serving Scotland Better: Scotland and the United Kingdom in the 21st Century, Final Report – June 2009.* Edinburgh: Commission on Scottish Devolution

Department of Health (2009) *The Government Response to the Welsh Affairs Committee interim report on the provision of cross-border health services for Wales, Cm 7531.* London: The Stationery Office

Greer SL (ed) (2009) *Devolution and Citizenship Rights in the United Kingdom* Bristol: Policy Press

Greer SL and Trench A (2008) *Health and Intergovernmental Relations in the Devolved United Kingdom* London: The Nuffield Trust

HM Treasury (1979) *Needs Assessment Study - Report* London: HM Treasury

HM Treasury (2009a) *Public Expenditure Statistical Analyses 2009 Cm 7630.* London: The Stationery Office

HM Treasury (2009b) *House of Lords Select Committee on the Barnett Formula: The Government's response, Cm 7772.* London: The Stationery Office

House of Commons (2008) *Welsh Affairs Committee Sixth Report of Session 2007–08 The provision of cross–border health services for Wales: Interim Report, HC 870.* London: The Stationery Office

House of Commons (2009) *Justice Select Committee, Fifth Report of Session 2008–09: Devolution: A Decade On, HC 529.* London: The Stationery Office

House of Lords (2009) *Select Committee on the Barnett Formula 1st Report of Session 2008–09: The Barnett Formula, HL Paper 139.* London: The Stationery Office

Independent Commission on Funding and Finance for Wales (2009a) *Funding devolved government in Wales: Barnett & beyond, First Report to the Welsh Assembly Government* Cardiff: Welsh Assembly Government

Independent Commission on Funding and Finance for Wales (2009b) *Working paper: Replacing Barnett with a needs-based formula, December,* Cardiff: Welsh Assembly Government

Marshall TH and Bottomore T (1992) *Citizenship and Social Class* London: Pluto Press

McEwen N (2002) 'State Welfare Nationalism: The territorial impact of welfare state development in Scotland', *Regional and Federal Studies,* 12:1, 66–90

McLean I, Lodge G and Schmuecker K (2008) *Fair Shares? Barnett and the politics of public expenditure* London: ippr: www.ippr.org.uk/publicationsandreports/publication.asp?id=619

Ministry of Justice (2007) *The Governance of Britain, Cm 7170.* London: The Stationery Office

Obinger H, Leibfried S and Castles F (eds) (2005) *Federalism and the Welfare State: New World and European Experiences* Cambridge: Cambridge University Press

Osborne G (2009) 'Defence of the Union and mutual respect key in debate over powers', *The Scotsman,* 26 November

Scotland Office (2009) *Scotland's Future in the United Kingdom. Building on ten years of Scottish devolution, Cm 7738.* London: The Stationery Office

Scottish Government (2008) News Release: 'Joint statement on NHS values', 3 April, available at www.scotland.gov.uk/News/Releases/2008/04/03120546

Scottish Government (2009) *Fiscal Autonomy in Scotland: The case for change and options for reform. Taking forward our National Conversation* Edinburgh: Scottish Government

Shah A (ed) (2007) *The Practice of Fiscal Federalism: Comparative Perspectives (Global Dialogue on Federalism Series)* Kingston and Montreal: McGill-Queen's University Press

Trench A (2007) 'The framework of devolution: the formal structure of devolved power' in Trench A (ed.) *Devolution and Power in the United Kingdom* Manchester: Manchester University Press

Trench A (2009a) 'Un-joined Up Government? Intergovernmental relations and citizenship rights' in Greer 2009 *op. cit.*

Trench A (2009b) 'Devolution in Scotland and Wales: Muddled Thinking and Unintended Results' in Facey P, Rigby B and Runswick A (eds) *Unlocking Democracy: 20 years of Charter 88* London: Politico's

5. Devolution in a recession: who'd have thought it would come to this?

David Bell

The UK economy enjoyed one of its longest periods of continuous economic growth between 1998 and 2008, a period that broadly coincided with the UK's first decade of devolved government. But in 2008 this growth came to an abrupt halt. Output dropped sharply. By late 2008 it was clear that the British economy was experiencing its deepest recession since the 1920s.

For almost a decade the devolved institutions in the UK reaped the benefits of this economic growth. Increased tax revenues allowed public spending to grow rapidly. Like other parts of the public sector, the devolved institutions enjoyed significant real increases in spending power. They applied this to the areas they had control over, such as health, education and transport.

Thus, during their first decade, the devolved bodies did not have to take unpopular spending decisions seriously. None embarked on significant reductions in the size of the public sector. They may have looked for efficiency savings, or reallocated resources at the margin between spending programmes. But they did not have to deal with the politics of withdrawing support from major public programmes. The next decade will be much more challenging for devolved government due to the public expenditure consequences of the recession.

This chapter looks at how the devolved administrations in the UK have dealt with the recession thus far. It considers the extent to which their existing powers enable them to institute policies to counteract its effects. It also details the types of measures that they have put in place and reflects on what the recession has revealed about the nature of the relationship between the UK government and the devolved institutions.

The recession

The genesis of the recession lay in the financial markets. Reckless expansion of credit in asset markets, particularly in housing and commercial property, led to a worldwide loss of confidence in financial institutions. This was particularly marked in the UK, Ireland and the United States. Central banks and national government had little option but to intervene to shore up these institutions, at great cost to the taxpayer. Forced by the authorities to reduce their exposure to risk, financial institutions cut back their lending drastically both to consumers and businesses. Businesses and households found it difficult to access loans: credit conditions moved from feast to famine almost overnight.

The result was not only a substantial cut in local demand for goods and services, but also a cut in the demand for exports, which had further adverse effects on output and employment. UK output fell by 5.4 per cent between the first quarter of 2008 and the second quarter of 2009, a decline unprecedented since the Great Depression. Between the second quarter of 2008 and the third quarter of 2009, UK unemployment rose by 841,000.

The recession has been especially harmful to the public finances. Borrowing increased at an alarming rate. The Chancellor of the Exchequer, in his 2009 Pre-Budget Report, forecast that the public sector deficit would be £178bn in 2009–10. This is in excess of 12 per cent of GDP, a peacetime record. The effects on the devolved institutions will come in the future: following the next election, whichever party is in power, the UK Government will have to put in place a credible plan to reduce the deficit, which will involve sharp cutbacks in Departmental Expenditure Limits (DEL). The Barnett Formula will ensure that the devolved administrations take their population share of these cuts.

The effects of the recession have thus far been broadly similar across the nations that comprise the UK. Figure 5.1 shows the path of unemployment in each of the home nations from January 2008: a broadly parallel increase in unemployment rates over

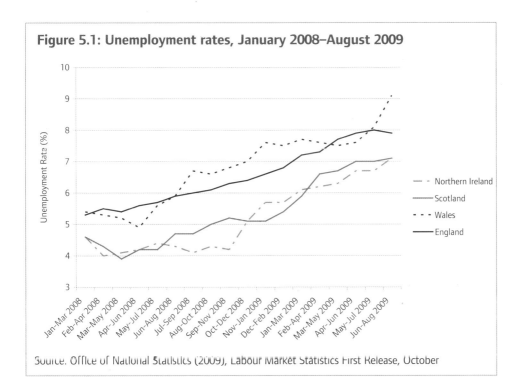

Figure 5.1: Unemployment rates, January 2008–August 2009

Source: Office of National Statistics (2009), Labour Market Statistics First Release, October

the period to August 2009. While there are some minor differences in starting points and timing, the increases are broadly the same across the home nations.

Figure 5.2 takes a longer-term perspective on the unemployment data. It shows how the claimant count unemployment rate has varied in the home nations since devolution began in 1999. The increase in the unemployment rate during 2008 was very marked and followed a long period of declining rates in all of the home nations. The recession has reversed these advances but in international terms, the UK labour market has been more resilient than countries such as Ireland, Spain and the US, whose recessions also originate with the difficulties of the financial sector.

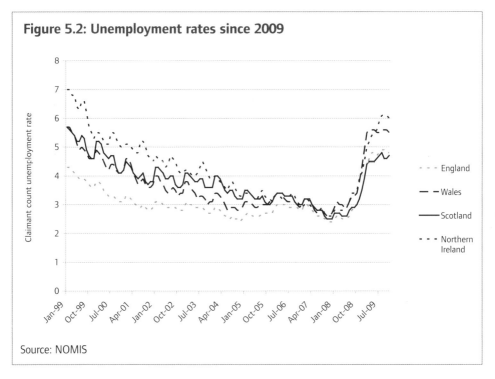

Figure 5.2: Unemployment rates since 2009

Source: NOMIS

Figure 5.3 illustrates the changes in unemployment within the home nations. It shows how the increase in the claimant count unemployment rate between March 2008 and November 2009 was distributed across the local authorities within each of the nations. It is evident that Northern Ireland has a larger share than the other nations of local authorities experiencing unemployment rate increases of 3 per cent or more.

Table 5.1 (on page 64) shows how broader labour market measures have performed across all parts of the UK during the recession. It gives the change in the numbers of economically active, employed, unemployed and inactive by region for the 12 months to August–October 2009. Since these data are based on the Labour Force Survey (LFS), they give a more complete picture of the labour market than the claimant

Figure 5.3: Distribution of unemployment rate changes by local authority, March 2008–November 2009

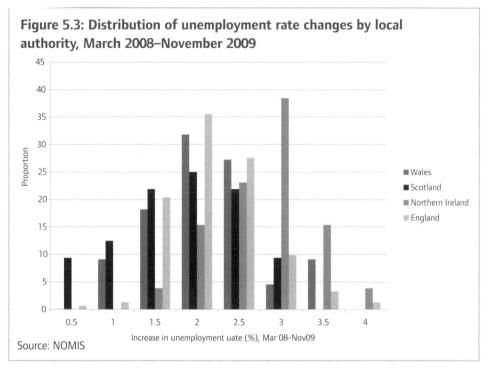

Source: NOMIS

count unemployment rate, which counts only those eligible for Job Seeker's Allowance. The rows are ordered by the increase in the broader LFS-based unemployment rate.

It is clear from the table that the West Midlands and South West have experienced larger increases in their unemployment rate than either Northern Ireland or Wales. However, the picture changes slightly when inactivity rates[1] are taken into account. In the UK as a whole, there has been very little increase in inactivity during the current recession. In previous recessions, the 'discouraged worker' effect led to large increases in the number of individuals, particularly older men, who dropped out of the labour market entirely. This effect was particularly strong in Wales and Northern Ireland during the 1980s. These areas still have high inactivity rates, but only in Northern Ireland has there been an increase during this recession (of 1.2 per cent). Thus, while the LFS-based unemployment measure implies that the Northern Ireland labour market is not performing as badly as the claimant count data show, the data on inactivity show that the overall effect of the recession on the Northern Ireland labour market has perhaps been worse than it has been elsewhere in the UK.

The downward path in economic activity is confirmed by data on output that are available only for Scotland, which show the decline in production there broadly matched that in the UK as a whole (Scottish Government 2009).

1. The economically inactive are those out of the whole population, including those not eligible to work, who are not in the labour force.

Table 5.1: Labour market changes, 12 months to August–October 2009

Age	Economically active		Employed		Unemployed		Economically inactive	
	16+ (000s)	16–59/ 64 (%)	16+ (000s)	16–59/ 64 (%)	16+ (000s)	16–59/ 64 (%)	16+ (000s)	16–59/ 64 (%)
North West	45	0.9	1	-0.1	44	1.2	-39	-0.9
London	64	-0.5	-5	-1.7	69	1.6	45	0.5
North East	14	-1.2	-33	-2.5	20	1.7	21	1.2
South East	1	-0.7	-77	-2.3	76	1.7	41	0.7
East Midlands	30	0.2	-15	-1.4	45	1.8	-3	-0.2
East	23	0.9	-35	-0.7	57	1.9	-27	-0.9
England	186	-0.1	-323	-1.6	510	1.9	60	0.1
Scotland	15	-0.3	-38	-1.9	52	1.9	12	0.3
Yorks & H'ber	5	-0.2	-47	-1.8	52	2	9	0.2
Wales	9	-0.1	-39	-1.8	30	2.1	?	0.1
N. Ireland	7	-1.2	-25	-2.7	18	2.2	14	1.2
South West	26	-1.7	-86	-3.5	59	2.3	53	1.7
West Midlands	61	1.3	-26	-1.3	87	3.1	-42	-1.3
UK	175	-0.2	-432	-1.7	608	1.9	96	0.2

Source: Office of National Statistics (2009), Labour Market Statistics First Release, November

There have been some small differences between the nations in the performance of the housing market (see Figure 5.4). The decline in house price values from the beginning of 2008 has been much more marked in Northern Ireland than in the rest of the UK. This may partly reflect its proximity to the extremely depressed housing market in the Republic of Ireland. But housing finance is not an area where the devolved institutions have a strong policy presence, reflecting the fact that the UK housing market has been lightly regulated in recent years.

The economic problems that the recession has caused seem to be broadly common across all of the home nations. Previous recessions were more focused on particular industries. Because these were not evenly distributed across the UK, past recessions were characterised by higher rates of unemployment in Wales, Scotland, Northern Ireland and the North of England. But it seems that this recession, perhaps because its origins are more financial than sectoral, is presenting the devolved authorities and the UK Government with broadly the same set of economic problems. For individuals,

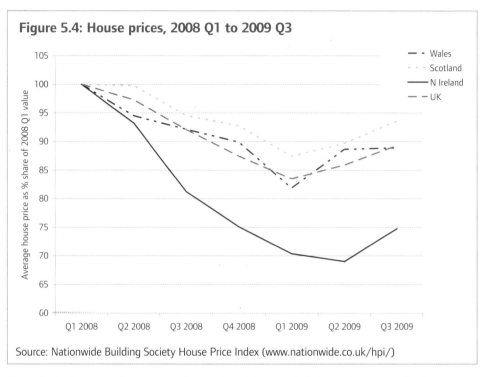

Figure 5.4: House prices, 2008 Q1 to 2009 Q3

Legend: Wales, Scotland, N Ireland, UK

Y-axis: Average house price as % share of 2008 Q1 value (60 to 105)

X-axis: Q1 2008, Q2 2008, Q3 2008, Q4 2008, Q1 2009, Q2 2009, Q3 2009

Source: Nationwide Building Society House Price Index (www.nationwide.co.uk/hpi/)

these include unemployment and associated issues of debt and poverty. Businesses are suffering not only from a drop in orders, but also from a sharp contraction in credit availability, which threatens their viability.

Employers' organisations and trade unions raise such difficulties with the devolved administrations, but their ability to respond is limited. They can offer advice and information, and have a limited ability to influence demand through government purchases of, say, affordable housing. But the policy instruments available to the devolved administrations are much less extensive than those held by Westminster, as will be shown.

Economic powers of the devolved institutions

The devolved administrations lack the economic powers needed to fight a recession on their own. Fiscal policy is reserved and monetary policy rests with the Bank of England. Furthermore, all policy matters relating to financial services and financial markets are reserved.

Most national or federal governments guard their right to control both fiscal and monetary policy, though different mechanisms exist to inform and/or consult sub-national governments about changes to these policies. The duty to consult might be seen as an impediment to decisive policy action by central government but international evidence suggests otherwise. In Germany, for example, the Financial Planning Council proposes fiscal policy actions at the Federal and Länder (state) level, and comprises Federal Ministers of Finance and of Economics, the Länder Ministers responsible for finance and four representatives of municipalities. The model has produced much greater fiscal discipline than in the UK. In the UK, there is ex-post explanation of the contents of the UK Budget by the Treasury in the devolved territories, but the devolved administrations have no defined ex-ante role in determining its contents. Determining how effective consultation is in changing outcomes is notoriously difficult to measure, but the fact remains that there are models outside the UK that seem to be more consensual in arriving at budget priorities whose fiscal outcomes are certainly no worse than those in the UK.

Most countries allow sub-national government to borrow as well as to raise some taxes. Part 3 of the Scotland Act restricts the Scottish Government's ability to borrow from the Treasury in Westminster to a maximum of £500 million. Such borrowing can be used only for temporary working capital. It cannot be used to fund public sector investment. The Wales and Northern Ireland Acts contain provisions for 'advances' by the Secretary of State to the respective Assemblies. In the case of Wales, the advance is not to exceed £500m and for Northern Ireland the limit is £250m. As in Scotland, these monies are to be used to meet temporary imbalances, rather than to fund capital spending. But in Northern Ireland a separate borrowing mechanism for capital expenditure does exist. This was agreed by the Prime Minister, Chancellor of the Exchequer and the First and Deputy Ministers in May 2002 and was introduced in the 2003 Budget. Known as the Reinvestment and Reform Initiative (RRI), it was designed to address infrastructure deficits and to modernise services following 30 years where security was the main focus of spending. The borrowing facility operates under the standard terms for borrowing from the National Loans Fund and is funded through revenue from rates. Recent borrowing from this fund has been around £200m per annum.

The Scottish Parliament, unlike its Welsh and Northern Irish equivalents, was granted the power to vary the basic rate of income tax by no more than 3p in the pound. In addition, it was granted powers over local authority taxation. These provide a modest control over aggregate taxation revenues raised in Scotland and so over the level of demand in the Scottish economy. However, the Scottish Government has never used this tax power, perhaps because it fears that it might lead the Treasury to reduce the level of Scotland's block grant.

The ability of the devolved administration to influence economic forces is therefore largely confined to the 'supply side' of the economy. For example, the Scottish Government can pursue economic development policies, such as improving transport or information infrastructure, and it can choose to spend resources on improving the quality of training and education. But it cannot make a significant impact on the demand side of the economy.

The workings of the Barnett Formula
On the spending side the devolved nations are funded by an annual grant from the Treasury. They have no control over the size of the grant but they do decide how it

should be spent. Its value is determined by the Barnett Formula, which relates changes in the grant provided to the devolved administrations to changes in spending on 'comparable' programmes in England. Within the UK public expenditure framework, this type of spending is part of Departmental Expenditure Limit (DEL). Its value is set during the Comprehensive Spending Review (CSR), which reflects public spending priorities for the UK over the short to medium term.

The grant to each administration comprises the 'baseline' plus 'increment'. The baseline is made up of the baseline in the previous year plus that year's increment. The increment is determined by applying the 'comparabilities' in the Statement of Funding Policy to changes in DEL. The recent report by the Lords Select Committee on the Barnett Formula points out that this means that previous increments become embedded in future allocations, irrespective of their relevance to current need:

> *Thus everything in the past is taken as given. The original baseline when the Formula was first applied now represents barely one tenth of the total expenditure but there are a culminating series of new baselines, which become increasingly out of date, leading to further anomalies. Together, these account for the vast bulk of the block grant.* (House of Lords Select Committee on the Barnett Formula 2009)

The Barnett Formula is a convention that has been accepted by successive Labour and Conservative governments. It has no legal status and could be replaced by some other funding mechanism without legislative difficulty. None of the devolved administrations can be assured of its longevity and, as we shall see subsequently, this uncertainty has perhaps been part of the motivation for the recent reviews of funding in the devolved territories carried out in Wales (the Independent Commission for Finance and Funding in Wales – chaired by Gerald Holtham), Scotland (the Commission on Scottish Devolution – chaired by Sir Kenneth Calman) and by the House of Lords Select Committee on the Barnett Formula.

As well as DEL, total public expenditure (also known as 'Total Managed Expenditure' – TME) in the UK includes 'Annually Managed Expenditure' (AME), which comprises those elements of spending that cannot be so readily controlled over a time horizon longer than a year. Recessions tend to result in upward pressure on AME, mainly because it includes both social security payments and interest on the national debt, and these tend to increase during recessions. When overall public expenditure is constrained by the state of the economy, upward pressure on AME implies downward pressure on DEL.

Thus, if economic circumstances warrant cuts in overall spending, the devolved administrations have to adjust not only to an overall reduction in resources, but also to a further squeeze arising from the diminishing share of DEL in total public expenditure. This is illustrated in Table 5.2, which shows how DEL and AME resource and capital spending together contribute to TME from 2008–9 to 2010–11. With an overall budget fixed by the need to reduce the rate of growth of the public debt and AME spending increasing because of increased social security spending and debt interest, the squeeze on DEL is particularly apparent between 2009–10 and 2010–11.

Table 5.2: Departmental Expenditure Limits (DEL) and Annually Managed Expenditure (AME), 2008–9 to 2010–11

	2008–9		2009–10		2010–11	
	Amount (£bn)	Share (%)	Amount (£bn)	Share (%)	Amount (£bn)	Share (%)
DEL resource	321.2	51.2	342.2	50.6	353.4	50.0
AME resource	242.7	38.7	264.8	39.2	293.6	41.6
Total resource	**563.9**	**89.8**	**607**	**89.8**	**647**	**91.6**
DEL capital	48.1	7.7	56.6	8.4	52.7	7.5
AME capital	15.9	2.5	12.1	1.8	6.8	1.0
Depreciation	-18.7	-3.0	-19.2	-2.8	-20.1	-2.8
Net capital	**45.3**	**7.2**	**49.5**	**7.3**	**39.4**	**5.6**
Total Managed Expenditure	**627.9**		**675.7**		**706.5**	

Source: HM Treasury (2009)

The squeeze will fall most severely on capital spending, perhaps because it is anticipated that this will be less unpopular than cuts to resource (current) spending. Cuts in resource spending often lead to cuts in frontline services and/or public sector jobs, both of which carry significant political dangers. Between 2009–10 and 2010–11, DEL capital spending will fall from 7.3 to 5.6 per cent of Total Managed Expenditure. In practice, this means that the share of capital purchases in UK public spending will fall by 23 per cent over this period – quite a dramatic downturn.

Comprehensive Spending Reviews have taken place at irregular intervals since 1998, but are normally expected to occur every two years and to look three years ahead. Given the framing of the Scotland, Wales and Northern Ireland Acts, it is not surprising that there has been no significant overspend on the devolved authorities' CSR allocations, although as we shall see, the Northern Ireland Executive is struggling to keep its spending within current DEL limits.

There has been some history of underspend. This mainly occurs when capital projects are delayed or postponed, resulting in actual spending falling short of budgeted amounts. Underspends are given the rather curious title of 'end year flexibility' (EYF). These are held by the Treasury, but remain part of the budgets allocated to the devolved authorities. The rules governing EYF are set out in the Statement of Funding Policy. The most recent version of this was published in 2007 and states that the devolved administrations 'have a full discretion over the use of these resources' (HM Treasury 2007). In practice, this does not seem to be entirely the case. For example, the devolved administrations cannot shift EYF funding between capital and resource budgets. Furthermore, as the Statement says, 'expenditure cannot be anticipated': EYF is solely for underspends. It cannot be used to bring expenditure forward. The rate at which it can be drawn down into devolved administration budgets has to be agreed with the Treasury.

Because it has had a history of underspend, the Scottish Government now typically over-allocates its budget by a small amount. This reduces the likelihood that EYF will be accumulated with the Treasury, but also runs the relatively small risk of overspend if all budgets are fully spent during the fiscal year.

The inability to bring expenditure forward is important because a Keynesian response to recession would be to increase the level of government spending and fund this through borrowing. The Statement of Funding Policy precludes the devolved authorities from using EYF as part of a Keynesian strategy to boost demand, unless they have built up a reserve of EYF at the Treasury either by accident or design. There is clearly a political case for the devolved authorities to have more extensive powers to influence demand. Interestingly, however, the recession does not seem to have significantly heightened demands for fiscal autonomy. One exception has been the specific demands by the Scottish Government for powers to bring forward capital expenditure.

There have been clear differences in the use of EYF in recent years across the devolved administrations. Some have been more willing than others to draw down from their accumulated 'savings'. The Scottish Government has run down its EYF reserves most rapidly. This is shown in Table 5.3, which gives the value of EYF at the end of each fiscal year and expresses this as a share of the relevant 2007–8 DEL. It

Table 5.3: End Year Flexibility (EYF) (£m) and as share of 2007–8 Departmental Expenditure Limit (DEL)

	Scottish Government		Welsh Assembly Government		Northern Ireland Executive	
	Value (£m)	Share of DEL (%)	Value (£m)	Share of DEL (%)	Value (£m)	Share of DEL (%)
2006–7	1,528.6	5.6	607.0	4.4	912.5	9.1
2007–8	952.3	3.5	899.9	6.5	915.6	9.1
2008–9	669.8	2.4	970.4	7.0	675.1	6.7

Source: HM Treasury Public Expenditure Outturn 2006–07 to 2008–09

thus gives an estimate of the value of accumulated savings to each administration. Between 2006–7 and 2008–9, the Scottish Government reduced its share from 5.6 to 2.4 per cent; the Welsh Assembly increased the relative value of its EYF by more than 50 per cent, while in Northern Ireland, its value fell from 9.1 to 6.7 per cent of DEL.

The motivation behind the reduction in EYF in Scotland had little to do with the recession. The SNP Government realised that there were opportunities to increase the level of public spending in Scotland beyond that available in current DEL by accessing previously accumulated EYF. It agreed a rundown of these funds with the Treasury shortly after the publication of CSR 2007, and well before the beginning of the recession. As a result, public spending in Scotland in 2008–9 was around 3.2 per cent (5.6 per cent, less 2.4 per cent) higher than it would have been, had the decision to reduce the EYF funding not been taken. But, looking forward, the unspent EYF available to Scotland is less than that in Wales or Northern Ireland. Thus, if the recession is prolonged, Wales and Northern Ireland will have more of a safety net which they may be able to draw on to maintain levels of public spending.[2]

In the next section, we discuss the specific responses that have taken place within the devolved administrations to the recession. These measures have to be seen in the context of the framework for public expenditure in the UK that has been discussed in this section.

Responses to the recession

By the end of 2008 it was clear that the UK economy was rapidly deteriorating. In the November 2008 Pre-Budget Report, the Treasury introduced a number of measures to maintain a balance between supporting aggregate demand on the one hand, and thus preventing the recession from getting worse, and protecting the UK's reputation as a reliable borrower on the other. These included:

a) Temporarily reducing the rate of Value Added Tax to 15 per cent

b) Bringing forward £3bn worth of capital spending from 2010–11

c) Introducing a new higher rate of income tax of 45 per cent for those with incomes above £150,000 from April 2011

d) Setting an additional £5bn worth of efficiency savings for 2010–11

Measures (b) and (d) had implications for the devolved administrations. Firstly, as a result of the Barnett formula, the bringing forward of capital spending had 'Barnett consequentials'[3] for the devolved administrations. Because of the regulations laid out in the Statement of Funding Policy, the consequentials had to be restricted to capital spending. Thus, the 2008 Pre-Budget Report changed the plans set out in the CSR

---

2. There are no detailed plans regarding how such monies might be used, perhaps because of uncertainty associated with the process of agreeing with the Treasury how EYF will be drawn down.
3. If baseline DEL is changed, allocations to the devolved bodies are changed by their population share of such changes – these changes are known as 'Barnett consequentials'.

2007 and triggered an increase in government-funded capital spending throughout the UK. In Scotland it facilitated the bringing forward of £346m of capital spending from 2010–11 to 2008–9 and 2009–10. The downside was the offsetting adjustment that had to be made in the 2010–11 budget. Similar adjustments applied to the Welsh and Northern Irish accelerated capital expenditure programmes.

This illustrates one of the most important properties of the Barnett Formula. Increases in spending at the UK level are reflected immediately in the devolved administration budgets. There is no need to negotiate the strength of the case for increases in Scotland, Wales or Northern Ireland relative to England. But, as we shall see, there is also no need for the Treasury to negotiate with the devolved administrations when spending is being cut.

Secondly, the efficiency savings, insofar as they affected 'comparable programmes', would have negative effects on the budgets of the devolved administrations in 2010–11. In Scotland, the costs directly attributable to the efficiency savings were £392m. But a downward adjustment of £1.3bn in the Department of Health's capital budget resulted in a further £129m cut in the Scottish budget. These cuts became a potent political issue, with the SNP government claiming that the Chancellor had imposed £500m worth of cuts in the Scottish budget. None of these were cuts specifically imposed on Scotland. Rather, they were the Barnett consequences of decisions made about levels of funding in England. Similar but smaller effects impacted on Wales and Northern Ireland.

Compared with 2008, the effects of the 2009 Pre-Budget Report on the devolved administrations were negligible. Much to the regret of the SNP administration in Edinburgh, there was no extension of the capital acceleration programme. Due to economic uncertainty, but probably also partly for electoral reasons, there were no specifics on DEL beyond 2010–11. This leaves the devolved administrations in limbo: they know that, whichever party is in power, there will be significant cuts in their block grants from 2011–12 onwards, but they do not know how large these will be.

We now look in more detail at the specific policy measures that the devolved administrations have introduced in response to the recession. It is too early, however, to determine definitively how economically effective these may have been.

Responses – Scotland
The policy response of the Scottish Government to the recession is described in the Scottish Economic Recovery Plan (Scottish Government 2009) and the 2008 and draft 2009 Scottish Budgets. The Economic Recovery Plan is interesting in the sense that it provides a list of actions that the Scottish Government intends to take, but makes no attempt to set the difficulties that the Scottish economy faces in the context of a worldwide recession; neither does it look at the factors that might influence the depth of the recession or assist any future recovery. The plan focuses on three areas – jobs and communities, education and skills, and investment and innovation, which we discuss below.

In the category of supporting **jobs and communities**, the highlights include:

- An additional £120m investment in affordable housing in 2008–9 and 2009–10. This was partly funded by shifting capital spending from other parts of the capital budget.
- £50m to invest in council house building – a radical step given the lack of support for council house building since the time of Mrs Thatcher.
- Reduced rates for small businesses and an extension to the agreement with local authorities to freeze council tax.
- £35m to support home owners in financial difficulty and £60m for a shared-equity scheme for first-time house buyers.
- £60m for town centre regeneration and £30m to improve household energy efficiency.

Not all of these schemes are new: the freeze on council tax had already been in place for two years. The town centre regeneration fund was a concession to the Conservatives, necessary to ensure their support for the 2009–10 Scottish Budget. The major innovation was the acceleration of capital expenditure. But, as mentioned above, the overall amount to be spent on capital between 2008–9 and 2010–11 remained fixed. If some spending was brought forward to 2008 9 and 2009–10, less could be spent in 2010–11. It was not clear what the net effects of this rescheduling might be on tackling the recession. In response to the Scottish Parliament Finance Committee, the Cabinet Secretary argued that:

> *The Government hopes and believes that by accelerating affordable housing investment, for example, we can try to stem some of the losses in the construction sector. By 2010–11, there may be some recovery in private sector activity that allows construction activity to fill some of those gaps in the programme.* (Scottish Parliament Finance Committee 2008: para 54)

The Cabinet Secretary's judgement was that capital acceleration would tide the economy over until it emerged from recession. The difficulty was that such a favourable outcome was conditional on the recession being shortlived, which turned out not to be the case. The basis on which this forecast was made is not explained in the Economic Recovery Plan.

The second component of the Economic Recovery Plan focuses on **strengthening education and skills**, including wage subsidies in some circumstances, help for people facing redundancy, an additional £16m to support 7,800 apprenticeships, improving services for the unemployed and spending £16m on helping young people seeking to work in the community or third sector.

The scheme for those facing redundancy, known as PACF (Partnership Action for Continuing Employment), was partly funded by the European Social Fund. PACE had already been in existence for nine years. The recession involved closer partnership working, but the basic mission to provide advice and assistance to those facing redundancy did not change. Thus, not all of the policy measures that are listed in the Economic Recovery Plan were initially designed as responses to the current recession.

The final part of the Economic Recovery Plan focuses on **investment and innovation**. It includes increased incentives for businesses to use and pursue innovation, to establish a Scottish Investment Bank with initial funds of £150m provided by Scottish Enterprise, and to work with the private sector to increase competitiveness. The Scottish Investment Bank would be the first of its kind in the UK. It was intended that it would receive some funding from the European Investment Bank but is being told by the Treasury that the funds should be administered privately, rather than in a public sector organisation.

The Economic Recovery Plan in Scotland contains some elements that were already planned, and some that were the result of deals made previously to enable the last Scottish Budget to receive parliamentary approval (the SNP formed a minority government in 2007). Many of the measures are rather small in the context of a Scottish government budget that totals around £34.8bn in 2009–10. Most also focus on the supply side of the economy, for which it is too early to judge their effects.

The Scottish Government is not the only agency with responsibility for economic issues in Scotland. Another key body is the UK Government's Scotland Office which has taken an active interest in the impact of the recession in Scotland almost entirely distinctly from the Scottish Government. Since the beginning of the recession, the Scotland Office has been involved in consultation with key groups in the Scottish economy, such as the Confederation of British Industry (CBI) and the trade unions, and has championed measures taken by the UK Government that have affected economic conditions in Scotland. An example is the Future Jobs Fund. Announced in the 2008 Budget, this is a UK-wide fund of around £1bn aimed at supporting the creation of jobs for long-term unemployed young people and others. In July 2009, the Secretary of State for Scotland was able to announce that 2,800 jobs would be supported in Scotland as a consequence of this measure.

The interesting political aspect of this development is that the Scotland Office provides a mechanism for the Labour Party to claim credit for the effects in Scotland of UK macroeconomic policies intended to stimulate demand. This is no doubt intended to convey a message to the Scottish electorate that the UK Government is responsible for many of the policy measures focused on alleviating unemployment and economic recovery. The Secretary of State, Jim Murphy, is the focus for the local delivery of this message.

Responses – Wales
One of the key measures taken by the Welsh Assembly Government was to set up a series of Welsh Economic Summits. The intention was to use these meetings to facilitate information flows and to develop policies to respond to the recession. Eight summits had taken place by November 2009. They have usually involved the Deputy

First Minister, senior officials, businesses, social partners, community representatives and others. This is a more corporatist response to the recession than in Scotland, perhaps reflecting a more cohesive political approach in Wales to the difficulties that the recession presents.

The summits have focused on issues including:

- Skills, interventions by the Department for Work and Pensions, Jobs Programme and initiatives from Jobcentre Plus
- The role of the Strategic Capital Investment Fund and brought-forward expenditure
- Release of Assembly land for affordable housing purposes
- Sustainable development
- Green jobs strategy
- Social implications of the recession
- The contribution of further and higher education
- Procurement and prompt payment of invoices
- Availability of bank finance.

A second response is via the ProAct policy, which arose from ideas generated at an economic summit (see Keep *et al*, Chapter 6). It aims to help businesses cope with the downturn, and develop staff skills ready for the upturn, by providing training for employees who are on short-term contracts, and to keep skilled staff who may otherwise be made redundant by offering wage support. It is initially available until March 2010 and offers to meet training costs of up to £2,000 per individual and a wage subsidy up to £2,000 (£50 a day) per individual during training.

This measure bears similarities to policies introduced at the national level in other European countries. For example, both Germany and Italy have introduced subsidies to support short term working: it has been argued that the relatively modest increase in unemployment in these countries is attributable to these policies. Nevertheless, because of their high cost, their longevity is in doubt. At a UK level, it is probable that such schemes have been rejected not only because of cost but also due to a belief that they may be ineffective. This is likely to be based on evidence from the past, such as the 1980s recession, when such schemes did form part of UK Government policy.

This touches on an important general principle. The devolved administrations are not necessarily familiar with the historical evidence of what does or does not work in terms of, say, labour market interventions. The same may even be true within Whitehall Departments (see for example Lodge and Rogers 2006). Even if the devolved administrations are familiar with the history, the use of evidence that is based largely on English experience may be politically problematic for them. The costs of gathering evidence on the effectiveness of policy in the devolved nations are also relatively higher than they are in England. Of course, the extent to which any policies reflect evidence is always in question at any level of government. But in the absence of effective mechanisms for sharing information, the devolved authorities are at a disadvantage in using such evidence to design policies compared with the UK Government.

A further initiative has taken the form of joint working between the Department for Children, Education, Lifelong Learning and Skills (DCELLS) and the Department for Work and Pensions. This initiative arose from a perceived need to harmonise the work these agencies perform in relation to supporting labour markets. This is also interesting in that it demonstrates a fairly high level of cooperation between a UK Government ministry and a devolved administration. In Scotland and Northern Ireland, cooperation with UK Government agencies is weaker than it is in Wales, perhaps reflecting the political difficulties which it might raise.

The Welsh response to the recession has emphasised partnership to a greater extent than the other devolved administrations. The ProAct initiative emerged from this. It provides the clearest example across all of the devolved administrations of direct intervention in the labour market to reduce the adverse effects of unemployment. While increases in unemployment in Wales have been relatively high, this does not mean that ProAct is not working, since unemployment might have risen further had it not existed. It cost £48m in 2009–10, a small fraction of the Welsh Assembly's budget.

As in Scotland, changes in the profile of capital spending announced in the UK Budget provided opportunities for additional capital spending in Wales. These were relatively modest: an additional £23m was announced in December 2008 and a further £41m in July 2009, with the spending being distributed across a large number of projects.

Another focus of the economic summits has been availability of finance for businesses. They have facilitated discussions between employer organisations and banks on the availability of credit. The Welsh Assembly has no direct powers in respect of bank lending, but has clearly been trying to persuade banks to increase lending. The devolved authorities may have limited policymaking powers, but this does not preclude them from trying to encourage stakeholders to take actions that would support recovery. They may have difficulty with the banks, however, since their immediate focus is on increasing their capital base rather than increasing lending.

Responses – Northern Ireland
The Northern Ireland Assembly published a three-year budget shortly after the publication of the Comprehensive Spending Review 2007 (Northern Ireland Executive 2007), meaning that this document did not anticipate the recession. After the stop-start history of devolution in Northern Ireland, this approach to budgeting marked a significant change. It anticipated the Northern Ireland Assembly would make its own decisions about priorities and resource allocation over a significant period of time.

However, progress on an economic agenda is difficult for the Assembly, while there are major unresolved political issues, such as responsibility for policing. As a result, specific actions to combat the recession have been more limited in Northern Ireland than in the other devolved nations. This is particularly problematic since, as we have seen, the province suffers from very high rates of economic inactivity as well as having experienced a rapid rise in unemployment during this recession. The Northern Irish economy has also been affected by its southern neighbour. Following the most rapid rise in house prices in any part of the UK in 2007, which to some extent mirrored the house price bubble in the Irish Republic, Northern Ireland has experienced a precipitous fall in house prices, creating difficulties for the construction sector and for those locked into negative equity.

The Budget has been dealt with somewhat differently in Northern Ireland than in the other devolved administrations. Thus, in March 2008, the Northern Ireland Executive decided to undertake a Strategic Stocktake of its budget position for 2009–10 and 2010–11. This was seen as an acceptable alternative to producing an annual budget for 2008–9 but the downside was that it meant that no immediate measures could be put in place to combat recessionary pressures. To counter this, the Minister for Finance and Personnel, Nigel Dodds, announced a number of measures in December 2008, which included:

- An acceleration of £9.4m of capital spending into 2008–9
- A review of the Northern Ireland planning system
- As in Wales, face-to-face meetings with local banks to encourage them to increase the flow of credit
- 20 per cent reduction in rates for those aged over 70
- Freezing of non-domestic rates
- £20m for the farm nutrient management scheme
- £15m for fuel poverty, which amounts to a £150 payment to 100,000 households in receipt of income support or pension credits
- £150 for pensioners on top of their winter fuel allowance of up to £250 for those aged 60 to 79 and £400 to those aged over 80.

The statement also notes that:

> As a consequence of sustained dialogue with the Chief Secretary to the Treasury and the Prime Minister, an assistance package has been secured that is worth more than £900 million over this year and next. That includes access to funding to assist with our response to the current economic position, and the removal of significant cost pressures that we would otherwise have faced. (Northern Ireland Assembly 2008)

This substantial payment, which is outside the Barnett Formula, is closely linked to the abortive attempt to privatise water services in Northern Ireland. The Northern Ireland Water Company was established in April 2007 on the basis of an agreement with the

Treasury that water charges would be introduced and the company would become self-financing. But the Northern Ireland Executive subsequently decided not to go ahead with this plan. In the absence of charge income, the Water Company's deficits have to be met from general public expenditure, costing the Northern Ireland Assembly more than £500m in 2009–10 and 2010–11 (Hewitt 2009). This expenditure reduces the latitude of the Assembly to introduce new policies in response to the recession, given that its total budget for 2010–11 will be around £9bn. Furthermore, the capital charges for water now have to be met from the Northern Ireland block grant. This will cost around £800m in 2009–10 and 2010–11 – thus using up a large share of the additional money provided by the Treasury in November 2008.

Additional budgetary difficulties were highlighted by the Committee for Finance and Personnel (2008) which, in its submission to the Strategic Stocktake, argued that some departmental plans were insufficiently detailed to be used as a basis for taking forward expenditure plans. Further, in his review of the public expenditure outturn in 2008–9, Sammy Wilson, Minister for Finance and Personnel, had to admit that several departments had exceeded their budgets (Wilson 2009). And, as Hewitt points out, further serious problems have arisen on the capital budget, with prospective shortfalls in the value of asset sales of £176m in 2009–10 and £435m in 2010–11, largely because of the collapse in property values mentioned above. In addition, there is around £100m in back-pay claims from civil servants that have not been budgeted for within or beyond the current CSR period. Further, transfer of policing and justice from the Northern Ireland Office to the Northern Ireland Executive is likely to have serious budgetary consequences. These functions are much more expensive in Northern Ireland than in the rest of the UK, but would fall within the remit of the Barnett Formula as a result of this transfer. This would result in significant downward pressure on other parts of the Northern Ireland Executive budget.

Thus the response to the recession in Northern Ireland is constrained by the difficulties that the Executive is having in managing its own budget. As Hewitt puts it:

> [T]he financial situation facing the Executive is very tight and, consequently, there is very little capacity to launch new and expensive initiatives to address the recession unless existing programmes are cut back. (Hewitt op.cit., p12)

Unlike in Scotland and Wales where social security benefits are administered centrally by the Department for Work and Pensions, Northern Ireland administers its own social security system. Though the rates and eligibility are largely the same as in Great Britain, Northern Ireland has recently broken rank with other parts of the UK by offering a significant top-up to Winter Fuel Allowance – boosting household incomes in the face of the recession.

To conclude, the Northern Ireland Executive is maintaining the level of demand in the local economy, but this is largely by accident rather than design. Spending not budgeted for in CSR 2007, changes in the planned privatisation of the water industry, and falls in the values of assets, mean that it has virtually no latitude to introduce specific measures to combat the recession. As mentioned previously, Northern Ireland's EYF is around 6.7 per cent of the value of DEL. It may have to further run down this source of funding to meet its commitments – and in an environment where the outlook for public spending in the UK is grim, there may be little option for the Executive but to cut back on its commitments to support public services, including those that may be aimed at alleviating recessionary pressures.

Northern Ireland may, however, benefit from events in the Irish Republic. In contrast to the lack of substantive recession-related policy action in the North, the Irish Government has been forced into making drastic cuts in the public sector and increasing taxes sharply to reduce its fiscal deficit. The Northern Irish economy is therefore benefiting from the acquiescence of the UK Government to the effective devaluation of sterling in relation to the Euro, which has given it a considerable competitive advantage over the Republic. This in turn has stimulated demand in the North, particularly in sectors such as retailing.

Conclusions

The recession has exposed the lack of powers within the devolved administrations to influence demand in their local economies and so stave off the adverse effects of falling incomes and increases in unemployment. But this is not unique to the UK version of sub-national governance. For example, although the German Länder appear to have more extensive taxation powers than the devolved authorities in the UK, their ability to differentiate fiscal policy is limited. They do control car tax and inheritance tax. But in relation to the major taxes, such as VAT, corporation tax and personal income tax, they receive fixed shares of total revenues collected. They cannot unilaterally increase or decrease the share that they receive when their particular economic circumstances change. Their ability to respond differentially to a recession is heavily constrained.

American states are able to exercise their tax powers more independently. But most are constrained from implementing expansionary policies because of their existing levels of debt. Indeed, part of the 2009 Federal Recovery Act is aimed at reducing levels of state debt by around $140bn, between 30 and 40 per cent of their aggregate indebtedness. Even with this subsidy, many states are already cutting back on spending due to worries over debt levels. Thus, 43 states have reduced spending on a range of services, including schools, colleges, universities and health-related programmes. Rather than maintaining demand, these states are taking active steps to reduce it. This illustrates that having greater political freedom to influence fiscal policy is no guarantee that there will be sufficient economic freedom to exercise such fiscal powers.

In most countries, federal or national authorities control macroeconomic policy. This is not necessarily harmful if national policy is sufficiently flexible to respond to differences in the impacts of the recession in different regions (known by economists as asymmetric shocks). One obvious danger with allowing devolved authorities the right to control demand at a local level is that of moral hazard: if devolved bodies overspend and debt accumulates, the federal authorities cannot guarantee such debt either implicitly or explicitly. Otherwise, there would be no incentive for the devolved bodies to control spending. Thus, for example, the granting of increased borrowing powers to the Scottish Government would have to be accompanied by cast-iron repayment guarantees based on tax-raising powers.

This discussion relates to the debate about extending fiscal powers, particularly in Scotland. This debate began prior to the onset of recession, but the recession has cast it in a new light. One major issue is that neither national nor sub-national governments can escape the constraints of the market in framing fiscal policy. If sub-national governments borrow from central government to fund expansion, then their policies will be constrained by the national policy stance, which inevitably will be influenced by the conditions under which central government can borrow. If sub-national governments borrow directly on the market, then these market constraints are more direct, as many American states have recently discovered.

The argument about whether additional fiscal powers would permit the devolved bodies to better deal with recession cannot be simply about their willingness to spend more than central government. All levels of government have to observe fiscal discipline either directly or indirectly. The argument for greater fiscal powers has to be more sophisticated: it might hinge on arguments that sub-national governments are better informed about local economic conditions than central government is and so may be able to adjust tax and spending plans to better align with the wishes of the local electorate and conditions in the local economy. This recession has perhaps shown that the freedom to make such adjustments is perhaps more heavily constrained by the market than had been imagined in the first decade of devolution.

The Calman Commission has made the case for extending the Scottish Parliament's fiscal powers. In particular, it argues in favour of giving Parliament a significant share of the income tax revenues it raises. This will lead to a reduction in the grant coming to Scotland via the Barnett Formula. The Commission acknowledges that ultimately the Barnett Formula may be replaced by a needs assessment. The case for a needs assessment has also been made strongly by the Holtham Commission, given that it is widely acknowledged that Wales is disadvantaged by the current funding arrangements.

It is also generally believed that carrying out a needs assessment for the nations of the UK would be an extremely complex process. However, a recent working paper by the Holtham Commission suggests that this may not be the case (Independent Commission on Funding and Finance in Wales 2009). It argues that a needs assessment could be carried out using only seven indicators of need and shows that these indicators could closely mimic the outcomes of the very complex needs assessments that are used to allocate funding to local government in England.

Using this small number of indicators and applying them to the devolved nations, the paper further shows that this surrogate needs assessment would result in a small improvement in funding for Wales relative to the current Barnett allocation. For Scotland, however, the effect would be dramatic: rather than receiving a Barnett-determined allocation of around 20 per cent per head more than in England, the gap would be squeezed to 5 per cent. Bell has pointed out that this would mean a reduction of around £4.5bn in the Scottish block grant, which would have very severe consequences for the provision of public services in Scotland and in turn significant political consequences (Bell 2009a). This effect would be independent of any reductions in Scotland's block grant that might result from recessionary pressures.

The devolved nations have been affected by the recession in broadly the same way as England has. This is perhaps the result of the origin of the crisis being in the financial sector: the consequent sharp reduction in lending has affected all parts of the private sector in the UK. The case for radically different policies in different parts of the Union to address the problems caused by the recession is not particularly strong. An argument might be made that policy experimentation should not be discouraged, since there are always opportunities for joint learning. But formal mechanisms to facilitate such learning within a UK context, such as the Joint Ministerial Committee, are not being used to their full potential.

In addition, the devolved nations find it relatively more expensive to properly evaluate policy interventions. There are also political barriers, in some cases, to the use of lessons from policy experience gained in England. An alternative approach is to utilise experience and advice from the social partners to develop policy. Wales has perhaps developed this mechanism to a greater extent than Scotland or Northern Ireland.

There is now little doubt that significant cuts to public spending will occur from 2011–12 onwards. The devolved administrations will feel their consequences through the Barnett Formula. Although there will be intense pressure to cut DEL, the effect on the devolved administrations' allocation will depend on how these cuts are distributed across UK Government departments. If, in the run-up to an election, political parties are unwilling to cut spending on health or education, the devolved administrations' budgets will also be to some extent protected, since these services account for more than half of devolved spending. The devolved administrations will not play any direct role in negotiating spending cuts, but may be prepared to forego that pleasure if, as a consequence of the Barnett Formula, they escape relatively lightly. In addition, as Bell argues, the 'Barnett Squeeze' goes into reverse when spending cuts are being made, so that the proportionate fall in spending in the devolved administrations is lower than that in England when DEL budgets are being cut (Bell 2009b).

Of course, there may be political consequences if Scotland, in particular, is perceived to be suffering less pain as a result of the idiosyncrasies of the Barnett Formula. This could hasten the formula's demise and bring forward an alternative funding mechanism, almost certainly needs-based.

Another political aspect of the recession is how UK policies are being presented within the devolved nations by their respective Secretaries of State. Whereas the Welsh and Northern Irish secretaries have played a low-key role, Jim Murphy, the Scottish Secretary of State, has been active in promoting any beneficial impact that UK Government policies have had on Scotland. This no doubt stems from a desire to counter SNP arguments about which institutions are having the greatest impact in alleviating the effects of the recession. However, there has also been some cooperation between the Scotland Office and the Scottish Government, with Jim Murphy attending a Scottish Government cabinet meeting for the first time.

But there is no doubt that UK central government has the strongest policy hand in dealing with recession. The weakness of the devolved bodies in responding to a demand shock is that they cannot significantly expand or reduce spending. Neither can they significantly change the tax burden. Instead the devolved authorities have limited powers to shift the time profile of spending, a policy likely to be of second-order importance in influencing aggregate demand. They may reallocate spending towards programmes that promote economic growth.

But again the effects are likely to be small given that all of the devolved bodies have claimed that they have used the promotion of economic growth as a guide to allocating spending even before the recession occurred. It is difficult to establish whether their influence on economic growth has been positive or negative, given that it is impossible to calibrate the counterfactual – that is, what economic growth would have been in the home nations had devolution not occurred. But at least the devolved authorities in the UK can console themselves with the fact that their relatively weak position in respect of the recession is not much different from that of many other sub-national governments around the world. National governments are rarely prepared to devolve macroeconomic policy.

References

Bell D (2009a) 'Countless Reasons to be Fearful if Barnett Goes', *The Scotsman*, http://news.scotsman.com/opinion/Countless-reasons-to-be-fearful.5891203.jp

Bell D (2009b) *The 2010-11 Draft Budget: Evidence to the Finance Committee*, www.scottish.parliament.uk/s3/committees/finance/budget/documents/2010-11adviserpaper.pdf

Center on Budget and Policy Priorities (2009) 'Policy Points: Recession Still Causing Trouble for States', December 18, www.cbpp.org/cms/index.cfm?fa=view&id=1283]

Hewitt V (2009) *Mitigating The Recession: Options For The Northern Ireland Executive*, Economic and Research institute of Northern Ireland

HM Treasury (2007) *Funding the Scottish parliament, National Assembly For Wales And Northern Ireland Assembly: Statement Of Funding Policy*, October, www.hm-treasury.gov.uk/d/pbr_csr07_funding591.pdf

HM Treasury (2009) *Pre-Budget Report* London: HMT

House of Lords Select Committee on the Barnett Formula (2009) *First Report,* www.publications.parliament.uk/pa/ld200809/ldselect/ldbarnett/139/13902.htm]

Independent Commission on Funding and Finance in Wales (2009) *Replacing Barnett with a Needs-based Formula,* http://new.wales.gov.uk/icffw/home/news/needspaper/?lang=en

Lodge G and Rogers B (2006) *Whitehall's Black Box: Accountability and Performance in The Senior Civil Service,* London: Institute for Public Policy Research, www.ippr.org/publicationsandreports

Northern Ireland Executive (2007) *Building a Better Future: Draft Budget 2008-11,* www.pfgbudgetni.gov.uk/draftbudget1007.pdf

Northern Ireland Assembly (2008) *Ministerial Statement 2008-09 December Monitoring Round and Executive Response to the Economic Downturn,* Proceedings, 15 December, www.niassembly.gov.uk/record/reports2008/081215.htm

Northern Ireland Assembly, Committee for Finance and Personnel (2008) *Submission to the Executive's Strategic Stocktake of the Budget Position for 2009/10 & 2010/11,* www.niassembly.gov.uk/finance/2007mandate/reports/report20_08_09R.htm

Scottish Government (2009a) *Gross Value Added In Scotland, Quarter2 2009,* www.scotland.gov.uk/Publications/2009/10/GDP2009Q2

Scottish Government (2009b) 'The Economic Recovery Plan', www.scotland.gov.uk/Topics/Economy/economic-situation

Scottish Parliament Finance Committee (2008) *Report on the 2009-10 Budget,* www.scottish.parliament.uk/s3/committees/finance/reports-08/fir08-07-vol1.htm

Wilson S (2009) *Public Expenditure Provisional Outturn 2008-09 & June Monitoring 2009-10,* www.dfpni.gov.uk/statement-to-the-assembly-by-sammy-wilson-mp-mla-minister-for-finance-and-personnel.pdf

6. Devolution and strategies for learning and skills: the Leitch Report and its alternatives

Ewart Keep, Jonathan Payne and Gareth Rees

In exploring the skills policy trajectories of the UK's four national governments, there are a number of points of explanation that need to be made at the outset. First, in the area of Education and Training (E&T), the move to devolved national governments in Scotland, Wales and Northern Ireland did not necessarily mark a wholesale shift in the locus and direction of policy formation. Put simply, much E&T policymaking was already devolved, and in some areas of policy, divergent.

For example, pre-devolution Welsh and Scottish policy retained an enthusiasm for comprehensive schooling that had been significantly diluted in England, whereas Northern Ireland continued with a mainly selective system that still revolved around the eleven-plus examination. Scotland already maintained its own qualifications structure, and operated a school system with no national curriculum, testing regime or league tables. Indeed, where there has been divergence, it has often been the result of Westminster pursuing neo-liberal policies around choice, diversity and competition that has taken England in a different direction to both Scotland and Wales, where a broadly social democratic consensus prevailed (Paterson 2003, Rees 2002, 2004, 2007).

In both Scotland and Wales, the role of local government and education professionals, who already enjoyed more influence and power than their English counterparts, has also tended to be further consolidated (Arnott and Menter 2006, Rees 2004, 2007), although as we shall see, the role being afforded to local authorities in England is currently in a state of flux. As a result, devolution since 1999 has often witnessed the continuation of previous trends rather than marking a sharp break with the past.

Second, underlying social and economic conditions differ across and within each of the four nations. As a result, the scale of the policy problems that each nation faces varies, as do the economic possibilities that might be pursued via a skills policy. For example, the Welsh economy generates a much lower average Gross Value Added (GVA) per worker per hour than England does (see Wales Employment and Skills Board [WESB] 2009: 13). If the UK average for GVA is 100, then Wales manages just 84.6 (see UK Commission for Employment and Skills [UKCES] 2009: 23), and Welsh

GVA per hour worked fell by 9.5 per cent relative to the UK average between 1996 and 2007 – the largest fall anywhere within the UK (ibid: 25). Wales also contains very few large domestically-owned and headquartered companies, and only a tiny native financial sector. As a consequence, the demand for skills within Wales differs from that in England, particularly London and the South East (which together account for over a third of UK GDP [ibid: 19]). The range of policy options in relation to skills and economic development is also very different.

Third, the four nations also allocate quite widely varying proportions of total public expenditure to skills policies. Scotland is traditionally a high spending nation, particularly in relation to schools, colleges and higher education. Wales, meanwhile, has fallen behind England in recent times in the funding of both schools and post-16 provision (although valid comparisons are difficult to make; see Reynolds 2008 and WESB 2009 respectively).

Fourth, Scotland has been and remains a relatively high performer in terms of qualifications in the workforce, for example outstripping England in terms of the proportion of the adult workforce holding level 4 or above (degree level) qualifications (see Table 6.1). By contrast, Wales has tended to perform worse than the UK average, along with Northern Ireland, both in terms of the proportion of adults with low-level or no qualifications and those holding higher-level qualifications.

Table 6.1: Levels of highest qualification[1] held by working-age adults (aged 19–64), 2007

	No qual's (%)	Below level 2 (%)	Level 2 (%)	Level 3 (%)	Level 4 and above (%)
Scotland	13	13	17	20	36
England	11	18	20	20	31
Wales	15	16	22	20	28
N. Ireland	20	11	21	20	27
UK	12	17	20	20	31

Source: Adapted from UKCES 2009: 59

1. The table uses Labour Force Survey categories (From Ambition 2020 Technical Report, 2009), as follows: Level 4 and above includes: RSA higher diploma, other higher education below degree, foundation or first degrees, recognised degree-level professional qualifications, NVQ level 4, teaching or nursing qualifications, HE diploma, HNC/HND or equivalent vocational qualification. Level 3 includes: RSA Advanced diploma or advanced certificate, Advanced Welsh Baccalaureate, International Baccalaureate, GNVQ/GSVQ advanced, Scottish CSYS (two thirds), Access qualifications, 3 or more SCE, 4 or more AS levels, trade, apprenticeship (half), Scotvec Full N. Level 2 includes: 1 A-Level, Intermediate Welsh Baccalaureate, Trade apprenticeship (half), Scottish CSYS (one third), 1 or 2 SCE, 2 or 3 AS levels, 1 Advanced Scottish higher, 1 or 2 Scottish highers. Below Level 2 includes: 4 or fewer GCSEs, O-Level or equivalent at grades A-C, SCOTVEC first/general, some other RSA (including Stage I, II and III), 1 AS level, City & Guilds Foundation/Part 1, YT, YTP certificate, Key Skills Qualification, Basic Skills Qualification, entry level qualificational certificate, 2 or more Advanced Scottish highers, 3 or more Scottish highers.

The combination of geography and distinct political forces operating in Northern Ireland introduces an additional dynamic to skills policies in the province. Northern Ireland shares no land border with the rest of the UK and its neighbour is the Republic of Ireland. This is recognised in the constitutional settlement, and the power-sharing Northern Ireland Government has chosen to frame skills policies in relation to both those set across the UK, but also those being established in Dublin (Department of Employment and Learning [DEL] 2007).

Finally, it is also important to note that right across the UK skills policy is currently passing through a period of volatile change and extreme instability. This was already the case before the recession struck, but has become even more pronounced since. Institutional and programmatic change is happening apace, in part as a response to changed economic conditions and the need to try to bolster training volumes and employment through the downturn. However, at a deeper level, we are also undergoing a period of general re-evaluation of skills policy, involving a contested reframing of the diagnosis of the underlying causes of our long-standing 'skills problem' (Payne 2008, Keep 2009).

Until quite recently, it could be argued that many of the variations between the four UK nations had tended to reside in institutional and programmatic design and configuration. To give one example, Scotland retained a joint funding council for further (FE) and higher education (HE) whereas England maintained a Learning and Skills Council that funded FE and training while HE was dealt with by a separate funding body. Divergence was 'in the detail' of programmes and institutions rather than in the fundamental philosophy or ideological stances that underpinned governmental policy and action in the field of E&T, where differences have emerged only since 2007.

This chapter concentrates mainly on these broader policy divergences because they have emerged more recently and have so far attracted relatively little attention within the 'devolution debate'. Over time, they are likely to become increasingly significant in terms of the overall direction that skills policies take within the devolved UK and the policies, programmes and projects that they give rise to. In reviewing skills policy developments across the UK, it can be argued that the main points of potential innovation and divergence might be:

1. Underlying ideology and purposes

2. Institutional and regulatory frameworks

3. The culture of management and control

4. Programmes and initiatives

5. Outcomes

This chapter, firstly, discusses the impact of the Leitch Review of Skills, which exposed tensions between the UK Government and the devolved institutions, before deploying the headings above to frame and structure its discussion. It draws on the limited stock of research that is available, and also on the authors' engagement with policymakers in government and agencies across three of the four UK nations (England, Scotland and Wales). It is beyond the scope of the chapter to consider changes in Northern Ireland.

Whitehall strikes back?

The Leitch Review of Skills was established by Her Majesty's Treasury in 2005 as one of a group of long-term UK Government policy inquiries, with others looking at housing and planning (Barker) and transport (Eddington). At the time, this development was interpreted as a move by the then-Chancellor of the Exchequer and Prime Minister in waiting, Gordon Brown, to lay the foundations for future policy moves in this area. The skills policy review was tasked with establishing the future skill needs of the UK economy to the year 2020 and how these might best be met. Partway through the inquiry, its remit was enlarged to cover employment and services to the unemployed. Lord Leitch, a Scottish financier and close associate of the Chancellor, was chosen to head the exercise.

It could be argued that one of the key sub-texts for the Review was that some within the English/UK Government harboured concerns that skills policy was too important to be left to the vagaries of the devolved administrations, and that a greater degree of coordination and centralisation, under the aegis of the Treasury, was required to secure the necessary and desired step-change in performance in this area. The Leitch Review was, then, by accident or by design, a potential vehicle for bringing about this shift in the locus for establishing the overall strategic direction for skills policy across the UK. In formal terms, the Review was directly sponsored by the Treasury (whose remit is UK-wide) and England's then Department for Education and Skills (DfES), with the three devolved administrations also signing up to cooperate with and support the Review in undertaking a UK-wide examination of policy and a benchmarking of UK performance against other developed and developing countries.

The degree of enthusiasm for the Review appears to have varied across the devolved administrations, with the greatest uncertainties residing in Scotland. There, concerns appear to have centred on a belief that if Leitch came to set the overarching strategic direction and goals for the E&T systems across the entire UK, then, in some respects, the 'high end' of policy formation would be partially recentralised around an English agenda. In essence, the stance of the devolved administrations was to acquiesce to the Review process, but with positions on any resultant policy recommendations reserved.

In terms of its analytical approach and preferred policy remedies, the Review tended to adopt many of the viewpoints and priorities favoured by the English DfES. Thus, the stress was on international benchmarking of qualification stocks, which tended to show the UK in a relatively poor light, and on the need for further supply-side interventions to boost the levels of E&T taking place (Keep *et al* 2006, Keep 2009).

As will be discussed further below, this stance did not meet with great enthusiasm from the devolved administrations.

After an interim report in 2005, the Leitch Review produced its final report and policy recommendations in December 2006. These included:

- A UK-wide set of targets (expressed as an 'ambition'), which by 2020 aimed to put the UK in the 'top quartile' of the Organisation for Economic Cooperation and Development (OECD) league tables at every different level of skill (as proxied by qualifications).

- Moves towards a more 'employer-led' E&T system, where employers and their representatives would, for example, be able to approve which qualifications should be eligible for public funding.

- A concern that the skills system was overly complex and bureaucratic and in need of simplification and streamlining.

- An end to the investment of considerable time and energy in 'manpower' planning systems, and the development of a more marketised and responsive, 'demand-led' E&T system.

- Contestability within the E&T system (i.e. marketisation of provision), particularly in terms of public funding being channelled through brokers to employers who would then choose which provider they wished to use. The aim was to encourage private training providers to compete for adult learning provision with FE colleges.

- The establishment of the UK Commission for Employment and Skills (UKCES), which was to be an employer-led body that would replace the Sector Skills Development Agency (SSDA) in its role in funding and managing the UK-wide network of Sector Skills Councils (SSCs), but also act as guardian of the Leitch 'ambition', monitor progress towards the Leitch targets and report to the four national administrations. As will be discussed later in this chapter, the UKCES may prove in the long term to be the most important and lasting of Leitch's ideas.

Although all four national governments welcomed the Leitch Review's final report, in reality the warmth and strength of reception varied enormously, as did the willingness to endorse its analysis and adopt the Report's recommendations. As the sections below discuss, with no UK Government powers to impose Leitch's recommendations, the four UK nations have treated Leitch more as a pick-'n'-mix menu than as a single prescriptive package, and some administrations have chosen to pick rather more than others.

Underlying ideology, analysis and aims of policy

One of the key reasons why the Leitch Review did not secure wholehearted enthusiasm across the UK was its choice of analytical framing. In essence, two quite distinct and implicitly conflicting explanatory narratives have emerged within the UK around central government's reasons for, and approaches to, interventions concerning workforce skills.

The English policy model, which has developed over the last quarter of a century (see Keep 2009), affords skills prime position in the governmental policy armoury in relation to both social and economic problems (see Keep and Mayhew, forthcoming). Its central assumption is that the 'skills problem' is one of inadequate supply; for example, that an insufficient proportion of the adult workforce is skilled to the equivalent of five good GCSEs, and that once a greater flow of skills is created, these skills will be used to productive effect within the workplace. Indeed, it is argued by proponents of this analysis that government-funded increases in skills supply can create a 'supply-push' effect, whereby a more qualified workforce leads employers to adopt high value-added product market strategies (HM Treasury 2002, Leitch Review of Skills 2006).

In Scotland and Wales, a radically different analysis has emerged, reflecting not only very different political priorities, but also much more difficult economic circumstances. This alternative analysis can be illustrated most clearly by reference to developments in Scotland following the election of a minority Scottish Nationalist Party (SNP) Government that provided the catalyst for a radical re-think of skills policy (Payne 2008). The earlier New Labour/Liberal Democrat coalition governments had tended to replicate both the underlying analysis prevalent south of the border, in terms of its stress on simple forms of human capital accumulation as the prime basis for policy, as well as mirroring English New Labour's enthusiasm for a plethora of new targets, schemes, initiatives and programmes (see Dutton *et al* 2005).

The arrival in power of the SNP proved significant for the direction of skills policy because it occurred at a moment when a significant number of senior officials and governmental advisers had concluded that traditional policy approaches did not seem to be delivering the scale of benefits expected, particularly in terms of the relative performance of the Scottish economy. On many measures of skill production, Scotland appeared to outperform England (see Table 6.1 above), yet, as Table 6.2 indicates, on economic measures, particularly those relating to relative productivity, England outperformed Scotland (for more detailed figures on this see UKCES 2009: 23-25).

Table 6.2. Economic performance across the UK

	GVA per hour worked (UK=100)	Employment rate, % (Jan 2007)
England	101.8	70.1
London	129.7	78.6
Scotland	95.6	76.4
Wales	84.6	72.1
Northern Ireland	84.1	70.3

Source: UKCES 2009: 23

Further increases in skills supply would not have the desired economic effect, it was argued, if they were not linked to efforts both to increase the underlying levels of demand for skill within the Scottish economy, and to improve the utilisation of existing skills within Scottish workplaces. In other words, on their own, more skills were not enough to transform economic performance, and much greater attention needed to be devoted to linking skills to economic development, innovation and business improvement, and to thinking through how skill utilisation might be improved (Payne 2008). For instance, new forms of job design and initiatives to improve work organisation might be needed (see below).

This analysis and policy approach was enshrined in both the Scottish Economic Strategy (Scottish Government 2007a) and, most significantly, its new skills strategy document, *Skills for Scotland – A Lifelong Skills Strategy* (2007b). It is important to note that the latter was essentially a strategic document outlining a broad policy reorientation and did not seek to develop in any detail the forms of policy intervention that this might give rise to.

In recommending the strategy to the Scottish Parliament, the then Cabinet Secretary for Education and Lifelong Learning, Fiona Hyslop, drew a direct comparison with Leitch, stating: 'Our problem is not characterised by the supply of skills but by employer demand for skills and how these skills are utilised in the workplace. Our strategy goes further than Leitch and is designed to suit Scottish needs and aspirations.' She added, 'We agree with Lord Leitch's analysis that we need to improve skills in order to unlock our economic potential but we do not agree that simply injecting skills in the labour market will have the economic effect we seek' (Scottish Parliament 2007).

Interestingly, English policymakers have quietly acknowledged this clash of paradigms and developed a response that seeks to reconcile the Leitch analysis with Scotland's experience of disappointing results from a heavy investment in certified human capital. One of the authors has heard both English civil servants and quango staff advance the argument that the Leitch analysis was founded on the importance of 'economically valuable' skills and that Scotland's failure to reap greater reward from its massive public investment in an expanded post-compulsory education system is the result of inappropriate qualifications that employers do not value and of failing to invest in the right kind of skills.

This line of thought has not been accepted in Scotland (Davis 2008). In some senses it is an odd argument to make, since Scotland's qualification system is not that radically different from England's and the areas, such as basic skills and higher education, where Scotland has increased publicly-funded skills supply are very similar to those currently targeted for expansion south of the border. Furthermore, this argument has not prevented policymakers in England from readily embracing Leitch's 'blanket' qualifications targets that have been arrived at without any meaningful consultation with employers and which can be viewed as a form of central planning (Wolf 2007).

The upshot is that there now exist two incommensurable theories of action, which can be compared and contrasted, and the relative effectiveness of the resultant policy interventions perhaps measured. One has been promulgated by the English/UK Government via the Leitch Review of Skills (2005, 2006); the other developed by the Scottish Government to support its own Skills Strategy (2007b) and, rather less definitively, by the Welsh Assembly Government in its Skills and Employment Strategy (WAG 2008). As will be suggested below, the latter analytical frame appears to be gradually gaining ground.

Management and control of E&T systems

The ways in which the different UK nations have chosen to configure their E&T systems vary radically. In Wales, the government opted early on to assume direct control of most E&T issues and funding (except for higher education). Quasi-autonomous agencies, notably the National Council/Education and Learning Wales (Elwa) – the Welsh equivalent of England's Learning and Skills Council (LSC) – were wound up and their functions incorporated within the Welsh Assembly Government (WAG) in what was known as the 'bonfire of the quangos' (Rees 2004, 2007). This has had a number of interesting implications, of which one of the most important is that Welsh civil servants have found themselves having to forge direct relationships with employers in receipt of government funding in a way that is uncommon elsewhere in the UK.

In Scotland there has been reconfiguration of the agencies, with Scottish Enterprise losing its skills funding to a new quango – Skills Development Scotland – which combines the funding of training with the provision of careers information and advice. In general, the Scottish system operates on a model that devolves considerable power to agencies (such as the Scottish Funding Council, which supports further and higher education), local authorities and individual educational institutions, with central government setting overall strategies, objectives and some targets.

England finds itself in a very different place, with a constantly changing but highly centralised, top-down, command-and-control system of governance that seeks to manage the E&T system in detail from Whitehall (Coffield et al 2008, Coffield 2008, Keep 2006, 2009). This has resulted in an unprecedented degree of institutional and programmatic change and a very complex skills system. Furthermore, as Coffield et al (2008) note, there exist few feedback loops through which educational professionals and those charged with delivering the policy 'on the ground' might influence higher level decisions. In marked contrast to Wales, the various quangos act as buffers that help insulate senior policymakers from direct contact with the bulk of ordinary employers and also with realities that do not fit their preconceptions (Keep 2009).

England is currently in the process of returning funding responsibilities for 16–19 education to local authorities, as the LSC is being replaced with a Young People's Learning Agency (YPLA) and Skills Funding Agency (SFA) (see DCSF/DIUS 2008). This follows a period in which local authority influence over local arrangements has been marginalised. FE colleges were removed from Local Education Authority control in 1992/3 and government policy has since encouraged competition and choice across a diverse range of essentially autonomous providers, some of which (for example, Academy Schools) are funded directly from the centre. There are issues, therefore, around how much influence and control local authorities will be able to exert in shaping local arrangements. A further question regards whether or not they will have the necessary capacity and skills to perform their new role as the 'single local strategic leader' for planning, commissioning and funding 14–19 provision. Although the talk is of a 'new localism' (Avis 2009), the underlying intents behind these developments and their real implications for greater decentralisation of power within the English E&T system are open to debate (Payne 2009, Keep 2009).

It is perhaps too early to say, therefore, if, or to what extent, these developments move England closer to Wales and Scotland. It is interesting that Wales has chosen not to follow England's example of returning post-16 funding to local authorities, despite the fact that Welsh local government has, in general, retained much greater powers than in England over recent decades. At the same time, there are few indications that local authorities in England are obtaining any greater input into, or influence over, national policy formation that would indicate convergence towards the situation in Scotland and Wales.

In relation to post-19 skills, the Skills Funding Agency, which will take charge of overall responsibility for the shape and direction of the FE sector and for the funding of adult learning, will be a 'Next Steps' agency and, in marked contrast to the LSC which it will be replacing, will have neither a chair nor a council. It will be directly accountable only to the Secretary of State, and represents yet another accretion in the powers of central government to direct and control the activities of the FE sector.

One of the explanations for these variations frequently cited by policymakers is the issue of scale. In contrast to England, which accounts for four-fifths of the total UK population, Northern Ireland, Scotland and Wales are all relatively small countries, with political cultures that engender opportunities for contact and connection between governed and individual members of government. Smaller scale and greater connectivity also help to create the possibility of higher levels of trust between the various actors, and between government and the agencies and organisations that have to deliver policy (although, of course, this is not a necessary outcome).

For example, in Scotland, Wales and Northern Ireland, it is possible for the relevant government minister to know all of the individuals who hold posts as FE college principals. With over 400 FE colleges, this is plainly not possible for their English counterpart. In England, the combination of a large population and a high degree of centralisation – the E&T system being run as though the country was a unitary authority – has tended to encourage low levels of trust and autonomy (Keep 2006, 2009).

Currently, there are no signs of any convergence around the single UK-wide model of system design and governance that the Leitch Review held up as an ideal – an outcome that will be a disappointment to the Review's supporters and those seeking less divergence across the UK in this field of policy. Leitch's enthusiasm for a responsive, demand-led system has secured general rhetorical buy-in, but how demand is defined often remains very vague, not least in terms of whose demand – individuals' or employers' – should be afforded primacy. Likewise, while all are keen to support the notion that employers should have a major role to play in the governance of the system, their respective approaches continue to differ.

Wales has tended, particularly in response to the recession, to rely on a form of social partnership model that revolves around national Economic Summits that embrace business, trade unions and community representatives. The Scots have been careful not to promise employers the same level of direct influence that has been afforded them in England. In terms of the contestability (between public and private providers) of public funding of E&T, only England has chosen to head down this road.

Programmes and initiatives

As ever, there is a plethora of more or less constantly evolving government schemes, programmes, and initiatives covering the provision and certification of skill across the UK. The onset of a severe recession has added a new layer of innovation in the shape of emergency training support measures on top of the pre-existing landscape of provision. There is not space here to review these in any detail, and any such review would almost certainly be out of date by the time that this volume is published, so rapid is the pace of change.

One scheme that is worthy of note, however, is Wales's ProAct, which offers one widely-praised model for responding to the recession. ProAct was established in March 2009, initially for a year, with funding of £48 million. It offers wage support to companies that have introduced short-time working, to retain the workers and to use the 'down time' to upskill the staff. Up to £2,000 is given for training per worker, and up to £50 per day per worker (up to a maximum of £2,000) in wage subsidy. So far, more than 5,000 workers have benefited.

The other issue of note has been the lack of a 'ripple effect' across the UK from England's decision to raise the learning age (in two stages, initially to age 17 by 2013 and then to 18 by 2015), which is to be backed by legal compulsion on young people to cooperate. Neither Scotland nor Wales has shown an inclination to copy this. Both are happy to try to encourage more youngsters to remain in education and training post-16, but neither has exhibited any enthusiasm for a policy of compulsion.

Performance and outcomes

The targets for qualification achievement by 2020 set by the Leitch Review were meant to provide a simple, UK-wide standard, against which 'national' performance could be gauged. Unfortunately, two problems intervened. The first was a fundamental disagreement about the value of deploying skills-supply measures, particularly specified in terms of whole qualifications achieved. As noted earlier,

Scotland's experience has unfortunately demonstrated (at least to the Scottish Government) that achieving high levels of qualification output does not necessarily generate the desired or expected outcome. Therefore, the utility of assigning over-riding importance to qualifications stocks has been disputed. Similarly, in Wales the Welsh Employment and Skills Board has noted:

> ...*our main concern is with developing skills relevant to, and applied in the workplace and in wider society, not with qualifications as an end in themselves. While we believe that progress towards the qualifications targets set by Lord Leitch in his report ... are important as an **indicator** of whether we are on the right track, what really matters is whether, as a nation, we develop the skills which are useful and are used to generate wealth and enrich society.* (WESB 2009: 9, emphasis as in the original)

The second problem was that the Leitch targets were not linked to demand for skills in the UK labour market (or constituent parts thereof), but were instead derived from international benchmarking and were designed to move the UK up the OECD league tables. Given the different patterns of economic activity (and qualification achievement) that existed across and within the four UK nations, the realism, achievability and utility of the targets appeared to vary widely. As a result, England has chosen to make the Leitch targets the centrepiece of its Public Service Agreement (PSA) targets for the E&T system (Department for Innovation, Universities and Skills [DIUS] 2007), but the other administrations have created their own priorities. In Scotland and Wales, the Leitch targets have not been adopted as policy benchmarks; while in Northern Ireland local targets are deemed to be contributing to UK targets (DEL 2007).

Even within England the relevance of the PSA targets to some regions, localities and sectors of economic activity (such as retailing, catering and hospitality, and transport) is open to serious doubt. In some areas, such as the North East and the Sheffield city-region, adverse economic conditions combine to create a 'wicked' set of problems that makes progress on the Leitch targets particularly challenging (North *et al* 2007, Jones and Etherington 2009).

If the Leitch targets are not the answer to measuring national performance, in either absolute or relative terms, then what judgements can be reached? Given their very different starting points, economic drivers and ability to fund interventions, the overall conclusion must be that it is hard to reach any useful judgement on the performance of the national E&T systems within the UK. In many senses, these are the result of an interplay of forces on both the supply and demand side. Regions and nations with lower levels of employer demand for skill are liable to generate lower levels of output within their E&T systems than those with stronger levels of demand. Moreover, in order to determine relative levels of performance, we would need a commonly agreed definition of success. Given the varying objectives at which the national skills policies are directed, such a yardstick is lacking. At present, the desired objectives range from a simple increase in the stocks of qualifications to higher levels of innovation, productivity, value added and social equity.

As a consequence, it is not at all clear what the correct measures for gauging the relative performance of national E&T systems ought to be. The tendency up until now has been to rely upon rather crude participation levels (usually expressed as percentages of any given age cohort or section of the workforce) and output measures (usually whole qualifications at different levels). The bulk of national targets for E&T systems in the UK have been expressed in these narrow terms, but there is a growing belief that these forms of performance measure are, on their own, inadequate, not least as they represent throughput within (participation) and outputs from the E&T system (qualifications achieved), rather than outcome or impact measures. In other words, they focus on the idea of large flows of students leading to large stockpiles of skilled labour within the workforce/population. The UKCES has noted this 'measurement gap' (UKCES 2009: 141) and has stated that one of its goals is to develop performance indicators that will allow us to move from measuring outputs to outcomes.

The UKCES as a trans-UK institution

One of the most interesting, radical and perhaps as yet unrecognised outcomes of the Leitch Review was the creation in April 2008 of a UK-wide, employer-led Commission on Employment and Skills (UKCES). The UKCES has a chair (Sir Michael Rake), a chief executive (Chris Humphries, who previously chaired the National Skills Task Force), and 23 commissioners, the bulk of whom are drawn from among employers, but with some trade unionists and educational leaders.

Each of the devolved administrations has one commissioner to represent them formally on the UKCES (though there may be additional commissioners from those countries, as is the case for Scotland). In Wales, this UK-wide apparatus has been augmented by the decision of the WAG to establish a Welsh Employment and Skills Board (WESB) to advise WAG 'on employment and skills policies, with a particular remit to articulate the employer perspective' (WESB 2009: 3). The UKCES reports to the three devolved administrations, as well as the UK Government's Cabinet Office, Treasury, the Department for Business, Innovation and Skills (BIS), and the Department for Work and Pensions (DWP). Commissioners and senior UKCES staff hold regular meetings with ministers from all four administrations.

The Commission has a number of roles. First, it is the guardian of, and monitors progress towards, the Leitch 'ambition'. Second, it is responsible for the licensing, funding and performance management of the UK-wide network of sectoral employer bodies (SSCs). A further role is what might be termed policy and information exchange, and it is in this capacity that it may have a particular significance.

In the field of E&T and skills, it was apparent fairly soon after the devolutionary settlement that, outside of a number of technical areas, such as the management of national qualification systems, formalised mechanisms for the regular updating and transfer of policy ideas across the UK were often lacking. English policymakers in particular appeared to be unaware of developments elsewhere. Although Welsh, Scottish, Northern Irish and sometimes Republic of Ireland officials convened to discuss developments, a UK-wide mechanism for policy comparison and interchange did not exist.

The UKCES helps to fill this gap. It also acts as a form of think tank attached to, but not part of, the UK nations' governments, with its own research programme, and both an in-house research function and advisory Expert Panel. It has a research budget that enables it to research and develop strands of policy independently of the governments to which it reports.

Although the Commission has not existed for very long, it has already proved to be a transmission mechanism for policy thinking and lines of development across internal UK borders. The most important example of this has been the ability of the Scottish commissioners to place skill utilisation on the UKCES's policy agenda, thereby broadening research and policy action in this field beyond the confines of Scotland.

Its direct impact is liable to be greatest in England, since the UKCES appears to be capable of a degree of independence of thought the like of which has been almost wholly absent from the English skills policy scene since the days of the old Manpower Services Commission (MSC) (Keep 2009). Thus, in its first 'state of the nations' annual report on progress towards the Leitch 'ambition', UKCES has suggested that with regard to the fundamental nature of the UK's 'skills problem':

> *Our view is that this problem lies largely on the demand side. The relatively low level of skills in the UK; the limited extent of skill shortages; and the potentially relatively low demand for skills relative to their supply taken together, imply a demand side weakness. The UK has too few high performance workplaces, too few employers producing high quality goods and services, too few businesses in high value added sectors. This means that in order to build an internationally competitive economy, the future employment and skills system will need to invest as much effort on raising employer ambition, on stimulating demand, as it does on enhancing skills supply...In the end, the demand for skills is a 'derived' demand. It depends on the shape of the economy and level of economic activity. This is why economic and industrial policy are crucial to achieving our 2020 employment and skills ambitions, and why achieving these ambitions are, in turn, a key route to a stronger economy.* (UKCES 2009:10)

In other words, the traditional thrust of English skills policies has been judged insufficient to deliver the Leitch 'ambition', and, following in the footsteps of Scottish and Welsh policy, UKCES is arguing for an approach that embraces not just the supply of skills, but also efforts to stimulate underlying levels of demand and to improve skill usage. In acknowledging the existence of a major 'policy gap' (UKCES 2009), it calls for a fundamental rebalancing of the emphasis afforded to skills supply and demand.

In its recent white paper, *Skills for Growth*, the Department for Business, Innovation and Skills offers a partial response from the English government (BIS 2009). It argues that the majority of the Leitch 'ambitions' or targets can be met on current policy trajectories, but there is also a muted acknowledgement that policy needs to address underlying levels of demand for skill and how skills are utilised. Although the white paper offers some minor policy initiatives in both these areas, its chief response is to offer a holding position, with the promise of major policy developments to come at some later date.

Where next?

As this chapter has already noted, UK skills policies are in a state of flux, partly due to the recession, but more fundamentally because old certainties about the causes, nature and policy responses to the UK's long-standing skills problem are being challenged. Perhaps as a result of economic circumstances and issues of political and ideological space, much of the energy for this rethinking of skills policy is coming from the devolved governments, particularly Scotland.

New points of departure are beginning to emerge from the ruins of traditional lines of policy. Unfortunately, it is far too early for evidence to show the relative success of these new policy models. In part, this is simply because most of the developments are relatively recent and are often (for example, in the case of Scottish initiatives on skill utilisation) still in a developmental phase. However, there is also a broader problem of measurement, in that the relationship between traditional output indicators for E&T outputs (for example, stocks of qualifications) and the impact on wider social and economic outcomes is both complex and indirect.

The arrival of the UKCES has provided both a UK-wide policy 'space' within which such ideas can be debated, and also a transmission mechanism for moving ideas around the UK. In English policy terms, it is capable and willing to think outside the box of established lines of policy 'orthodoxy'. That said, the fate of UKCES itself (as with many aspects of the devolution settlement) remains uncertain, not least if a general election in 2010 brings the Conservatives into power, as they have offered (as this is being written) no public assurance that UKCES will survive under their rule.

In terms of likely developments, three key issues can be identified. First, the Scottish Government has chosen to take the UK policy lead on the issue of skills utilisation and is now beginning to move forward on this agenda. It has established a Skill Utilisation Leadership Group, and constructed a policy statement on encouraging employer engagement in improved skill utilisation (Scottish Government 2009). More significantly perhaps, the Scottish Funding Council has set up a suite of skill utilisation action research projects involving a number of Scottish colleges and universities. In Wales too, the Welsh Assembly Government has for some time been addressing issues of skills utilisation through initiatives such as its Workforce Development Programme, albeit on the basis of very modest levels of funding (Keep 2008).

In beginning to grapple with skill utilisation, Scottish and Welsh policymakers are entering largely uncharted territory, where a steep learning curve beckons. The more progress they can make in moving this agenda forward and in demonstrating clear and positive outcomes (and again there are issues here in terms of how one might measure such impact), the more pressure this is likely to bring to bear on an English policy community that remains wedded to a relatively narrow skills-supply approach (Payne 2008).

Second, the UKCES, Wales and Scotland have all stressed the need for closer connections between skills and economic development. In England, the creation of the Department for Business Innovation and Skills (BIS), in June 2009, through a merger of DIUS and BERR, offered an opportunity for the emergence of a more integrative policy approach. With New Labour in England having rediscovered industrial policy (or 'industrial activism') in response to the economic downturn, new models of skills and business improvement interventions may emerge if time allows. As noted above, the BIS 2009 white paper on skills offers some early hints that attempts to bring policies on skills, economic development, the workplace and employee relations closer together are being contemplated, though to what concrete effect remains to be seen.

If such policies are to emerge, one challenge will be joining up a skills delivery system and a governance regime for economic development in England, both of which have been characterised by complexity, fragmentation and incoherence (Payne 2009, Pike and Tomaney 2009, Jones and Etherington 2009). At present, the UK/English government is developing cities and city-regions as engines of economic development and devolving new roles and responsibilities to local authorities (HM Treasury et al 2007, Pike and Tomaney 2009, Mawson 2009). As Pike and Tomaney (2009) have argued, however, the current policy rhetoric around the new localism downplays the shadow of the nation state and the pushing down of responsibility for economic development to lower levels without concomitant shifts in authority and resources. They highlight problems in relation to issues of multi-level and multi-agency coordination, the potential over-burdening of local authorities and a tendency to absolve central government of its responsibilities for spatial equity.

As Buchanan et al (2009) note, institutions matter because they 'shape the character of competition in both product and labour markets', together with the quality and distribution of jobs across industries and space. Clearly, there is a danger in devolving responsibility for economic development to local actors (whose capacity to deliver this may be limited), particularly where the wider institutional framework does little to limit low-skill, low-wage options for employers, and where central government minimises its responsibility for addressing issues of regional imbalance and inequity.

It is important, too, to remind ourselves that these challenges are not confined to England and also present themselves to those parts of the UK that have embraced a skill utilisation agenda. Policy levers that might be used to push firms away from 'low road' strategies, such as raising the level of the minimum wage, along with wider aspects of employment relations policy and labour market regulation, are reserved matters which lie firmly under the control of Westminster (see Payne 2008).

Finally, it is important to end by emphasising that for the immediate future the most pressing issue facing skills policies across the whole of the UK is that of funding. In this context, it is not surprising that the devolved administrations have become increasingly concerned about the Barnett Formula as the basis of financial allocations from the UK to the Scottish and Welsh levels of government, as is reflected for example in the deliberations of the Calman and Holtham Commissions (both 2009). How far such deliberations will actually lead to funding systems that reflect economic and social needs more accurately remains to be seen. And certainly, any changes of this kind will be complicated by more general economic circumstances. Given the parlous state of the public finances, major cuts in public spending on skills seem inevitable. How these cuts will be calculated and apportioned will vary across the four governments, but however constructed, their impact on the direction, shape and levels of public policy interventions on skills will be drastic.

In the longer term, the hope must be that the current financial and economic crisis engenders a major policy re-think not only of skills policies but also of the wider model of economic development to which they have been linked for so long. This model, built on excessive and unsustainable levels of private and public debt, a booming housing market, a deregulated labour market and over-reliance on the financial services sector, has been found sorely wanting. What the political response to this challenge will be remains to be seen. What is certain is that skills policies across the devolved UK, however divergent, will operate within the context of these wider political choices and the constraints and opportunities that they present.

References

Arnott M and Menter I (2006) 'The same but different? Post-devolution regulation and control of education in Scotland and England', *European Educational Research Journal*, 6 (3), 250-264

Avis J (2009) 'Further Education in England: the New Localism, Systems Theory and Governance', paper presented at the 8th International Conference of the Journal of Vocational Education and Training, Oxford, 3-5 July

Buchanan J, Yu S, Marginson S and Wheelahan L (2009) *Education, Work and Economic Renewal: An issues paper prepared for the Australian Education Union* Sydney: Workplace Research Centre, University of Sydney

Business, Innovation and Skills (BIS) (2009) *Skills for Growth – The national skills strategy, Cm 7641*, London: The Stationery Office

Coffield F (2008) *Just suppose teaching and learning became the first priority,* London: Learning and Skills Network

Coffield F, Edward S, Finlay I, Hodgson A, Steer R and Spours K (2008) *Improving Learning, Skills and Inclusion: The Impact of Policy,* London: Routledge/Falmer

Commission on Scottish Devolution (Calman Commission) (2009) *Serving Scotland Better: Scotland and the United Kingdom in the 21st Century,* Edinburgh: CSD

Davis M (2008) 'Briefing on the Skill Utilisation dinner, 27 May', www.scotland.gov.uk/Topics/Education/skills-strategy/making-skills-work/utilisation

Department for Employment and Learning (DEL) (2007) *Statement of Skills in Northern Ireland,* Belfast: DEL

Department for Children, Schools and Families (DCSF)/Department for Innovation, Universities and Schools (DIUS) (2008) *Raising Expectations: enabling the system to deliver, Cm 7348,* London: the Stationery Office

Department of Innovation, Universities and Skills (DIUS) (2007) *World-Class Skills: Implementing the Leitch Review of Skills in England,* Norwich: HMSO

Dutton E, Warhurst C and Fairley J (2005) *New Britain: old politics – devolved post-16 education and training. SKOPE Research Paper No. 57.* Coventry: University of Warwick, SKOPE

HM Treasury (2002) *Developing workforce skills: piloting a new approach,* London: HMT

HM Treasury, BERR and CLG (2007) *Review of Sub-National Economic Development and Regeneration,* Norwich: HMSO

Independent Commission on Funding and Finance for Wales (Holtham Commission) (2009) *First Report: Funding Devolved Government in Wales: Barnett and Beyond,* Cardiff: ICFFW

Jones M and Etherington D (2009) 'Governing the skills agenda: Insights from the Sheffield City-Region', *Local Economy,* 24, 1, 68-79

Keep E (2006) 'State control of the English education and training system – playing with the biggest train set in the world', *Journal of Vocational Education and Training,* 58, 1, 47-64

Keep E (2008) 'A Comparison of the Welsh Workforce Development Programme and England's Train to Gain', *SKOPE Research Paper 79,* Cardiff: Cardiff University, SKOPE

Keep E (2009) 'The Limits of the Possible: Shaping the Learning and Skills Landscape Through a Shared Policy Narrative', *SKOPE Research Paper,* Cardiff: Cardiff University, SKOPE

Keep E and Mayhew K (forthcoming, 2010) 'Moving Beyond Skills as a Social and Economic Panacea?', *Work, Employment and Society*

Keep E, Mayhew K and Payne J (2006) 'From Skills Revolution to Productivity Miracle – Not as Easy as it Sounds?', *Oxford Review of Economic Policy,* 22, 4, 539-559

Leitch Review of Skills (2006) *Prosperity for all in the global economy – world class skills,* London: HMT

Mawson J (2009) 'Local economic development and the sub-national review: old wine in new bottles', *Local Government Studies,* 35, 1, 39-59

North D, Syrett S and Etherington D (2007) *Devolution and Regional Governance: tackling the Economic Needs of Deprived Areas,* York: Joseph Rowntree Foundation

Paterson L (2003) 'Three educational ideologies of the British Labour Party 1997-2001', *Oxford Review of Education*, 29 (2), 165-186

Payne J (2008) *Divergent skills policy trajectories in England and Scotland after Leitch, SKOPE Research Paper*, Cardiff: SKOPE, Cardiff School of Social Sciences

Payne J (2009) 'Scoring opportunity or hospital pass? The changing role of local authorities in 14-19 education and training in England', *SKOPE Research Paper*, Cardiff: Cardiff University: SKOPE

Pike A and Tomaney J (2009) 'The state and uneven development: the governance of economic development in England in the post-devolution UK', *Cambridge Journal of the Regions, Economy and Society*, 2, 13-34

Rees G (2002) 'Devolution and the Restructuring of Post-16 Education and Training in the UK', in Adams J and Robinson P (eds.) *Devolution in Practice: Public Policy Differences Within the UK*, London: ippr

Rees G (2004) 'Democratic Devolution and Education Policy in Wales: the Emergence of a National System?', *Contemporary Wales*, 17, 28-43

Rees G (2007) 'The impacts of parliamentary devolution on education policy in Wales', *Welsh Journal of Education*, 14 (1), 8-20

Reynolds D (2008) 'New Labour, education and Wales: the devolution decade', *Oxford Review of Education*, 34, 6, 753-765

Scottish Government (2007a) *The Government Economic Strategy*, Edinburgh: Scottish Government

Scottish Government (2007b) *Skills for Scotland – A Lifelong Skills Strategy*, Edinburgh: Scottish Government

Scottish Government (2009) *Reaping the Benefits: Encouraging Employer Engagement in Skills Utilisation*, www.scotland.gov.uk/Topics/Education/skills-strategy/making-skills-work/utilisation

Scottish Parliament (2007) *Time for Reflection, Office Report 12* December 2007, www.scottish.parliament.uk/business/officialReports/meetingsParliament/or-07/sor0912-02.htm

UK Commission for Employment and Skills (UKCES) (2009) *Ambition 2020: World Class Skills and Jobs for the UK*, Wath-upon-Dearne: UKCES

Welsh Assembly Government (WAG) (2008) *Skills that work for Wales: A skills and employment strategy*, Cardiff: WAG

Welsh Employment and Skills Board (WESB) (2009) *A Wales that Works – First Annual Report*, Cardiff: WESB

Wolf A (2007) 'Round and round the houses: the Leitch Review of Skills', *Local Economy*, 22, 2, 111-117 ·

7. 'Doing things differently'? Rhetoric and reality in regional economic development and regeneration policy

John Adams

The level of economic growth is perhaps the most important issue facing the United Kingdom at present. It has also consistently been one of the most high-profile and politically-salient issues in the devolved territories, both before and since the creation of devolved institutions in 1998 and 1999. Not only are politicians and officials judged on traditional economic measures – levels of GDP, productivity and employment – but the issue has been politicised to such an extent that numerous non-economic policy domains – health, education, culture, climate change – tend to be framed and evaluated in terms of their economic impact (Morgan 2006).

One of the main arguments put forward in the referendum debates of the late twentieth century was that devolved institutions would significantly improve economic growth in their respective territories: that devolved institutions would bring forward an automatic 'economic dividend'. In truth, the relationship between the two is far from straightforward.

Devolution clearly has the potential to improve economic growth. It can allow industrial policies to be developed that reflect the specific needs, problems and potential of a devolved economy, rather than having to fit the requirements of a national template. It can empower local knowledge and build local capacity, buttressing the institutional capacity that we know is crucial for economic performance (Russell Barter 2000). It can enable devolved institutions to lead high-profile lobbying campaigns in the corridors of power – in London, Brussels or further afield. It can also create the conditions for a more democratic and locally accountable system of governance, avoiding scandals and controversy that can undermine the effective delivery of industrial policies (as happened in Wales to the Welsh Development Agency in the late 1980s).

But this does not mean that the creation of devolved institutions will in and of itself lead to regional economic success. Many academics and commentators now cast a sceptical eye over the claims that devolution brings with it an automatic 'economic dividend'. Morgan feels that evidence of this dividend is 'at best ambiguous and at worst absent' (2006), while studies of the economic impact of devolution across a number of nation states conclude that there was no inevitable promotion of welfare (Rodrigeuz-Pose and Gill 2005). One study into the impact of devolution on the Scottish economy concluded that the relationship between devolution and development is 'likely to be complex, subtle and difficult to measure' (Ashcroft *et al* 2005). Official figures discussed later in this chapter indicate that the gap in economic performance between the UK average and that of the devolved areas has worsened since the creation of devolved institutions.

Certainly some of the claims for an economic dividend were overstated in the past, notably in the White Paper *A Voice for Wales* (Welsh Office 1997). But while there is no evidence of an economic dividend, neither is there any of an economic penalty. We will never know whether or not the economies of the devolved territories would be stronger in 2010 had power not been decentralised and political responsibility devolved from Whitehall in 1999. But what we do know is that there would have been less scope for policy differentiation, both in industrial policy and in attempts to link employment generation to the needs of deprived areas.

This chapter attempts to highlight some of the policy divergences in economic development and industrial policy that we have seen post-devolution, as well as setting out some of the pressures for convergence. It is in three parts. First, it discusses the long-term economic strategies for sustainable economic growth of the different administrations.[1] Second, it looks at attitudes towards multiple deprivation and neighbourhood regeneration. Finally, it briefly discusses the economic performance of the four constituent parts of the UK and the implications of the devolution of power within the Union, a nation state with a persistently uneven economic geography.

Devolution, economic development and policy differentiation
A common approach to development?
All other things being equal, we would expect the economic history of the devolved territories to promote divergence. The devolved territories are grappling with the consequences of deindustrialisation and the decline of the so-called heavy industries – coal, steel, shipbuilding and manufacturing. The areas that were more dependent on these traditional sectors (the North of England, Scotland, Wales and Northern Ireland) are those areas that today lag behind the most prosperous part of the UK (the Greater South East).

This could have led to the policies being pursued by the three devolved administrations being very different from those pursued by Whitehall acting on behalf of England. The economies of the North of England and the West Midlands might have much in common with those of the devolved areas, but the English authorities also have to ensure sustainable economic growth in the Greater South East, which not only has a very different industrial structure to the rest of the UK but also has to

---

1. For a discussion of how the devolved administrations have responded to the recession see David Bell, Chapter 5.

grapple with the problems that economic success brings – congestion, lack of water resources, pressure on housing, and so on.

However, despite rhetoric of 'clear red water' or 'Scottish solutions to Scottish problems', perhaps the most striking aspect of economic development in the different territories of the UK is the similarity in the approaches taken by the different administrations. In short, the ambition is for a high-value-added, export-orientated business sector, creating or attracting well-paid jobs that require high levels of qualifications. The emphasis is on globalisation and productivity, and this is largely to be achieved through tackling market failures, with limited intervention in industrial policy and a phobia of 'picking winners'.

At first, this may seem the only sensible policy option for devolved and regional institutions, but in fact different options do exist and have been utilised in the past. Industries have been nationalised and privatised in the name of greater efficiency, and 'surplus' growth in the South has been identified and moved northwards by the man in Whitehall. The high levels of public expenditure on financial assistance for industry and on bail-outs for politically or strategically important companies rose to record levels in the 1970s and were then cut back in the 80s. In turn many of the Thatcherite policies of the 80s – Enterprise Allowance Schemes, developing business parks and Enterprise Zones, and subsiding overseas investment – have become unfashionable in their own right. The recent emphasis on employment growth in the business and financial services sector now looks unwise in light of the crisis in the world's financial system.

In France, President Sarkozy has backed a report written by Joseph Stiglitz and Amartya Sen which recommends shifting our emphasis from simple GDP and the production of goods to a broader measure of citizens' well-being, income inequality and the impact of sustainability (Stiglitz et al 2009). This would imply employment growth in locally traded services, which would suggest some of the sectors that matter most in our everyday lives: for example, the caring profession, childcare, food and transport (Morgan and O'Hara Jakeway 2009). Arguments rage as to the merits of each of these approaches, and the effectiveness of the policy tools used, but what is clear is that the devolved administrations have not chosen any of these approaches.

Instead, they have adopted a common approach that can be traced back to the arrival of Michael Heseltine at the Department of Trade and Industry in 1992. He was responsible for initiating the 'competitiveness' agenda, offering a middle way between intervention and laissez-faire economics and focusing on the supply side in order to address market failures (Gillespie and Benneworth 2002). It stresses the importance of globalisation, recognises that firms in the UK are unlikely to compete with firms based in India and China on the basis of cost, and argues that future economic growth lies in high-value-added economic activity and developing comparative advantage in the global economy. Fundamentally this approach was UK-wide, focused on generating national wealth and less concerned with geographical disparities. However, the election of a Labour government in 1997 brought with it a concern about spatial inequalities, so devolved and regional institutions were created and the UK Government set itself a long-term goal of reducing regional economic disparities (HM Treasury/Department of Trade and Industry 2001).

The rhetoric used by politicians in the different parts of the UK is remarkably similar. Alex Salmond argues that Scotland needs to generate 'new high quality, high value jobs in the vital knowledge industries' (Salmond 2009a), while the Northern Ireland Executive states in its *Programme for Government* that 'we will focus on increasing productivity and supporting growth in well-paid high-skilled jobs' (Northern Ireland Executive 2008). Peter Mandelson believes that: 'globalisation is going to continue to push us to improve productivity and carve out our specialisations and comparative advantages in the global economy. Those specialisations should be based on the high levels of value-added we bring to what we produce' (Mandelson 2008). The Welsh Assembly Government has a clear vision for a 'strong and enterprising economy and full employment based on quality jobs' (Wyn Jones 2008).

The impact of the credit crunch and recession is discussed in Chapter 3 by David Bell, but it is worth noting that this has not fundamentally affected the approach of the four administrations, at least not yet. While some experts predicted wholesale changes in the nature of capitalism in the UK, a retreat from a crude reliance on market forces and a greater role for state planning and mutualism, in reality the response has been to support private sector companies in protecting their markets and remaining profitable. The different administrations still have faith in the market as a producer of wealth, and so they also have a common emphasis on tackling the market failures that constrain the performance of individual businesses.

Two obvious examples of market failure are the funding of small and medium sized companies (SMEs) and investment in Research and Development (R&D).

There are many economic development schemes that provide either debt or equity investment to SMEs. The rationale is that entrepreneurs with perfectly sound business ideas cannot find the money to start up or expand their activity and that market forces are failing to effectively allocate resources to this profitable opportunity. Reasons for this market failure include a preference among venture capitalists for short-term investments (sensible for them, damaging to the economy as a whole). Alternatively, transaction costs could be too high, for example if expensive prototypes are necessary but deter interested investors. If these situations are seen as market failures due to asymmetrical information, then devolved and regional institutions have a clear rationale to tackle this problem.

In Wales, such funds are provided through Finance Wales, a public limited company fully owned by the Welsh Assembly Government, whereas Scottish Enterprise runs a number of different funds providing the same services: the Scottish Seed Fund, the Scottish Co-Investment Fund and the Scottish Venture Fund. Invest Northern Ireland runs the Northern Ireland Spin Outs (NISPO) initiative and a 'proof of concept' fund and there are a huge variety of schemes available in England, both at the national and the regional level. These schemes are generally run at arms-length from Ministers and the civil service, often funded by European money (Structural Funds and/or the European Investment Bank). It is also the case that the individual investment decisions are commonly made jointly with representatives of private sector funders (banks, business angels, venture capitalists).

Another relevant market failure concerns the promotion of innovation, knowledge transfer and investment in R&D. The role for the public sector arises here because inventors, creators and innovators cannot hope to capture all the value that their work creates. Other firms or individuals may profit from their insight and hard work independent of paying for it (the 'free-rider' problem). Consequently, less innovation takes place than would be ideal (Hutton and Schneider 2008).

As such, all English regions have regional Science Councils, partly inspired by the Scottish Science Advisory Committees, and each devolved area is trying to improve the links between business and universities. Another common approach is for the development agencies to create sectoral networks, which can bring together people, firms and organisations active in particular industries. By strengthening such relationships in a non-competitive environment the hope is that we shall see more joint investment in areas such as training and R&D. Similarly, much of the devolved and regional investment in training and skills could be justified on the basis of market failure – without state intervention firms would refuse to adequately invest in up-skilling staff because they might be poached by another, free-riding, employer.

These are quite straightforward examples of what an economist would recognise as market failure, and constitute much of the activities of devolved and regional institutions in economic development. However, the devolved, regional and UK-wide institutions also have ambitions to shape the future economy to achieve more of the high-value-added economic activity so desired by those working in regional economic development. The approach here is to identify growth sectors for additional support, for example through funding basic research, providing pump-priming finance, or by improving skills. Through this form of industrial activism, the various institutions hope to strengthen productivity and international comparative advantage.

Again, much of the rhetoric is similar across the UK. Whitehall argues that, 'well-designed and well-implemented policies, when focused on particular sectors and markets, can be a source of enormous competitive advantage and benefit, both to businesses and to the competitive profile of the economy as a whole' (BERR 2009), while the Scottish government pledges to identify sectors where 'government intervention can make a significant difference to future success by facilitating or accelerating development in areas where the market alone cannot deliver the best outcome' (Scottish Government 2007). The Welsh Assembly Government 'wants to create a situation where the Welsh economy does not merely survive, but thrives. In order to achieve that, we have to be more focused on the sectors that can achieve the desired outcomes and generate the greatest wealth' (Wyn Jones 2008). Invest

Northern Ireland is also trying to effect a 'shift in the sectoral mix towards higher value-added activities' (Invest NI 2008). Table 7.1 contains an outline of the sectoral priorities of the devolved administrations.

While there is a clear desire to 'pump-prime' these sectors which have high-growth potential, there is also a concern that taxpayers' money is not wasted in the modern-day equivalent of the 1970s policy of bailing out failing companies like British Leyland. Ministers in each of the four territories would probably agree with the Scottish Government's statement that: 'the strategy should not be to pick individual companies as winners – the market does that. Rather, the job of government should be to facilitate and accelerate the growth sectors and to provide the necessary environment to make sure that it happens in Scotland' (Scottish Government 2007). The UK Business Secretary put it another way: 'One person's useless bail-out and inappropriate use of taxpayer's money is another person's vital bridging loan to secure a company's future. And ministers have to take very difficult decisions based on officials' advice as to when to put money in, for how long to sustain it and at what cost to the taxpayer' (Mandelson 2009).

Naturally, such an approach raises the question of whether or not the 'new' industrial policy is really all that different from the policies pursued in the 1970s and 80s. It is not clear what the practical difference is between an approach that 'pump primes growth sectors' or 'supports emerging industries' and one that 'picks winners'. Policies aimed at particular industries are by definition aimed at the firms that make up that sector. Another difficulty arises in defining sectors and classifying firms. For example, take a software company helping to build an offshore wind turbine tower. Depending on where the statisticians draw the lines, this firm could count as part of the creative industries or the energy sector; it could form part of our manufacturing base or part of the service sector. Defining these categories is more difficult than it first appears.

The fact that the different parts of the UK have a broadly similar approach to each other in industrial policy is not necessarily a cause for concern, and it may well be the best possible approach in order to promote productivity, create well-paid jobs and improve the well-being of citizens. However, it is interesting that this common approach is taken in territories whose economic challenges differ significantly from one to the next.

Perhaps over time we shall see greater divergence, but the pressure for convergence may mean a common approach continues across the nations and regions of the UK. The economies of the constituent parts of the UK are highly integrated, with goods and services traded within it all the time. Furthermore, the devolution settlement places the major macroeconomic policy levers in the hands of the UK authorities, as the response to the credit crunch and the recession has shown. Whether shoring up banking sector liquidity, stabilising the financial system, easing monetary policy, allowing the depreciation of the pound or using taxation powers to support demand and provide a good old Keynesian stimulus, it

Table 7.1: Sectoral priorities in the devolved territories and North East England

Scotland

Particular attention to be given to building a 'critical mass of activity' in the following key sectors:
- Creative industries (including digital content and technologies)
- Energy (with a particular focus on renewables)
- Financial and business services
- Food and drink (including agriculture and fisheries)
- Life sciences (including biotechnology and translational medicine)
- Tourism

Advantage also to be sought in the opportunities presented by Scotland's strengths and opportunities in public sector dominated industries, including education and healthcare. *Source: Scottish Government 2007*

Wales

The following three core or enabling sectors are considered of significant importance to the economy and, therefore, top priorities:
- Energy and the pursuit of clean and renewable energy generation and supply
- Environmental management based on the need to minimise energy use and maximise energy efficiency, both in industry and in domestic settings
- Telecommunications and ICT, 'which is the backbone and key enabler of the knowledge economy'

Six further sectors are considered 'not necessarily enabling', but strategically important:
- Bioscience
- Health
- Financial services/products and professional services
- Creative industries
- Automotive
- Aerospace

Five further sectors have been identified that are economically important to Wales 'and the world', but less strategic for developing Wales's competitive advantage: construction, food, defence, retail, and leisure and tourism. *Source: Wyn Jones 2008*

Northern Ireland

The plan is to: 'drive a shift towards high-value economic activity by attracting FDI [foreign direct investment] in target industries, notably financial services, software and ICT, and by boosting indigenous businesses and start-ups in high-value sectors including certain tradable services, niche manufacturing, life sciences and the creative industries.' *Source: Invest NI 2008*

North East England

Key manufacturing sectors identified through research:
- Chemicals and pharmaceuticals
- Automotive
- Defence and marine
- Food and drink

Key service sectors identified through research:
- Knowledge-intensive business services
- Tourism and hospitality
- Commercial creative
- Health and social care. *Source: One NorthEast 2006*

is the UK authorities who have responsibility in these crucial economic policy areas.

However, it is also true that many of the powers of the devolved authorities are important for promoting economic growth and even in areas with scope for policy differentiation there is a largely common approach. Today's economic strategies are the result of partnership working and an inclusive approach, and perhaps UK-wide interest groups – such as the business lobby or the trade union movement – will prove a force for convergence. Furthermore, there is to some extent a UK-wide labour market for the individuals who work in economic development. Those individuals who are employed in the civil service or quangos often move from region to region, but more important may be the independent freelance consultants who advise devolved, regional and local institutions. These people travel widely across the UK, and will be a significant force for convergent approaches. Finally, the fact that there are dominant trends and fashionable notions in policy thinking will also help bring about a convergent evolution of policy.

Some divergent approaches in policy and delivery

While it is true that the constituent parts of the UK have taken a broadly common approach to economic development, there are still some significant areas of policy divergence. For example, there are significant differences in the following four areas:

- Changes that have been introduced to the institutional structure of public bodies and the various agencies charged with pursuing economic development
- Attitudes to creating a 'tax-friendly' business environment
- Attitudes to demand-side labour market issues
- The importance of population growth.

To take the first of these, there have certainly been substantial change and divergence in the institutional structure of the agencies charged with delivering the policy agenda. Perhaps most notable has been the decision to abolish the Welsh Development Agency (WDA), announced by the WAG in 2004 with all its functions brought into the civil service from April 2006. This move was political in nature, drawing on the experience of the scandals of the WDA in the late 1980s and the devolution debates of the 90s (and the commitment of the then Labour opposition to hold a 'bonfire of the quangos'). Ironically, England and Northern Ireland had created Regional Development Agencies (RDAs) in large part because of the perceived success of the Welsh and Scottish agencies. Scottish Enterprise remains the lead economic agency in Scotland, but that too has been subject to structural reforms, losing its training programmes to the new body Skills Development Scotland in 2008.

Another area that has seen institutional reform has been in the administration of European Structural Funds. In England, Whitehall's Government Office for the Regions was in charge of their administration until they were moved into the RDAs for the 2007–13 period. In Scotland the civil service of the Scottish Government administers the funds, and similarly in Northern Ireland the Department for Finance and Personnel is the lead organisation. Northern Ireland also receives a distinctive Structural Funds Programme – PEACE II – designed to help address the legacy of the conflict. The availability (or lack) of funding for Structural Funds led to the resignation of Wales's first First Minister, Alun Michael, and EU funds are a major political issue in Wales. Administration was passed over to the Welsh European Funding Office (WEFO) in April 2000, and WEFO is an executive agency of the Assembly, arms-length but not quite with the independence of a quango.

There are other reforms, organisations and policy areas that could be mentioned – including Ministerial portfolios and civil service structures – but even this brief discussion illustrates that divergence in institutional structure is more common than divergences in policy. Structural reforms of this type can have a profound effect on the delivery of public policy, by encouraging coordination and cooperation between different policy areas. Furthermore, it can signify a different approach to the policy issue – for example, if skills were placed in business-led agencies we might see a very different approach than if they were located in local government. But in the case of economic development, and with the exception of the abolition of the WDA, these differences in structure do not seem to reflect divergent approaches in values or policy. Rather, they seem a practical and pragmatic response to day-to-day administration, depending on the particular circumstances of the territory and the character of the individuals involved. What impact these changes will have over time is impossible to judge.

Moving on to the second area of divergence, one feature of the economic debates in Scotland and Northern Ireland that is not seen in England or Wales to anything like the same degree is that over whether or not lower business taxes would help promote economic growth. In both cases, these debates are influenced by the experience of the Republic of Ireland, which until recently was seen as a nation experiencing well-above-average levels of economic growth (it is now in severe difficulties).

The transformation in the Irish economy between the mid-1980s and the mid-2000s was truly remarkable, and was dubbed an 'Irish economic miracle' and a 'Celtic Tiger economy'. Policymakers across the globe turned to Ireland to see if they could discover for themselves the secret of success, and different people were attracted to different aspects of the story. Some felt that the high-tech inward investment of companies such as Dell and Microsoft was the crucial factor; others believed that the social partnership was key (the voluntary agreements between the employer groups, trade unions and government for wage moderation, social protection, and so on). Some felt that European Structural Funds were the main cause of the boom, while others considered the lower rates of corporate taxation to have been the deciding factor.

It was this latter issue that was taken up by numerous politicians and business people in Northern Ireland and Scotland. All of the main parties, business leaders and the

Belfast Telegraph lobbied for a reduction in corporation tax in Northern Ireland, and in March 2007 HM Treasury established the Varney Review to examine the extent to which tax policy dissuaded firms from locating in Northern Ireland. However, the Varney Review dismissed these arguments, concluding that 'a clear and unambiguous case for a 12.5 per cent rate of corporation tax cannot be made' (Varney 2007). The SNP has also advocated a low business-tax agenda, drawing on the Irish experience. One of the overarching objectives of the SNP economic strategy is for Scotland to be the Celtic Lion to the Irish Tiger. In part this would be achieved by creating 'a competitive tax regime which incentivises business growth and attracts mobile factors of production' (Scottish Government 2007).

On the other hand, the issue is not much discussed by individuals working in economic development in England or Wales. It seems to run in contrast to the general principle that the road to regional prosperity is through higher skills, better infrastructure, more R&D and innovation, and so on. And as the Varney Review stated, in many of these areas taxation needs to be raised in order to fund these public goods (Varney 2007).

The third area of divergence is on demand-side labour market issues. One of the most important and enduring criticisms of the regional economic policies of both the Conservative and Labour UK Governments has been that policy has failed to recognise the lack of labour demand in the poorer areas of the country. Traditional Treasury analysis argues that 'almost without exception, areas of high unemployment lie within easy travelling distance of areas where vacancies are plentiful' (HM Treasury/DWP 2000). If this analysis is accepted, the solution to unemployment is to focus on supply-side measures, such as improving skills, providing advice and support to jobseekers or using conditionality within the benefit system.

Critics of this approach argue that jobs are not plentifully available, and that if regional and local economies were stronger the extra demand for labour would draw the unemployed and workless into the labour market. Generally advanced by economic geographers and organisations such as the Alliance for Regional Aid, this approach stresses that the unemployed are active jobseekers, but that it is a shortage of opportunities that causes regional disparities in employment (Regional Studies Association 2001, Martin and Sunley 2002).

The Welsh Assembly Government has adopted the second approach, and Rhodri Morgan has argued that, 'whether you are going to actively participate in the labour market to some extent is determined by your perception of whether there are lots of jobs available. That's going to be very different if you live in Mountain Ash than if you live on the outskirts of London' (Morgan 2008). This analysis would be completely refuted by the Treasury and the Department for Work and Pensions (DWP). In theory the Welsh approach should focus less on supply-side measures aimed at increasing employability, skills and enterprise, and more on interventionist policies designed to boost labour demand, particularly in jobs that are relevant to the skills of workless groups. The practical implications of this divergent analysis are not yet clear, as policy on both sides of the border contain aspects of both supply and demand-side interventions. However, over time this may well lead to more significant policy divergences.

The fourth area is population growth. One distinctive feature of economic development in Scotland has been the political importance of demographic change, leading to attempts to ensure that Scotland's population does not fall beneath the 5 million mark. This was seen in the Fresh Talent Initiative of the previous Labour administration (McConnell 2004), an attempt to encourage people to live and work in Scotland, which included measures such as help with work permits, visa extensions for overseas students and the establishment of a Relocation Advice Service. As immigration was reserved to Westminster, agreement had to be obtained from the Home Office for key parts of the proposals, although it ended in 2008 when the UK Government brought forward its new points-based immigration system. Similarly, one of the key aspirations of the SNP's economic strategy is to at least match the average population growth in the Western European nations (Scottish Government 2007).

In contrast, population politics is almost entirely off the political agenda in Westminster, associated as it is with the 'nanny state' and the one-child policy of China. The impact of an ageing society and immigration may be politically salient issues, but there is no desire for demographic targets or aspirations. Some nations, France for example, have traditionally favoured population growth and there has been a trend in a number of OECD countries in recent years for a more proactive approach to countering low fertility (d'Addio and d'Ercole 2005). One reason why Britain may not be pursuing these population growth targets is that our fertility rate remains relatively high by international standards, chiefly fuelled by population growth in the Greater South East. The fact that Scotland faces a different population growth trajectory to the UK as a whole is perhaps the main reason for this diverging population politics.

Devolution and regeneration

Devolved and regional differences in economic performance are marked, but there is often greater variation between local areas within a region or a city than between UK regions themselves. The devolved and English authorities have set themselves the ambition to both grow the size of the aggregate economy and tackle disparities at a neighbourhood and community level. The two policy areas have traditionally been pursued separately in the UK, but they are in fact intimately intertwined because deprived communities are the physical manifestation of inequalities in the labour and housing markets.

Inequalities in the labour market mean that those individuals who are without work, or who are poorly paid, find themselves with less choice in the housing market; and market forces operate to sift a high proportion of these people into the areas where house prices and rents are low, or where social housing is concentrated. This 'residential sorting effect' therefore concentrates lower income groups in particular areas. These areas also tend to have poorly performing schools, higher levels of crime, limited job networks and employment ambitions and lower levels of private amenities. These effects can become self-reinforcing. While not all people who live in deprived communities are poor, and while not all poor people live in these areas, they have been the subject of much policy and academic interest in recent years.

All corners of the UK have brought forward a plethora of initiatives designed to tackle this neighbourhood deprivation. Some interventions have been short term, others have been long term; some have been focused quite narrowly, while others have taken a holistic cross-cutting approach. We have seen schemes designed to be implemented at the street level, and attempts to link deprivation to regional and international economies. Person-based and place-based policies have both been brought forward, and there has been much earnest debate as to which is the more important. This section will highlight the high-profile cross-cutting initiatives designed to improve economic, social and environmental outcomes at a relatively small geographical scale, typically at the level of a local authority ward or what can be termed the 'neighbourhood' or 'community'.

Flagship schemes tackling neighbourhood deprivation

As with regional and industrial policies, there are many similarities in the approaches adopted by the different parts of the UK. Many of the historic complaints about frontline practitioners – a 'silo approach', a lack of long-term funding, a lack of partnership working – have been addressed, suggesting that academic and policy research and pressure from community and third sector organisations have proved to be significant forces for convergence.

Whether we are talking about the New Deal for Communities or the National Strategy for Neighbourhood Renewal in England (Social Exclusion Unit 1998), Communities First in Wales (WAG 2000), or Social Inclusion Partnerships (Scottish Executive 1999) or Community Planning Partnerships in Scotland (Scottish Executive 2002), the objectives for each of these programmes are broadly similar and wide-ranging. Objectives include improving a locality's performance in areas such as worklessness, crime and community safety, health, housing, the physical environment, educational achievement and community spirit. As the problems of social exclusion were seen to be multi-faceted and inter-connected, it was felt that the policy prescriptions also had to take a joined-up approach.

Similarly, each part of Great Britain has adopted a 'partnership approach', where different institutions are expected to work together to improve their local community. The different parts of the public sector were required to engage and contribute towards a joint strategy and action plan, whether Local Strategic Partnerships in England, Community Planning Partnerships in Scotland or local Communities First partnerships in Wales. This brings together the local representatives of diverse organisations such as local authorities, the NHS, the police, Jobcentre Plus, economic development agencies, environmental bodies, further education colleges and so on. The local community and voluntary sectors have also been invited to contribute towards the joint strategies and action plans, with much success. However, in each of the three territories there have been difficulties in bringing the private sector into the process; and there have also been difficulties in integrating elected councillors into these structures (Audit Scotland 2006, Adams 2008).

This emphasis on partnership working arises from a recognition that it is easier to tackle the problems and achieve the potential of an area if all local organisations work together. For example, the police may find solving and preventing crime easier if the local council prioritised the maintenance of street lights or tackled problem tenants. It also recognises that regeneration budgets are dwarfed by mainstream public sector budgets, and in each territory mainstream organisations are expected to 'bend the spend' in order to help achieve local regeneration outcomes. For example, the NHS may build a walk-in centre in the heart of a deprived community rather than choose an out-of-town site, contributing to local economic and environmental outcomes in a way that a local regeneration initiative would find unaffordable.

This was an explicit part of the National Strategy in England, Communities First in Wales and Community Planning Partnerships in Scotland. Interestingly, it signals a move from the traditional pattern of 'government', in which authority is centralised and exercised hierarchically, to a more pluralistic pattern of 'governance'. This term is used to describe a system where authority and accountability are exercised through informal networks, and where boundaries between different tiers of government, between the public and the private sectors, and between the state and civil society are blurred. (This more pluralistic approach can still retain some of the bureaucratic elements of the traditional approach, such as audit trails, targeting and performance management.)

Another traditional frustration for regeneration practitioners was the short-term nature of public sector funding. While the public sector traditionally works to annual budgets, or sometimes to two- or three-year timescales, this is woefully insufficient to transform a deprived community. A local scheme would only just become known to the local population before its funding was wound up. In each of the devolved territories there has been an attempt to take a longer term approach. The New Deal for Communities and Communities First were 10-year programmes, and Community Planning Partnerships were explicitly designed with a longer timescale than their predecessors.

In essence, therefore, the broad thrust of regeneration policy is similar across the different parts of Great Britain, but there are also some interesting divergences. Below we address two of these: the relative importance given to this policy area in the different territories, and the relationship between economic and social policy initiatives.

On the first count, the relative importance of deprived communities, it seems that it is England that has given the highest political commitment to neighbourhood renewal. As this policy area was closely associated with Tony Blair when he was Prime Minister, the problems of deprived communities were taken seriously both at the centre of government and in Whitehall departments. During most of the first 10 years of the Labour Government, the Social Exclusion Unit was influential within the Whitehall machine, and developed a relatively high profile in stakeholder circles and in the media. The Government set itself ambitious objectives, not just at the purely rhetorical level ('no one should be disadvantaged by where they live') but also in specific targets designed to close the gap between deprived communities and the rest of the country.

The approach seems to be having some impact, and one recent report from the Joseph Rowntree Foundation concluded that services and key indicators in poor communities were improving and on some indicators they were also closing the gap with more prosperous areas (Hills and Stewart 2005). In contrast, the One Wales document (setting out the terms of the coalition between Plaid Cymru and Wales Labour) did not make mention of tackling the gap between the rich and the poor or the gap between rich and poor communities.

At a financial level, however, it seems that Scotland is the most generous contributor to these types of regeneration programmes. It is not always easy to draw comparisons between the different nations, because programmes can have a different scope, or cover different time periods. Often even the most basic information is extremely difficult to get hold of. However, we do know that the Community Regeneration Fund amounted to £318 million over three years, and from 2008 the Fairer Scotland Fund will total £435 million over three years. In England, the Working Neighbourhoods Fund will be allocated £1.5 billion over the three years from 2008, so it seems we can make a comparison between the Fairer Scotland Fund and the Working Neighbourhoods Fund. As the population in England is about 10 times larger than Scotland's, a £435 million programme in Scotland would cost roughly £4.35 billion to fund in England. It seems, therefore, that the Scottish Community Regeneration Fund is much larger than its English equivalent.

Wales, by contrast, seems to have allocated less money to this policy area, even accounting for the smaller size of its population. We know that in England the New Deal for Communities cost £2 billion over 10 years, the Neighbourhood Renewal Fund cost nearly £3 billion over six years (2001/02 to 2007/08) and the various neighbourhood management programmes total about £500 million. In Wales, figures provided by the Welsh Assembly Government reveal that Communities First cost £174.5 million over six years (2001/02 to 07/08). It is therefore possible to make a financial comparison between the Neighbourhood Renewal Fund and Communities First. As the population of England is roughly 17 times bigger than Wales, a £174.5 million programme in Wales would cost roughly £3 billion to fund in England. Therefore, Communities First was allocated roughly the same resources as the Neighbourhood Renewal Fund in England.

But Wales did not have sister programmes, such as the New Deal for Communities or the various neighbourhood management programmes.

While these comparisons are 'rough and ready', they do indicate that there has been a greater emphasis on neighbourhood renewal in Scotland and England than in Wales, which has preferred to focus on a larger geographical unit.

On the second question, of integrating economic and social policies, one of the arguments consistently advanced in favour of devolution was that it would be easier to achieve 'joined-up government', bringing together different parts of the public sector in a manner that would be impossible in a much bigger Whitehall machine with more entrenched policy silos. If we examine the integration between the industrial policies discussed above and the neighbourhood policies discussed in this section, it does seem that there is some justification for this claim.

The economic development and social exclusion agendas are split between different government departments in each of the three territories, and naturally there is an underlying tension between the two different policy areas. Wales and England have Ministers who work in both the economic and social departments, and there are attempts by the devolved authorities and the RDAs to develop an economic inclusion strand, mostly around the issue of worklessness, which does transcend the economic and social. However, there will always be some problems in trying to integrate the two areas.

In England, the RDAs are in charge of economic issues, while the Government Offices and local authorities are in charge of regeneration, neighbourhood renewal and social exclusion. The Sub-National Review of Economic Development and Regeneration recognised that there were substantial and persistent failures of integration between the two (HMT/BERR/DCLG 2007). In Wales, on the other hand, the Spatial Plan does seem to have been a more successful mechanism to integrate the social and economic agendas (WAG 2004). The Spatial Plan has defined six sub-regions in Wales, albeit with fuzzy boundaries, which then set the context both for local and community planning and for broader economic development strategies. It aims to be cross-cutting in nature, aiming for decisions to be made with regard to their impact beyond the immediate sectoral or administrative boundaries.

Certainly experience on the ground suggests that there is a high degree of integration between the numerous strategies produced in the various parts of the public sector, including those produced for EU Structural Funds, for local government, for the economic and other documents produced by the Welsh Assembly Government itself (Adams forthcoming). However, some feel that this has the consequence that producing and implementing strategies has become bureaucratic and time-consuming, and hinders innovation at a local level.

Conclusion

The solution to neighbourhood deprivation is not necessarily found within the deprived communities themselves, as the problems are ultimately caused by inequalities in the wider labour and housing markets. As the 1970s Community Development Programme found, community action could not, alone, address complex and deep-seated problems, and what is needed is local action coupled with major changes in wider policy and delivery (Penn and Alden 1977).

There is a balance to be struck between local action and wider economic restructuring, and that balance is struck slightly differently in the different parts of the UK. England has had more emphasis on local neighbourhood action, while in Wales the revitalisation of the sub-regional economy has perhaps more priority. Neither approach is necessarily correct or wrong, but it is an interesting divergence.

Impact and importance of initiatives

Devolution is a little over 10 years old, which is too short a timescale to judge the impact of the economic initiatives brought forward. The modern approach to economic development is inherently long-term in nature, focusing on building indigenous capacity rather than attracting international investment. Nevertheless, it is important to start considering the impact that the devolved administrations have had on improving outcomes for their citizens. This section will not be able to conduct a voluminous examination of economic indicators, but it will highlight performance in the basic building blocks of economic prosperity.

The best (or more accurately, the least-worst) indicator of economic performance we have is Gross Domestic Product or Gross Value Added (GVA) per head. This does not measure social or environmental progress, but it is an accurate measure of narrow economic output. Figure 7.1 shows levels of GVA per head in each of the four territories for the 10 years leading up to the creation of devolved administrations, and

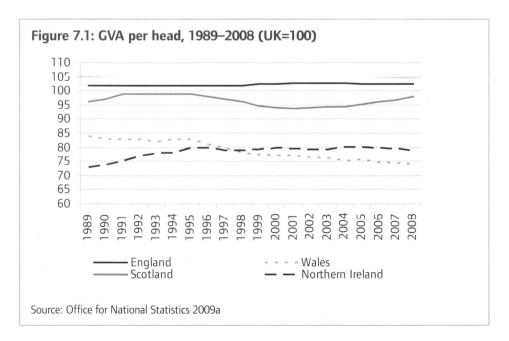

Figure 7.1: GVA per head, 1989–2008 (UK=100)

England
Scotland
Wales
Northern Ireland

Source: Office for National Statistics 2009a

the eight years post-devolution. Scotland, England and Northern Ireland have seen little change to their relative economic standing post-devolution, although Wales has seen its relative decline continue. GVA per head in Wales stood at only 74 per cent of the UK average in 2008.

Figure 7.2 contains productivity data for the four nations of the UK. We only have data for a few years prior to devolution, but post-devolution we can see that each of the three devolved territories have lower levels of productivity per hour worked in the post-devolution era than they did at the time the institutions were created in 1998/99. Again, this is most notable in the case of Wales, where productivity in 2007 was less than 85 per cent of the UK average.

In contrast, the employment data tell a different story (see Figure 7.3). They reveal that levels of employment among the working-age population grew in each of the devolved territories, until the impact of the recession was felt towards the end of 2008. Until that time employment rates were growing in each of the devolved areas, and Wales and Northern Ireland narrowed the gap with the English average. Scotland now has the highest working-age employment rates of the four territories, passing the English average in 2006.

So the information provided from these most basic economic indicators seems to indicate that the performance of the devolved territories has been relatively poor in terms of GVA and productivity but much more positive in terms of employment (at least until the start of the recession). But of course, it is impossible to determine the extent to which devolved and UK-wide institutions are responsible for these trends.

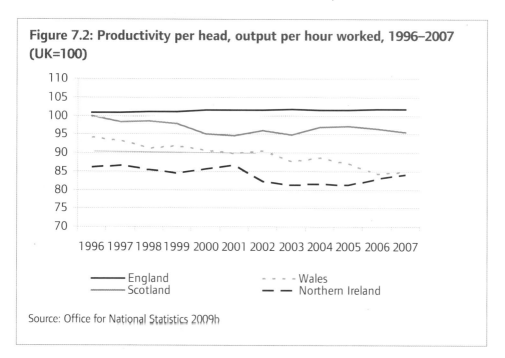

Figure 7.2: Productivity per head, output per hour worked, 1996–2007 (UK=100)

Source: Office for National Statistics 2009h

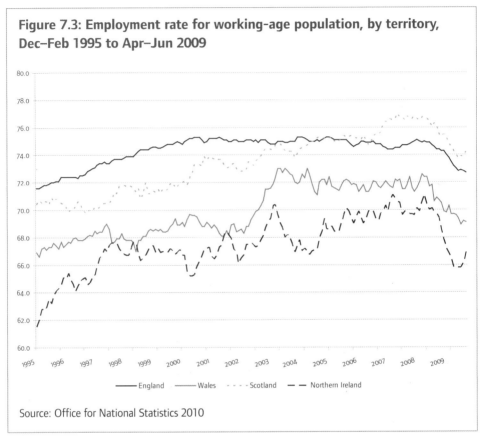

Figure 7.3: Employment rate for working-age population, by territory, Dec–Feb 1995 to Apr–Jun 2009

Source: Office for National Statistics 2010

First, it is almost impossible to measure the impact of public sector interventions on economic growth. We can never really know if changes in GDP are the result of state action or global economic forces. Second, the devolution settlement did not create a watertight division of competences and the different tiers of government will each have some impact on economic performance. For example, even if we assume that the state helped cause the employment growth in Wales we cannot know if this was due to the Treasury's macroeconomic policies, the DWP's policies on active labour market initiatives, National Minimum Wage and tax credits, WAG's stress on supporting new industries or local authorities' efforts to regenerate their local areas. Each of the UK-wide policies will have differentiated regional impacts and implications, and each tier and/or each department will have played some role, whether for good or bad.

Due to a lack of rigourous evaluation it is just as difficult to judge the impact of devolution on neighbourhood regeneration. However, the Jospeh Rowntree Foundation has analysed a series of social and economic indicators in order to judge the impact of devolution on low income people and places. Table 7.2 contains its assessment of changes in the relative position of Scotland, Wales and Northern

Ireland, as well as a number of English regions. Its conclusion was that the most improved parts of the UK over this period were Scotland and the North East of England. Northern Ireland improved most on two indicators and Wales on one. This is due to the fact that child, pensioner and working age poverty decreased most in Scotland, unemployment decreased most in Northern Ireland and the number of infant deaths decreased most in Wales. Conversely, Wales saw the lowest decline in pensioner poverty, and Northern Ireland the lowest decreases in the number of infant and premature deaths.

However, while this assessment is interesting it says little about the impact of devolution. For example, the areas Scotland improved in the most are influenced more by UK reserved powers than by devolved policies – by the reserved responsibilties on welfare-to-work and tax-benefit reforms.

Table 7.2: Progress on poverty and exclusion indicators: the most and least imropoved countries and English regions (1998–2008)

Nation/region	Most improved	Least improved	Net
Scotland	6	0	+6
North East	5	0	+5
Wales	1	1	0
Northern Ireland	2	2	0
London	2	2	0
East Midlands	0	4	-4
East of England	0	4	-4
West Midlands	0	5	-5
South East	0	5	-5

Note: Northern Ireland rankings based on seven indicators for which trend data is available.
Figures add to more than 16 due to the inclusion of joint rankings.
Source: McCormick and Harrop 2010

Devolution and solidarity

If we have not seen the clear economic dividend some argued would follow devolution (or at least, not yet) what evidence is there of two other traditional concerns of academia? The first is the argument made by some that devolution weakens the basis and motives for spatially redistributive regional policies, and indeed can in some respects be seen as an alternative to these. The second is that devolution inevitably promotes bottom-up forms of territorial competition (Gordon 2002). The evidence so far suggests that neither of these concerns has been borne out yet.

Each of the constituent parts of the UK has taken a broadly similar approach to the others in response to the recession, but there is also evidence of a cooperative approach. After a meeting between Gordon Brown and the devolved leaders in February 2009, a new series of meetings of the Joint Ministerial Committee was instigated after a period of abeyance. This is the forum that brings together ministers of the UK Government with ministers of each of the devolved administrations. Welsh Secretary Paul Murphy was given the task of overseeing this, and plenary sessions were held on energy policy and public expenditure in June 2009 and the economy in September 2009. Furthermore, Alex Salmond has called for a joint UK and Scottish Cabinet meeting to discuss the economy, arguing that it is in the 'national interest' for both administrations to work together (Salmond 2009b). In turn, Gordon Brown has hosted an economic summit at his house in Fife, with Alex Salmond, Iain Grey and other Scottish political and civic leaders.

On the policy front, the UK Government has taken a number of initiatives that have benefited businesses in the devolved territories. England-based banks such as Northern Rock and Bradford and Bingley have been nationalised (or part nationalised) and the fact that the Royal Bank of Scotland Group was based in Edinburgh did not stop the Treasury injecting billions of pounds into the bank to prevent its closure. Similarly, the £340 million loan to aeroplane manufacturer Airbus will protect jobs in both Filton in Bristol and Broughton in North Wales. Furthermore, schemes such as the Enterprise Finance Guarantee, where the Department for Business, Innovation and Skills guarantees lending to businesses to ensure that they can get the working capital and investment they need, operate across the UK.

If there is little evidence that devolution of economic development functions has increased territorial competition among political elites, neither does it seem to have affected public attitudes. The Scottish social attitudes surveys ask a question that should help gauge attitudes to the economic consequences of devolution: 'on the whole, do you think that England's economy benefits more from having Scotland in the UK, or that Scotland's economy benefits more from being part of the UK, or is it about equal?'

This question has been asked on a fairly regular basis since 1992, and the evidence suggests that the creation of the Scottish Parliament has actually helped foster a more positive attitude to the economic benefits of the Union. Table 7.3 shows that, up to and including the referendum in September 1997, around half of Scots felt that England's economy benefited more from the Union while no more than one in seven thought that Scotland's economy benefited more (Bromley et al 2006). But after 1999, attitudes changed. By 2003, 30 per cent thought that England's economy benefited more, only six points higher than the 24 per cent who thought that Scotland's economy did. Both figures are less than the two in five who think that the two economies benefit equally. There is evidently no longer a clear perception that Scotland's economy loses out from the Union, indicating that devolution has not fostered bottom-up forms of competition; if anything it has been rather the reverse.

Table 7.3: Perceptions of which economy benefits more from the Union, 1992–2003

	1992	May 1997	Sept 1997	1999	2001	2003
England	49	50	48	36	38	30
Scotland	14	11	14	22	18	24
Both equally	32	31	32	36	39	40
Sample size	957	882	676	1482	1605	1508

Source: Bromley et al 2006

Conclusion

In economic development terms, devolution has not proved to be a 'divergence machine'. While it has facilitated important but somewhat limited policy divergences, perhaps its most significant impact has been to increase local ownership of strategy and decision-making. Interestingly, the recession has not exacerbated territorial rivalries, and even though the different administrations of the UK are made up of politicians from different political parties, we have not seen political buck-passing and point scoring. This was not necessarily an inevitable outcome – the shock to the economy was unprecedented, and we now know that in the autumn of 2008 the UK came within hours of a banking shutdown and the closure of cash machines.

Perhaps counterintuitively, the recession has increased the desire for the four constituent parts of the UK to work together in the 'national interest', for example through the resurrection of the Joint Ministerial Committee and the invitation of Gordon Brown for Alex Salmond to dine at his house and discuss the economic crisis. Rather than undermine a UK-wide sense of solidarity, devolution seems to have helped buttress a pre-existing desire to share some economic risk on a UK-wide basis.

References

Adams J (forthcoming) *Regenerating the Afan Valley* Tredgear: Bevan Foundation

Adams J (2008) *Working Together: perceptions of and attitudes to LAAs and partnership working in North East England* Newcastle: Improvement Partnership for North East Local Government

d'Addio A C and d'Ercole M M (2005) *Trends and Determinants of Fertility Rates: The role of policies* Paris: OECD

Ashcroft B, Swales K and McGregor P (2005) *Is Devolution Good for the Scottish Economy? A Framework for Analysis, Devolution Briefings* 26, Swindon: ESRC

Audit Scotland (2006) *Community Planning: An Initial Review* Edinburgh: Audit Scotland

BERR (Department for Business, Enterprise and Regulatory Reform) (2009) *New Industry, New Jobs: Building Britain's Future* London: BERR

Bromley C, Curtice J, McCrone D and Park A (eds) (2006) *Has Devolution Delivered?* Edinburgh: EUP

Calman K (2009) *Serving Scotland Better: Scotland and the United Kingdom in the 21st Century* Edinburgh: Commission on Scottish Devolution

Gillespie A and Benneworth P (2002) 'Industrial and regional policy in a devolved united Kingdom' in Adams J and Robinson P (eds) *Devolution in Practice: Public policy differences within the UK* London: ippr

Gordon I (2002) 'Industrial and regional policy: a London perspective' in Adams J and Robinson P (eds) *op. cit.*

Hills J and Stewart H (2005) *A More Equal Society: Policies towards poverty, inequality and exclusion since 1997* Abingdon: The Policy Press

HMT/BERR/DCLG (HM Treasury/Department for Business, Enterprise and Regulatory Reform/Department for Communities and Local Government) (2007) *Review of sub-national economic development and regeneration* Norwich: TSO

HM Treasury/DWP (Department for Work and Pensions) (2000) *The Goal of Full Employment: employment opportunity for all throughout Britain - Trends in regional and local vacancies and unemployment* London: HM Treasury

HM Treasury/DTI (Department of Trade and Industry) (2001) *Productivity in the UK: 3 - The Regional Dimension* London: HMT

Hutton W and Schneider P (2008) *The Failure of Market Failure: towards a 21st century Keynesianism* London: NESTA

Invest NI (2008) *Corporate Plan 2008–2011* Belfast: Invest NI

Mandelson P (2008) 'A new industrial activism', speech to the RSA,18 December, London: BIS

Mandelson P (2009) *World at One,* BBC Radio 4, 11 August

Martin R and Sunley P (2002) *The Geography of Workfare: Local Labour Markets and the New Deal* Swindon: ESRC

McConnell J (2004) *First Ministers Statement on Fresh Talent,* 25 February, www.scotland.gov.uk/News/News-Extras/191

McCormick J and Harrop A (2010) *Devolution's impact on low-income people and places* York: Joseph Rowntree Foundation

Morgan K (2001) 'The new territorial politics: Rivalry and Justice in post-devolution Britain', *Regional Studies* 35.4

Morgan K (2006) 'Devolution and Development: Territorial Justice and the North-South Divide', *Publius* 36.1

Morgan R (2008) 'Ministers' benefit reform worries', BBC website, http://news.bbc.co.uk/1/hi/wales/7773960.stm

Morgan K and O'Hara Jakeway J (2009) 'Mutualism – an idea whose time has come (again)' in Tomaney J (ed) *The Future of Regional Policy* London: The Smith Institute

Northern Ireland Executive (2008) *Building a Better Future: Programme for government 2008–2011* Belfast: Northern Ireland Executive

One NorthEast (2006) *Leading the way: Regional Economic Strategy 2006–2016* Newcastle: ONE

Office for National Statistics (2010) *Regional Labour Market Summary – Statistical Bulletin Dataset,* www.statistics.gov.uk/statbase/product.asp?vlnk=8281

Office for National Statistics (2009a) 'Regional, sub-regional and local gross value added 2009', *Statistical Bulletin*, 9 December Newport: ONS

Office for National Statistics (2009ba) 'Productivity measures by region', www.statistics.gov.uk/downloads/theme_economy/regional-prod-table8-Feb09.pdf

Penn R and Alden J (1977) *Upper Afan CDP Final Report to Sponsors: Joint Report by the Action Team and the Research Team* Directors Cardiff: UWIST

Regional Studies Association (2001) *Labour's New Regional Policy: An assessment* Seaford: RSA

Rodrigeuz-Pose A and Gill N (2005) 'On the "economic dividend" of devolution', *Regional Studies* 39.4

Russell Barter W (2000) *Regional Government in England: a preliminary review of literature and research findings* London: DETR

Salmond A (2009a) Speech to Scottish Council for Development and Industry International Seminar, 20 March, Edinburgh: Scottish Government

Salmond A (2009b) 'Alex Salmond calls for joint cabinet on economy', press release, 13 April, Edinburgh: SNP

Scottish Executive (1999) *Social Justice: A Scotland where everyone matters* Edinburgh: Scottish Executive

Scottish Executive (2002) *Better Communities in Scotland: Closing the gap* Edinburgh: Scottish Executive

Scottish Government (2007) *The Government Economic Strategy* Edinburgh: Scottish Government

Scottish Government (2009a) 'Statistics Publication Notice – Gross Domestic product for Scotland for the 1st Quarter of 2009', press release, 22 July, Scottish Government: Edinburgh

Scottish Government (2009b) *Preparing for Recovery: Update on the Scottish Economic Recovery Programme*, 15 June, Edinburgh: Scottish Government

Sentence A (2009) 'Monetary Policy and the Current Recession', speech to the Institute of Economic Affairs State of the Economy Conference, 24 February

Social Exclusion Unit (1998) *Bringing Britain Together: A National Strategy for Neighbourhood Renewal* London: Social Exclusion Unit

Stewart H, Mathiason N, Webb T, Wood Z and Davies C (2008) 'It's grim down south' *The Observer*, 19 October

Stiglitz J, Sen A and Fitoussi C (2009) *Report by the Commission on the Measurement of Economic Performance and Social Progress* www.stiglitz-sen-fitoussi.fr

Summers D (2009) 'Food for thought: Gordon Brown invites Alex Salmond to dinner summit', *The Guardian*, 15 April

Varney D (2007) *Review of Tax Policy in Northern Ireland* London: HMT

Welsh Assembly Government (WAG) (2005) *Wales: A Vibrant Economy – The Welsh Assembly Government's Strategic Framework for Economic Development – Consultation document*, November, Cardiff: WAG

Welsh Assembly Government (WAG) (2004) *People, Places, Futures: the Wales Spatial Plan* Cardiff: WAG

Welsh Assembly Government (WAG) (2000) *Communities First: Regenerating our most deprived communities* Cardiff: WAG

Welsh Office (1997) *A Voice for Wales: The Government's proposals for a Welsh Assembly* Cardiff: Welsh Office

Wyn Jones I (2008) 'A New Approach to Economic Development - recommendations from the Ministerial Advisory Group', Statement by the Welsh Assembly Government, 24 June, Cardiff: WAG

8. Devolution and approaches to social policy

Derek Birrell

The devolved administrations were handed significant powers to influence social policy. Health, social care, education, housing and planning, along with aspects of employment, criminal justice and delivery structures, were devolved to each nation. The priority afforded by the devolved administrations to social policy is reflected in the pattern of public expenditure in Scotland, Wales and Northern Ireland: Table 8.1 shows that the devolved governments choose to dedicate a high proportion of their spend to health and education, and to a lesser degree, personal social services. Social policy could therefore be identified as constituting the main remit of the Scottish Parliament, Welsh Assembly and Northern Irish Assembly (Chaney and Drakeford 2004, Stewart 2004, Scott and Mooney 2004 and Mooney *et al* 2006). Such a focus might even justify labelling them the 'social policy parliament' and 'social policy assembly(s)'.

This chapter explores the different approaches taken by the devolved administrations in the field of social policy. It highlights the main policy innovations of the last decade, and assesses the degree to which devolution has created a genuine laboratory of democracy.

Table 8.1. Total identifiable expenditure on services in the devolved nations, 2006–7

Service	Scotland (%)	Wales (%)	N. Ireland (%)
Health	26	28	25
Education	20	21	21
Social protection – personal social services	15	17	14
Total	61	66	60

Source: HM Treasury (2008)

The role of social policy

The role that social policy plays and the priority afforded to it can be assessed via an analysis of the programmes of government of each administration and the underlying principles used to inform each approach. A brief overview of each is provided here.

Principles of social policy

To turn first to principles, there is some evidence of differences in the principles and values that underpin the approach to social policy in each of the devolved administrations, although how this translates into policy outcomes is not always clear. In Scotland and Wales the values of social justice and equality have provided a touchstone in the narratives and rationales for their policy agendas (see for example Drakeford 2007). The promotion of social justice has been frequently cited as central to Welsh Assembly policies and initiatives in tackling disadvantage and social exclusion (WAG 2007b). The Labour/Plaid Cymru government formed in 2007 has not altered this focus. The Scottish Executive's commitment to placing social justice at the heart of political and civic life was recorded as early as 1999 (Scottish Executive 1999b). For a period the Scottish and Welsh administrations both published social justice annual reports, promoted as a means of highlighting their commitment to social justice, and a way to monitor their progress.

In terms of equality, the Welsh Assembly Government has made reducing inequalities among children a statutory duty for public agencies in Wales. In Scotland a strong emphasis has been placed on equality in government strategies to tackle poverty and health and education inequalities (Scottish Government 2008b). The 2008/9 programme for government and the Scottish Government's economic strategy both highlighted combating inequality as a core principle. This approach involves a golden rule of 'solidarity' to reduce inequality and increase the position of low income groups through a fairer distribution of wealth, and a golden rule of 'cohesion' to achieve growth across Scotland and regenerate communities suffering from multiple deprivation (Scottish Government 2008c; see also Ben Galim *et al* in this volume). It should be noted, however, such rhetoric overlooks the fact that the Scottish government lacks important levers needed to reduce inequality.

Narratives in Northern Ireland Assembly and departmental papers have differed somewhat, and lack such explicit commitments to social justice, although the 2008 programme for government did use the term 'fairer society'. The programmes for government in Northern Ireland have not specified a strong egalitarian value but instead an aim of increasing prosperity to help reduce poverty and disadvantage. The focus of political parties on constitutional issues and communal identities means that 'policies lack the political compass that the left–right divide provides in normal democratic society' (Wilford and Wilson 2008).

Priority afforded to social policy

Despite the emphasis on key principles and values differing to some degree, a brief review of the devolved administrations' programmes of government over the last 10 years reveals the importance they have all afforded to social policy.

The first programme for government for Scotland, *Making It Work Together* (Scottish Executive 1999a), contained 12 policy areas, eight of which can be described as social policy. The 2003 programme for government, *A Partnership for a Better Scotland*, set out similar policy areas and supportive activities (Scottish Executive 2003). In 2007 the ruling SNP produced a programme of government with a slightly different narrative, emphasising the need for economic growth and the overarching importance of a future independent Scotland (Scottish Government 2008a). But the details – presented under five headings of a wealthier and fairer; smarter; healthier; safer and stronger; and greener Scotland – in practice reaffirmed the importance of social policy measures.

To date all three Welsh programmes for government have entailed a significant role for social policy. *A Better Wales* (Welsh Assembly Government [WAG] 2000) committed WAG to new and improved services, reducing inequalities and shared prosperity. In 2003, *Wales, A Better Country* (WAG 2003) set out a vision of a fairer, more prosperous, healthy and better educated country, accompanied by a list of 10 priorities, nine of which were social policies. In 2007 the programme of government *One Wales* was drawn up by a new coalition and described as radical but deliverable. *One Wales* has an eight themed framework, five of which can be firmly located as social policies (WAG 2007c).

Northern Ireland has had only two programmes for government. The 2001 document was based on a five-themed framework with three covering health, education and equality, and community relations (Northern Ireland Executive [NIE] 2001). The new document for the restored devolved government was much briefer (NIE 2008) and reflected the difficulty in reaching a policy consensus in the coalition. Five priority areas were identified: growing the economy, promoting inclusion and health, protecting the environment, building the infrastructure and delivering high quality services. These were translated into Public Service Agreements and sub-objectives which still represented a significant range of social policy topics (Table 8.2).

An analysis of government programmes and other documents show a number of common social policy themes across all three nations, which have continued to be important in setting much of the policy agenda. These common objectives can be described as including:

- Tackling child poverty, health inequalities, social exclusion, public health issues and mental health advocacy
- Improving standards of educational achievement in early years provision
- Encouraging collaboration between health and social care
- Reducing hospital waiting times
- Addressing problems associated with affordable housing, homelessness and urban regeneration
- Support for the voluntary sector.

There have not been extensive changes to the list of priorities over the first decade of devolution. However, the political circumstances in each government make aspects of consensual policymaking more difficult, with coalition government in Wales and minority government in Scotland requiring deals with other parties. A lack of consensus in the Northern Ireland Executive has caused an impasse for core social policies including an anti-poverty strategy, single equality legislation, and a community relations strategy.

Another significant factor affecting the ability of the devolved administrations to continue to place such high priority on social policy, at least in terms of spending levels, is the recession. This has resulted in a recalibration of priorities from 2007/8. Budget reductions and requirements for efficiencies have reduced the scope for major new policy initiatives. The Scottish Government, for example, has reneged on some commitments such as grants for first-time house buyers and reducing school class sizes (Jones 2008). In Wales, there have been changes to the grant offsetting fees for Welsh domiciled students, and in Northern Ireland cuts to health services. The devolved administrations have made assisting with economic recovery and helping those in financial difficulty a priority; for example via the Mortgage to Rent Scheme in Scotland and the Low Income Household Fuel Payment in Northern Ireland.

While the major economic levers are not devolved, there are mechanisms available to the devolved administrations to help with economic recovery through the use of their social policy powers (see Bell in this volume). These include capital spending on hospitals and schools, financing social housing, advice for people made redundant, maximising uptake of benefits, measures to address fuel poverty and help with debt management. Other measures have included prompting public service providers to make efficiency savings to protect frontline services; an example is the innovative Invest-to-Save fund in Wales. Some initiatives have had a stronger financial emphasis with freezes on council tax, promotion of economic investment and incentives for businesses to retain staff.

The response to the economic crisis has also drawn more attention to the limits on the powers of devolved governments. The SNP government stated in 2009 that sustainable economic development was its overarching goal and argued that the current framework has constrained its ability to take measures to stabilise the economy. The White Paper *Your Scotland. Your voice: A national conversation* stated the clear need to enhance the taxation, spending and borrowing responsibilities of the Scottish Parliament (Scottish Government 2009).

In Wales the devolved administration has committed itself to measures to lead Wales out of recession but the cumbersome process for obtaining Westminster approval for new Welsh legislation has drawn attention to the limitations of the existing devolution arrangements. The report of the All Wales Convention, set up to assess public views on primary law-making powers, found that transferring legislative powers from Westminster in one go would offer substantial advantages (All Wales Convention 2009). Finally, while the Northern Ireland Executive has agreed on measures to combat the recession, it has drawn attention to its lack of economic powers, for example, to alter the rate of corporation tax.

This brief review would seem to reaffirm the view that the devolved administrations have been dominated by social policy, although the recent economic turmoil, combined with the presence of Nationalist parties in government, has sparked some debate about the need for wider powers.

Key policy innovations and divergence

Much of the debate about the impact of devolution on social policy has centred on the emergence of significant policy differences between the administrations. These policies can be divided into two categories:

- New and innovative policies, which have been created where none previously existed in the UK
- Policies that alter the nature of existing service entitlements, for example by extending provision so it is universal rather than targeted, or removing charges on existing services.

Table 8.2. Key innovations in social policy

Scotland	Wales	Northern Ireland
• Free personal and nursing care	• Commissioner for Older People	• Abolition of statutory 11-plus transfer test
• Student fees	• Children's Commissioner for Wales	• Abolition of prescription charges
• Free bus travel for older people	• Abolition of Prescription charges	• Free train and bus travel for people aged 60-plus
• Abolition of prescription charges	• Free car parking at hospitals	• Fully integrated health and social care
• Free eye and dental checks	• Primary schools free breakfast initiative	• Childcare expenses for lone parents to family members
• Free pre-school places for all three and four year olds	• Welsh baccalaureate qualification	• Low-income-household fuel payment
• Community schools	• Foundation phase curriculum	
• Minimum alcohol pricing	• Flying Start for children 0–3 in deprived communities	
• Abolition of hospital car parking fees	• Student support	

Source: Adapted from Birrell (2009)

A further consideration in relation to social policy and the delivery of public services is the type of service delivery model that should be used. Each of these issues is addressed in turn below.

New policy innovation
Though limited in number, devolution has nonetheless generated some important new policies. Some of the most notable social policy innovations are outlined in Table 8.2.

For Wales, these include the Children's Commissioners and the Older People's Commissioner, which were both initiated by the Assembly Government. The Welsh Voluntary Sector scheme is claimed to be unique in the UK (WAG 2007c) and established a statutory relationship between the WAG and the voluntary sector involving regular ministerial meetings, consultations and support (see Alcock, this volume). The development of the Welsh Baccalaureate qualification is also unique in the UK.

In Scotland, direct elections to Scottish health boards are underway, with possible implications for the democratisation of quangos (see Greer and Parry, this volume). Scotland also led the way – just – in reintroducing the building of social housing by councils (see Wilcox, this volume). Furthermore, there are potentially significant legislative innovations in public health currently under consideration, most notably further restrictions on tobacco sales and minimum pricing of alcohol (see Muir, this volume).

Northern Ireland too provides some innovative examples. Although the very radical fair employment legislation was introduced before devolution, the 1998 Devolution Act saw the amalgamation of the various equality bodies into one unified equality body, separate from the Human Rights Commission, and there were also innovative equality provisions in the Northern Ireland Act 1998, Section 75. The strong commitment after devolution to Northern Ireland's unique integrated structure of health and social care, although initiated prior to devolution, should also be noted. More recent developments have been a fuel allowance scheme, and restorative justice practices that bring together offenders and victims of crime (see Muir, this volume).

Changes to entitlements
The most common means of changing entitlements in the devolved administrations has been to extend services through universal provision – in other words providing comprehensive free services for everyone, irrespective of income. This is traditionally exemplified by core NHS services. The selective approach has become more widespread in recent welfare developments, especially in England, meaning that services, benefits and resources are free to those targeted as in greatest need and may involve means-testing, charges and restricted access.

Scottish social policy appears to favour universalistic, undifferentiated public services (Keating 2005). Since devolution Scotland has seen an expansion of universalist non-means-tested approaches, with free nursing, personal care, prescriptions, hospital car-parking, bus travel and school meals, and the abolition of student fees. Scotland has also made certain drugs available that were denied to patients in the other nations because the National Institute for Health and Clinical Excellence (NICE) ruled against their cost-effectiveness. This commitment to universality has also entailed a critique of selectivity made on the grounds of low uptake, means-testing acting as a deterrence, the stigma associated with being deemed eligible, and the possibility of two standards of services emerging.

Wales has a similar history of support for universality in the old Labour party tradition. Like Scotland there are numerous examples of charges being removed, for example prescription charges, hospital car parking charges, free bus travel for older people and there have been (limited) changes to university fees. It has been argued that in Wales a distinctive form of universalism has developed, what is known as progressive universalism, with the progressive element a top-up to universally provided services to help those who need it most (Drakeford 2007). Examples can be found in the top-up to the child trust fund in Wales and extra early-years education and childcare provision, but generally additions to universalist services are not that common in Scotland or Wales.

Northern Ireland presents a different scenario: there has been little debate on the issue there and on balance there is more political support for selectivity. There have been only a few examples of universalist measures being introduced, including free prescriptions and free bus and train travel for older people. In other respects Northern Ireland looks more like England. For example, university tuition fees remain in place, and the Executive has decided to target free hospital car-parking rather than abolish charges altogether.

It is worth dwelling briefly here on Scotland's approach to social care for older people here, as this is perhaps the boldest example of extending entitlements. In Scotland, free nursing and personal care in both the home and care home has become the major flagship policy since devolution, and has been described as its major achievement (Dickenson 2007). It is the policy that has most distinguished Scottish from UK social policy. A review in 2008 found it was working to deliver better outcomes for Scotland's older people, was extremely popular and was affordable (Sutherland 2008; see also McCormick *et al*, this volume). Neither Wales nor Northern Ireland has followed suit because of the cost but the Scottish success has put pressure on England to produce alternatives to the status quo. The Department of Health (2009) has committed to developing a national care service in England that is fair and affordable and Gordon Brown has promised to introduce free domiciliary care for the most needy. This suggests devolution can provide a laboratory for different approaches. It also demonstrates that extensions to entitlements in one part of the UK can put pressure on others to provide a similar level of service.

Divergence in delivery

There is also scope for divergence in terms of the delivery mechanism used. This relates to the nature and composition of the service provider, whether it is the state, the private or voluntary sector, or a combination of delivery partners. In general, Scotland and Wales have continued their tradition of state provision and devolution has not affected the major provider role of local government. We look briefly here at approaches to delivering health policy, education and capital projects.

As Greer shows in this volume there has been substantial reorganisation of healthcare delivery structures across the four nations since devolution. Scotland moved to a flatter integrated structure for all health services by creating 14 area health boards and localised community health partnerships. In Wales a reorganisation of health into seven health boards took place and Northern Ireland also reorganised into a smaller number of delivery bodies although these are integrated structurally with social care. Closer collaboration between health and social care is a major issue throughout the UK and arrangements have differed under devolution. Evans and Forbes (2009) have argued that overall, Scotland has been making more progress with integrated work than England.

The attitude of the devolved countries to internal markets differs, with Scotland and Wales generally rejecting such an approach. In Scotland, the commissioner/provider split was ended in 2004, and action was taken to eliminate the use of the private sector in the NHS in 2008 (Sturgeon 2008). This is in stark contrast to the policy of Department of Health in England of delivering more NHS services through the private sector. Wales too followed the direction of Scotland, restructuring in 2009. In contrast, Northern Ireland has restructured around a commissioner/provider split and thus is more similar to England (see Greer in this volume).

Some significant differences in strategies and structures for public health and public involvement in health and social care can also be indentified. Mental health strategies are another area of some divergence in policies. Scottish legislation has placed less emphasis on compulsion than England and Wales, and has also conferred a right to advocacy (Cairney 2009).

Historically, of course, the education systems have differed significantly between all four nations of the UK. Devolution has continued the process of divergence which can be identified in: the types of schools, in examinations, curriculum development, parental and pupil participation in governance, class sizes, pilots with free school milk and meals, and literacy and numeracy measures. The Scottish and Welsh administrations have also demonstrated little enthusiasm for private sector involvement in education, and there are only small numbers attending fee-paying secondary schools. Northern Ireland has even fewer pupils attending fee-paying schools than Scotland or Wales. A substantial area of divergence in delivery is the role that the private sector plays through the academy schools system. The real outlier here is England, which has diverged significantly in its decisions to pursue academy schools. This approach has not been followed in Scotland and Wales, which have emphasised comprehensive schools serving the local community. Northern Ireland is slightly closer to the English position, with the private sector playing a part in the specialist schools scene there, although in a much more limited way compared to England.

A further area of divergence is in relation to the use of public–private partnerships for capital projects. These have also been rejected in Scotland and Wales, with the Welsh Assembly Government deciding that there would be no Private Finance Initiative (PFI) schemes introduced for the NHS in Wales (Roy 2008). In Scotland, new schools and a new hospital in Glasgow are being built from public capital. This has however created difficulties due to the devolved administrations' lack of real borrowing powers. The SNP has sought to develop alternative proposals through a Futures Trust and a non-profit distribution model, but there have been problems in establishing this, and it is not yet working as an alternative to conventional public funding (Hallowell and Pollock 2009). The position in Northern Ireland is somewhat ambiguous, and no serious debate about this issue has taken place, although there have been few objections to the use of PFIs for building new schools and hospitals.

Finally, it is important to note that more subtle differences can emerge during the implementation stage of some polices (Birrell 2009). These are the result of differences in delivery systems and action plans, shifts in emphasis, minor innovations and variations in need. Wincott (2005) has said that differences in early-years education and care reflect different approaches to circumstances in Scotland and Wales rather than fundamental variations (see Ben-Galim, this volume). Similarly, housing policies in Scotland, Wales and Northern Ireland have been implemented differently, with different approaches to stock transfer, homelessness, affordability, decent housing, tenant participation and the right to buy (see Wilcox, this volume). Public health strategies, the operation and use of the voluntary sector, and regulation and inspection in health and social care are other areas of low-level differences in implementation.

Convergence, collaboration and policy transfer
Devolution does not simply generate policy difference: on the contrary, it can force convergence across the UK. This convergence tends to arise in two circumstances: firstly where there are interconnected and overlapping functions between devolved administrations and the UK government; and secondly where one devolved government decides to copy a policy from another devolved administration or from UK government practice.

Shared responsibility

The first circumstance often arises as a consequence of the important powers that remain reserved to the UK government, particularly social security benefits and tax credits. Social security is unified throughout England, Scotland and Wales, although there is certain ambiguity in relation to Northern Ireland, as constitutionally social security is a devolved matter but in practice benefit rates have matched those in Great Britain. A clause in the Northern Ireland Act 1998 specified that the two governments consult to agree that there is a single system of social security, child support and pensions for UK citizens but that Northern Ireland passes its own legislation. UK equality legislation also applies to Great Britain but not Northern Ireland, whereas UK human rights legislation does apply to all four countries in the UK. A number of other subjects are controlled by UK-wide legislation, for example regulation of health professionals, licensing of medicines and human genetics.

UK decisions on non-devolved areas of social policy particularly in social security and employment have major implications for closely related areas of devolved social policy and lead to a requirement for cooperation which can produce similar policies and strategies in all four countries. Anti-poverty policies demonstrate a clear need for the UK government programmes to join up with devolved programmes (see Ben-Galim *et al*, this volume). The Scottish government (2008c) in setting out a policy to tackle poverty and deprivation addressed the issues of interface and overlapping responsibilities. It defined levers where the Scottish government could support UK policies on tax and benefit arrangements and the national minimum wage and where devolved and reserved policies could work together to complement each other. Thus the Scottish government identified its complementary role in addressing educational under-achievement, early years provision, child poverty, area deprivation, substance misuse, uptake of benefits, fuel poverty and take-up of free school meals.

In Wales it has also be recognised that a shared effort and close collaboration was necessary to achieve goals in abolishing child poverty (Gibbons 2008). The Welsh Assembly referred to similar devolved activities as in Scotland, for benefit maximisation, benefit advice, school meals, skills and a strong focus on early years. The older Northern Ireland anti-poverty strategy has also referred to a benefit uptake campaign.

The UK government 'welfare-to-work' policies mean that providing access to the labour market involves both the devolved and UK government. The Scottish administration identified many devolved matters as having an impact on employability, including health, skills, children and regeneration. There has been close working with the DWP and Jobcentre Plus Scotland to develop jointly owned targets to get people into employment. The DWP paper *Ready for Work* (2007), revising the welfare-to-work strategy, acknowledged that policies for skills, childcare, health, local government and advice were all closely linked to the proposals in the paper but were the responsibility of devolved administrations. Northern Ireland was formally different in that both benefits and employment were devolved but similar welfare-to-work programmes were adopted including New Deal and Pathways to Work. More generally, policies for tackling social exclusion reflect a mixture of devolved and reserved matters although some distinctive strategies have been developed by devolved administrations, for example in early years provision. A further convergent pressure in the area of social exclusion is the EU requirement for a national action plan for social inclusion in which the UK strategy integrates the contributions of the devolved administrations.

Fuel poverty has also been referred to as 'a complex mix of reserved and devolved issues' (Scottish Fuel Poverty Forum 2008) with the UK government responsible for energy market issues, prices, regulation, social tariffs and winter fuel payments but assessment of energy assistance insulation and energy efficiency and financial assistance measures can rest with devolved administrations.

Another example concerns equalities legislation. Although equality and anti-discrimination legislation are reserved matters, the Scottish government has the power to encourage equal opportunities and to place duties on public bodies The Government of Wales Act 2006 requires Welsh ministers to have arrangements to ensure their functions are exercised with due regard to the principle that there should be equality of opportunity for all. The Equality and Human Rights Commission has jurisdiction in England, Scotland and Wales to promote equality of opportunity and challenge discrimination. There is a Scottish and Welsh Commissioner and committee of the Equality and Human Rights Commission (EHRC) and in practice they have to find a synergy between the EHRC and devolved administrative activities (EHRC 2006). The EHRC has influence on Scottish and Welsh practices, promoting some similar strategies with England on issues such as domestic violence, equal pay and hate crime. The Northern Ireland Equality Commission is separate but often follows similar initiatives.

Policy transfer
The other main influence on convergence concerns policy transfer: when one of the devolved governments or UK government decides to implement a policy that one of the others has tried out first. Examples include the Children's Commissioner which was originally introduced in Wales in 2001, and then subsequently rolled out in Northern Ireland in 2003 and Scotland a year later, and then in England in 2005. Free bus travel for older people is another, introduced in Northern Ireland in 2001, Wales in 2002, Scotland in 2006 and England in 2008.

Policy experimentation also allows nations to reject ideas tried out elsewhere For example the Welsh have moved ahead with an Older People's Commissioner, which the Scots and English looked at but decided against. Northern Ireland still may emulate Wales and is holding a consultation on a Commissioner for Older People (see McCormick et al, this volume).

Policy transfer may not always be clearly identifiable. For example, Scotland did lead the way in banning smoking in public places but it was fairly certain that Wales and Northern Ireland would follow suit.

Clear-cut examples of policy emulation can be found in decisions by the Scottish Government to accept Westminster legislation to cover devolved matters in Scotland rather than introduce separate legislation in the Scottish Parliament. In opting for these legislative consent motions the Scottish Government is making a decision to adopt parity in policy with England and often with Wales as well. What were originally called Sewel motions have advantages of saving time, convenience and speed of action. This form of policy transfer is often used for more technical matters, for example, the regulation of health professionals or community pharmacies or closing loopholes between the two jurisdictions in criminal legislation. It is sometimes also used to avoid possible controversy, for example, on civil partnerships. Formally, Northern Ireland legislation can use a similar device but there are few examples and Northern Ireland has a stronger tradition of separate legislation. One example, however, is the Child Poverty Bill currently going through Parliament, which each of the devolved administrations has backed with a legislative consent motion.

Inter-governmental relations

A number of inter-governmental arrangements also have a role in promoting cooperation and the sharing of ideas. It was originally intended that a formal mechanism, the Joint Ministerial Council, would act as a forum between all four countries to promote cooperation and resolve any disputes but between 2002 and 2007 no use was made of this mechanism except for European matters (Trench 2007). The Joint Ministerial Council was reconvened in 2008 and possibly can be seen as a mechanism that will encourage sharing ideas and more similar approaches.

A different body has In practice fulfilled the role of encouraging shared practice and exchanging policy ideas. The British-Irish Council was established to provide a forum for the UK and Irish Governments, the devolved governments in Northern Ireland, Scotland and Wales, together with the governments of the Isle of Man, Guernsey and Jersey. Its role was to exchange information, discuss and cooperate on matters of mutual interest and work through meetings of ministers and officials. The participants have found this activity useful, and the work has expanded in the areas of social exclusion, drugs, demography, tourism and early years. Thus it is possible to trace some elements of policy and ideas transfer under these work-stream headings, for example on credit unions, smoking bans and criminal assets recovery (Birrell 2009: 119).

Regular meetings between ministers may also encourage policy copying as well as more formal meetings of all four finance ministers. A number of networks of statutory bodies also exist, for example of the UK equality and human rights bodies and the Children's Commissioners, which can again promote convergent practice.

When devolution was introduced there was a view that in some respects a policy laboratory was coming into existence, in which new policy ideas would be tried and each country would learn from each other and copying could become extensive (Stewart 2004). Emulation of innovations emerging from one devolved country has not been extensive, and in practice London may still be the source of much policy development given the location there of the large Whitehall machine, national advisory bodies, policy networks and think tanks. The civil service based in Whitehall may also be a source of initiatives and the unified Home Civil Service may contribute to convergence in policies and strategies. However, there is no formal system for the exchange of policy information and practice. The 10-year review of devolution by the House of Commons, reported that there was not a full understanding in Whitehall of the policy areas that had been devolved (House of Commons 2009). A more precise external influence has been EU Directives in requiring uniform policy approaches although many fall outside social policy, related more to the environment, food, and health and safety. A stronger influence for social policy has been similar interpretations of international conventions, particularly relating to children and older people.

Conclusions
Social policy still plays a major role in the operation of devolution as demonstrated in policy, strategy, legislation and expenditure. It may not quite have the dominant role conferred by some commentators at the beginning of devolution. The position of social policy has and will be effected by an increase in other new devolved powers and by the dominance of economic and environmental agendas. It can also be noted that social policy has never been seen or accepted as a dominant feature of devolution in Northern Ireland as it has in Scotland or Wales.

Innovative social policies have been introduced and have had an impact throughout the United Kingdom, such as free personal care in Scotland, the Children's Commissioner in Wales and the Equality Agency in Northern Ireland. However, there may not be quite enough examples to justify proclaiming devolution as a policy laboratory. There are significant constraints; the Block Grant determined by the UK Government; uncertainties and compromises produced by political coalition; and a growing recognition as devolution develops that overlapping powers requires collaboration and agreement with the UK Government on issues such as employment at different levels of governance.

Such factors have meant that it is difficult to identify very different approaches to social policy. There has been a stronger commitment to universalism in Scotland and Wales, and less enthusiasm for involving the private sector in delivery. But despite these differences many key new social policy commitments are shared throughout the UK, such as tackling child poverty, reducing waiting lists, developing early years provision, promoting affordable housing, improving educational achievement. So it seems narratives on social justice and citizen empowerment have not always led to major differences between Scotland and Wales on the one hand and England and Northern Ireland on the other. Devolution therefore allows the governments in Scotland, Wales and Northern Ireland to influence, innovate and experiment with core social policies within identifiable constraints.

References

All Wales Convention (2009) Report available at www.allwalesconvention.org

Birrell WD (2009) *The Impact of Devolution on Social Policy*, Bristol: Policy Press

Cairney P (2009) 'The British Policy Style and Mental Health: Beyond the Headlines,' *Journal of Social Policy*, 38.4. pp 671-688

Chaney P and Drakeford M (2004) 'The primacy of ideology: social policy and the first term of the National Assembly for Wales', in Ellison N, Bauld L and Powell M (eds) *Social Policy Review* 16, Bristol: The Policy Press

Department of Health (2009) *Shaping the future of care together. Cm 7673,* London: The Stationery Office

Dickenson H, Glasby J, Forder J and Beesley L (2007) 'Free personal care in Scotland: a narrative review,' *British Journal of Social Work* 37.3, pp 459-474

Drakeford M (2007) 'Social justice in a devolved Wales', *Benefits*, 15,2, pp 171-178

Equality and Human Rights Commission (EHRC) (2008) *Wales programme 2008/9: Bringing people together:* www.equalityhumanrights.com/en/wales/publications/pages/walesprogramme

Evans D and Forbes T (2009) 'Partnership in health and social care,' *Public Policy and Administration*, 24.1, pp 67-83

Gibbons G (2008) 'Child poverty,' written statement: http://new.wales.gov.uk/about/cabinet/cabinetstatements/?lang=en

Hallowell M and Pollock A (2009) 'Non-profit distribution: The Scottish approach to private finance in public service,' *Social Policy and Society*, 8.3, pp 405-419

House of Commons Justice Committee (2009) *Devolution: A Decade On, HC529-1,* London: Stationery Office

Jones P (2008) 'Scotland: The nationalist phoenix,' in Trench A (ed) *The State of the Nations 2008* Exeter: Imprint Academic

Keating M (2005) *The government of Scotland: Public policy making after devolution,* Edinburgh: Edinburgh University Press

Mooney G, Scott G and Williams C (2006) 'Rethinking social policy through devolution', *Critical Social Policy*, 26.3, pp 483-97

Northern Ireland Executive (NIE) (2001) *Programme for government: Making a difference,* Belfast: The Office of the First Minister and Deputy First Minister (OFMDFM)

Northern Ireland Executive (NIE) (2008) *Building a better future: Draft programme for government 2008-11,* Belfast: OFMDFM

Roy E (2008) *The Private Finance Initiative and Public Private Partnerships,* Paper no. 08/005, Cardiff: National Assembly for Wales: www.assemblywales.org/bus-home/bus-guide-docs-pub/bus-assembly-publications-research

Scott G and Mooney G (2009) 'Poverty and Social Justice in the devolved Scotland: neoliberalism meets social democracy,' *Social Policy and Society,* 8.3, pp 379-300

Scottish Executive (1999a) *Making it work together: A programme for government:* www.scotland.gov.uk/Resource/Doc/158140/0042788.pdf

Scottish Executive (1999b) *Social justice, a Scotland where everyone matters: Milestone sources and definitions:* www.scotland.gov.uk/publications/1999/11/SocialJustice

Scottish Executive (2003) *A partnership for a better Scotland: Partnership agreement:* www.scotland.gov.uk/publications/2003

Scottish Fuel Poverty Forum (2008) *Towards 2016: The future of fuel poverty policy in Scotland:* www.scotland.gov.uk/publications/2008/10/09155649/0

Scottish Government (2008a) *Moving Scotland forward: The government's programme for Scotland 2008/9:* www.scotland.gov.uk/publications/2008/09

Scottish Government (2008b) *Achieving our potential: a framework to tackle poverty and income inequality in Scotland,* Edinburgh: Scottish Government

Scottish Government (2008c) *Taking forward the economic strategy: A discussion paper on tacking poverty, inequality and deprivation in Scotland:* www.scotland.gov.uk/publications/2008

Scottish Government (2009) *Your Scotland. Your voice: A national conversation:* www.scotland.gov.uk/publications/2009

Stewart J (2004) *Taking stock: Scottish social welfare after devolution,* Bristol: The Policy Press

Sturgeon N (2008) *Future of the NHS in Scotland:* www.scotland.gov.uk/news/releases/2008

Sutherland (Lord) S (2008) *Independent review of free personal and nursing care in Scotland,* Edinburgh: Scottish Government Publications

Trench A (2007) 'Washing dirty linen in private: The processes of intergovernmental relations and the resolution of disputes,' in Trench A (ed) *Devolution and power in the United Kingdom,* Manchester: Manchester University Press

Welsh Assembly Government (WAG) (2000) *A better Wales,* Cardiff: WAG

WAG (2003) *Wales: A better country: The strategic agenda of the Welsh Assembly Government,* Cardiff: WAG

WAG (2007a) *One Wales: a progressive agenda for the government of Wales:* www.new.wales.gov.uk/about/strategy/publications/onewales/?lang=en

WAG (2007b) *Communities First guidance 2007:* www.wales.gov.uk/topics/housingandcommunity/regeneration/publications/cfguidance2007/?lang=en

WAG (2007c) *Voluntary sector scheme, Annual Report 2006-07:* www.swanseasthirdsector.com/wag

Wilford R and Wilson R (2008) 'Northern Ireland: Devolution once again,' in Trench A (ed) *The State of the Nations,* Exeter: Imprint Academic

Wincott D (2005) 'Reshaping public space? Devolution and policy change in British early childhood education and care', *Regional and Federal Studies,* 15.5, pp 453–470

9. Devolution and health: structure, process and outcomes since 1998

Scott L. Greer

People writing in the years ahead about health in the UK will agree that the 10 years after 1999 were enormously important. They will also agree on the two most important acts: devolution, and the decision to hugely increase spending on health in England. Both changed the face of health policy for good, bequeathing politics, staff, problems and infrastructure that will last for decades.

There is no immediate prospect of another flood of new spending on health care, so the investments and staffing decisions made between 1999 and 2009, and the cuts in the subsequent decade, will shape quality, access, and costs for decades to come[1]. The political energy is also gone; another phenomenon like the Blair majorities is unlikely. Finally, the policy changes since 1 May 1997 have put the four systems on different trajectories, with different values, styles and management approaches entrenched in them. All four systems, as they retrench in the face of the UK's enormous new debt burden, will have to use the resources, structures and infrastructures they built up in the last decade.

This chapter uses the classical language of health policy to review UK-wide health policy since 1999. Health policy analysts often speak of structure, process, and outcomes (Donabedian 2003, Wyszewianski 2009). *Structure* is the distribution of power, materials and responsibility in the system. It starts with the constitutional legislation that created devolution and goes on to include the different sets of organisations that make up the different systems. It also includes budgets and resources such as hospitals or surgical gloves. *Outcomes* are, of course, what we want: good health or at least good health care. *Process* is how a system, given its organisation, goes about doing its job. The gaps between structure, process and outcome repeatedly frustrate policymakers, who find that a change in one can have unpredictable or no effects on another.

We have long known about changes in structures; they are the staple of health politics because ministers are ill positioned to affect process or outcomes. Useful, comparable, data on process and outcomes are much harder to collect and need to be

---

1. Even if the English NHS retains a stable budget, the Barnett formula is quite capable of turning other cuts in the English budget into reductions for devolved budgets.

quite finely grained to distinguish between populations and practice in systems as closely connected as those of the UK. For a decade, analysts have complained about data problems and have had difficulty comparing outcomes with much precision (the best early comparisons had to be very cautious, for example Dixon *et al* 1999, Alvarez-Rosete *et al* 2005; or had to focus on quite narrow indicators: Hauck and Street 2007, Propper *et al* 2008, Bevan and Hamblin 2009, Andrews and Martin 2007). Investments by charities, especially the Commonwealth Fund, Health Foundation and Nuffield Trust, have started to pay off in real data (Connolly *et al* 2010, Sutherland and Coyle 2009). There are still serious and worsening problems in matching pan-UK statistics with policies or indeed anything governments do, but the situation, despite deteriorating government statistics, is much better for their work. Our sections below on outcomes and structures, in particular, use Sutherland and Coyle's invaluable chart book of comparative data.

The effect of the data, naturally, is to make the picture more complex. The findings are often provisional, and much of the data remind us that health care and health policy are but a small part of the influences on health. Therefore the first message is that many of the most popular headline variables for comparison do not work, and the best comparisons are often narrow.

The second message is that many of the most flamboyant ideologies have not had much impact on the major outcomes. They are political visions and weapons and explanations of policies. We should not confuse them with the actual changes in structure, process and outcome. 'Flagship' policies are defined by political salience rather than impact, and are often aimed at redirecting priorities rather than changing existing indicators. A list of politically salient health service issues looks rather strange (see also Birrell 2009): for example, free prescriptions for mostly healthy people, mental health policies, long-term personal care, foundation trusts and the absurdly salient issue of car-parking charges. All of them matter, but they hardly add up to a whole health system.

Insofar as there are policy-relevant messages, they do not give obvious answers about the superiority of one system or another or about the ideologies of 'choice' and so forth. They are about the importance of management (of whatever kind), about the impressive democratic responsiveness of the various governments, and about the difficulty of changing NHS systems. Devolution, health policy shows, was a victory for democracy and a challenge to management and clinical engagement.

Structure: reorganisations and reforms

The years between 2000 and 2004 saw a striking range of health policy innovation, with major reforms creating important structural differences between the health systems of England, Scotland and Wales. That left a rather less changed Northern Ireland as divergent by default (for one perspective see Greer 2004, Greer 2009, Greer 2010b). The basic reason this could happen was that the governments were all relatively strong and well-funded. The NHS systems are historically not particularly well funded by the standards of other rich countries and health care cannot continue to grow so much in absolute or proportional terms, so the wave of money spent on them will shape their infrastructure and priorities for years to come.

Furthermore, the elites of all four systems now see themselves as sharing a challenge with the rest of the rich world: they have to move care into the community, reduce costly and debilitating hospital stays, and integrate primary care. Their debates are about how to deliver such localised, personalised, integrated care within the financial, demographic, staff, political and infrastructural constraints that have long defeated joint working or a focus on primary care.

Two forms of constraint deserve special notice. All four systems are bound by the same doctors' contracts. The contracts are among the biggest cost drivers across the UK. They were negotiated early in devolution and the three devolved governments delegated them to the Department of Health (Greer and Trench 2008). John Reid as Secretary of State then signed the contracts with almost no negotiation – solving a political problem before the 2005 general election at a staggering and probably needless cost. These expensive contracts also had some serious drafting flaws that worked against the four governments, and set constraints on all future policy[2]. They created special problems for out-of-hours services, driving patients across the UK into hospital A&E departments and undermining other policies designed to keep treatment out of the dangerous and expensive A&E environment.

They are also, differently, bound by their Private Finance Initiative (PFI) obligations. PFI, while bringing no appreciable management benefits, was a useful technique to get buildings built quickly and keep spending off government balance sheets. A price of PFI is rigidity. Because PFI facilities are built and operated around long, usually 30-year, contracts, they constrain policy far into the future. It is easy to see the future of hospital services in places as different as North Lanarkshire and South East London because policymakers have PFI obligations to some facilities and not to others. PFIs weigh particularly heavily on England and Scotland. Wales is already reaping the benefit of devolution; its devolved governments never liked PFI as much and now are freer of at least that constraint.

The four health systems are less bound by political institutions than we might imagine (Greer 2007). Health services are relatively free of the entanglements and overlaps that make policymaking in areas such as higher education or population ageing so complicated (Birrell 2009, Trench and Jeffery 2007, Trench 2008, Greer and Trench 2008). They exist and are not always well managed, but have not yet constrained devolved policy much.

Likewise, it turns out that the devolved governments, including Wales, have had significant powers over health care services since devolution started (Drakeford 2007).

---

2. Separately, there are the vertiginous NHS pension cost estimates, which account for much of what was counted as 'new' NHS spending.

The first Wales-only legislation after devolution was about health care services – but the reorganisation that justified it had mostly been carried out by provisions slipped into an earlier UK health bill. Suspension of devolution in Northern Ireland was a problem for much of the decade. But otherwise, the real problems for devolved health policy are in affecting determinants of broader population health such as the interaction between health and disability benefits, not in their ability to make health care services policy.

Inputs

Tony Blair's decision to push UK spending up to the 'European average' (Smee 2005) was a momentous commitment. Budgets did indeed go up, as did staffing.

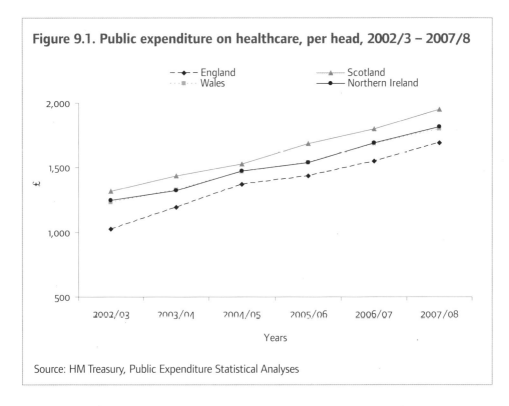

Figure 9.1. Public expenditure on healthcare, per head, 2002/3 – 2007/8

Source: HM Treasury, Public Expenditure Statistical Analyses

The total increases in health spending per capita between 2002–3 and 2007–8 were impressive: 55 per cent in England, 48 per cent in Wales, and 45 per cent in both Northern Ireland and Scotland. The very limited degree of convergence is striking. There is nothing in the Barnett formula that obliged devolved governments to put Barnett consequentials of English health allocations into their own health budgets. But politically it was hard for devolved (Labour) ministers to follow a UK Government announcement about health spending with a devolved announcement to spend the money elsewhere. Devolved health spending increases came close to matching UK increases, preserving higher per-capita spending, regardless of whether or not that was the best use of funds. The funding increases raise a simple but dangerous question: did all four systems really need roughly equal percentage increases, given different baselines?

The different per-capita spending did not necessarily lead to different levels of professional employment or staffed beds. All of the UK systems have lower numbers of professionals per 1000 than comparable systems around the world (Sutherland and Coyle 2009). Only Scotland had higher numbers of GPs per 1000 of population: 0.82 as against 0.64–0.65 for the UK as a whole. Consistent figures on average daily available beds are, interestingly, difficult to find as the Office for National Statistics and four health departments do not always agree. We have one well-funded health system with high employment and perhaps more beds in Scotland; one less well-funded system with fewer resources per capita in England; and a reminder of the problems with health care data in the UK today.

Scotland

Scotland's health policy has shown the most coherence and consistency since 1997, which was when Labour's Scottish Office team began to pursue a distinctive health policy agenda that focused on integrating organisations and reducing competition and fragmentation in favour of reliance on professionals and good management. Subsequent policies opted for more integration: eliminating hospital trusts, abolishing the purchaser-provider split, and organising the whole system into 14 health boards (plus specialist boards) that are responsible for planning, organising and providing the whole range of care in a given area.

Scottish health politics has since evolved in a different direction. Abandoning the internal market does not produce apolitical stability. It produces new, different, politics. First, the relative lack of managerial tools relative to England has paradoxically refocused NHS Scotland on management. There are not as many carrots and sticks as in England, but there are far fewer misaligned incentives. So NHS Scotland's results depend on good management and clinical engagement. That does not mean clinical engagement or management in Scotland is especially good. It just means that it must be good if Scotland is to deliver, and many Scottish professionals, managers and officials know this.

Second, it has meant that local availability of services became an even more central issue. Scotland, like the UK as a whole, has a long tradition of fighting about hospital 'reconfigurations'. This often meant supporters of local general hospitals raged against managers who on financial and technical grounds supported centralisation (as in, for example, Glasgow's centralisation of services at the Southern General, or more recent battles over A&E and maternity departments in Ayrshire, Inverclyde and Lanarkshire). A small, threatened hospital is a terrible financial problem because doctors will not take permanent posts and it becomes dependent on very expensive locums – a dependency that makes it even harder to sustain quality.

The 2005 Kerr report (Kerr 2005, Kerr and Feeley 2007) started to move Scotland beyond the managers vs populations stand-offs that so marked Scottish health politics for several years (Jervis 2008), by focusing on the need for community services and intermediate facilities ('community hospitals') that combine primary care with more specialised services. In the abstract, both big parties agree with the Kerr report and it guides policy thinking. In practice, however, politicians cannot always resist championing local hospitals against reconfiguration, especially in the run-up to an election.

Third, the obvious clash between professional and managerial elites and local communities produced a call for the democratisation of the Health Boards. Both Labour and the Scottish National Party supported this call in the 2007 elections. It was the SNP that had to grapple with the problem of implementing elected boards. The legislation for half-elected boards with local government representation (which creates a majority for elected representatives) nevertheless passed, and two boards are piloting the new model in 2010 alongside two other boards that are experimenting with alternative models of public engagement.

It is also worth noting the impressive extent to which Scottish policy has paid attention to the determinants of population health. As the next section will show, the health of the Scottish population and the financial sustainability of the Scottish economy and health services depend on improved population health but the problem is that many public health interventions have only long-term effects. Their political support must depend on conviction or other merits of the policies (such as promotion of income equality or healthier food) because the short-term effects are often small. It is also often difficult to identify public health interventions in the making because they are about priorities; the evidence for effective 'effort' on public health determinants is often about priorities within existing organisations. The efforts put into diet, reduction of smoking, childhood interventions and other such priorities is impressive compared to the other three systems and might show in Scottish population statistics in 20 years.

England

Reform in England, especially under Blair, was more radical as policymakers increasingly tried to break the NHS as a state-provided service. To begin with the reform process was, depending on its portrayal, either an attractively pragmatic focus on 'what works', or a mark of drift under ministers who had no clear ideas.

Regardless, the tone and focus of health policy shifted dramatically after Alan Milburn became Secretary of State. On every level – from theory to law to the very make-up of the Department of Health – there was revolution and lots of new spending. The best single statement of the theory came from Blair's adviser Simon Stevens, now an executive with a US health care firm (Stevens 2004), but others put forth coherent versions (Barber 2007)[3]. Simplified, the theory was that there were different tools for affecting health services: working with the staff (hiring lots, paying them well, and relying on professionalism or a public sector ethos), Stalinism (giving orders and making failure to meet targets a sackable offence), and creating systems that would give them the incentives to improve without direct government intervention or shirking by employees.

The argument ran that all the new money should provide the benefits of good staffing, the famous Labour focus on targets was providing the Stalinism, but at a high cost, and the final piece would be to build in the competitive mechanisms that would outlast the funding surge and the Government's ability to impose targets. Beyond the public administration argument, the improved efficiency and sensitivity to middle-class voters would entrench the NHS. Not only would it make the NHS keep pace with the level of customer service that the middle classes had learned to expect from dealing with modern enterprises like airlines and mobile phone companies: it would also produce consensus on a mixture of market and regulation that the Conservatives would not be able to alter.

The theory was a political work of art, combining party-political strategies, historical references, and a variety of theories of public administration in order to create a coherent narrative that could unify officials, managers, journalists, MPs and others. It made the relatively marginal electoral value of choice (see Curtice, this volume) into a theory of public management that would convince informed elites. Above all, it turned contradiction into a virtue.

Policy contradiction, and an overall excess of policy, was indeed a more serious problem in England than elsewhere. The many policies that Labour promoted over the years defied any easy characterisation and it was never clear how they really all fitted together. Imposing waiting targets, choice, private sector entrants, foundation trusts, tariffs, and competition was energy-intensive and costly. An increasingly chaotic Department of Health, just as reorganised as the NHS, was less and less help (Jarman and Greer 2010).

The money and political energy both began to run out at the end of the Blair government, and new teams at the Department of Health began to draw back from their previous reforming energy even before Gordon Brown became Prime Minister. This meant giving up on most efforts to bring in more private sector competition and generally paying less attention to structure and more attention to process. Under Brown, it also meant pressure on Foundation Trusts. The autonomy of Foundation Trusts was a key part of the Blair agenda of extracting government from NHS management and adding competitive discipline, but it was always vulnerable to pressure from future governments that would want their planning capacity back (useful in making rational cuts) and from everybody annoyed by the tendency of foundation trusts to unbalance finances all around them by 'overtreating' and hoarding cash.

---

3. Historians trying to figure out the debate should compare Le Grand 2007 with Hunter 2008.

The story since 2006 has increasingly been the reassertion of traditional NHS management people and techniques as money and reforming energy have dissipated. The English experiment, just like Kenneth Clarke's original internal market, only attained theoretical coherence for a couple of years before the Government became too poor and weak to force it through. Perhaps in a decade or two there will be a government young, rich and powerful enough to try it all again.

As for lessons about health care, the data below strongly suggest that the distinctive English improvements were down to money, priorities and management rather than to the market. Competition was at best a tool for improving NHS management, and at worst a costly ideological distraction from managerial initiatives such as National Service Frameworks that did much of the real work (Healthcare Commission and Audit Commission 2008, Appleby and Coutts 2009, Ham 2009).

Wales
Welsh health policy after devolution was also radical, but in a very different way. If English policy deepened and extended the purchaser–provider split, the National Assembly for Wales picked up a different kind of health policy thinking (Drakeford 2006), an approach associated with social medicine and the 'new public health'. It is probably best captured by the comment that the NHS is really a 'National Sickness Service' – and that policymakers should pay more attention to reducing ill health if they want to avoid dedicating more and more of their budgets to treating its consequences.

The problem that public health activists always find is that many of the most important determinants of health are outside the control of health ministers: taxes, benefits, labour relations, overall economic strategy. Many are also outside the control of the devolved governments. As a result, the Welsh strategy was almost automatically confined to promoting joint working between the health services and local government. The incentive for the NHS was to resolve some major problems such as delayed transfers of care – what newspapers call bed-blocking. The incentive for local government was access to health services policymaking, a reward that in this and most other cases was more attractive before councillors actually got to enjoy it. The result was a difficult and energy-consuming reorganisation, leading to commissioning and fragmentation of local health services into local boards coterminous with local government. The problems were immediately apparent. It was difficult to staff the boards, and there was an imbalance between their power and the power of the trust hospitals.

The new system does not appear to have resolved the most serious problems of NHS Wales that devolution inherited: staffing problems, problems with service design, weakness in primary care, striking differences in performance between different areas, and questions about resource allocation. Devolution, by creating democratic accountability, has created a mechanism for the Welsh to demand better. It did not initially produce structures that resolved the problems.

2005 was a bad year for the WAG. Not only was Wales coming out worse on key waiting time indicators than Scotland was, but the penetration of the English media and greater weight of English debates during a UK general election also meant that Welsh policymakers were under more pressure than their Scottish counterparts to explain why they were failing the exam that English policymakers had set themselves. A very negative report from the Auditor General for Wales was the last straw. Like Scotland, the Welsh government changed ministers and made some moves in the 'English' direction of greater choice and market mechanisms. The result was two years of management focus and strategic drift built around the *Designed for Life* document (Welsh Assembly Government 2005).

After the 2007 elections, matters took a turn for the better. Part of the coalition agreement called for an end to the internal market. There had never been a market in NHS Wales, but the demand (made by Plaid Cymru) was for a reorganisation that would reduce the number of bodies, encourage planning and service integration within NHS Wales, and get rid of a number of senior managers.

The plan, much amended after consultation, reshaped almost all of NHS Wales's management from October 2009. It turned NHS Wales into a set of seven integrated health boards that strongly resemble the Scottish health boards, complemented by three trusts for the ambulance service, public health, and special services. This essentially abandons commissioning, opting instead for integration and planning as in Scotland. While the Welsh Assembly Government chose not to use it as an opportunity to lay off managerial staff, it reduces the imbalance of power in favour of trusts and creates more scope for integration and prioritisation within the NHS. Now the challenge is to manage the system well.

Northern Ireland

Northern Irish politics is not about any kind of public policy. So, health and other public services occupy an uncomfortable position in the province's political life. Health receives constant political attention and is the subject of intense debate – until there is an election, at which point the logic of sectarian voting pushes it aside. Few or no voters will reward the DUP for its performance in the health portfolio, just as Sinn Fein's scores have probably had nothing at all to do with its. Furthermore, the twists and turns of the peace process have meant that devolution was suspended for much of the decade, with decisions made by direct rule ministers who had limited incentive to even be physically present in Northern Ireland.

The result was a situation that one local politician described to me as 'the replacement of self-rule with self-review'. A variety of Northern Ireland and UK politicians opted, repeatedly, to push off decisions with further review, and then to push off implementation of those decisions that were made. This behaviour, particularly notable in hospital reconfiguration debates, was immensely frustrating for most key actors within the Northern Ireland health service, who were left leaderless, incapable of fixing major problems, and publicly exposed in a system whose reorganisation was constantly being proposed. Many people working within the system have persistent worries about their legitimacy. Its lack of mechanisms for responding to public preferences exacerbates the class and sectarian divides that plague Northern Irish society (Birrell 2009).

Finally, after long debates and delays a relatively unified new system came into operation in 2007. This model divides Northern Ireland into five large trusts, each of which combines health and social care, and a single large ambulance trust. The Belfast trust, which employs one in 30 in the whole of Northern Ireland's workforce, dominates. A single large commissioning agency covers the entire area. There is no reason to expect that its 'commissioning' will differ much from what the world knows as planning. Again, part of the challenge is to manage the system well. Like Wales, Northern Ireland got its new system in its last year of plenty. But the immediate challenge of the new system, and above all the devolved ministers, is to prioritise amidst unfamiliar financial constraint.

Outcomes

Health outcomes are tricky things; there is an entire discipline, epidemiology, that focuses on gathering, analysing, and interpreting population health data. Likewise, the complexities of health care data are exactly what keep health service researchers busy. There are often multiple ways to discuss the same issue and multiple indicators. And even the most technologically boastful health care systems around the world have problems providing data that is not two or three years old, giving everybody a good argument that bad statistics reflect a situation that has since changed. The statistics included in this chapter are credible and broadly representative of what other indicators show, but make no claim to inclusiveness. A few of the statistics, such as five-year cancer survival rates, are also being floated as policy goals for England by the Conservatives, so it is worth seeing what they say.

Population health

The first and simplest indicators, and arguably the most important ones, are 'population health indicators'. They are popular with uninformed analysts. But they are also, unfortunately, the worst statistics to use for parsing the differences between health systems, let alone ones as similar as those of the UK.

The problem is that they tend to capture much more than the effects of the health care system, meaning that it is hard to isolate the impact of a particular government policy. To make the problem worse, the effects of policies can be lagged for decades. Healthy life expectancy therefore makes more sense as a replacement for GDP as a measure of social success than as a tool for scoring health policy.

The main thing that Table 9.1 shows is that the North–South divide is alive and well and bisects England. Southern England is healthier, richer and generally more fortunate. Anything north of the proverbial line from the Severn to The Wash is relatively troubled (see also Trench 2008). In general, this makes the point that for

Table 9.1. Population health indicators

	SMR* (UK=100)	Male life exp. at birth	Male life exp. at age 65	Infant mort. (under 1 yr, per 1000)	Lung cancer M (UK=100)	Lung cancer F (UK=100)
UK	100	77.3	17.3	4.8	100	100
North East	109	76.3	16.5	4.8	134	144
North West	110	76.0	16.6	5	120	125
Yorks & H'ber	104	76.9	17.1	5.6	114	117
E. Midlands	99	77.6	17.3	5.3	101	91
W. Midlands	101	76.9	17.1	5.9	100	87
East	92	78.7	18	4.3	86	78
London	92	77.9	17.8	4.5	101	96
SE Coast	92	78.9	18.2	3.9	83	78
SE Central	88	same	Same	3.9	Same	Same
South West	90	78.7	18.2	4.2	81	77
England	97	77.7	17.5	4.8	96	96
Wales	104	76.8	17.1	5.3	105	107
Scotland	118	74.9	16.1	4.7	134	150
N Ireland	106	76.3	16.9	4.9	96	94

*SMR = standardised mortality ratio
Source: Regional Trends 41, ONS

most questions of outcomes, finely-grained answers will come from working with English regional data. Better English data usually shows immense internal variation within England, makes London a more remarkable outlier than Scotland (McLean *et al* 2009), and makes North East England stand out for both social problems and good public services[4].

Efficiency
There are all sorts of questions about the meaning of efficiency in health care services. One of the basic facts about personal services such as medicine, nursing, and therapy – or teaching, management consultancy, lobbying, private banking, and MP

---

4 Andrews and Martin (2007) developed the clever technique of creating an alter-ego for Wales within England by matching Welsh to English local areas. Their analysis is limited to the statutory indicators, mostly about waiting times, but broadly confirms the messages here – specifically, that Wales has long waits.

surgeries – is that their quality can be a simple function of time spent. This means that efficiency measurements are tricky because if policymakers measure higher efficiency as a simple matter of higher throughput, they might reduce quality, the satisfaction of patients and carers, or both.

Furthermore, 'efficiency' always drops when spending increases, and increases when spending stops, because organisations will cut down on the less efficient activities in times of stress. Loss of that marginal activity will improve throughput in leaner coming years while costing the public in access, care or quality. There is, after all, no good reason to decide that the socially valuable service of health care should be provided at the point of maximum marginal productivity rather than some other measure more closely related to effectiveness and value (Spicker 2009)[5].

Simple throughput measures such as full beds also ignore supply-created demand, which is a major issue in health economics; if there is available capacity, it takes powerful rationing to keep it from filling up. Using full beds alone as an indicator of success ignores day and outpatient treatments. It is strange to focus on throughput when every UK system, and almost every health system in the developed world, is focused on reducing hospitalization through better preventative and primary care. Finally, infectious disease specialists will note that spare capacity can be good – empty beds are useful in epidemics, and some research finds correlations between lower facility usage and lower levels of hospital-acquired infection. With those caveats, admissions per bed are relatively high across the UK (Figure 9.2)[6].

There are more beds going unused in Northern Ireland and Wales than in Scotland and England. The latter two countries have remarkably high bed utilisation (a study comparing the English NHS to the lauded US provider Kaiser Permanente found that the English NHS

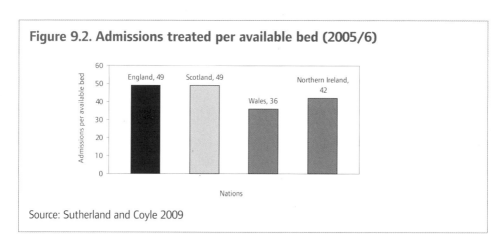

Figure 9.2. Admissions treated per available bed (2005/6)

Source: Sutherland and Coyle 2009

5. The right way to proceed is to determine how much health care we want and then focus on designing and managing systems to produce it at the least cost. I owe this point to Paul Spicker.
6. See Connolly *et al* 2010 for more detailed comparisons, modified after publication to reflect additional Scottish Government data.

gets many more occupied beds for comparable spending [Feachem *et al* 2002]). The higher Scottish spending and larger number of beds comes with high utilisation of hospital beds. This is not necessarily much of a blessing, because on current data Scotland has rates of day surgery for simple procedures (such as hernias) that are very low by international standards or compared with England (Castoro *et al* 2007: 4)[7].

Comparative health outcomes

While cancer mortality is really a population health measure, cancer treatment and support for cancer patients, and lifestyle changes such as smoking cessation and better diets after diagnosis, explain much of cancer survival rates.

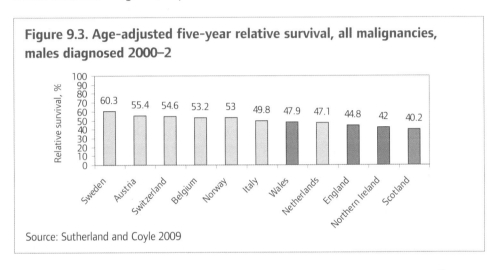

Figure 9.3. Age-adjusted five-year relative survival, all malignancies, males diagnosed 2000–2

Source: Sutherland and Coyle 2009

The differences in performance follow no obvious pattern in structure or spending. Scotland has very bad outcomes and Wales has very good outcomes by UK standards (all have mediocre results compared with the rest of Western Europe). It is worth remembering that treatment of cancer, like most other diseases, is often driven by professional networks and goals that politicians barely understand. It is also worth remembering that because five-year data is (obviously) lagged, these data might not show improvements from the focus on cancer across Great Britain in recent years.

Another promising way to view the effect of devolution is by looking at the data over (more or less) the time period of devolution. To save space, Figure 9.4 shows only cancer mortality for men. Mortality for women dropped less but the results otherwise look similar.

Internationally, England's 18 per cent reduction in male cancer mortality was impressive. The smallest reduction was in Northern Ireland at 13 per cent, but what is striking is that the lines drop almost in parallel. In specific cancers, the trends vary.

---

7. Scotland has had a problem with coding erstwhile day surgery as outpatient treatment. It is not clear how much of the low rate is coding error, how much is divergent medical practice, and how much is a response to patient preferences.

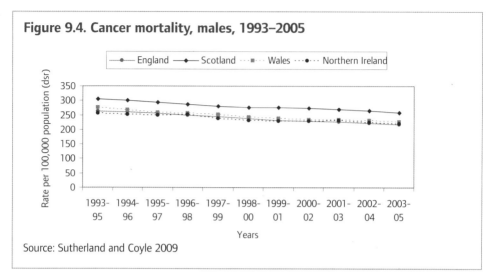

Figure 9.4. Cancer mortality, males, 1993–2005

Source: Sutherland and Coyle 2009

Comparing 1993–95 data with 2003–05 data, prostate cancer mortality has been dropping across the UK despite increasing incidence. The biggest drops were in England and Scotland, which also initially had the highest mortality rates. So cancer care probably got better even if cancer itself remains a serious population health problem.

Waiting times

Waiting times were a central part of devolved health policymakers' 2005 *annus horribilis*. Northern Irish, Scottish, and Welsh policymakers had not put much emphasis on reducing waiting times. Labour fought the 2005 general election on its health policy performance in England, and that meant emphasising the reduced waits in England. Not only did this give Labour MPs from Scotland and Wales an opportunity to comment negatively on devolved Labour governments: it also guaranteed that the three systems would constantly be compared to England on waiting times – and look bad. The result was a change of minister and direction in both Scottish and Welsh health policy.

How, then, do our four systems perform? While we cannot compare overall waiting lists due to (intentionally) non-comparable reporting, there are a few procedures for which we have independent survey data and can escape flawed government sources. Of them, hip replacements are simply so famous as to demand inclusion. Sadly, the data is not longitudinal.

The data for hip replacements and other procedures (angiographies, cataract surgery) confirms what most observers thought: waiting times are longer in Wales and Northern Ireland; they are relatively short in Scotland (probably due to greater spending and staffing); central pressure and new money pushed them down in England; after the traumas of 2005, devolved policymakers began to push them down as well. Determination produced dramatic improvements, with direct-rule ministers winning the prize with a 45 per cent year-on-year drop in Northern Ireland!

English policy achieved the waiting times target through sheer relentless managerial pressure and targeted expansion capacities. The Government, Department of Health, and every level of NHS management knew that waits were the key target, and the first priority. This approach enabled the multiple micro-reforms (such as changing skill mixes or staff rota) that actually produce such important improvements (Willcox *et al* 2007, Propper *et al* 2008).

England's performance on waiting times also clearly shaped those of the others because England's political agenda affects the others. The biggest (messiest, nastiest) public debate about comparative health system performance that the UK has had pushed devolved ministers to change health system performance. The people have spoken, governments listened, and they produced results.

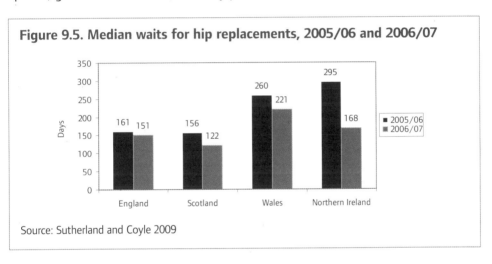

Figure 9.5. Median waits for hip replacements, 2005/06 and 2006/07

Source: Sutherland and Coyle 2009

Public health outcomes

Public health is the field of activity that specifically tries to address the causes of morbidity in society, and is the source of much of the evidence base on the relationship between different social factors and population health. In terms of trends in smoking (the world's biggest cause of avoidable mortality), use of ecstasy (not necessary the most serious public health threat, but a proxy indicator for more damaging drug use); binge drinking; and notified tuberculosis cases, which are a proxy for the extent of communicable disease challenges, there are, on average, very slightly bigger public health problems in northern England, with Scotland, Wales and Northern Ireland lying between the north and the south of England – and London lives up to expectations with a strikingly high incidence of each kind of problem.

There has been substantial change in tobacco and alcohol policy. Devolution produced convergence on late-night drinking in smoke-free pubs. It is harder to identify any one policy that has enabled the ongoing increase in alcohol consumption, and much alcohol comes from supermarkets, but the spread of 24-hour drinking probably contributes.

Smoking is the world's leading cause of avoidable mortality and tobacco one of the rare products with no good use. Bans on smoking in public places were introduced from March 2006 in Scotland, April 2007 in Northern Ireland and Wales, and July 2007 in England. The politics are fascinating and show a clear case of devolved leadership of a UK agenda (Donnelly and Whittle 2008, Asare *et al* 2009). They also show a clear benefit to Scotland: during the gap when the Scots had the ban and England did not, acute coronary syndrome cases dropped by 17 per cent in Scotland and only 4 per cent in England (Pell *et al* 2008). This is not just a strikingly effective public health policy: it is a strikingly effective health policy by any standards. England has since adopted the ban; every part of the UK now enjoys its effects, and devolution politics can take part of the credit for pushing it onto the agenda.

Equalities outcomes

Equalities policy is born of the conviction that one's state of health should not reflect one's social class, ethnicity or gender. The problem with equalities policy is partly that the sources of health inequalities are the same as the sources of population health problems. The three devolved governments would need access to social security and the income tax code to promote equality seriously. So they are left with efforts to make sure that appropriate medical care is equally available, often with special arrangements for the less well-off or otherwise vulnerable, and that the staff deal well with diversity.

The data compares the differences in outcomes between people in different quintiles of deprivation. While the people in a given quintile may be very different, the measurement of inequalities is the gap between outcomes in different local areas – comparing the outcomes in the most and least distressed quintiles of local areas.

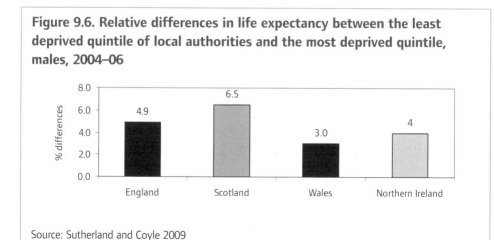

Figure 9.6. Relative differences in life expectancy between the least deprived quintile of local authorities and the most deprived quintile, males, 2004–06

Source: Sutherland and Coyle 2009

Figure 9.7. Cancer mortality by deprivation

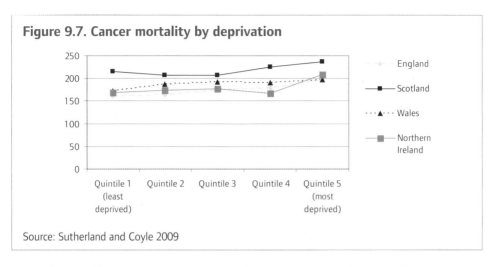

Source: Sutherland and Coyle 2009

Inequalities in life expectancy incorporate all sorts of issues – for example, the working poor are more likely to have on-the-job accidents, keep peculiar hours, or be exposed to pollution than the wealthier quintiles.

While Scotland's record with inequalities in overall life expectancy is awful, its cancer inequalities are smaller. The shocking differences are in England and Northern Ireland. The mortality rate among the poorest quintile of Scots from cancer is 10 per cent worse than for the richest. Among cancer sufferers in England, the poorest quintile is 22.3 per cent more likely than the richest to die. The comparable statistics are 21.9 per cent in Northern Ireland and 14.2 per cent in Wales (Sutherland and Coyle 2009). What this provisionally suggests, once again, is that Scotland has reasonably good health services that are doing their bit for equality against the backdrop of some serious social problems. Their cancer treatment is relatively egalitarian by UK standards, even if their society is clearly not.

The broader point is that we should not be surprised that devolved government commitments to reduce health inequalities have not had much effect, and have even struggled to manifest themselves in concrete policies. Devolved governments, and health departments in general, lack the tools to affect many of the key causes of inequality in society, and inequalities in life expectancy reflect that. This should be obvious, but most commentary and policy pronouncements on inequalities tend to obscure it and overstate what devolved governments can do (Greer 2010a).

It is better to focus on access to health care and treatment, which is what the Scottish and Welsh formulas were explicitly recalibrated to do, and where policies in England actually managed to produce faster treatment for the poorest quintile than for the rest – an outcome that should make Labour proud (Cooper *et al* 2009).

Satisfaction

The last word on outcomes can go to the public.

Public satisfaction is a mixture of expectations, process, and outcomes. There is more dissatisfaction in Northern Ireland. A 17-point increase in satisfaction with the English NHS under Labour is a kind of vote for Labour's policies (Appleby and Phillips 2009). But with the exception of higher dissatisfaction in Northern Ireland, the differences are small.

Public opinion is not easily correlated with other outcome indicators. On one hand, people value things our data captures poorly, such as being treated with care and respect. On the other, a nice doctor and a caring nurse can be inefficient and even dangerous. The key issue with public opinion on outcomes is that even if it frustrates health policy specialists, it reflects viewpoints that are often just as sensible and sometimes more powerful. Comparing system with system, it looks like most people in Britain are about equally happy.

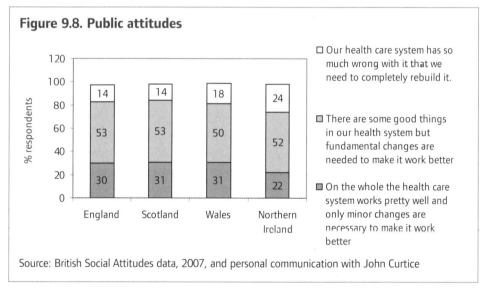

Figure 9.8. Public attitudes

Source: British Social Attitudes data, 2007, and personal communication with John Curtice

Process: management and treatment

Population health outcomes are not just very hard to shift: they also obscure all sorts of important variation in how well patients are treated. So what researchers and clinicians do is focus on process – whether or not the health system is carrying out its defined tasks well.

There are different measurement problems here: there are comparability problems in process as well as outcomes indicators, but while outcomes indicators tend to be too crude, process indicators run the risk of not measuring anything at all. By and large, the medical procedures that are simple enough to generate good process data are ones that are usually done by computers, phones, and a few nurses. Process data

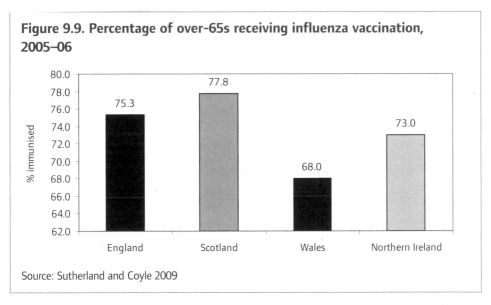

Figure 9.9. Percentage of over-65s receiving influenza vaccination, 2005–06

Source: Sutherland and Coyle 2009

measure nursing and bureaucracy more than medicine, and primary care more than specialist care.

The bulk of useful quality indicators are in the UK-wide Quality and Outcomes Framework for primary care, which is part of the GP contract. Performance on QOF indicators tells us that primary care in general is somewhat better in Northern Ireland and Scotland than in England and Wales. That is a useful baseline to keep in mind.

Consider influenza immunizations: a combination of logistics, record-keeping, and outreach efforts and therefore an indicator of local health system administration. There are significant variations, with Scotland narrowly showing the best performance (and the much-reorganised English local level turning in an extremely good performance, given its turbulence and the presence of ever-problematic London).

Penetration and use of information technology is an indicator of government success in changing process, since an adopted IT project necessarily changes the organisation of work. Health care around the world is notable for low investment in IT[8]. Furthermore, health care everywhere, including the UK, has a record of serious IT failures. In the UK, Northern Ireland does best overall for IT.

The likeliest lesson of this outcome is a simple one: IT projects are best done in and by smaller units – learning is easier, trust is easier to establish, users are easier to integrate, communication is easier, and there can be more competition because more firms have enough capacity to enter the market. England's NHS Connecting for Health would undoubtedly be working better if it had not been set up as one of the

---

8. Health care observers become excited about pilot projects using technology that is absolutely standard in other sectors. The average delivery driver or airline gate agent has better IT than the average hospital consultant.

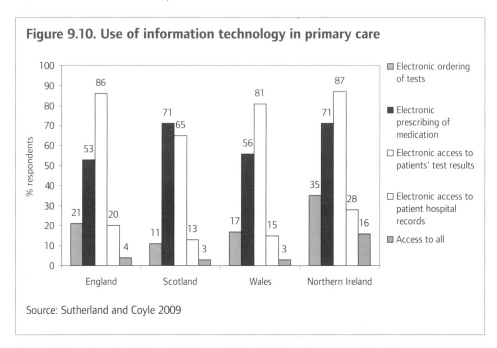

Figure 9.10. Use of information technology in primary care

Source: Sutherland and Coyle 2009

largest IT projects in history. Northern Ireland's IT performance is best in areas connected with primary care, reflecting a history of GP fund-holders banding together to invest in systems – a good example of medical networks producing improvements.

Despite the problems of survey research, some of the best and most important process and quality indicators come from asking patients about the experience of medical care itself. These are issues such as follow-up of adverse events (such as drug reactions) and non-delivery of correct lab results.

These and similar statistics tell us that there are some problems in Wales. In fact, the elites of NHS Wales told us that. Only 31 per cent said in a 2004 survey that they that they would want to have themselves or their loved ones treated in Wales (Longley and Beddow 2005). This is not a surprise because there is not a lot of evidence that Welsh health care overall was particularly good before devolution.

It is also shown that Northern Ireland had excellent follow-up to adverse events in 2006 – just after some very public disasters that focused policy attention on the issue. That is a nice testament to democracy in Northern Ireland. Otherwise, reports of health care coordination and quality tend to favour Scotland and reflect badly on England.

Finally, infections acquired in health care settings are a serious health problem and the source of some recent press scandals (focused on the mediagenic methicillin-resistant staphyloccoccus aureus, better known as MRSA). In each system the MRSA infection rates had not taken much pattern until press and political attention fixed on them, at which point they all started to turn down[9]. Any decline is impressive because

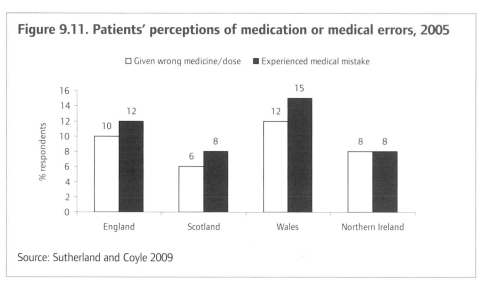

Figure 9.11. Patients' perceptions of medication or medical errors, 2005

□ Given wrong medicine/dose ■ Experienced medical mistake

Source: Sutherland and Coyle 2009

discoveries of MRSA, like medical errors, tend to increase when people pay attention to the issue. Reporting improves at the same time that policy tries to reduce the incidence of the problem. The lines in Figure 9.12 give us a testament to democracy in action.

England's performance is particularly inspiring, given that its MRSA policies were classic top-down 'Stalinism' driven by a government that was loudly abjuring anything of the sort.

Conclusion

Waiting times, MRSA, per-capita spending, blocked hospital reconfigurations, smoking in public places and response to adverse events in Northern Ireland: they all show that democracy works in health care policy. When the media–political spotlight turns on a specific issue in health policy, health care systems swing into line. That is the virtue of NHS systems – politicians can produce effects if they actually specify what effects they are trying to produce. England in particular shows that spending and clear political direction can produce good outcomes in short periods of time, even if it is not clear that the Blair government's headline contestability and other reform policies helped. Money and management delivered the outcomes ministers wanted (Bevan 2009a).

The evidence of politicians' effectiveness is one of the ultimate justifications for devolution. It is easy to forget that devolution was not just about nationalism. It was also about democratisation – giving the people of Northern Ireland, Scotland and Wales a voice in decisions previously made by the obscure officials and ministers of the territorial offices. We can argue about whether a given political intervention was sensible or whether it was fair for English waiting times to hijack Welsh health policy,

9. Wales has had the most difficulty holding MRSA steady or pushing it down, which is not surprising.

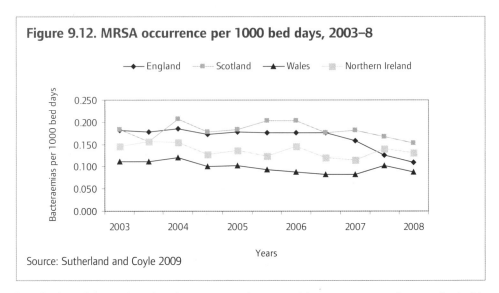

Figure 9.12. MRSA occurrence per 1000 bed days, 2003–8

Source: Sutherland and Coyle 2009

but the key thing is that devolution created responsible governments that can be held to account for their outcomes. Even in Northern Ireland, popular outrage has an impact. In Scotland, professional elites and once-mighty quangos must change their basic approach to meet popular preferences. And everywhere, it is harder to close a hospital. Democratic accountability, and the diffusion of unpopular decisions, should be particularly important in the coming years of retrenchment that the UK faces.

And how does democratic accountability work? Through good management and clinical networks. It is no accident that the English and Welsh, after their extended experiments, are refocusing on the verities of good health management. Reducing the waste found in every health care system and planning service cuts that will be cost-effective takes the knowledge and engagement of professionals and serious, disciplined managers. It takes the confidence and coherence to argue that investing in 'Cinderella services' like foot care for diabetics, sexual health strategies, or mental health nurses is better than almost any capital expenditure. It takes engagement between managers and the networks of professionals that are both unchangeable and a great asset (Ham 2003). It takes, as all systems now agree, the hard work required to create service integration that reduces hospitalisations.

New organisations, new incentives and new forms of accountability for one category or another of manager are luxuries for the fat years. In a crisis, what NHS systems need are priorities, responsiveness to voters, transparency, clinical engagement and good management (including ministers). Devolution, and a decade's learning from our four experiments, should help make that possible.

Health policy researchers and advocates can provide the comparisons, try to affect the policy agendas of the laggards, and proffer solutions. Naming and shaming can work within networks of public sector professionals, even if it leaves voters undisturbed

(Downe *et al* 2007, Bevan 2009b). Governments, if they are responsible and honest, should provide comparable data that would let all of us compare and benchmark these four systems. But if league tables are to be credible and work, they cannot rank entire health systems or societies; they have to be on a more practical level such as individual cancer survival rates. A 'league table' of entire health systems cannot be much more than a political weapon and will always look arbitrary.

But ultimately democratic (dis)satisfaction is what drives political activity, and when there is directed political activity, health systems respond. Devolution, by increasing the opportunities for people to put pressure on their governments, makes it more likely that underperformance will be unstable. That is not such a bad contribution to health policy, and it is one that should operate through feast and famine alike.

The author would like to thank John Curtice, Peter Donnelly, Heather Elliott, Holly Jarman, Guy Lodge, Paul Spicker and the participants in the ippr seminar held in Edinburgh in October 2009. The research underpinning this paper has been funded over the years by the King's Fund, Leverhulme Trust, Nuffield Trust, and National Science Foundation.

References

Alvarez-Rosete A, Bevan G, Mays N, and Dixon J (2005) 'Effect of diverging policy across the NHS', *British Medical Journal* 331: 946-950

Andrews R and Martin S (2007) 'Has devolution improved public services?' *Public Money and Management* 149-156

Appleby J and Coutts A (2009) 'NHS, health and well-being', in Uberoi V, Coutts A, McLean I, and Halpern D (eds) *Options for New Britain*, Basingstoke: Palgrave Macmillan

Appleby J and Phillips M (2009) 'The NHS: Satisfied now?' in Park A, Curtice J, Thomson K, Phillips M, Johnson MC, and Clery E (eds) *British Social Attitudes Survey: The 25th Report*, Beverly Hills: Sage

Asare B, Cairney P, and Studlar DT (2009) 'Federalism and multilevel governance in tobacco policy: The European Union, the United Kingdom, and devolved UK institutions', *Journal of Public Policy* 29 (01): 79-102

Barber M (2007) *Instruction to Deliver: Tony Blair, the Public Services, and the Challenge of Delivery* London: Politico's

Bevan G (2009a) 'Have targets done more harm than good in the English NHS? No', *British Medical Journal* 338: a3129

Bevan G (2009b) 'Performance measurement of "knights" and "knaves": Differences in approaches and impacts in British countries after devolution', *Journal of Comparative Policy Analysis*

Bevan G and Hamblin R (2009) 'Hitting and missing targets by ambulance services for emergency calls: Impacts of different systems of performance measurement within the UK', *Journal of the Royal Statistical Society* 172 (1): 1-30

Birrell D (2009) *The Impact of Devolution on Social Policy* Bristol: Policy

Castoro C, Bertinato L, Baccaglini U, Drace CA, and McKee M (2007) *Day Surgery: Making It Happen* Brussels: European Observatory on Health Systems and Policies

Connolly S, Mays N, and Bevan G (2010) *The Impact of Devolution on Health Care Systems in the UK* London: The Nuffield Trust

Cooper ZN, McGuire A, Jones S, and Le Grand J (2009) 'Equity, waiting times and NHS reforms: Retrospective study', *British Medical Journal*, 339b: 3264

Dixon J, Inglis S, and Klein R (1999) 'Is the English NHS underfunded?' *British Medical Journal* 318: 522-526

Donabedian A (2003) *An Introduction to Quality Assurance in Health Care* Oxford University Press

Donnelly P and Whittle P (2008) After the smoke has cleared – reflections on Scotland's tobacco control legislation', *Public Health* 122:762-766

Downe J, Grace C, Martin S, and Nutley S (2007) *Comparing for Improvement: Local Government Performance Regimes in England, Scotland and Wales* Swindon: ESRC PSP Discussion Paper Series

Drakeford M (2006) 'Health policy in Wales: Making a difference in conditions of difficulty', *Critical Social Policy* 26: 543-561

Drakeford M (2007) 'Governance and social policy', in Williams C (ed) *Social Policy for Social Welfare Practice in a Devolved Wales*, Birmingham: Venture Press

Feachem RGA, Sekhri NK, and White KL (2002) 'Getting more for their dollar: A comparison of the NHS with California's kaiser permanente', *British Medical Journal* 324: 135-143

Fox DM (2003) 'Population and the law: The changing scope of health policy', *Journal of Law, Medicine and Ethics* 31: 607-14

Greer SL and Trench A (2008) *Health and Intergovernmental Relations in the Devolved United Kingdom* London: The Nuffield Trust

Greer SL (2004) *Territorial Politics and Health Policy: UK Health Policy in Comparative Perspective* Manchester: Manchester University Press

Greer SL (2007) 'The fragile divergence machine: Citizenship, policy divergence, and intergovernmental relations', in Trench A (ed) *Devolution and Power in the United Kingdom*, Manchester: Manchester University Press

Greer SL (2009) 'How does decentralisation affect the welfare state?' *Journal of Social Policy* 39 (2)

Greer SL (2010a, forthcoming) 'Introduction: Health departments in health policy', *Social Policy and Administration*

Greer SL (2010b) 'Options and the Lack of Options: Healthcare Politics and Policy', in Uberoi V, Coutts A, McLean I, Halpern D (Eds.) *Options for Britain II: cross-cutting challenges for policy-makers. Special Issue of Political Quarterly*

Ham C (2003) 'Improving the performance of health services: The role of clinical leadership', *Lancet* 361: 1978-1980

Ham C (2009) *Health Policy in Britain,* 6th ed., Basingstoke: Palgrave Macmillan

Hauck K and Street A (2007) 'Do targets matter? A comparison of English and Welsh national health priorities', *Health Economics* 16: 275-290

Healthcare Commission and Audit Commission (2008) *Is the Treatment Working? Progress with the NHS System Reforms,* London: Healthcare Commission and Audit Commission

Hunter DJ (2008) *The Health Debate* Bristol: Policy Press

Jarman H and Greer SL (2010, forthcoming) 'The eye of the storm: Reorganising the Department of Health, 1998-2009', *Social Policy and Administration*

Jervis P (2008) *Devolution and Health* London: Nuffield Trust

Kerr D (2005) 'Building a health service fit for the future', in *Building a Health Service Fit for the Future* Edinburgh: Scottish Executive

Kerr D and Feeley D (2007) 'Values in NHS Scotland: A tale of two c-words', in Greer SL (ed) *Devolving Policy, Diverging Values?: The Values of the National Health Services* London: The Nuffield Trust

Le Grand J (2007) *The Other Invisible Hand: Delivering Public Services Through Choice and Competition* Princeton: Princeton University Press

Longley M and Beddow T (2005) *NHS Wales Barometer 2004* Pontypridd: Welsh Institute of Health and Social Care, University of Glamorgan

McLean I, Lodge G and Schmuecker K (2009) 'Social citizenship and intergovernmenal finance', in Greer SL (ed) *Devolution and Social Citizenship in the United Kingdom* Bristol: Policy

Pell JP, Haw S, Cobbe S, Newby DE, Pell ACH, Fischbacher C, McConnachie A *et al* (2008) 'Smoke-Free legislation and hospitalizations for acute coronary syndrome', *New England Journal of Medicine* 359: 482-491

Propper C, Sutton M, Whitnall C, and Windmeijer F (2008) 'Incentives and targets in hospital care: Evidence from a natural experiment', *University of Bristol Centre for Market and Public Organisation Working Papers Series,* 08-205

Smee C (2005) *Speaking Truth to Power: Two Decades of Analysis in the Department of Health* London/ Oxford: The Nuffield Trust/Radcliffe

Spicker P (2009) 'The nature of a public service', *International Journal of Public Administration* 32 (11): 970-991

Stevens S (2004) 'Reform strategies for the English NHS', *Health Affairs* 23 (3): 37-44

Sutherland K and Coyle N (2009) *Quality in Healthcare in England, Wales, Scotland, Northern Ireland: An Intra-UK Chartbook* London: The Health Foundation

Trench A (2008) *Devolution and Higher Education: Impact and Future Trends* London: Universities UK

Trench A and Jeffery C (2007) *Older People and Public Policy: The Impact of Devolution* London: Age Concern

Welsh Assembly Government (2005) *Designed for Life: Creating World Class Health and Social Care for Wales in the 21st Century* Cardiff: Welsh Assembly Government.

Willcox S, Seddon M, Dunn S, Tudor Edwards R, Pearse J, and Tu JV (2007) 'Measuring and reducing waiting times: A cross-national comparison of strategies', *Health Affairs* (Millwood) 26 (4): 1078-87

Wyszewianski L (2009) 'Basic concepts of healthcare quality', in Ransom ER (ed) *The Healthcare Quality Book* (2nd ed), Chicago: Health Administration Press

10. Crime and justice after devolution

Rick Muir

Questions of crime and justice are always near the top of the political agenda. Indeed, before the impact of the recent recession, 'law and order' was felt by the British public to be the most important issue facing the country (Ipsos Mori 2009).

But how has the process of devolution affected the criminal justice systems in the different nations of the UK? Have the devolved governments taken different approaches to tackling crime? If so, what has been the impact on crime itself? This chapter asks if and in what way devolution has led to a divergence in criminal justice policy and crime trends since the late 1990s.

The chapter comes in three parts:

- First, it sets the context by sketching out some of the key differences in crime patterns in the different jurisdictions of the UK.
- Second, it asks whether the different countries took different approaches to questions of crime and punishment, highlighting policy innovations and any transmission of ideas, policies and learning across the union.
- Third, it examines whether these policy differences had any impact on outcomes, by examining whether crime trends differed across the union.

The chapter compares the three separate criminal justice systems of the UK:

- England and Wales are treated as a common unit because they share the same legal system and a common framework for the administration of justice and policing.
- Scotland has had its own system of law and justice, going back centuries before the Act of Union. Upon devolution in 1999 crime and justice were devolved fully from Westminster to the Scottish parliament[1].
- Northern Ireland also has its own framework of laws dating back before 1921, but also resulting from the period of devolved government that ran from 1921 to 1972. At the time of writing, responsibility for policing and justice is about to be devolved from the Westminster government to the Northern Ireland Assembly, following agreement between the Northern Ireland parties.

---

1. There are some important exceptions: drugs and firearms laws remain with Westminster.

Crime patterns across the UK

Patterns of crime vary across the union, meaning that the different administrations face different challenges. There are two main ways of measuring crime. The first is to look at crimes recorded by the police. This method is problematic because most crimes go unreported and there have been changes to recording rules, meaning that the figures tend to rise and fall because of changes in the type of data collected by the police. For example, new crime recording standards were introduced across police forces in England and Wales in 2002 and in Scotland in 2004. At both of these points we see a rise in the overall recorded crime figures in both jurisdictions (Scottish Government 2009a, Walker *et al* 2009).

The second way of measuring crime is to ask a representative sample of the public whether they have been a victim of crime in the last 12 months – something that is now done annually through the British Crime Survey (BCS) for England and Wales, and also separately through the Scottish Crime and Justice Survey (SCJS) and the Northern Ireland Crime Survey (NICS) (see Box 10.1 for details). This method is the one generally favoured by criminologists because it gets at the majority of offences that go unrecorded.

In what follows we compare the data from the victimisation surveys to assess differences in the patterns of crime in different parts of the union. We should be cautious when comparing crime patterns across countries, simply because the criminal law differs across jurisdictions. For example, one reason the number of assaults per head is higher in Scotland may be because assault is always given priority in the Scottish survey when two crimes have occurred simultaneously, which is not the case in the British Crime Survey. Similarly, part of the reason burglary might be higher per head in England and Wales is because it is a more encompassing offence than housebreaking in Scotland, including for example incidences without forced entry.[2] Having said that, much of what comes under 'burglary' in England and Wales gets coded under 'other household thefts' in Scotland – and burglary and other household thefts are *both* proportionately higher in England and Wales than in Scotland.

While making comparison of individual crime types like burglary or assault is more problematic, we can be more confident about differences between the larger categories of criminal activity (such as 'property crime' and 'violent crime'), which cover all offences of a certain broad type, whatever the legal definition of a particular crime in each country.

The first finding is that crime has always been and remains higher in England and Wales than in Scotland or Northern Ireland – and that Northern Ireland has much lower levels of crime than its UK neighbours. In 2008/9 23.4 per cent of people were the victim of a crime in England and Wales, compared with 20.4 per cent of people in Scotland and just 13.4 per cent in Northern Ireland (Walker *et al* 2009, MacLeod *et al* 2009 and Toner and Freel 2009).

2. See MacLeod *et al* 2009: 212 for a detailed discussion of the comparability of these surveys.

Box 10.1. The UK crime surveys

The British Crime Survey (BCS) is a face-to-face victimisation survey in which people aged over 16 resident in households in England and Wales are asked about their experiences of crime in the 12 months prior to interview. Respondents to the survey are also asked about their attitudes towards different crime-related issues such as the police and criminal justice system, and perceptions of crime and anti-social behaviour.

The BCS excludes fraud and those crimes termed as victimless (for example, possession of drugs). As it is a survey that asks people whether they have experienced victimisation, murders cannot be included.

The survey has been run regularly since 1981 and is now carried out every year. BCS estimates for 2008/9 are based on face-to-face interviews with 46,286 respondents.

The Scottish Crime and Justice Survey (SCJS) is a large-scale continuous survey measuring people's experience and perceptions of crime in Scotland, based on 16,000 face-to-face interviews conducted annually with adults (aged 16 or over) living in private households in Scotland. It is the latest phase of a number of Scottish crime surveys that have been carried out since 1993.

The latest 2008/9 survey represents a major shift in design and methodology from previous surveys, principally involving a large increase in sample size – which makes the latest survey much more reliable. There was also a move to continuous interviewing using a rolling reference period, asking people about 'the last 12 months', rather than a fixed period. Although the basic structure of the questionnaire remained the same, this latter change cannot be discounted as an explanation for changes in trends compared with the preceding survey.

The Northern Ireland Crime Survey (NICS) is a representative, continuous, personal interview survey of the experiences and perceptions of crime of 3,856 adults living in private households throughout Northern Ireland. Previously conducted on an ad hoc basis in 1994/95, 1998, 2001 and 2003/04, the NICS began operating on a continuous basis in January 2005. It is similar in structure and methodology to the BCS.

Sources: Walker et al (2009), MacLeod et al (2009) and Toner and Freel (2009)

The overall distribution of crime is also different across the different countries. Whereas violent crimes make up just 20 per cent of total crime in England and Wales, it makes up 29 per cent of crime in Northern Ireland and 30 per cent in Scotland. At the same time property crimes make up 80 per cent of crimes in England and Wales, but just 71 per cent in Northern Ireland and 70 per cent in Scotland. All property crimes (burglary, other household theft and vehicle related theft) are higher in England and Wales than in Scotland or Northern Ireland. Finally, vandalism is much higher in Scotland than in the rest of the UK.

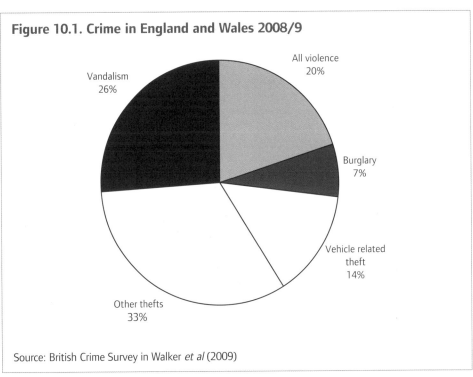

Figure 10.1. Crime in England and Wales 2008/9

- All violence 20%
- Burglary 7%
- Vehicle related theft 14%
- Other thefts 33%
- Vandalism 26%

Source: British Crime Survey in Walker *et al* (2009)

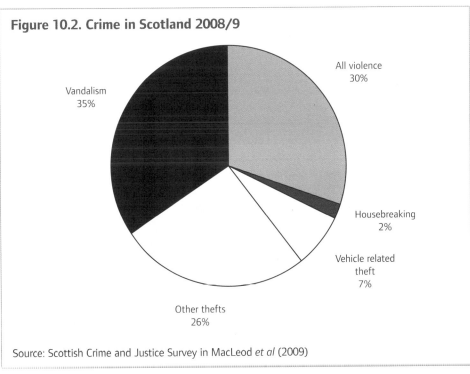

Figure 10.2. Crime in Scotland 2008/9

- All violence 30%
- Housebreaking 2%
- Vehicle related theft 7%
- Other thefts 26%
- Vandalism 35%

Source: Scottish Crime and Justice Survey in MacLeod *et al* (2009)

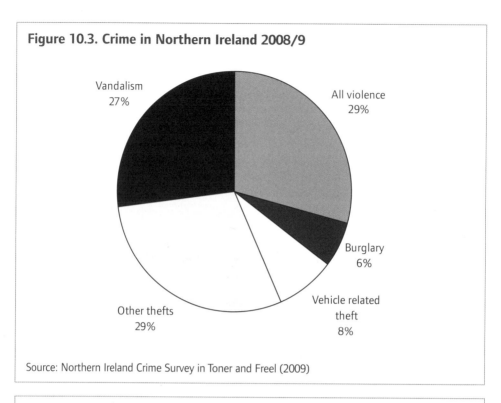

Figure 10.3. Crime in Northern Ireland 2008/9

Vandalism 27%

All violence 29%

Burglary 6%

Vehicle related theft 8%

Other thefts 29%

Source: Northern Ireland Crime Survey in Toner and Freel (2009)

Figure 10. 4. Crime in England and Wales, Scotland and Northern Ireland compared, 2008/9

Percentage of overall crime

- England and Wales 2008/09
- Scotland 2008/09
- Northern Ireland 2008/09

All violence   Burglary   Vehicle related theft   Other thefts   Vandalism

Sources: British Crime Survey, Scottish Crime and Justice Survey (and predecessor crime and victimisation surveys in Scotland) and Northern Ireland Crime Survey in Walker *et al* (2009), MacLeod *et al* (2009) and Toner and Freel (2009)

In this context, how has criminal justice policy diverged or converged across the UK since devolution? And what has been the effect, if any, on the crime rates of each jurisdiction?

Criminal justice policy across the UK

This section briefly sketches out some of the key characteristics of criminal justice policy in the devolved territories of the UK. In doing so it sketches out the similarities and differences, and highlights examples of policy innovation and learning.

England and Wales

In opposition, Tony Blair sought to distinguish his approach to 'law and order' both from the Conservatives' focus on enforcement and from the Labour party's traditional focus on crime's wider social causes, which had left it open to accusations of being 'soft on crime'. In an extremely successful act of political triangulation Blair labelled his approach 'tough on crime and tough on the causes of crime'. It is this basic approach that has characterised the Westminster government's philosophy towards tackling crime in England and Wales since 1997.

Of course, most of what was done to tackle crime's causes had little to do with the work of the criminal justice system. Economic growth and low unemployment are widely believed to be responsible for most of the fall in crime during the Blair years. Indeed, one government report argued that 80 per cent of the fall in crime over this period was due to economic growth (*The Sunday Times* 2006). Other initiatives, such as introducing the New Deal which helped lower unemployment and policies that reduced poverty levels in the UK, are also likely to have helped lower the crime rate.

Criminal justice policy delivered the 'tough on crime' component of Labour's strategy in England and Wales. Below we examine three key components of the Government's approach: investment in and reform to the police service, a tough penal policy and a coordinated effort to reduce 'anti-social behaviour'.

New Labour and the Old Bill

Labour massively increased the resources available to the police: spending on the police service in England and Wales increased by 19 per cent in real terms between 1997/8 and 2008/9 (Home Office 2009a). Most of this money was spent on raising the number of police officers, responding to a widespread public perception that there were too few police officers out on the beat in local neighbourhoods. Police numbers increased by 11 per cent or by 16,326 officers between 1997 and 2009, meaning that there are more police now than at any time in the past (Home Office 2009b, Solomon *et al* 2007).

In addition to these new constables, the Government recruited over 16,000 police community support officers (PCSOs), uniformed officers without the full powers of a warranted constable but who are able to conduct regular foot patrols and provide a visible reassurance to the public. PCSOs were first criticised as being 'policing on the cheap' by the Police Federation, but they have played a critical role in delivering the

Government's neighbourhood policing programme. There are now over 3,000 neighbourhood policing teams in England and Wales, made up of constables, PCSOs, local authority wardens and special constables. These teams are designed to provide policing that is visible, reduces fear of crime, engages actively with the public and works jointly with other local agencies.

Has any of this been effective? The early neighbourhood policing pilots (known as 'reassurance policing' pilots) showed impressive results. The pilot areas saw higher reductions than elsewhere in the number of reported victims, falls in some types of recorded crime, decreases in perceptions of anti-social behaviour, a rise in feelings of safety after dark and a big rise in public confidence in the police (Tuffin et al 2006). It is also true that since the rollout of neighbourhood policing nationwide, the proportion of people in England and Wales saying the police do a good or excellent job increased from 50 per cent in 2005/6 to 53 per cent in 2008/9 (Walker et al 2009).

Nevertheless, a recent nationwide assessment of the neighbourhood policing programme found that after two years it had yet to have a statistically significant impact on key factors like detection rates and public confidence (Mason 2009). This should be a disappointment given the amount of money spent, although the report notes that two years is too short a period to come to a fair assessment of the impact of the programme and that it is not yet fully developed in all areas. The report points to international evidence that this style of policing can have a significant impact over time.[3]

In addition to putting 'more bobbies on the beat', Labour introduced a system of centrally set targets that all police forces had to follow. This involved quantitative targets, such as increasing the number of offences brought to justice, and ceiling targets to keep specific recorded crimes under certain levels. Strong performance was rewarded through bonuses to some senior officers, increased status and funding – while poor performance could be sanctioned through Home Office interventions (Gash 2008).

This framework was certainly accompanied by falling crime rates (see below) although most experts argue that this was in the main due to wider social factors such as the growing economy during the 2000s (Pearce 2007, Solomon et al 2007). At the very least these targets focused police effort on tackling certain types of crime. However, in its 2008 policing green paper the Government itself recognised that this centralised approach had reached the limits of its useful life: policing targets set in Whitehall reduced the flexibility forces needed to respond to local people's concerns about crime. They have now been replaced by a single target to improve people's confidence in the ability of their local police to reduce crime (Home Office 2009b).

---

3. For example, the Chicago Alternative Policing Strategy in the United States, known for its beat meetings between police and members of the public and its problem-solving approach, led to significant increases in public confidence in the police and reduced worry about crime over a 10-year period (Mason 2009).

Punishment

The second main characteristic of criminal justice policy in England and Wales has been that it has become increasingly punitive. It has been estimated that Labour has introduced over 3600 new criminal offences since 1997, an average of over 320 a year (*The Daily Telegraph* 2008).

The Government gave the police new summary powers to punish low-level disorder through on-the-spot fines: after 2004 the number of Penalty Notices for Disorder issued rose from 63,639 to 176,200 in 2008 (Hansard, 26 January 2009, Ministry of Justice 2008). Most of these were for drunk and disorderly behaviour, minor shoplifting and causing harassment, alarm or distress.

The judicial process has been speeded up in some areas: Labour set targets to ensure that the courts dealt with persistent young offenders more quickly, delivering a reduction in the amount of time between arrest and sentence from 142 days in 1997 to 72 days in 2006 (Solomon *et al* 2007).

The sentences passed down by the courts have become tougher, with a 40 per cent rise in the use of custodial sentences between 1997 and 2007 (Centre for Social Justice 2009). Custodial sentences in England and Wales have become longer: the average sentence length increased from 14.7 months in 1995 to 16.8 in 2005. The number of people serving sentences of over 12 months rose 70 per cent from 32,000 in 1995 to 54,000 by 2005 (House of Commons Justice Committee 2008). The average length of sentences handed down by magistrates courts for robbery rose from 3.7 months in 1997 to 8.4 months by 2009. In the crown courts immediate custodial sentences for burglary increased by one month and drugs offences by five months over the same period (Centre for Social Justice 2009).

The increased use of custodial sentences and the greater length of prison sentences have not been due to a deliberate policy intervention by government (Pearce 2007). Rather they reflect an increasingly punitive climate of public opinion, very likely intensified through sensationalist media reporting of crime, and consequent pressure on both politicians and the courts to act tough. In fact, while the Government has made it clear that it expects only serious and violent offenders to be sent to prison, the courts in England and Wales remain reluctant to use alternative non-custodial sanctions such as community orders. The House of Commons Justice Committee found that this was because the courts do not feel the public have confidence in community sentences, but also because they are not sufficiently resourced so that the courts can be sure that they will be effectively implemented (House of Commons Justice Committee 2009).

The consequence of all this is a massive expansion in the prison population, leading to serious overcrowding. The prison population in England and Wales increased from 61,000 in 1997 to over 84,000 in 2009, with estimates indicating that it will reach 100,000 by 2013 (Pearce 2007, *The Independent* 2009). England and Wales have the second highest imprisonment rate in Western Europe, with 149 prisoners for every 100,000 people, compared to the European Union average of 102 per 100,000 (although that is in the context of one of the highest crime rates) (Centre for Social Justice 2009). This is despite the fact that most experts believe that prison is an ineffective way of reducing crime, with reoffending rates running at 60 per cent for ex-offenders within two years of leaving prison (*The Independent* 2008).

Anti-social behaviour
There was unquestionably growing public concern over what has been termed 'anti-social behaviour' during this period. In response the Government introduced a number of new legal measures designed to control low-level disorder. These include the famous anti-social behaviour orders (ASBOs) to control undesirable behaviours, which if breached can result in a prison sentence. They also include parenting orders, late night curfews, group dispersal orders and crack house closure orders (Home Office 2007). The programme has had an impact: public perceptions of anti-social behaviour since the inception of this programme are that it has decreased: 21 per cent of people were concerned about high levels of anti-social behaviour in 2002/3, falling to 17 per cent in 2008/9 (Walker *et al* 2009).

However, critics argue that ASBOs have become a motor for youth incarceration and criminalisation. Between 2000 and 2007 a total of 14,868 ASBOs were imposed in England and Wales, of which 40 per cent (6,028) were on persons aged between 10 and 17 years old. The breach rate for ASBOs imposed on under-18s across that whole period was 64 per cent, of which 41 per cent resulted in a custodial sentence, supporting the view that the legislation is fast-tracking young people into the criminal justice system (Home Office 2009). Critics have argued that these enforcement measures ignore the real causes of youth offending and misbehaviour, which lie in poor parenting, dysfunctional households and a lack of alternative, structured youth activities (Margo *et al* 2006).

In England and Wales, then, we have an approach characterised by a massive investment in the criminal justice agencies (especially the police) and a tough approach to punishing offenders and clamping down on anti-social behaviour, particularly that committed by young people.

Scotland
Scotland has for centuries had its own system of law and justice, pre-dating the Act of Union. There are substantial differences between Scots and English law in areas such as property law, criminal law, trusts law and family law. Some of the most significant differences in criminal law include a different age of criminal responsibility, the fact that the accused has no right to choose a judge or a jury trial in Scotland and the fact that judges and juries have a third option of 'not proven', which does not exist in English law. Prior to devolution criminal justice was therefore an area in which the Scottish Office and the relevant policy communities in Scotland had long adopted a distinctive approach to that taken in England and Wales.

One can broadly distinguish between three phases of criminal justice policy since devolution in Scotland, which correspond with the different political administrations during this period:

- *The first Parliament, 1999–2003:* during this period the Labour and Liberal Democrat coalition maintained a policy of continuity with the approach to criminal justice long adopted in Scotland, taking a less activist – critics might say less authoritarian – approach to these issues than the government in England and Wales. This approach may in part be due to the fact that the Liberal Democrats held the Justice Ministry.

- *The second Parliament, 2003–2007:* in this period there was greater convergence between the approaches taken in Scotland and in England and Wales. The First Minister Jack McConnell made tackling crime a key priority and Labour took control of the Justice Ministry for the first time. There was a flagship Anti-Social Behaviour Act in 2004, which heralded a tougher new approach to the issue, bringing in ASBOs for under-18s, crack house closure orders and dispersal orders. This was followed by legislation to clarify the system of early release from prison, introduce football banning orders, extend electronic tagging of prisoners out on licence and increase the penalties for knife crime.

- *The third Parliament 2007– :* the election of the SNP administration led to some significant changes in criminal justice policy, meaning that this area of policy has started to diverge once more from the approach taken in London. Although there is considerable continuity with the approach of the previous administration – in particular, wanting to increase the numbers of police officers out on the beat – there have also been some substantive changes of direction. The SNP plans to raise the age of criminal responsibility from 8 to 12 (it is 10 in England, Wales and Northern Ireland), replace short-term custodial sentences with community sentences and curtail the use of ASBOs.

In what follows we highlight some of the key areas of divergence and convergence between criminal justice policy in Scotland and that in England and Wales since 1999.

Policing

Police officer numbers have risen in Scotland, as in England and Wales: from 15,400 in 2003 to an historic high of 17,048 in 2009 (Scottish Government 2009). The SNP made recruiting a further 1,000 officers a manifesto pledge, although it is one it has struggled to deliver.

However, as Figure 10.5 demonstrates, although police spending has risen since devolution, Scotland continues to spend less of its resources on policing than the other parts of the UK. An independent analysis of expenditure figures on key public services in Scotland (commissioned by the Scottish Police Federation) found that police spending per capita is the lowest in Scotland of all the nations of the UK with England spending 20 per cent more, and Wales 13 per cent more (2006–7 figures). Northern Ireland spends 122 per cent more than Scotland for obvious reasons. Police expenditure in the UK as a whole is 21 per cent higher than in Scotland – despite the fact that overall public spending per head is significantly higher in Scotland than in the rest of the UK (Midwinter 2007, McClean *et al* 2008).

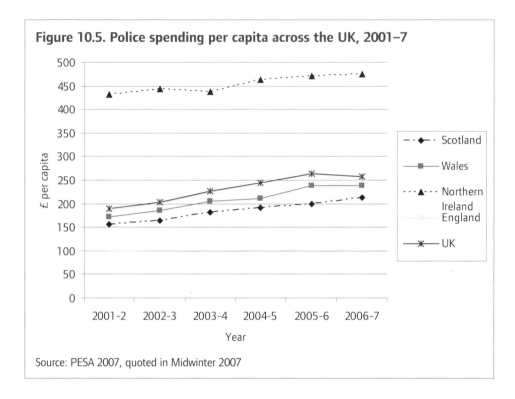

Figure 10.5. Police spending per capita across the UK, 2001–7

Source: PESA 2007, quoted in Midwinter 2007

Moreover, this gap in police spending across the union has widened over time: whereas Scotland was spending £33 per head less than the UK average on policing in 2001–2, by 2006 it was spending £44 per head less than the rest of the country. Policing has received less of a priority compared with other services in Scotland: although Midwinter found that police spending has grown at 3.4 per cent a year in the Scottish budget, that compares to 5.6 per cent a year for all services (Midwinter 2007).

A further difference between Scotland and the other two UK jurisdictions is the absence of a national neighbourhood or community policing strategy. This is not to say that there is no community policing in Scotland – clearly there has been for decades. But Her Majesty's Chief Inspector of Constabulary Scotland found in a 2004 report that 'a lack of any consistent or standardised approach to community policing is evident, largely due to the continuing challenge of meeting reactive resource and operational demands' (HMICS 2004). This has since been reiterated by a report from the Scottish Parliament's Justice Committee which concluded: 'while in some forces community policing is at the core of everything the police do, the priority accorded to community policing varies from force to force' (Scottish Parliament Justice Committee 2008). The Committee opposed rolling out a uniform model as has occurred south of the border, but did call for the Scottish Government to push all forces to develop proactive community policing strategies.

One final related difference between Scotland and England and Wales, is that police community support officers have not been adopted north of the border. Local authority wardens to help the police patrol and engage with communities have been rolled out, however.

Youth offending

Scotland has long had a less punitive approach to youth offending. The Social Work (Scotland) Act of 1968 introduced the innovative Children's Hearings system which meant that children's welfare hearings took over from the courts responsibility for dealing with children and young people under 16 who commit offences or are in need of care and protection (Youth Justice Scotland 2008).

The paramount concern during these hearings is the welfare of the child, rather than punishment for an offence – a completely different philosophy to that taken to youth offending south of the border. Local councils run the system, with decisions being made by a panel of trained community volunteers. If the panel members decide that compulsory supervision is required, in most cases this will entail the child continuing to live at home under the supervision of a social worker. In others cases, they may be directed to live away from home with relatives of foster parents or in a local authority children's home or secure accommodation. Children under 16 are only considered for prosecution in court for serious offences such as murder, an assault that puts a life in danger or very serious road traffic offences.

The 2004 Antisocial Behaviour (Scotland) Act – heralding a so-called 'war on neds' – did introduce a 'tougher' approach to youth offending. This was a case of policy convergence with Westminster, although one motivated by public and political concern in Scotland about youth crime and disorder – in particular in the deprived urban areas that make up Scottish Labour's heartlands. The Act required local authorities to adopt anti-social behaviour strategies, introduced ASBOs for under-16s (unlike in England and Wales, until then an ASBO could only be imposed on someone over 16), brought in dispersal orders and gave the police powers to close down 'crack dens' and other premises where anti-social behaviour has been continuously taking place.

However, even though the 2004 Act did mark a 'tougher' turn in Scottish youth offending policy, it remained more liberal than the anti-social behaviour legislation south of the border. Importantly, unlike in England and Wales, the breach of an ASBO, while a criminal offence, cannot lead to a prison sentence in Scotland. More importantly, even after the introduction of the Act, hardly any ASBOs have been imposed on children: between 2004 and 2007 only six ASBOs were granted against under-16s in the Scottish courts, which is in stark contrast to the situation south of the border where 40 per cent of the ASBOs granted between 2000 and 2007 were on children.

The arrival of the SNP in power marked a return to Scotland's traditional welfare-oriented approach to youth offending – although, perhaps conscious of public demand for action on crime, the administration has not sought to repeal the 2004 Act. The Government has agreed with the Convention of Scottish Local Authorities (COSLA) updated guidance which emphasises that ASBOs should only be used as a last resort, and only with appropriate supportive packages in place.

Penal reform

A further key area of policy divergence is in sentencing policy, which has become a significant political hot potato since the SNP came to power. Scotland faces a similar prisons crisis to England and Wales: the prison population in Scotland currently stands at around 8,100, many more than the estate was built to accommodate – and this is estimated to rise to 9,600 by 2018/19 (Scottish Government 2010).

The recent rise in numbers is largely down to rising numbers of people imprisoned for less than four years. These have increased from approximately 2,600 in 2007 to 3,000 in 2008, with the rate of increase accelerating during 2008 and 2009 to reach 3,500 (Scottish Government 2010).

This has led to a wide-ranging debate about sentencing policy, with the previous Labour-Liberal Democrat coalition establishing a Sentencing Commission. The Commission recommended that a clear set of national sentencing guidelines should be established to determine the balance between custodial and non-custodial sentences. The Government is setting up the Scottish Sentencing Guidelines Council to do just this.

More radically, the nationalist administration has put forward legislation to replace prison sentences of under six months with a set of 'tough' community sentences. These would include a new Community Payback Sentence, to enable the court to impose one or more of a range of requirements on the offender, including unpaid work, supervision, alcohol or drug interventions or a requirement to take part in a programme to address offending behaviour.[4] This issue has provoked furious debate – in particular Labour and the Conservatives have argued that the proposals will make Scotland a 'soft touch' and that it will mean that those convicted of knife crime will no longer go to prison.[5]

On the question of penal policy there is then now a clear divergence between Edinburgh and Westminster: the Scottish government has explicitly stated that it believes that prison is ineffective at rehabilitation and that community-based

---

4. It should be noted that these options are also available in England and Wales under their system of community orders – the major difference in Scotland is the action to discourage short-term prison sentences by law.
5. The legislation is still before Parliament at the time of writing.

alternatives should be actively pushed on the courts. Despite provisions for community justice being in place south of the border they remain under-resourced and there is no comparable legislative action to reduce the use of short-term custodial sentences.

Alcohol-related crime

A final area of innovation in Scotland is in relation to alcohol misuse – relevant in this chapter because alcohol is a cause of crime, especially violent crime. To put this into some context, sales data for the year 2007 estimate that Scots over the age of 16 drank, on average, the equivalent of almost 23 units of alcohol per week, compared with just over 19 units in England and Wales (Scottish Government 2009c). Scotland is eighth in the world for alcohol consumption per head of population (Alcohol Focus Scotland 2008).

This is very likely to affect Scotland's crime rate: violent crime as measured by the Scottish Crime and Justice Survey (SCJS) makes up a higher proportion of overall crime in Scotland than it does in England and Wales (see Figures 10.1–4 above). And we know that for 58 per cent of violent crime measured by the SCJS 2008/9, victims said the offender(s) were under the influence of alcohol. This was a significantly higher proportion than found in the BCS in England and Wales in 2008/9, where victims reported that the offender(s) were under the influence of alcohol in 47 per cent of violent crime.

The SNP government has responded to this by adopting an aggressive alcohol-reduction strategy, with an Alcohol Bill currently before Parliament. This contains many similar measures to those being proposed by the Home Office in Westminster, in particular a clampdown on irresponsible discounts and promotions. The most radical proposal in the bill is to set a minimum price for a unit of alcohol to stop strong drink being sold at very low prices. This move, vociferously opposed by the drinks industry, prompted the Chief Medical Officer for England and Wales Sir Liam Donaldson to call for a similar reform south of the border. However, the Prime Minister quickly ruled out minimum pricing, arguing that it would also punish moderate drinkers on low incomes.

Northern Ireland

This section is inevitably rather different from the previous two simply because so much of what might be discussed under the heading of 'criminal justice policy' in Northern Ireland concerns the gradual implementation of the Good Friday Agreement. This includes, for example, the establishment of a new cross-community police service, the decommissioning of paramilitary weapons, the release of prisoners, and the devolution (still pending at the time of writing) of crime and justice powers from Westminster to the Northern Ireland Assembly.

Rather than go over that familiar terrain, this section focuses on those aspects of criminal justice policy where there are clear comparisons to be made with policy in England, Scotland and Wales – and lessons to be learned.

Community policing

One of the most important components of the Good Friday Agreement was the establishment of a new cross-community and non-sectarian police force. The 1999 Patten Report called for the establishment of the Police Service of Northern Ireland (PSNI), to replace the Royal Ulster Constabulary. The new police service began operations in November 2001, although Sinn Fein refused to recognise it or join the governing Policing Board until all of Patten's recommendations were implemented. Following the St Andrew's Agreement of 2006, Sinn Fein voted to recognise the PSNI in 2007 and its Members of the Legislative Assembly (MLAs) have now taken their seats on the policing board.

The purpose behind the establishment of the PSNI was to create a legitimate cross-community police service. So, the symbols of the service are neutral between the different religious communities. Recruitment has been undertaken on a 50 per cent Catholic and 50 per cent Protestant basis, which has led to an increase in the number of Catholic police officers from just 8 per cent in 1999 to 26 per cent in 2009 (*The Guardian* 2009).

In the Northern Ireland context police/community relations are clearly crucial, not just for reducing crime, but for underpinning the stability and legitimacy of the state. The PSNI has now adopted an extensive neighbourhood policing strategy similar in approach to that implemented in England and Wales. Each policing district is divided into a number of small geographic areas, which are allocated a dedicated team of police officers. Each neighbourhood is to set up a consultative forum through which residents can agree local priorities with the police. Where the programme differs from England and Wales is that it is not currently supplemented by Police Community Support Officers (PCSOs). This is not because of any ideological opposition and indeed the policing board had planned to start recruiting PCSOs, but a funding shortfall led to the plans being dropped.

Police accountability

The accountability of the Chief Constable to the Policing Board is arguably much clearer in Northern Ireland than in England and Wales. In England and Wales a chief constable is said to be 'operationally independent' – although this is a long-standing constitutional convention and has never been fully defined in law. As a result there have been a series of recent controversies regarding the politicisation of the police, most prominently London Mayor Boris Johnson's alleged attempt to take greater political control of the Met.

By contrast, in Northern Ireland the Patten Commission codified the different roles and responsibilities of the police, on the one hand, and politicians, on the other. The report argued, 'no public official, including a chief of police, can be said to be "independent"' and that they need to be held to account for their decisions. Rather, chief constables should have "operational responsibility", being solely responsible for decisions to enforce the law in particular cases' (Independent Commission on Policing for Northern Ireland 1999). However, the chief constable is then answerable for their decisions afterwards to the Northern Ireland Policing Board. The Policing Board, made up of elected and appointed members, sets the budget and the three to five year strategic priorities for the police service. Politicians in England and Wales might do well to lay out in similarly clear terms the different roles and responsibilities of elected politicians and police officers.

A declining prison population
Northern Ireland's prisons system has not been under the same sort of pressures as its counterparts in the rest of the UK. Reflecting its lower crime rate, Northern Ireland has a much lower prison population per capita than the other parts of the union. Moreover, rather than experiencing a growth of prison over-crowding, the province's prison population grew smaller in the aftermath of the Good Friday Agreement as many paramilitary prisoners were released. Indeed one of the most controversial questions discussed in the Northern Ireland Assembly has been over what to do with vacant prison sites such as the Maze prison, closed in 2000.

The prison population increased very rapidly from an annual average of 686 in 1967 to a high of 2,946 in 1978. The next two decades were characterised by a generally declining trend, which was accelerated further from 1998, following the Good Friday Agreement. A low of 910 prisoners was reached in 2001, followed by an increase bringing the prison population up to 1,379 in February 2010 (Amelin and O'Loan 2005).

Despite this comparative lack of pressure on the system, the province has experimented in some interesting penal reforms in recent years.

Restorative justice
Northern Ireland's youth justice system was reformed in the aftermath of the Good Friday Agreement. The most important element of that reform was the introduction of restorative justice into the heart of the youth justice system. The Restorative Justice Consortium says that 'Restorative Justice (RJ) processes give victims the chance to tell offenders the real impact of their crime, to get answers to their questions and to receive an apology. It gives the offenders the chance to understand the real impact of what they've done and to do something to repair the harm. RJ holds offenders to account for what they have done, personally and directly, and helps victims to get on with their lives' (Restorative Justice Consortium 2010).

A Youth Conference Service was introduced which organises 'youth conferences' at which the victim and victim's supporters (or representatives) are brought together with the offender and offender's supporters in a meeting facilitated by professionals. The aim of the conference is to discuss the offence and its repercussions, and to agree on an action plan for the offender. Youth conferences are fully integrated within the criminal justice process: a young person can be referred for a conference either before conviction (after an admission of guilt to a prosecutor) or after conviction – and they have been very effective. A recent report from the Prison Reform Trust found that in 2006 youth conferencing led to a one year reoffending rate of just 37.7 per cent, compared to 52.1 per cent from community-based sanctions and 70.7 per cent for custodial sentences (Jacobson and Gibbs 2009).

Restorative justice schemes have also been operated in working class communities, run in part by former loyalist and republican paramilitaries. Forms of paramilitary self-policing continued for years after the Good Friday Agreement. An American group, Atlantic Philanthropies, provided the finance to effectively co-opt this informal system of justice into the democratic system and reform it to protect the rights of the accused and make it more open and transparent.

The loyalist programme Northern Ireland Alternatives has worked intensively with young people accused of crime or anti-social behaviour including elements such as mediation between victims and offenders, reparation and purposeful activity to change offending behaviour. The Republican-based project Community Restorative Justice Ireland operates in over a dozen locations. Volunteers engage with problems or disputes brought to them by members of the public or by other agencies. They organise mediation sessions where alleged perpetrators, direct victims and community representatives try to work out solutions.

The Northern Ireland Office has deemed the projects a success and is now formally accrediting and financing schemes provided they cooperate with the wider criminal justice system and include safeguards to protect the rights of the accused. Partly building on its success in Northern Ireland the Prison Reform Trust is now pushing for the role of restorative justice to be expanded in the criminal justice system in England and Wales (BBC News Online 2009).

Outcomes

Having surveyed the differences in approach taken across the UK we can ask: has any of this led to differences in outcomes? This is complicated terrain given that most observers believe the operation of the criminal justice system exerts a relatively small influence on the crime rate. The Prime Minister's Strategy Unit estimated that 80 per cent of the fall in crime in England and Wales in the Blair years was due to economic and social factors (*The Sunday Times* 2006). So that would lead us to conclude that just 20 per cent of the fall in overall crime rates is due to the work of the criminal justice agencies. If there are differences between the crime trends between the different nations, this may be because of differences in the drivers behind crime, or differences in the approach of the criminal justice agencies.

In what follows we look at the crime survey data for England and Wales, Scotland and Northern Ireland to assess any differences in their crime trends since devolution.

Figure 10.6 shows trends in the percentage of people who were victims of crime in the different nations, over time. In England and Wales crime rose steadily from 1981 to reach a peak of 40 per cent in 1995, then falling fairly steadily to just 23.4 per cent in 2008/9, well below its 1981 level. Similarly, crime has fallen consistently in Northern Ireland since 1998, from 23 per cent to just 13.4 per cent today.

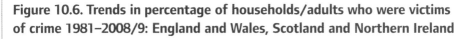

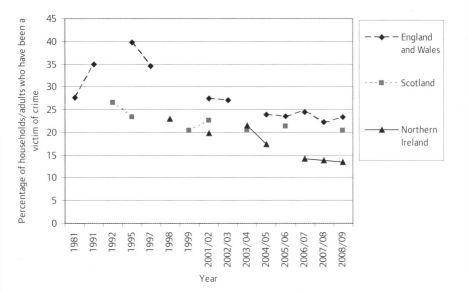

Figure 10.6. Trends in percentage of households/adults who were victims of crime 1981–2008/9: England and Wales, Scotland and Northern Ireland

Sources: British Crime Survey, Scottish Crime and Justice Survey (and predecessor crime and victimisation surveys in Scotland) and Northern Ireland Crime Survey in Walker *et al* (2009), MacLeod *et al* (2009) and Toner and Freel (2009)

The main contrast is with Scotland: although crime in Scotland is 6.2 percentage points lower than it was in 1992, unlike the rest of the UK the Scottish crime rate has not changed much since devolution in 1999. In fact, the crime rate in 2008/9 was almost exactly the same as in 1999.

Figure 10.7 helps shed some light on this issue by showing trends in different types of crime since devolution. Taking the closest crime victimisation survey to devolution as the benchmark it shows that whereas crime fell by 11.2 percentage points in England and Wales and by 9.2 percentage points in Northern Ireland, it remained almost the same in Scotland (increasing by a statistically insignificant 0.1 percentage points).

Turning to different types of crime we find that while vandalism fell by 0.6 percentage points in England and by 1.1 percentage points in Northern Ireland, it rose by 2.9 percentage points in Scotland. Scotland also saw increases in 'other household thefts', which include thefts from garages and outside areas, and in the number of assaults, despite falls in these types of crimes in the rest of the UK. Burglary or housebreaking, and vehicle theft, fell across all parts of the UK during this period.

We should note that the 2008/9 phase of the Scottish survey used a different methodology, asking people on a rolling basis to recall crimes 'in the last 12 months' rather than for a fixed period. This cannot be discounted as a possible explanation for

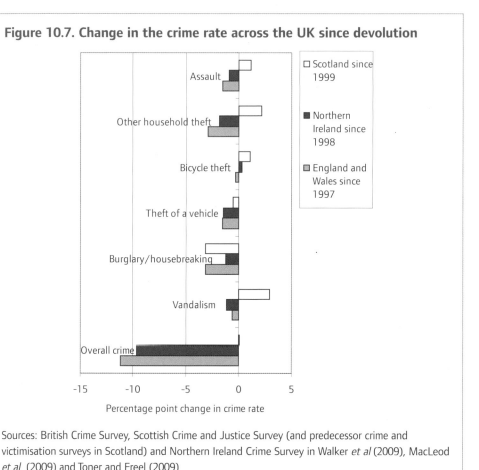

Figure 10.7. Change in the crime rate across the UK since devolution

Sources: British Crime Survey, Scottish Crime and Justice Survey (and predecessor crime and victimisation surveys in Scotland) and Northern Ireland Crime Survey in Walker *et al* (2009), MacLeod *et al* (2009) and Toner and Freel (2009)

change. Nevertheless the latest figures are largely consistent with the trends identified in the previous Scottish crime surveys (see MacLeod *et al* 2009).[6]

It is important to note that the results of the SCJS contrast with the overall trends for police recorded crime in Scotland, which shows that crime is lower now than it was at the time of devolution. The total number of crimes reported to the police fell from 435,481 in 1999–2000 to 414,214 in 2003–4. They then rose with the introduction of a new recording standard in 2004–5 to 438,121 but then fell to 377,433 in 2008–9 (Scottish Government 2009). Still, criminologists generally prefer victimisation surveys for measuring crime overall, given that they cover the vast swathe of crimes that are not reported to the police.

A final group of outcomes are public attitudes: how has public confidence in the criminal justice system changed since devolution? Have the various policy measures

6. The exception is vandalism, which had been declining in the last two surveys but which shows a large spike in the latest 2008/9 figures (MacLeod *et al* 2009).

satisfied the public? From the victimisation surveys, we only have data from the BCS and the SCJS. First, in terms of perceptions of anti-social behaviour in England and Wales, policy may have had some effect: the proportion of people saying that there is a high level of anti-social behaviour in their area fell from 21 per cent in 2002/3 to 17 per cent in 2008/9 (Walker et al 2009). Similarly, in Scotland the proportion believing that anti-social behaviour is 'very' or 'fairly' common also decreased slightly, from 48 per cent in 2005/6 to 46 per cent in 2008/9 (MacLeod et al 2009).

Second, across the UK, trends in worrying about particular types of crime have improved. In England and Wales, the proportion of people with a high level of worry about burglary declined from 19 per cent in 1998 to 11 per cent in 2008/9, about car crime from 22 to 12 per cent and about violent crime from 25 to 14 per cent (Walker et al 2009). In Scotland, the proportion 'very' or 'fairly' worried about having their home broken into declined from 45 per cent in 2000 to 35 per cent in 2008/9 and about having your car or vehicle stolen from 31 to 28 per cent. Interestingly, given the reported increase in assaults in Scotland, the proportion of people in Scotland fearing that they will be physically assaulted in the street has not really declined, going from 32 per cent in 2000 to 31 per cent in 2008/09 (MacLeod et al 2009).

Finally, perceptions of the criminal justice system in England and Wales have improved. In England and Wales the proportion of people saying that the local police do a good or excellent job has seen a slight increase from 50 per cent in 2005/6 to 53 per cent in 2008/9. Overall confidence in the police has improved, from 63 per cent in 2005/6 to 67 per cent in 2008/9. Interestingly, following the adoption of neighbourhood policing the proportion saying that the police 'are dealing with things that matter to the local community' rose from 49 to 54 per cent over the same period. As for the wider criminal justice system, although we do not have long-term trend data, we should note that only 38 per cent thought the criminal justice system as a whole was effective (Walker et al 2009).

We do not have data over time for Scotland, but it is worth noting that a relatively high proportion (53 per cent) thought that the criminal justice system was effective at bringing people to justice and 61 per cent felt the police in their area did a good or very good job – significantly higher than the 53 per cent saying so in England and Wales (MacLeod et al 2009).

What are we to make of all this? England, Wales and Northern Ireland appear to follow the international trend during the last decade of falling crime rates, especially in relation to the 'volume crimes' like burglary, minor violent offences and car crime. The standard explanation for this cross-national trend was that the global economy was expanding, eating away at the social drivers of crime. Scotland, by contrast, records increases in vandalism, some forms of household theft and assaults – and overall its crime rate as measured by victimisation surveys stayed fairly constant.

This divergence requires further research – and we can only speculate here. One explanation might be that Scotland's economy performed less well than the rest of the UK during this period. It is true that Scotland's trend of growth as measured by GDP generally lagged behind the overall UK rate of growth, but the Scottish economy grew and unemployment fell continually from devolution until 2008, which should rule out this explanation (see Bell, this volume).

Another hypothesis would be that increases in crimes like vandalism and assault, both linked with alcohol misuse, were driven by Scotland's relatively greater problem with excessive alcohol consumption (discussed above). We know from the victimisation surveys that victims of violent crime in Scotland are much more likely to say that the perpetrator had been drinking when the crime took place than in England and Wales. If so this lends greater support to the Scottish Government's much more proactive strategy to reduce alcohol misuse.

Two final hypotheses relate to the criminal justice system itself. Might it be that Scotland's relatively lower rate of investment in the police service had an impact? Some would dispute that spending on the police has any significant impact on crime rates, but the divergence in spending is notable (Solomon *et al* 2007). Finally, might it be that Scotland was not 'tough' enough on crime? Many would contest this, given the large body of evidence that tougher penalties and greater use of custody are largely ineffective at reducing crime – for example, recidivism rates are generally lower from community penalties than from custodial sentences. It is not possible to resolve this question here, but clearly the divergence in crime patterns between Scotland and the rest of the union warrants further investigation.

Conclusion
This chapter has set out where criminal justice policy diverged between the different parts of the union following devolution. It has also examined differences in crime rates across the different nations over this period. It found that there were notable differences in approach, some of which reflected long-standing philosophical approaches to questions of crime and punishment in different countries.

It is not clear if the overall approaches to criminal justice policy in the different countries had a differential impact on the crime rate in those countries. This is a question that demands further research.

What is clear, however, is that policymakers in different parts of the UK would do well to learn from the approaches taken by their near neighbours. For example, we have seen how restorative justice projects have had greater success than custodial sentences at reducing reoffending in Northern Ireland. In another example, lessons should be learnt from the rollout of neighbourhood policing in England and Wales, which appears to have improved satisfaction with the police service. Finally, Scotland's relatively radical policies to reduce the use of short-term prison sentences and to reduce excessive alcohol consumption will have clear lessons for the rest of the union. Devolution has opened the prospect for the cross-fertilisation of policy ideas and cross-national learning from different practices. Policymakers would do well to make the best use of that opportunity.

References

Alcohol Focus Scotland (2008) Web page at www.alcohol-focus-scotland.org.uk/alcohol_information/facts_amp_statistics/

Amelin K and O'Loan C (2005) 'Northern Ireland Prison Population Projections 2005 –2009', *Research and Statistical Bulletin 12/2005*. Belfast: Northern Ireland Office

BBC News Online (2009) 'Victim meetings "cut" youth crime', 29 October. http://news.bbc.co.uk/1/hi/uk/8328529.stm.

Centre for Social Justice (2009) *Locked Up Potential: A Strategy for Reforming Prisons and Rehabilitating Prisoners.* London: Centre for Social Justice

Daily Telegraph (2008) 'Labour has created 3,600 new offences since 1997', 29 October. www.telegraph.co.uk/news/uknews/2679148/Labour-has-created-3600-new-offences-since-1997.html.

Gash T (2008) *The New Bill. Modernising the Police Workforce.* London: ippr. www.ippr.org.uk/publicationsandreports/publication.asp?id=586

Guardian (2009) 'Catholics still joining Northern Ireland police force despite attacks, says minister', 31 March. www.guardian.co.uk/uk/2009/mar/31/northern-ireland-police-force-recruiting-catholics

Hansard (2009) 'Number of Penalty Notices for Disorder issued to all persons aged 16 and over, by outcome, England and Wales 2004 – 07', 26 January. www.publications.parliament.uk/pa/cm200809/cmhansrd/cm090126/text/90126w0042.htm

Her Majesty's Inspectorate of Constabulary in Scotland (2004) *Local Connections – Policing within the community* Edinburgh: HMICS

Home Office (2009a) *Protecting the Public. Supporting the police to succeed.* London: Home Office

Home Office (2009b) 'Police Service Strength' *Police Service Statistical Bulletin 13/09* London: Home Office

Ipsos Mori (2009) *Issues facing Britain: Long-term trends.* www.ipsos-mori.com/Assets/Images/Polls/trend-issues-facing-britain-current-top-5.png

Home Office (2009c) 'Persons proved in court to have breached their ASBO at least once between 1 June 2000 and 31 December 2007 by age group and CJS area'. www.crimereduction.homeoffice.gov.uk/asbos/asbos2.htm

Home Office (2007) *Cutting Crime – a new partnership.* London: Home Office

House of Commons Justice Committee (2008) *Towards Effective Sentencing. Fifth Report of Session 2007-2008.* London: The Stationery Office

Independent (2008) 'Re-offending rates rise as the prison population expands', 20 July. www.independent.co.uk/news/uk/crime/reoffending-rates-rise-as-the-prison-population-expands-872411.html

Independent Commission on Policing for Northern Ireland (1999) *A New Beginning: Policing in Northern Ireland.* Belfast: Independent Commission on Policing for Northern Ireland

Jacobson J and P Gibbs (2009) *Out of Trouble. Making Amends: restorative youth justice in Northern Ireland.* London: Prison Reform Trust

McLean I, Lodge G and Schmuecker K (2008) *Fair Shares? Barnett and the politics of public expenditure.* London: ippr. www.ippr.org.uk/publicationsandreports/publication.asp?id=619

MacLeod P, Page L, Kinver A and Iliasov A (2009) *2008/09 Scottish Crime and Justice Survey: First Findings.* Edinburgh: Scottish Government Social Research

Margo J and Dixon M with Pearce N and Reed H (2006) *Freedom's Orphans. Raising youth in a changing world.* London: ippr

Mason M (2009) *Findings from the second year of the national Neighbourhood Policing Programme evaluation.* London: Home Office

Midwinter A (2007) *Police Funding In Scotland: A Review Of Trends In The Post-Devolution Period.* Edinburgh: Scottish Police Federation

Ministry of Justice (2009) 'Number of Penalty Notices for Disorder issued to offenders aged 16 and above by offence, 2004 – 2008'. www.justice.gov.uk/publications/docs/criminal-stats-2008-chapter-2.xls.

Pearce N (2007) 'Crime and Punishment. A New Home Office Agenda' in N Pearce and J Margo (eds) *Politics for a New Generation. The Progressive Moment* Basingstoke: Palgrave Macmillan

Restorative Justice Consortium (2010) 'What is Restorative Justice?' www.restorativejustice.org.uk/?What_is_Restorative_Justice%3F

Scottish Government (2010) 'Statistical Release: Crime and Justice Series. Scottish prison population projections: 2009-10 to 2018-19'. www.scotland.gov.uk/Publications/2010/01/21104150/0

Scottish Government (2009a) *Statistical Bulletin Crime and Justice Series: Recorded Crime in Scotland, 2008-09.* www.scotland.gov.uk/Publications/2009/09/28155153/26

Scottish Government (2009b) 'Police officer numbers reach record high'. www.scotland.gov.uk/News/Releases/2009/06/09095519

Scottish Government (2009c) 'Changing Scotland's Drinking Culture'. www.scotland.gov.uk/Topics/Health/health/Alcohol/culture

Scottish Parliament Justice Committee (2008) *Report on Inquiry into Community Policing.* Edinburgh: Scottish Parliament. www.scottish.parliament.uk/s3/committees/justice/reports-08/jur08-10.htm#11

Solomon E, Eades C, Garside R, and Rutherford M (2007) *Ten Years of Criminal Justice Under Labour. An independent audit.* London: the Centre for Crime and Justice Studies

Sunday Times (2006) 'Secret memo warns Blair of crime wave', 24 December. www.timesonline.co.uk/tol/news/uk/article1264341.ece

Toner S and Freel R (2009) *Experience of Crime: Findings from the 2008/09 Northern Ireland Crime Survey. Research and Statistical Bulletin 7/2009,* November

Tuffin R, Morris J, Kershaw C and Moon D (2006) *An Evaluation of the Impact of the National Reassurance Policing Programme* London: Home Office

Walker A, Flatley J, Kershaw C and Moon D (2009) *Crime in England and Wales 2008/09: Volume 1, Findings from the British Crime Survey and police recorded crime* London: Home Office

Youth Justice Scotland (2008) *Services for Young People Who Offend.* www.youthjusticescotland.gov.uk/theme.asp?ID=13

11. Devolution and housing

Steve Wilcox

This chapter explores the impact of the 1999 devolution settlement on the operation of key aspects of housing policies in the four nations of the UK over the decade to 2009. In all four nations there have been extensive reviews of housing policy in this period. However, the chapter focuses on the key of aspects of housing policy for which it is possible to examine evidence on the substantive outcomes of the distinctive policies adopted by the four nations.

Housing in the 1999 devolution settlement

Housing is itself a wholly devolved function under the devolution settlements for Scotland, Wales and Northern Ireland (each of which has a distinctive constitutional structure). However, its pursuit by the devolved administrations is hedged around by a number of related functions and policies that continue to be operated by the UK Government.

Of the continuing UK-wide functions, perhaps the most significant is the regulation of mortgage lenders. In addition, provisions for housing and related welfare benefits are made for Great Britain as a whole through the Department for Work and Pensions (DWP). In formal terms welfare benefits are a devolved function for the Northern Ireland Assembly, but in practice there is a 'concordat' whereby welfare benefits are operated within Northern Ireland in essentially the same way as applies throughout Great Britain.

More generally, the devolved administrations have to operate within the fiscal rules and financial provisions for overall departmental budgets set by HM Treasury. While the devolved administrations are free to set their own priorities within the total budget provisions made by the Treasury, those budgets reflect decisions in Westminster not just about the total levels of UK public spending provisions, but also about the priorities between different areas of expenditure (see McLean *et al* 2008).

The budgets for the devolved administrations are determined by a complex set of formulas based on the budget provisions made for England. These are only partly determined by the Barnett Formula, which adjusts previous levels of spending on a per capita basis (thus tending towards per capita equivalence over time); for some functions other rules apply.

Arrangements for council housing subsidies are dealt with separately, and reflect differences in the financial regimes in Scotland compared with England and Wales, which date back to 1989. There is also a different arrangement for Northern Ireland, where the Northern Ireland Housing Executive (NIHE) rather than local authorities acts as the primary social sector landlord across the province.

There are further 'concordats' that would enable the Treasury to recoup additional housing benefit costs in the event of council rents in Scotland or Wales (or NIHE rents in Northern Ireland) being increased more rapidly than in England. In practice this has not happened since 1999. There are no similar arrangements in respect of housing association rent levels.

Devolved budgets

If overall budget constraints for the devolved administrations are set by the Treasury, the priority given to housing expenditure within those budget constraints are entirely a matter for the devolved administrations. A measure of the relative priority given to housing by the devolved administrations can be seen in the proportion of housing expenditure (gross housing investment plus revenue subsidy) they devote to housing and how that has changed over the decade of devolution. This can be seen in Figure 11.1.

There have been some changes in the different levels of relative priority given to housing within the national budgets over the period. Both Scotland and Northern Ireland continue to give a far higher budgetary priority to housing than England and Wales do. However, while in England the priority given to housing expenditure increased over the decade, in Wales it declined, so that by the end of the decade Wales gave the lowest priority to housing expenditure of any of the four nations.

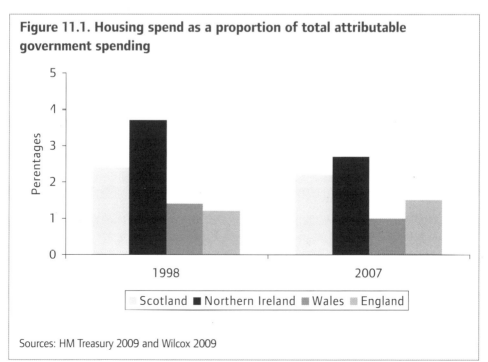

Figure 11.1. Housing spend as a proportion of total attributable government spending

Sources: HM Treasury 2009 and Wilcox 2009

The decline in Wales partly reflected views on the relative priorities of different policy areas but also the view that stock transfer provided an available route to funding for local authority stock improvements that would make less demand on the Welsh budget.

These public expenditure figures do not take account of the impact of stock transfers that switch investment to the private sector. However, this had a broadly similar impact on the proportion of retained council housing stock in England, Scotland and Wales over the decade. These differences in budgetary priorities have clear implications for the housing policies and outcomes in the four nations.

The supply of social sector dwellings

The devolved administrations can impact on the supply of social sector dwellings in a number of ways. The primary measures are the funding and provision of additional dwellings for, and policies regulating the sale of dwellings from, the sector. Both of these have a net impact on the stock of dwellings and the numbers of lettings becoming available each year for new tenants.

The changes in the size of the social sector stock in each of the four nations over the devolution decade are shown in Figure 11.2, which contrasts the 2007 and 1998 stock levels. It clearly shows that the size of the stock declined in all four nations over the decade, with losses to the social rented sector stock through sales (and demolitions) exceeding the additions to the stock through new provision. Proportionately, the decline was most rapid in Scotland and Northern Ireland, but nonetheless even at the end of the decade the social rented sector stock in Scotland formed a much larger proportion of the total stock than in the other three nations.

The decline in the levels of the social sector stock are also reflected in the levels of lettings available for new housing applicants. It should be noted, however, that there is a long time lag in the impact of right-to-buy sales on re-lets. While the immediate impact of sales on re-lets from vacancies in the remaining stock is quite small, it builds up gradually over several decades.

Figure 11.3 shows that the levels of re-lets available to new tenants declined in all four nations over the decade (although some caution is required with the data). That decline is not, however, solely a function of sales and new-build levels. Re-let rates also tend to rise and fall over the housing market cycle, as housing market affordability constraints reduce the capacity of existing tenants to move out of social housing, as well increasing the demand from households wishing to enter the sector.

Precise figures on total numbers of new additions to the social rented stock, in a comparable format across all four nations, are not readily available. Figures on new build are available for all nations; but figures on outputs from national government budgets, or stock additions through the acquisition, improvement and/or conversion of existing dwellings, are not so readily or consistently available. Data for Scotland, however, show that over the last eight years additions to the stock from acquisitions and rehabilitation were some 10 per cent of the level of new-build completions.

Figure 11.2. Social rented stock declines, 1998 and 2007

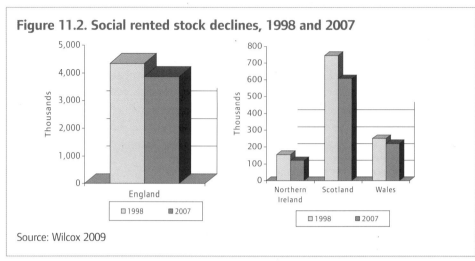

Source: Wilcox 2009

Figure 11.3. Decline in social sector lettings to new tenants, 1998–2007

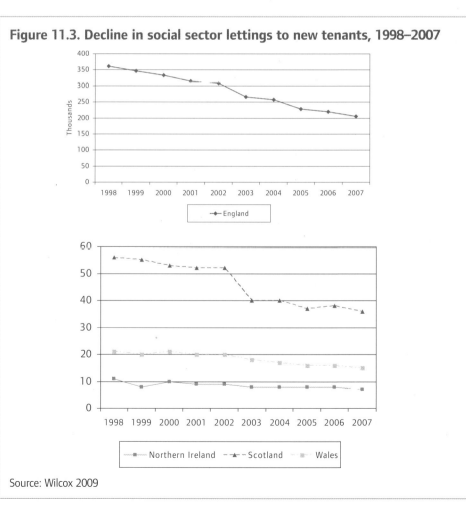

Source: Wilcox 2009

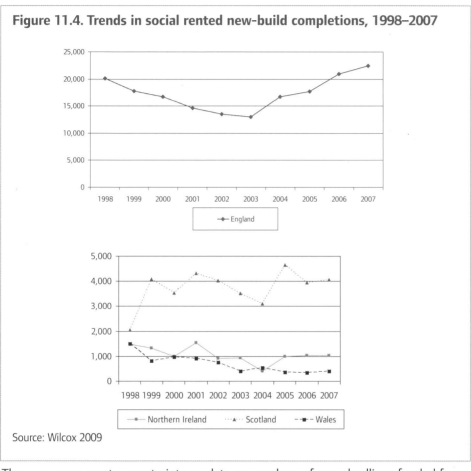

Figure 11.4. Trends in social rented new-build completions, 1998–2007

Source: Wilcox 2009

There are even greater constraints on data on numbers of new dwellings funded from housing associations' own resources, or as part of planning agreements. Analysis of the 'S106' planning agreements in England suggest that very few new social rented dwellings are funded without any government grant input (compared to a greater but still small – number of shared ownership dwellings) (Monk 2005). A more recent analysis in Wales, however, suggests that in the last year before the credit crunch, S106 agreements had added at least a quarter to the numbers of new social rented dwellings provided in that year (Welsh Economy Research Unit 2008).

Subject to the above caveats, Figure 11.4 shows the trends in provision of newly built social housing in each of the four nations over the last decade.

In all four nations funding for new housing association dwellings has increased since devolution, although not smoothly. Funding in Wales initially declined, and this only began to be reversed from 2005/6, and the overall net increase was less pronounced than in the other three nations. In Northern Ireland a substantial new-build contribution was also made by the NIHE in the early devolution years. Consequently, in both those nations the increased housing association funding was insufficient to support any increase in new social rented sector outputs over the decade to 2007.

The impact of the right to buy

The other policy impacting on the stock of social rented sector dwellings, and over time on levels of lettings, is the right to buy (RTB). This is a policy area in which there have been significant policy changes post-devolution, which have over the decade begun to impact on levels of sales, and levels of discounts.

The RTB enables council tenants with moderate incomes to purchase their homes at a substantial discount from open market vacant possession values. Thus, while there are some positive arguments in favour of the RTB, it is not a policy that directly assists a significant number of low-income households. Tenant purchasers tend to have higher incomes than households that become, or remain, social sector tenants – albeit they also tend to have lower incomes than households moving into shared ownership and other low-cost home ownership schemes.

In all four nations RTB sales (including NIHE sales to sitting tenants) rose in the early devolution years, in response to rising house prices (and house price expectations). However, from 2003 they began to fall (Figure 11.5), partly as prices had moved beyond the reach of tenants (particularly in Northern Ireland), and partly in response to the new policies introduced to limit the impact of the right to buy.

Sales fell over the decade in all four nations but to different degrees: they fell most in Northern Ireland and least in Scotland. However, over the decade as a whole sales in Northern Ireland were highest as a proportion of the social sector stock remaining in

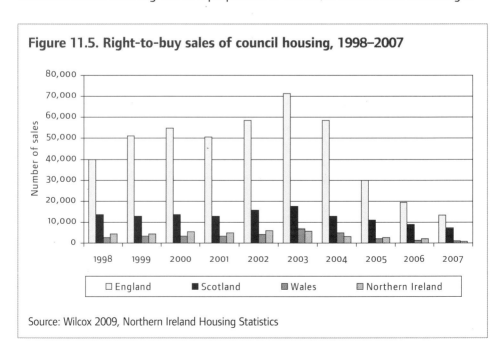

Figure 11.5. Right-to-buy sales of council housing, 1998–2007

Source: Wilcox 2009, Northern Ireland Housing Statistics

2007 (32 per cent), compared with 23 per cent in Scotland, 15 per cent in Wales and 13 per cent in England.

All the devolved administrations have since 1999 introduced measures designed to limit the impact of the RTB, but the policy approaches have differed between the four nations, and in particular between the policies adopted in Scotland and those in England, Wales and Northern Ireland. In the latter three, effective discount levels have been reduced with the introduction of lower national, regional or local 'caps' on maximum discounts (Table 11.1), while the Housing Act 2004 lengthened the qualifying time for RTB eligibility to five years and made a number of other detailed amendments to its operation in England and Wales.

Table 11.1. Maximum limits on right-to-buy discounts

Country or region	Year introduced	Discount limit
Northern Ireland	2002	£24,000
Scotland (Modernised RTB only)	2002	£15,000
Wales	2003	£16,000
London and South East	1999	£38,000
East	1999	£34,000
South West	1999	£30,000
North West and West Midlands	1999	£26,000
East Midlands and Yorkshire & Humber	1999	£24,000
North East	1999	£22,000
High-pressure areas in South East	2003	£16,000

Scotland introduced the 'modernised RTB' in 2002, under which tenants qualify for a 20 per cent discount after five years, and then an extra 1 per cent discount for each subsequent year of their tenancy, rising to a maximum of 35 per cent after 20 years. There is also a maximum cash limit of £15,000. However, the 'modernised' RTB only applies to new tenants from 2002, and existing tenants are still eligible for the higher discounts under the old RTB, which in Scotland has never had any provisions for imposing a cash cap on maximum discounts.

Scotland has also taken (and applied) the power to suspend the operation of the modernised RTB in selected high housing-pressure areas (but not the old RTB). In contrast, in 2003 England introduced a lower maximum £16,000 discount cap in selected high housing-pressure areas (most of London and a number of other areas in the South East). Wales has also recently sought the power to amend the RTB.

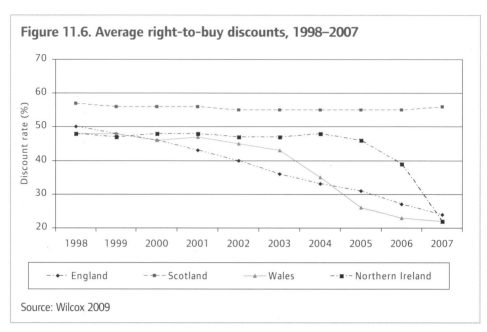

Figure 11.6. Average right-to-buy discounts, 1998–2007

Source: Wilcox 2009

These various measures have resulted not just in the substantial decline in the numbers of sales, but also the average level of achieved RTB discount in England, Northern Ireland and Wales (see Figure 11.6). However, average discount rates have not yet fallen in Scotland, as to date the great majority of sales have been under the old uncapped RTB, rather than the modernised version.

An economic assessment of the RTB suggests that the 'discount' levels of the modernised RTB are broadly in line with the economic value of RTB sales (Wilcox 2006). This is because they are sales to sitting tenants with an entitlement to a sub-market rent, who on average remain in residence for a further 15 or so years following the RTB sale. They are not open market sales with vacant possession.

On that basis, sales that provide sufficient receipts to invest in two new social rented dwellings from day one broadly balance out with the loss of three re-lets 15 years hence (based on HM Treasury investment methodology). There is no need for a 'one for one' replacement as the RTB households are the same households allocated their rented dwellings on the basis of housing need; it is just that post-RTB they occupy the dwellings as owners rather than tenants.

The critical issue arising from RTB sales is that in the past; discounts have been at excessive levels, and that receipts from sales have not been used to re-invest in new rented stock. Rules on the use of receipts vary from nation to nation, but in all cases they have in practice been used predominantly either to reduce new central government financial provisions and/or to invest in the refurbishment of the retained council stock.

In the short run the cash limits in England, Northern Ireland and Wales have provided a 'quick fix' to bring down discount levels to a point where they represent value for money to the public sector. In the first decade of devolution Scotland has continued with sales at high values that impose a substantial net replacement cost on the public sector.

Nonetheless the modernised RTB in Scotland offers a better longer-term balance between providing tenure choice to existing social sector tenants, and protecting public sector finances, and thus the resources available for low income households. If there is a case for Scotland to consider further measures to reduce discount levels for pre-2002 tenants, there is a similar case for the other three nations to consider the case for structural reforms to the RTB along similar lines to the Scottish 'modernised' RTB. However, the economic evaluation above does not support the case for the suspension of the RTB in high pressure areas, provided that discounts are not excessive.

Homelessness

The differences in approach to homelessness policy, and in particular between policy in Scotland and the rest of the UK, have been one of the more significant divergences of the post-devolution decade. There has been substantial legislative divergence on homelessness since devolution. Most notably, Scotland has significantly strengthened its statutory safety net, culminating in the highly ambitious target that virtually all homeless people in Scotland will be entitled to re-housing by 2012. This target is to be achieved, principally, by the gradual expansion of the categories of households defined to be in 'priority need'; subsequently leading to the abolition of any distinction between priority and non-priority households, so that all households have the rights previously only available to those defined as being in priority need.

The Homelessness etc. (Scotland) Act 2003, which provided the legislative basis for the phasing out of priority need, also allowed for a significant softening of the impact of the intentionality provisions and for suspension of the local connection referral rules (although neither of these amendments has been brought into force as yet). This expansion of the statutory safety net was made possible, in part, by the relative advantage that Scotland enjoys compared with other parts of the UK with a proportionately larger stock of social housing (albeit a relative advantage that has diminished over the last decade).

However, on balance, England (and to a lesser extent Wales) has been moving in the opposite direction. On the one hand the Homelessness Act 2002 repealed the two year time limit on the main homelessness duty in England and Wales (introduced by the Conservative government in the Housing Act 1996), and secondary legislation also expanded the categories of 'priority need' in both nations to include, for example, 16 and 17 year olds, care leavers and vulnerable adults (due to violence or to having an institutional background). On the other hand, the vigorous implementation of the 'homelessness prevention' approach, with its emphasis on making greater use of the private rented sector, could be seen as a de facto measure that effectively raises the statutory assessment threshold.

Trends in statutory homelessness

In England, the number of statutory homeless acceptances rose steeply in the late 1990s and early 2000s, as housing affordability deteriorated, squeezing many low income households out of the market. Since 2003/4, however, there has been an unprecedented reduction in homeless acceptances in England, with the total halving by 2007/8. In Wales, similarly, there was a sharp upward trend in homelessness acceptances until 2004/5, but this has since reversed. In Scotland, the number of homelessness acceptances grew steadily up to 2005/6, but has since evened out, and a broadly similar pattern is evident in Northern Ireland (Figure 11.7).

Current rates of both homelessness presentations ('decisions made' on those seeking assistance) and acceptances (those assessed as owed the main duty) differ significantly across the UK nations – both are much higher in Scotland and, especially, in Northern Ireland than in England and Wales. However, there is only a limited degree of difference in the relationship between presentations and acceptances in the four nations. In Scotland just over a half of all presentations result in acceptances, compared with just under a half across the rest of the UK.

With respect to Northern Ireland, the explanation for this exceptionally high level of statutory homelessness may lie in the particularly sharp deterioration in housing affordability experienced in the province in recent years compared with the rest of the UK. House prices in Northern Ireland rose by 287 per cent between 1998 and 2007, against 173 per cent for the UK as a whole.

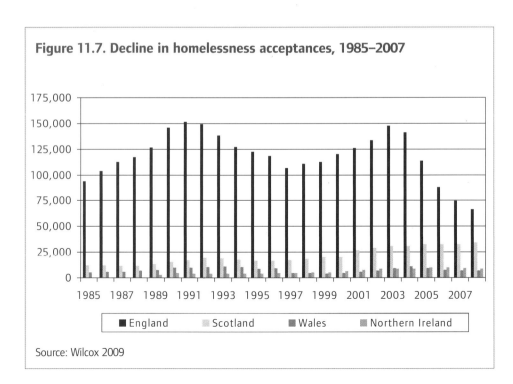

Figure 11.7. Decline in homelessness acceptances, 1985–2007

Source: Wilcox 2009

With regard to Scotland, it is likely that its more extensive statutory safety net encourages a higher proportion of homeless households, particularly single homeless households, to approach their local authority for help. Such 'single' households (those without dependent children or a pregnant woman) comprise approximately two thirds of those accepted as statutorily homeless in Scotland, as compared with only around one third in England, and about half in Wales and Northern Ireland.

The decline in homeless acceptances in England and Wales since 2003 can be understood partly in terms of the opportunities available with the rapid growth of the private rented sector, but primarily in terms of the constraints on the availability of social sector housing and the policy drive to assist households to secure accommodation in the private rented sector.

A key driver of much recent homelessness policy has been concerns about the large numbers of statutorily homeless households in temporary accommodation awaiting re-housing. As Figure 11.8 shows, the number of households in temporary accommodation rose sharply in England and Wales in the early 2000s before beginning to fall (albeit not as quickly as homelessness acceptances), whereas temporary accommodation placements have continued to climb in Scotland.

Housing homeless people
The ultimate test of this statutory system is, of course, the extent to which households accepted as homeless are actually re-housed and sustain that housing.

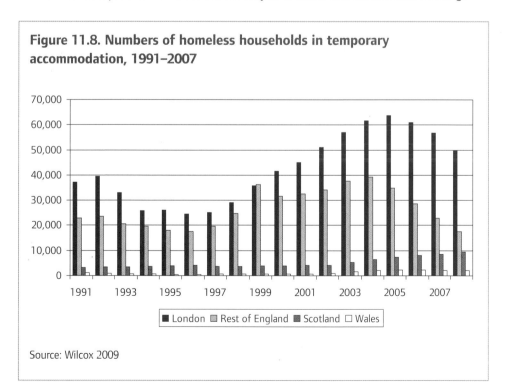

Figure 11.8. Numbers of homeless households in temporary accommodation, 1991–2007

Source: Wilcox 2009

Statutorily homeless households are entitled to 'reasonable preference' in the allocation of local authority housing throughout the UK.

In Scotland they are also entitled to reasonable preference in housing association allocations. Again in Scotland only, there is a legal duty on housing associations to re-house statutorily homeless households referred to them by a local authority within six weeks, unless they have a 'good reason' not to do so (with the exemptions narrowly drawn). Elsewhere, housing associations are required to assist local authorities with respect to their homelessness duties, and local authorities have substantial nomination rights in respect of the lettings made by housing associations.

In all parts of the UK, the main homelessness duty can be discharged via the offer of an 'assured' tenancy in the private rented sector (with security of tenure), as well as via the offer of a social tenancy. The Scottish Government has recently consulted on legislative amendments which would also allow for discharge of duty into fixed-term private tenancies ('short assured tenancies') with the applicant's consent, so long as certain other conditions were met (for example, with respect to tenancy length). This would bring Scotland broadly into line with the current position in England and Wales. There appear to be no plans in Scotland for 'compulsory' discharge of duty into fixed-term private tenancies (that is, without the applicant's consent) as have been mooted in England.

While data on discharge of duty is not directly comparable across the UK, it is clear that by far the most common outcome of the statutory process is acceptance by the household of a social rented tenancy. Only very small proportions of households owed the main duty accept a tenancy in the private rented sector (around 6 per cent in England and less elsewhere).

Significant numbers of statutorily homeless households (up to one third in total across the UK) 'leak' out of the statutory system without being re-housed because they voluntarily leave temporary accommodation, refuse a 'suitable' tenancy, return to previous accommodation, lose contact with the local authority before duty is discharged, and so on.

'Crowding out' other groups in housing need?

A longstanding concern with the statutory system is the extent to which lettings to homeless households 'crowd out' lettings to other households, potentially exacerbating 'perverse incentives' to take the 'homeless route' as a 'fast track' to a social tenancy (Hills 2007). The available evidence, while limited, is not suggestive of widespread manipulation of the homelessness provisions, but questions of 'fairness' with respect to social housing allocations to this group remain.

As Figure 11.9 shows, the proportion of local authority lets to new tenants made to statutorily homeless households has risen in all four nations in the UK in the period since devolution. However, in England this increase started to reverse from 2004/5, so

Figure 11.9. Percentage of local authority lettings made to homeless households, 1990–2006

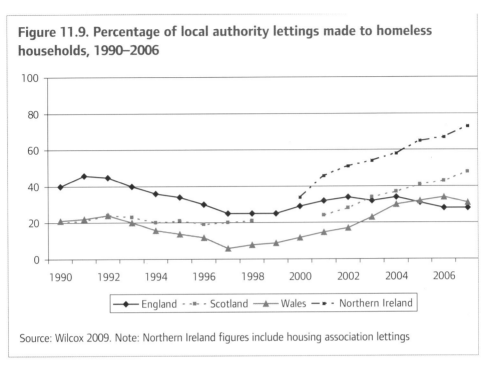

Source: Wilcox 2009. Note: Northern Ireland figures include housing association lettings

that by 2007/8 it stood at 28 per cent (not far off the figure back in 1998/9 of 25 per cent). The proportion of lets allocated to statutorily homeless households remains much larger in some high demand areas in England – particularly inner London.

In Wales, there has been an extraordinary four-fold increase in the proportion of local authority lets made to statutorily homeless households since devolution – from 8 per cent in 1998/9 to 34 per cent by 2006/7, although this figure did drop back to 31 per cent in 2007/8.

In Scotland, too, the proportion of local authority lets made to homeless households has grown rapidly over the past decade. While the national figure stood at 48 per cent in 2007/8, this masks strong variations between Scottish local authorities. The proportion of local authority lets absorbed by statutorily homeless households seems set to grow further in many areas of Scotland, as the widening of priority need takes place.

The proportion of NIHE and housing association allocations in Northern Ireland made to statutory homeless households has doubled in the period since devolution. It now stands at 73 per cent of all social lettings to new tenants in the province – the highest level in any of the UK nations by some margin.

The proportion of housing association lets to new tenants made to statutorily homeless households has also risen sharply in recent years: from 11 per cent in England in 1998/9 to 23 per cent by 2007/8; and in Scotland, from 13 per cent in 2003/4 to 25 per cent by 2007/8. In Wales, the equivalent figure was 14 per cent in 2006/7 and 16 per cent in 2007/8.

Thus, across the UK there are often relatively high, and in some cases growing, proportions of social housing lettings absorbed by statutorily homeless households. This is linked to the decline in the overall number of lets available to new tenants in all four nations (see Figure 11.3 above). In an allocation system based primarily on 'housing need', the extent to which this trend is of concern turns in part on whether statutorily homeless households are in fact more 'needy' than other households seeking social housing.

Data from CORE (The COntinuous REcording System) confirms that statutorily homeless households are a more socially disadvantaged group than other new social tenants in England. Tenants who are re-housed as statutorily homeless are much more likely to be lone parents than other new tenants, are less likely to be in work, and have a lower average weekly income (Table 11.2).

Table 11.2. Characteristics of new social housing tenants in England, by homelessness status, 2007/8

	Statutorily homeless	Other homeless	Not homeless
Proportion of lets to BME* households	14%	17%	13%
Proportion of lets to lone parents	36%	18%	20%
Proportion of lets to people not in work	77%	68%	63%
Mean weekly household income	£121.08	£133.56	£145.18

*Black and minority ethnic
Source: CORE Lettings Log (includes both housing association and local authority new general needs lettings only)

While debates about the balance of priorities in the allocations system involve many other dimensions, particularly in areas of acute housing shortage such as London, this evidence provides important support for the view that in broad terms the 'reasonable' priority given to statutory homeless households is about right.

Devolution and social sector rents

The devolved administrations have full formal control over social sector rent levels and policies. They are, however, subject to financial constraints under the various concordats, which in effect would mean that if they chose to increase council rents more rapidly than was the case in England, the devolved administrations would be required to meet the consequential additional housing benefit costs from within their own budgets. That constraint does not apply, however, to housing association rents.

In practice council rents in Scotland and Wales, and NIHE rents in Northern Ireland, have increased less rapidly than those in England over the devolution decade. However, while in the initial years of devolution this led to the UK Treasury making additional payments to the devolved administrations (for the consequential housing benefit savings), that arrangement was subsequently suspended, on the grounds that it was only intended to protect the Treasury in the event of higher rent increases by the devolved administrations.

The changes in the levels of average council and housing association rents are shown in Figures 11.10 and 11.11. In England council rents increased in line with median full-time earnings over the decade, while in Scotland and Northern Ireland the lower rate of rent increases meant that they declined relative to median full-time earnings over the decade. While rent increases in Wales were less rapid than in England, earnings growth in Wales was lower over the decade, with the net result that Welsh council rents rose slightly relative to earnings over the decade.

While lower council rents are clearly more affordable for tenants, they also represent less income being available for expenditure on repairs and improvements, and in both Scotland and Northern Ireland there would have been the opportunity to increase rental income by almost 1 per cent per annum without either increasing rents relative to earnings or doing so more rapidly than in England (and thus incurring budgetary costs).

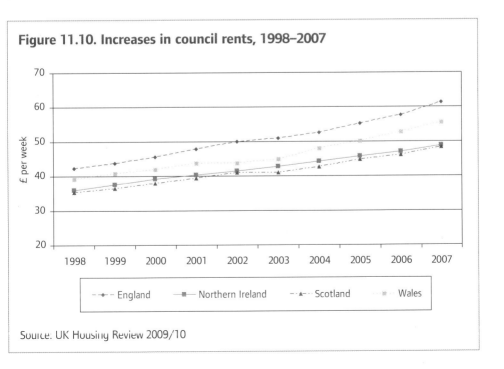

Figure 11.10. Increases in council rents, 1998–2007

Source: UK Housing Review 2009/10

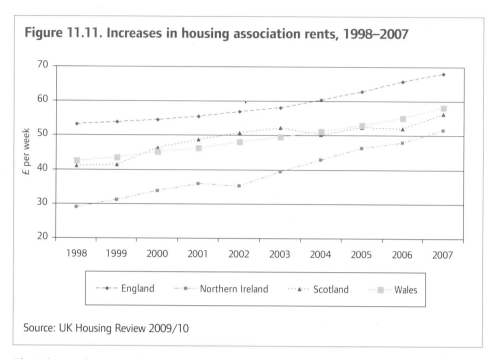

Figure 11.11. Increases in housing association rents, 1998–2007

Source: UK Housing Review 2009/10

The relative changes in housing association rents over the period were quite different. Housing association rent increases over the decade were lowest in England, under the impact of the 'rent restructuring' policy intended to create more consistency in rent levels both between the council and housing association sectors, and between individual landlords.

While housing association rents in England remained higher than council rents by the end of the decade, the gap between rent levels in the two sectors was significantly smaller. In Scotland housing association rents increased at the same rate as council rents over the decade and consequently also became more affordable relative to earnings.

In Wales housing association rents increased a little more slowly than council rents, and in consequence moved broadly in line with earnings over the decade.

In Northern Ireland, under pressures to maximise outputs from a limited grant budget, housing association rents increased sharply over the decade. However, by 2007 they still remained the lowest in the UK, although by then they were some 5 per cent higher than NIHE rents, whereas at the beginning of the devolution decade they had been substantially lower than NIHE rents (Figure 11.11).

Improving housing quality
The final section of this chapter explores the impact the devolved governments have made in improving the quality of the housing stock.

Measuring housing quality
New housing quality standards have been introduced in each of the four jurisdictions:

the Decent Homes Standard in England and Northern Ireland, the Scottish Housing Quality Standard, and the Welsh Housing Quality Standard. While the standards differ in detail, they commonly concern serious disrepair, modern facilities and insulation standards. The Welsh standard includes provisions relating to the neighbourhood as well as the individual dwelling, while the Scottish standard has more exacting energy efficiency requirements. More recently the decent homes standard adopted in England has become more exacting, as the requirement for a property to meet minimum 'fitness' standards has been replaced by a requirement to meet more wide ranging health and safety standards.

In England the target, adopted in 2000, was to make all social homes 'decent' by 2010, with most of this improvement occurring in deprived areas. In 2002 a further target to increase the proportions of 'vulnerable' households living in private sector decent homes to 70 per cent by 2010 (and 75 per cent by 2020) was adopted. The cross-tenure Scottish Housing Quality Standard was adopted in 2004, with a target for all social housing to reach this standard by 2015. The Welsh standard is also focused only on social housing and the target year for compliance is 2012. The Decent Homes standard in Northern Ireland was adopted in 2004 with a target for all social housing to meet it by 2010.

While the standards and targets may differ between the four nations, in each case they have focused their newly developed, higher quality targets primarily on improving the social sector stock, with much weaker targets and/or standards set in respect of private sector stock. The extent to which improvements towards those higher standards has been achieved over the devolution decade is considered below.

Investment in stock improvements

The achievement of these quality objectives has been linked to the future ownership models for social housing. In England councils were required to assess whether they could achieve the 2010 decent homes standard for their stock through the options of stock transfer, arms-length management organisations (ALMOs), or the use of Private Finance Initiatives (PFIs), with conventional stock retention only being viewed by central government as an option if the target could be achieved on the basis of planned levels of public sector funding.

This approach was also followed by the Scottish and Welsh councils but without the option of ALMOs. However, in Scotland the 'prudential' borrowing regime introduced in 2004 has also provided councils with the potential to access capital funding to improve stock that has not been transferred. The more restrictive council finance regimes that operate in England and Wales limit the extent to which councils in those nations can take advantage of prudential borrowing. Attempts by NIHE to upgrade stock have been inhibited both by the absence of stock transfers and borrowing constraints.

Figure 11.12 shows the increase in investment for each country over the decade as an annual expenditure per dwelling. At the commencement of the decade expenditure

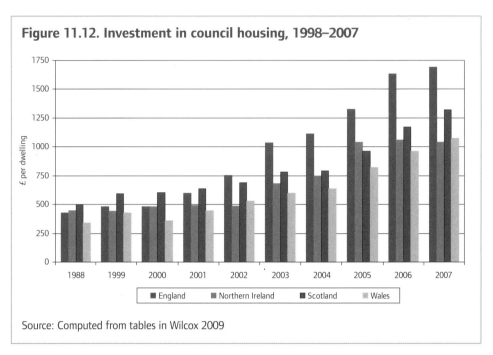

Figure 11.12. Investment in council housing, 1998–2007

Source: Computed from tables in Wilcox 2009

per dwelling was highest in Scotland and lowest in Wales. By the end of the decade it was highest in England and marginally lower in Northern Ireland than in Wales, with investment in Scotland at an intermediate level.

The increase in funding to improve the council stock within England was a conscious policy priority in the early years of the new Labour government; it was only from 2003/4 that there was any significant increase in the budget for new social sector housing. Those increased provisions for council borrowing were, in turn, reflected in the Barnett Formula computations of the overall budgets for Scotland, Wales and Northern Ireland.

However, post-devolution neither the Scottish nor Welsh government made any provision for increased borrowing for investment in council stock improvements. In Wales the council housing capital budget was effectively frozen in cash terms at pre-devolution levels. Similarly, there was very little change in the provision for council house borrowing in Scotland, before the advent of the prudential borrowing regime.

In effect, the Scottish and Welsh governments had other priorities within their devolved budgets, and clearly viewed stock transfer as a preferred source of funding for stock improvements that would make fewer demands on those budgets. Scottish councils were, however, permitted to make full use of their receipts from council house sales, and without the constraints of a redistributive revenue regime were also able to fund investments directly from their revenue streams. The relaxation of council borrowing controls with the introduction of the prudential borrowing regime was also particularly favourable for Scottish councils.

In Northern Ireland investment levels in NIHE estate renovation did not increase post-devolution until 2002/3, following a sharp rise in the funding available from sales receipts in the preceding years. Currently, however, the budget is now constrained by the subsequent fall in sales receipts.

There was little change in the levels of provision for private sector improvement grants post-devolution in England, Scotland or Northern Ireland. In real terms budgets fell. In Wales the budget was reduced sharply post-devolution, albeit from a much higher level in the pre-devolution years.

Figure 11.13 shows the expenditure on private sector improvement grants in the four nations in 1998 and 2007 as an amount per private sector dwelling (excluding grants for the installation of disabled facilities). While it would have been better to show this expenditure in terms of poor quality private sector dwellings this is precluded by the use of different quality standards in the four nations.

It is notable that expenditure per dwelling on improvement grants is much lower in England; although the differences between the nations reduced over the devolution decade. Even so, by 2007 the average grant per private sector dwelling in England was at only half the level of Scotland and Wales and only a quarter of the level in Northern Ireland.

If policy targets and investment provisions clearly prioritised improvements to the social sector stock relative to provision for private sector improvements in all four

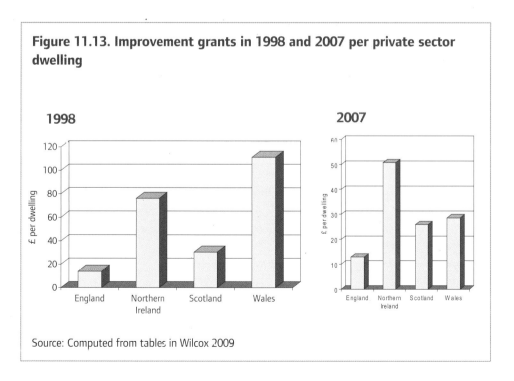

Figure 11.13. Improvement grants in 1998 and 2007 per private sector dwelling

Source: Computed from tables in Wilcox 2009

nations over the last decade, it was in England where that difference in priorities was most pronounced.

Impacts on measured housing quality

Measuring the outcome of these policies and investment levels in each country is complicated not just by the different stock condition standards in each nation, but also because of the differences in the timing of the stock condition surveys undertaken separately by each nation. Within these constraints the development of housing quality measures and changes in stock condition are outlined in turn below for each.

There has been a very significant fall in the proportion of social rented houses that do not meet the Decent Homes standard in England. In 2001, there were 1.64 million non-decent homes in the English social rented sector, and by 2006 this had been reduced to 1.13 million. Taking into account the fall in the total stock of social housing over the period these figures imply a fall in the proportion of non-decent homes in the English social rented sector from 39 to 29 per cent.

The proportion of vulnerable households living in non-decent private sector homes fell from 43 per cent in 2001 to 32 per cent in 2006. While the definition of 'vulnerable' households in this context includes all households in receipt of means-tested benefits, it does not include the substantial numbers of low income pensioners in the private sector that are entitled to, but do not claim, those benefits (Cuthbertson *et al* 2009).

Within the private sector overall the proportion of dwellings failing to meet the decent homes standard fell from 51 to 41 per cent in the private rented sector, and from 29 to 24 per cent in the owner-occupied sector. All these measures are based on the decent homes definition requiring housing to be fit, rather than the new standard that requires them to meet specified health and safety standards.

The proportion of all dwellings failing the Northern Ireland Decent Homes standard fell from 32 per in 2001 to 23 per cent in 2006. The failure rate for NIHE dwellings halved from 50 to 25 per cent, while the failure rate for the housing association stock increased a little from 7 to 9 per cent.

There was also a sharp decline in the failure rate for dwellings in the private rented sector in Northern Ireland, from 47 to 27 per cent, while the failure rate for owner-occupied dwellings fell from 23 to 20 per cent. In all cases these comparable measures show far fewer non-decent homes in Northern Ireland than in England, and a more pronounced rate of progress over the devolution decade.

The Scottish and Welsh Housing Quality Standards are not comparable to the English and Northern Irish Decent Homes standards, and these are reflected in the much higher proportion of dwellings that fall below the adopted standards. In Scotland the primary reason for the far higher failure rate is the more exacting energy efficiency standards in that nation.

In 2002 only 23 per cent of Scottish social sector housing met the Scottish Housing Quality Standard (SHQS) and this rose only slowly to about 29 per cent in 2007. Over the same period the proportion of private sector dwellings meeting the SHQS rose from 23 to 33 per cent. The proportions among housing association housing rose from 34 to 38 per cent, which represents a higher standard than both the owner-occupied sector (27 and 35 per cent) and the private rented sector (18 and 20 per cent).

Within the private sector in 2007 there was also a higher level of 'extensive disrepair' in the private rented sector (37 per cent), than in the owner-occupied sector (27 per cent). This compares with 31 per cent in the local authority sector and 28 per cent in the housing association sector.

There were very high rates of failure to meet the Welsh Housing Quality Standard (WHQS) in 2004, with 86.5 per cent of social homes failing to meet the standard (with almost all of the balance being accounted for by dwellings that were not surveyed). However, it should be noted that to meet the standard, a dwelling had to pass all 19 'primary' elements and 18 (out of 23) 'secondary' elements. More than 90 per cent of the social sector stock met most of the 'primary element' requirements, with high failure rates only for a limited number of elements, such as some thermal efficiency measures. As the WHQS has only been set as a standard for the social rented sector the analysis did not cover private sector stock.

Housing quality and energy efficiency
One of the few direct comparisons on the stock condition of the devolved nations that can be made is in respect of energy efficiency ratings. 'SAP' (Standard Assessment Procedure) ratings are available for England, Northern Ireland, Scotland and Wales, although the Welsh data are only currently available for 2004.

These results put the different national quality measures into perspective. While very high proportions of social sector dwellings in Scotland and Wales fail the nationally adopted quality standards, the SAP ratings provide a different picture to that provided by the proportion of social sector dwellings failing the Decent Homes standard in Northern Ireland and England.

On that energy efficiency measure dwellings in the social sector in Scotland have the highest rating, followed by social sector dwellings in Northern Ireland, while the average rating for Wales is only marginally below that for England. The average rating for private sector dwellings is lower than that for social sector dwellings in each country, but nonetheless the average rating for private sector dwellings in Scotland is still higher than the rating for social sector dwellings in England and Wales (see Figure 11.14).

The relative SAP ratings for each nation are not, however, solely a reflection of policies and investment to improve stock condition and energy efficiency. In part they also reflect the association between higher SAP ratings and flatted dwellings, as opposed to houses. In Northern Ireland, for example, the average SAP rating for a flat was 63 in 2006, but just 49 for a detached house.

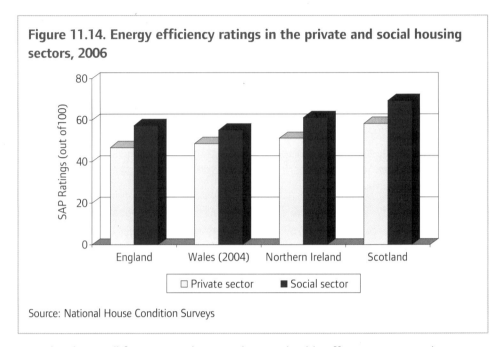

Figure 11.14. Energy efficiency ratings in the private and social housing sectors, 2006

Source: National House Condition Surveys

Post-devolution all four nations have made considerable efforts to improve the energy efficiency of social sector dwellings, both through broader improvement programmes and more specific energy efficiency programmes. In contrast there have been limited, and predominantly means-tested, programmes aimed at improving energy efficiency in private sector dwellings.

Those means-tested programmes are also hampered by the low take-up of pensioner credit and council tax benefit, as those benefits are used as qualifying criteria for the means-tested energy efficiency grants available in each country.

Conclusions
One of the critical measures of the success of the 1999 devolution settlement is the satisfaction each nation derives from the greater control it gives them over public policies, and the ability to develop them to reflect their own context and culture. That satisfaction was palpable in all our discussions with members of the policy communities in each.

But devolution does not, in itself, mean that devolved policies will deliver better housing outcomes. The devolved administrations have made different choices about the priority afforded to housing within their devolved budgets. Within a more constrained budget Wales also gave a lower priority to housing than the other three nations of the UK.

With a full decade with wider powers under its belt, Scotland has been able to make more of a difference in developing a distinctive policy agenda, infused with a wider vision for the public realm. If Wales has achieved rather less, this should be seen in the context of the greater budget constraints, and the current limitations of its powers. And in Northern Ireland the long interruptions in the operation of the devolved government effectively mean that devolution is still only just getting started. Critical decisions lie ahead about the future of the NIHE.

But underlying the differences in approach there are also some common themes with respect to the ways in which policies in the post-devolution period have impacted on the housing circumstances and opportunities of low income households. The availability of social sector lettings has declined in all four nations, as investment in new housing has lagged behind stock losses through RTB sales.

Scotland has grasped the nettle of fundamentally reforming the RTB but only in respect of new (post-2002) tenants. In contrast, England, Northern Ireland and Wales have simply introduced lower cash limits on maximum discounts for both new and existing tenants, while leaving the underlying structure of the RTB relatively unchanged. If the new Scottish 'modernised' RTB offers a model for the future that England, Wales and Northern Ireland might usefully consider, at the same time Scotland could usefully consider applying the modernised RTB to all council tenants, and not just those who entered the sector from 2002.

While Scotland and Wales have adopted distinctive (and higher) housing quality standards than those in England and Northern Ireland, the quality of the social sector stock has improved in all four nations over the decade, both as a result of new stock additions, and investment in the existing stock funded both by the administrations, and, in England, Scotland and Wales, by stock transfers.

However, less attention, and less funding, has been provided for improvements to poor-condition dwellings in the private sector, and in all four nations the majority of low income households living in poor-condition dwellings now reside in the private sector. Particularly in the light of growing concerns about energy efficiency issues, all four nations will need to focus more than they are currently on delivering improvements for those households (Wilcox 2008).

Devolution will evolve and mature, and the impact of distinctive policies will emerge more fully over time. It will also face new challenges in the post-credit crunch era, in particular in responding to the growing concerns around environmental issues, and the housing, social and health requirements of an ageing population. But perhaps the most significant measure of the success of devolution in the housing sphere is that there is a sense that it can only go forward; no one now wants to go back.

This chapter draws extensively on a wider and more detailed report undertaken for the Joseph Rowntree Foundation: What has devolution done for low income households? The case of housing, *by S Wilcox and S Fitzpatrick, with N Pleace, A Wallace and D Rhodes (Joseph Rowntree Foundation 2009). It also draws extensively on data from the UK Housing Review's Compendium of Tables.*

References

Communities and Local Government (Various Years) *English House Condition Survey reports* London: Communities and Local Government

Cuthbertson S, Smithson E, Herring I and C Wait (2009) *Income Related Benefits: Estimates of take Up in 2007/08* London: Department for Work and Pensions.

Hills J (2007) 'Ends and Means: the future roles of social housing in England', *CASE Report 34,* London: London School of Economics and Political Science

HM Treasury (2009) *Public Expenditure Statistical Analyses 2009, Cm 7630,* London: The Stationery Office

McLean I, Lodge G and Schmuecker K (2008) *Fair Shares? Barnett and the politics of public expenditure* London: ippr

Monk S (2005) 'Making Planning Pay?', in 2005/6 edition of *UK Housing Review*

Northern Ireland Housing Executive (Various Years) *Northern Ireland House Condition Survey reports* Belfast: Northern Ireland Housing Executive

Scottish Government (Various Years) *Scottish House Condition Survey reports* Edinburgh: Scottish Government

Welsh Assembly Government (2005) *Living in Wales 2004 – Report on Unfitness and Repairs* Cardiff: Welsh Assembly Government

Welsh Economy Research Unit (2008) *The Housing Associations of Wales: Measuring the Impact* Cardiff: Welsh Economy Research Unit, Community Housing Cymru

Wilcox S (2006) 'A financial evaluation of the right to buy', in 2006/7 edition of *UK Housing Review*

Wilcox S (2008) 'Adventures in environmental housing policy', in 2008/9 edition of *UK Housing Review*

Wilcox S (ed) (2009) *UK Housing Review 2009/10,* Building Societies Association and Chartered Institute of Housing

12. Child poverty and early years provision

Dalia Ben-Galim, Kayte Lawton and Emma Norris

In September 1999, then Prime Minister Tony Blair pledged that his government would halve child poverty by 2010 and eradicate it completely by 2020 (Blair 1999). This ambitious, historic commitment followed a significant rise in poverty that occurred across the population of the United Kingdom from the 1980s. Concerns about the long-term effects of growing up in poverty, coupled with a belief that an emphasis on children would elicit greater public support for anti-poverty measures, meant the focus of much of Labour's work on poverty has been families with children, as well as pensioners.

The pledge has since been adopted by all the devolved administrations and has driven considerable action on child poverty across the UK over the last decade. This chapter explores the different approaches of the devolved administrations across the UK in tackling child poverty. This is a difficult task since poverty is a policy area that cuts across devolved and reserved powers, although most of the policy tools that government has traditionally used to tackle poverty are reserved. We focus primarily on policy and practice surrounding early years provision, which encompasses early years education and childcare, usually up to the age of five. There is strong evidence demonstrating that early years services can reduce the affects of child poverty, both in terms of parental employment and children's life chances, providing opportunities for the devolved administrations to have a clear and active role in tackling child poverty.

We begin by briefly explaining how poverty is measured and set out recent trends in child poverty before outlining UK-wide strategies on both child poverty and early years. We then examine the approaches to early years provision adopted by the devolved administrations over the last decade and finish by considering the key points of convergence and divergence.

Child poverty in the UK: definitions, patterns and trends
Poverty is a complex concept with many different measures. The UK Labour Government has opted for a combination of measures against which to monitor UK-wide progress, based on both income and material deprivation. The headline measure has been a relative one: households with an income of less than 60 per cent of median household income are defined as experiencing poverty (Department for Work and Pensions [DWP] 2003)[1]. This measure has been complemented by two further

1. Income poverty can be measured before and after housing costs ('BHC'/'AHC') have been taken into account. There are arguments for and against both approaches. The Government's preferred measure uses income BHC and this is the measure we use in this chapter when we refer to child poverty.

indicators, one measuring absolute low income, and one using a combined measure of material deprivation and low income (ibid).

The Child Poverty Bill, which had its first reading in Parliament in June 2009, aims to put the goal of eradicating child poverty into legislation. All parts of the UK have committed to this goal, which explicitly addresses the issue of measurement as well as requiring each devolved administration to develop and monitor a child poverty strategy. The Bill includes reference to the three measures of poverty outlined above and adds a fourth indicator to measure persistent poverty. The Child Poverty Bill means that the targets to eradicate child poverty will remain a goal for any future UK government.

Trends in child poverty

The extent of child poverty increased rapidly across the UK during the 1980s, which left a legacy of high child poverty rates, both in historical terms and when compared to other wealthy countries. Broader measures of child well-being, which include income as well as subjective measures, also tend to see the UK somewhere near the bottom of league tables among the advanced countries (see for example Unicef 2007). Figure 12.1 shows the trajectory of child poverty (as measured by relative income poverty) since 1979. After rising up to 1992, the proportion of children living in poverty fell slightly and then levelled off before falling almost consistently from 1997/8. A major fall was achieved in the year after Tony Blair's pledge was made. However, rates of poverty began to creep up again from 2004/5, adding 200,000

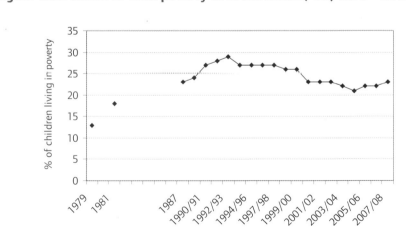

Figure 12.1: Trends in child poverty in Great Britain/UK, 1979 – 2007/8

Note: Data source changed in 1994, with a further small change in 1998/9, so figures are not exactly comparable. Data between 1994/5 and 1996/7 excludes Northern Ireland. Data before 1994/5 was not collected annually, hence breaks in the series. Poverty is measured as household income below 60% of contemporary mean household income, before housing costs.

Source: DWP 2009

children to the poverty count by 2007/8. Despite this recent and disappointing reversal in progress, Labour can still claim to have lifted 500,000 out of poverty since 1999/2000.

Analysis carried out by the Institute for Fiscal Studies (IFS), which takes account of the likely impact of the 2008/9 recession and financial commitments, suggests that the 2010 goal of halving child poverty will not be met (Brewer *et al* 2009). The IFS forecasts that the target will be missed by 600,000 children, a considerable number, leaving 2.3 million children living in poverty in the UK. This will make the goal of eradicating child poverty by 2020 even more challenging.

Regional and national patterns of child poverty
There are considerable disparities in the level of child poverty experienced in the regions and nations of the UK, along with sizeable differences in progress since 1999/2000 (Figure 12.2). Some of the largest falls in child poverty have taken place in the parts of the UK where child poverty was highest in 1999/2000, including Scotland, Northern Ireland and the North East of England. Scotland stands out as having witnessed the largest fall in child poverty rates (a 25 percentage point change) between 1999/2000 and 2007/8 (Table 12.1). At the same time, some parts of the UK that began the period with high levels of child poverty have experienced much smaller falls, particularly Wales and North West England. In the Midlands, no progress has been made, with child poverty remaining at identical and relatively high levels in both 1999/2000 and 2007/8. Eastern England and the South East have retained relatively low levels of child poverty, at around 15 per cent in 2007/8.

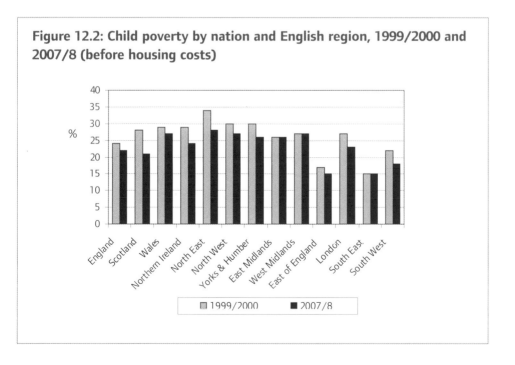

Figure 12.2: Child poverty by nation and English region, 1999/2000 and 2007/8 (before housing costs)

Overall, as well as a fall in the rate of child poverty, there has been some convergence in child poverty rates across the UK. The most progress has been made in many of the regions and nations with the highest levels of poverty in 1999/2000, with no change or a smaller fall in those regions that began the decade with lower levels of child poverty. Table 12.1 provides a summary of key child poverty statistics for the four countries of the UK.

Table 12.1: Key data on child poverty in the four nations of the UK, 1999/2000 to 2007/8

Country	Child poverty rate (%), 1999/00	Child poverty rate (%), 2007/8	% change 1999/00 to 2007/8	No. of poor children, 2007/8
England	24	22	- 8.3	2,400,000
Wales	29	27	- 6.9	160,000
Scotland	28	21	- 25.0	210,000
N. Ireland	29	24	- 17.2	100,000
UK average	26	23	- 11.5	2,900,000

Source: DWP 2009

Explaining the divergence in regional and national trends in child poverty is complex. Research by the Joseph Rowntree Foundation (JRF) concluded that devolution was unlikely to be the primary explanation for the above-average progress made in reducing child poverty in Scotland, since most of the relevant powers remain reserved (McCormick and Harrop 2010; see also Bell, this volume). Employment levels were also found to be insufficiently different across the four nations of the UK to explain the varying trends in child poverty up to 2007/8 (Bivand *et al* 2010).

The JRF research suggests that the benign economic conditions in the UK before the recession began in 2008 are a more likely explanation for the relatively impressive fall in poverty in the devolved administrations of Scotland and Northern Ireland. However, this theory does not really explain why Wales and Scotland in particular, which started the decade with high levels of child poverty, have experienced such contrasting paths up to 2007/8.

Tackling child poverty: the balance between devolved and reserved powers

The devolution settlement reserved key policy levers to the UK, leaving the UK Government with a vital role in tackling child poverty, and a number of the most important initiatives over the last decade have originated from this level. Examples include the National Minimum Wage in 1999, tax credits to support the incomes of low earners; greater opportunities for flexible working, and increasingly 'active' labour market policies designed to enable parents to return to work. These have all been crucial policies to combat disadvantage. Much of the approach has focused on work as a route out of poverty. While this been very effective in increasing, for example, the lone parent employment rate and therefore reducing the risk of poverty among lone parent families (Office for National Statistics 2009), there are limits to what a work-based poverty strategy can achieve. This is most notable in the stark fact that, in 2007/8, over half of poor children lived in working families (DWP 2009; see Cooke and Lawton 2008a, b and Lawton 2009 for more on the relationship between low pay, in-work poverty and child poverty). There have also been some measures to benefit families without work, as the value of some benefits and tax credits for families with children – both in and out of work – have also been raised, playing an important part in helping to lift some families out of poverty.

Table 12.2 sets out the division of devolved and reserved powers relevant to tackling child poverty. Many of the policy tools that have been used to directly reduce income poverty are reserved, including tax and benefit policy, welfare to work, employment law and equalities legalisation. This limits what devolved administrations can accomplish on child poverty, given the focus on meeting narrow income targets.

The table also shows, however, that the devolved administrations do have considerable autonomy over many public services and programmes that can help to reduce the negative impacts of poverty, with early years education and childcare policies important policy areas. Our focus on it is driven by the strength of evidence

Table 12.2: Devolution status of key policy areas relevant to child poverty

Reserved
Social security (including benefits and tax credits)*
Employment law (including parental leave and flexible working)
Welfare to work
Child maintenance (not Northern Ireland)
Equalities legislation (not Northern Ireland)
Tax**

Devolved
Health
Education
Skills
Local government
Social services
Housing and planning
Economic development

*In Northern Ireland, social security is in theory devolved but the Treasury insists on parity in benefit levels and entitlement as a condition of the financial support that it provides to Northern Ireland. **Scotland's devolution settlement gives the Government the ability to raise or lower the basic rate of income tax by up to three pence in the pound (though it has never used this power).

around the link between early years provision and child poverty, and the fact that it is an area where the devolved administrations have considerable devolved responsibility.

Access to affordable, high quality early years education and childcare not only enables parents to return to work, helping to make work a viable route out of poverty, but evidence also suggests it plays an important part in improving outcomes for poorer children and tackling social inequalities. For example the large-scale Effective Provision of Pre-School Education (EPPE) study found that children who participated in high-quality early years provision had higher achievement in language, reading and numeracy, even once family background had been accounted for (Sylva 2004). Children who began pre-school at age two also had greater developmental gains and children from deprived backgrounds tended to benefit most (ibid). Children who have benefited from high-quality care and education in the early years are then more likely to go on to do well at school, helping to close the attainment gap between children from poorer and more affluent households (Esping-Andersen 2005). These findings are reinforced by studies undertaken within the devolved administrations, further demonstrating the benefits of early years education and childcare in those particular localities (see for example Bradshaw and Wasoff 2009 on Scotland, and Melhuish *et al* 2006 on Northern Ireland).

It is important to note that early years provision is rarely the only or even the most important reason for a family living in poverty, so these policies alone will not overcome child poverty. However, analysis for JRF estimated that getting early years provision right could move between one sixth and half of children who are currently poor out of poverty (Waldfogel and Garnham 2008). This highlights the vital role of early years education, particularly as part of wider packages of support for low-income families, and outlines an important policy area where the devolved administrations have the power to contribute to tackling child poverty.

Direct financial support for parents to help with the cost of childcare remains reserved. This support, through the tax and benefits system, has focused almost exclusively on working families, reflecting the UK Government's primary vision of early years provision as a tool for improving parental – and particularly maternal – employment rates.

The key mechanism for directly supporting parents with the costs of childcare and early years education has been the childcare element of the Working Tax Credit (previously the Childcare Tax Credit, which formed part of the Working Families Tax Credit until April 2003). Working Tax Credits are available to working parents on low wages if they usually work 16 hours or more each week, and are responsible for at least one child[2]. The childcare element of the Working Tax Credit (WTC) covers up to 80 per cent of childcare costs, up to a maximum of £175 a week for one child, and £300 a week for two or more children.

---

2. Working Tax Credits are also available to people without children if they are 25 or over and usually work 30 hours or more a week, and to disabled people with or without children if they work 16 hours a week or more.

Although the childcare element of WTC provides vital support for childcare costs, it also has a number of drawbacks:

- It does not cover 100 per cent of costs and is capped, leaving some parents, particularly those with large families, struggling to pay the costs of childcare.
- There is only a four-week 'run-on' period when a parent's eligibility to WTC ends (if they lose their job or increase their earnings), which can mean that children are removed from early years settings.
- The requirement for parents to be working 16 hours a week excludes many children whose parents work fewer hours or live in workless families.

Tax exemptions on childcare vouchers provided by employers also provide help with childcare costs for working parents, although low income households are less likely to benefit significantly from tax relief.

This intersection of devolved and reserved powers creates scope for considerable tension between the UK Government's approach towards direct financial support for childcare, and the policy aspirations of the devolved administrations.

Devolution and early years policy

Outside the key area of direct financial support for childcare costs, the devolved governments have considerable policy responsibility for the delivery of early years education and childcare. Here, we discuss the main development of early years policy in England, Wales, Scotland and Northern Ireland, and in the next section we highlight common themes as well as areas of divergence.

England

Although the UK Government has talked about national childcare strategies and action plans since 1997 as if they applied to the whole of the UK, they have in large part only been relevant to England. Since 1997, early years policy in England has sought to deliver universal free entitlement to part time early years places, with a focus on integrated care, education, health and family support services. This is also the broad path followed by the governments of the devolved administrations.

The initial vision for England was set out in the 1998 National Childcare Strategy (NCS), the first of its kind, which emphasised the need to intervene in what had previously been an almost exclusively market-led service, focusing on three key challenges – quality, cost and availability (Department for Education and Employment 1998). Although the NCS set the tone for early years policy across the UK, the proposals only applied to England.

The step change in delivery of early years services began with a small number of Early Excellence Centres, proposed in the NCS, and continued when Sure Start Local Programmes (SSLP) were introduced in 1999, which were run by local partnerships in deprived areas responding to local needs (Department for Children, Schools and Families [DCSF] 2008). The Sure Start programme marked a major shift towards publicly-funded (but not necessarily delivered) early years provision and has worked on a model of providing integrated services to families with young children. Initially, the programme was targeted at low-income neighbourhoods but it has since expanded into most parts of England. Although policy in this area is devolved, in practice the three devolved governments chose, at least initially, to deliver a Sure Start programme which operated on similar principles to the English system and offered similar services.

Following on from the SSLP, the Neighbourhood Nurseries Initiative was launched in 2001 with the specific goal of tackling child poverty and reducing unemployment in deprived neighbourhoods (Smith *et al* 2007). Neighbourhood Nurseries were then rolled into Sure Start Children's Centres, which replaced the locally-focused SSLP with a more mainstream national programme, but still initially based in deprived areas (DCSF 2008). This formed a central plank of the 2003 Every Child Matters initiative, which placed childcare and early years provision at the heart of the Government's strategy to improve children's life chances.

Labour has been criticised for the confusing plethora of early years initiatives in England which characterised its first two terms (Wincott 2004). Many early years policies were pursuing the dual goals of parental employment and improving child outcomes, but these goals can be in tension. It resulted in an initiative overload. Given the lack of precedence for this level of government intervention in early years services, it may have been necessary to test out different models of provision. However, there is probably some truth in the criticism as Scotland and Wales appeared less prone to 'initiative-overload', developing more stable early years policy.

In common with the devolved administrations, an offer of free early care and education places to all three- and four-year-olds has been a core part of the Government's early years policy. England achieved this goal in 2004, initially offering a guarantee of 12.5 hours a week for 33 weeks of the year, increasing to 38 weeks in 2006. The Government plans to extend provision to 15 hours in 2010 and from 2011 all children will be entitled to start school in the September after their fourth birthday, or have 25 hours of free early years care and education a week.

Policy developments in England in the first half of the 2000s culminated in the 10-year cross-departmental strategy for childcare, published in 2004 (HM Treasury *et al* 2004). The document sought to promote flexibility, accessibility, affordability and quality in early years provision, and set out key milestones for the future. Proposals included a rapid expansion of Sure Start Children's Centres, taking it from a targeted to a universal programme; an extension of free places for three- and four-year olds to 15 hours a week (with a long-term goal to increase this to 20 hours), and a fully integrated early education and care service for children from birth to age five.

Many of these proposals were taken forward by the 2006 Childcare Act, a landmark piece of legislation which was the first to deal specifically with early years provision.

The Act established new obligations on local authorities in England and Wales (working with their partners) to improve outcomes for all young children and to monitor the local childcare market to ensure sufficient supply of childcare places appropriate to local needs. As with the countries in the UK, this means early years services have been largely delivered by local authorities.

The Act also introduced the Early Years Foundation Stage (EYFS), which brought together different national standards into one unified framework for children from birth to age five. The development of the EYFS was designed to improve the quality of provision, alongside measures to increase the accessibility of early years provision. Workforce development has also been key to improving quality in England, with a number of targets for up-skilling the workforce, including a requirement for all early years workers to be qualified to level 2 by 2015 and for all settings to be led by a graduate by 2015. This reflects evidence that more qualified early years workers tend to ensure better outcomes for children (Sylva 2004).

The Children's Plan took forward the Government's investment in free places by pledging to extend them to two-year-olds in deprived areas (DCSF 2007). This has been a recent feature of early years policy across the UK, although provision has developed at different speeds. The Children's Plan included a pilot to provide 20,000 places for two-year-olds and funding for a further 23,000 places was announced in 2009's *New Opportunities* White Paper (HM Government 2009). As yet, there is no universal provision of free places for two-year-olds in England or a guarantee of a place in deprived neighbourhoods. The pace of reform remains uncertain given the squeeze on public sector finances.

Scotland

In 1999, in a paper entitled *Social Justice: A Scotland where everyone matters*, the Scottish Executive committed itself to achieving Tony Blair's ambition to end child poverty by 2020 (Scottish Executive 1999). The presence of Labour in government in both Westminster and Holyrood meant that Scotland's anti-poverty strategy followed a broadly similar path to that of England between 1999 and 2007, focusing on parental employment and investment in family support, including early years provision.

Since the election of the SNP in 2007, the Scottish Government has sought to distinguish its approach to tackling child poverty. Most notably, it has reframed its discussions of poverty and inequality, adopting 'solidarity' as the key concept. The focal point of Scotland's post-2007 anti-poverty strategy has been the 'Solidarity Target', which commits the Government to increasing the proportion of income that goes to households in the bottom three deciles, an explicit target to reduce inequality (Scottish Government 2008a). Despite the presence of the Solidarity Target, in practice its anti-poverty strategy remains remarkably similar to the UK Government's, by stressing interventions directed at low-income families (Sinclair and McKendrick 2009).

At the same time, the SNP minority government has argued for greater powers over tax and benefit policy in order to have more control over how financial support is targeted at low-income families. The Scottish Government has used Labour's inability to meet its child poverty targets to make the case for a different approach to welfare policy in Scotland, including a demand for a single system for supporting parents with childcare costs (Scottish Government 2008a).

Scotland had its own legal and education structures in place before the 1998 Scotland Act, and in some senses early years provision was more advanced here than elsewhere in the UK (Wincott 2006). Scotland moved particularly early to adopt an integrated approach to early years services, bringing together health, education and social services more coherently than was the case in England, although this is perhaps easier in a smaller administration. *For Scotland's Children*, published in 2001, aimed to create a shared vision across children's services through a single service system (Scottish Executive 2001). One of the key documents on integration was the 2003 *Integration of Early Years Services*, which set out an ambitious strategy for how a range of services could be more closely aligned (Scottish Executive 2003, Wincott 2004). The 2008 Early Years Framework takes this forward, for example, by proposing the creation of joint roles which span a range of different services (Scottish Government 2008b).

Sure Start Scotland delivers a similar programme to the English version, through funding allocated to each Scottish local authority. The new Early Years Framework introduced in December 2008 will guide Scottish Government services for children from conception to age eight, including the delivery of Sure Start Scotland (Scottish Government 2008b). As well as building on Scotland's integrated delivery approach, the Framework continues to develop the country's focus on providing universal early years services combined with targeted measures, and emphasises the role of universal services in prevention and early intervention.

This reflects the fact that Scotland has led the UK in providing universal free childcare places for all three- and four-year-olds, achieving this in 2002, two years before England and Wales. The current offer is 475 hours a year, which is equivalent to 38 weeks at 12 hours a week. The offer will be increased to 570 hours a year in August 2010, equivalent to 15 hours a week, which will bring it into line with England. Scotland has also begun to investigate the potential for a targeted programme of free places for deprived two-year-olds, with a £2 million investment in pilot programmes in Glasgow, Dundee and North Ayrshire announced in 2006 (Woolfson and King 2008).

Wales

The Welsh Assembly Government's (WAG) strategy for tackling child poverty and commitment to the UK targets was published in 2005, some years after Scotland, and work began in 2009 to refresh the strategy (WAG 2005a). The 2007 elections produced a coalition government which published *One Wales,* a five-year plan that stressed the high priority that would be given to the eradication of child poverty

(WAG 2007). In income poverty terms, Table 12.1 above shows that Wales has the highest rate of child poverty of the four nations, by some margin. Since there is little evidence that devolution has contributed to dramatic reductions in child poverty in Scotland, it is also unlikely that ineffective action at the devolved level can explain Wales's relative lack of progress on tackling child poverty.

Wales stands out for adopting a strongly rights-based approach to tackling child poverty, underpinned by the United Nations Convention on the Rights of the Child. This has driven a greater emphasis on children's social participation and emotional well-being. Wales was also the first country in the UK to create the role of Children's Commissioner, an innovation that reflects a rights-based approach and the idea of a Children's Commissioner has since been adopted by Scotland, England and Northern Ireland.

Wales's current child poverty strategy focuses in particular on the early years and highlights affordable and appropriate childcare as key to both raising the employment prospects of parents and improving children's outcomes. The 2005 strategy provided extra resources for childcare places, a guarantee of at least one Integrated Centre in each local authority area, and a commitment from the Cabinet to produce an annual child poverty progress report (WAG 2005a). The WAG has also called on the UK to tackle child poverty by raising the level of Child Benefit.

The Government's commitment to the early years was set out in the 2002 strategy paper *Childcare is for Children*, which focuses on the common threads of availability, affordability and flexibility. *One Wales* further strengthened the WAG's vision for childcare and, following England and particularly Scotland, re-confirmed Wales' commitment to the universal provision of childcare (WAG 2007, Winckler 2009).

In the early years sector, Wales has led the way in creating an integrated curriculum framework which joins up early years with the primary school curriculum, with one curriculum stage from ages three to seven (Wincott 2004). Wales was also ahead of the rest of the UK in seeing education (through structured play) as central to early years provision, rather than just the provision of care. The Welsh curriculum does not create a clear distinction between learning through play up to age five, and then formal learning from age five. This has differed from the policy approach in England, which has increasingly focused on formal learning and earlier school entry. It also recognises evidence from Scandinavia about the benefits of non-formal learning and a later school-starting age (Sodha and Margo 2008).

Wales's early years services were delivered under the Sure Start branding until April 2003, when Sure Start funding was merged with two other children's funding streams to form a new unified fund called Cymorth – the Children and Youth Support Fund. The Fund is administered through local Children and Young People's Partnerships, which operate within each Welsh local authority. Part of the agreement with each local partnership is that they must run at least one integrated children's centre, as set out in *A Fair Future for Our Children*. Early years provision under the Cymorth fund mirrors Sure Start programmes elsewhere in the UK to a large extent, with an obligation on local authorities to provide locally appropriate education, care, health and family support services.

Like England, Wales was able to offer free places to all three- and four-year olds by 2004. In addition to mainstream early years funding provided through Cymorth, the Flying Start programme has been taking forward the provision of free part-time childcare places in Wales by extending the offer to two-year-olds in deprived areas. Flying Start will run from 2007 to 2011 as a separate and targeted grant to local authorities, and can be used flexibly to fund local services like parenting programmes and expanded health visiting as well as free places (Save the Children and the Bevan Foundation 2008, WAG 2005b). The proposal to extend targeted provision to two-year-olds under Flying Start was first put forward in 2005, making Wales the first country in the UK to demonstrate this level of ambition. There is also draft legislation to guarantee the provision of free places to all two-year-olds in specified deprived areas.

Northern Ireland
The Northern Ireland Assembly was the last of the devolved administrations to formerly adopt the UK Government's child poverty targets. The legacy of conflict in Northern Ireland adds a further layer of complexity to the Northern Irish case and its devolution settlement. The geographical areas where the conflict was most acutely felt are often those that are now experiencing high rates of poverty and deprivation (Horgan and Monteith 2009). The Northern Irish Executive set out its child poverty strategy in 2006 in *Lifetime Opportunities* (Office of the First Minister and Deputy First Minister 2006). The strategy is structured around four life stages: early years, children and young people, working-age adults and older citizens, with early years provision recognised as being a key area for investment (ibid). However, despite the relatively late adoption of child poverty targets, Northern Ireland has experienced one of the largest falls in child poverty over the 2000s, as discussed above. This adds further weight to the argument that devolution is not the primary explanation of different trajectories in child poverty over the last decade.

A Northern Irish childcare strategy was set out in *Children First* in 1999 (Department of Health, Social Services and Public Safety [DHSSPS] 1999). It highlighted the need for the integration of early years and care and identified the policy challenges so often associated with early years provision: affordability, accessibility and quality. Sure Start was introduced into Northern Ireland in 2000/1 and is delivered through four local partnerships. Horgan and Monteith (2009) suggest that funding for Sure Start, extended schools and other childcare programmes is considerably less generous in Northern Ireland compared to elsewhere in the UK.

Northern Ireland has also had a Pre-School Education Expansion Programme since 1998 which has created 10,000 new early education places (Horgan and Monteith

2009). Under the period of direct rule, extra resources were announced in 2006 for a programme of targeted free places for some two-year-olds, alongside additional funding for the expansion of Sure Start provision. However, progress on early years provision in Northern Ireland has been mixed. An official review published in 2005 found that childcare provision lacked a clear vision, had failed to adequately integrate care and education, and would benefit from more mainstream funding and stronger leadership (DHSSPS 2005). Northern Ireland has not pursued some of the key innovations rolled out in England, Wales and Scotland. In particular, Northern Ireland has not set a target to provide a children's centre in every local area.

The 2005 childcare review promised a new early years strategy but this was yet to materialise by early 2010, meaning that the review's recommendations have not been coherently implemented. In 2008, the Northern Ireland Assembly's Committee for the Office of the First Minister and Deputy First Minister reported that childcare provision in Northern Ireland was 'woefully inadequate' and called on the Northern Ireland Executive to commit to the development of a childcare strategy for Northern Ireland as a high priority (Committee for the Office of the First Minister and Deputy First Minister 2008).

The provision of free early education places in Northern Ireland is affected by the fact that the compulsory school age is four, so provision is not required for four-year-olds. Northern Ireland's Pre-School Education Expansion Programme meant that, by 2007, free places for three-year-olds were available for 90 per cent of all children. Given that not all parents will want to take up this offer, the Northern Ireland Assembly (NIA) argued that this would be sufficient to enable all parents who want to obtain a free place. However, the NIA does not offer an explicit guarantee of a free place to all three-year-olds in the same way that England, Wales and Scotland do.

The results of the lack of investment and clear strategy for early years provision in Northern Ireland appear to be higher costs and more scarce provision, with childcare costs the most expensive in the UK outside of London (Horgan and Monteith 2009). However, given the stalled process of devolution in Northern Ireland, responsibility for poor progress is likely to be shared between the NIA and the UK Government.

Divergence and common themes in child poverty and early years policy

The analysis above highlights the many shared themes running through the child poverty and early years strategies of both the UK Government and the devolved administrations. On the child poverty front, these include:

- *Commitment to the UK Government's goal of ending child poverty by 2020*
  Although adopted at different stages, and although there are differences of emphasis in child poverty strategies, each of the devolved administrations has signed up to the income-based target for ending child poverty.
- *Shared approaches to tackling child poverty*
  Child poverty strategies in each country have tended to reflect the same central

themes: work as the best route out of poverty, a multi-dimensional approach that recognises the importance of high-quality services as well as incomes, and a recognition of the 'double role' of early years provision – in improving outcomes for poor children and helping to increase family income. At the same time, programmes have continued to target low-income families and neighbourhoods.

The devolution settlements give considerable scope for the devolved governments to pursue different approaches to early years provision. Although they have clearly done this in some areas, they have also broadly adopted a similar approach on the key issues:

• *A multi-purpose vision for early years provision*

Each of the childcare strategies of the four nations has emphasised the dual role of early years provision in supporting parental employment and helping to reduce the effects of child poverty. These two goals are often in tension, and governments have tended to prioritise parental employment – and particularly maternal employment – over child outcomes. This has meant a focus on expanding provision with less attention on improving quality.

• *A universal service and the provision of free places for all*

The goal of providing universal free places has been at the core of all four early years strategies. This may reflect evidence about the benefits of universal provision in narrowing the gap in life chances between children from different backgrounds (Esping-Andersen 2005). It also reflects a desire among each administration to bring early years provision fully into the mainstream of public service delivery. More recently, the Welsh and Scottish governments have been clearer in reaffirming their commitment to universal provision. Fiscal constraints mean that there will be increasing pressure on universal services in the early years sector.

• *Targeted measures for poor children*

Alongside the goal of universal provision, each of the four governments began by targeting early years services in deprived areas and has continued to adopt targeted measures as early years provision has expanded. The targeting of children living in deprived communities continues to be evident in plans for the expansion of free places to two-year-olds. Each of the four countries is experimenting with this provision through pilots in specified areas.

• *Integration and centre-based provision*

Integration in early years has been a key watchword across the four nations, although each has taken forward the approach at different speeds. Integration has taken two broad forms: bringing together care and education in a single setting, and bringing together different services for families with young children, also in a single setting. Integration has also driven centre-based provision, where families can access a range of services in a convenient location. But this has also created challenges for families not comfortable with centre-based provision or when it fails to provide the flexibility and 'wrap-around' care that working families require.

- *Local delivery of early years services*

  Each of the four countries relies on local authorities, working with their partners, to deliver early years services and work with local private and voluntary-sector providers to achieve this. There is therefore more local input into services than in some other policy areas, but the strategy is still centralised.

Divergence

Despite these broad areas of convergence, the four nations of the UK have differed in the ways in which they have approached some of the challenges of addressing child poverty and expanding early years provision. Some of the key areas of divergence are set out in Table 12.3.

Although the devolved governments have taken different approaches in some areas, there is not always a particular pattern behind all of the decision-making. For example, Scotland led the way in providing free places to all three- and four-year-olds but it has been Wales that is now leading on expanding provision to two-year-olds. This suggests that devolution has not been used by the devolved administrations to implement unique and divergent policy solutions, but rather they have taken a more pragmatic and incremental approach. Table 12.3 also shows that most of the divergence has been within broad and shared policy goals such as universal provision and the integration of care and education, rather than any of the governments adopting a radically different approach. However some of the seemingly small divergences may, over time add up to larger differences.

Common challenges

Although much progress has been made across the four nations of the UK in the provision of early years care and education, the many common approaches adopted by the UK and devolved administrations means that they continue to face shared challenges. We finish this chapter by briefly setting out the key long-term challenges and areas for further investment.

Affordability

The high level of care and attention needed by young children makes childcare a labour intensive sector, resulting in high costs. Surveys consistently reveal high childcare costs in each of the four nations, with annual price increases usually above inflation. Table 12.4 provides the latest data on costs of childcare in Britain.

The high cost of childcare can make it more difficult for parents to cope with the fragmented and complex system of central government funding, with parents often having to combine the free entitlement with additional care paid for by the childcare element of WTC, childcare vouchers and their own earnings. This can be a particular source of frustration for the devolved administrations given their lack of control over direct cash support.

Access to appropriate and flexible provision

Problems also remain with ensuring sufficient provision of early years places, despite

Table 12.3: Areas of divergence in early years policy across the UK

	Major differences in approach	
	Child poverty	Early years
England	Focus on income measures and relative poverty	Fragmented and ever-changing delivery models, especially early on in the Labour government Preference for earlier school entry and more formal learning
Wales	Rights-based approach Wider understanding of poverty and exclusion, with more focus on participation and well-being alongside income	Earlier focus on learning through play Emphasis on integration of early years and primary education Earlier efforts to expand free provision to two-year-olds Greater integration and joint working across departments
Scotland	Early adoption of child poverty targets Change in strategy after 2007, reframing social justice in terms of 'solidarity' and using poverty targets to call for more powers over tax and benefit policy	Earlier achievement of universal provision for three- and four-year-olds More focus on delivering integrated services across departments
Northern Ireland	Similar to England Relatively late adoption of child poverty targets	Lack of investment and clear strategy has hampered progress

Table 12.4: Average yearly expenditure on childcare for a child under 2, 2010

England	£4576
Scotland	£4368
Wales	£4056

Source: Daycare Trust 2010

the guarantees of free entitlement. Just over two thirds of local authorities in England and Wales say that parents in their area have reported a lack of suitable childcare in the last 12 months (Daycare Trust 2009). Various studies have found a significant number of parents who continue to have difficulty accessing childcare places in each of the four nations of the UK (see for example Winckler 2009, Bradshaw and Wasoff 2009).

Quality and workforce development
The quality of early years provision is vital if it is to fulfil its potential in combating child poverty, with some studies even finding that poor quality provision can be damaging for some children (Waldfogel 2005). Early years provision in the UK has been rated relatively poorly compared to other OECD countries, with the UK lacking high standards for childcare workers and a highly trained workforce (Unicef 2008). But workforce development brings additional costs, both in providing funding for qualifications and supporting the higher wages that more qualified practitioners will expect. All four countries have struggled with this tension, particularly as all four parts of the UK aspire to make the provision of childcare a universal service. This will only become more difficult in a period of fiscal tightening. In future, greater targeting may be required.

Uptake among low-income families
Problems with quality, affordability and accessibility can have a particular effect on the uptake of childcare by low-income families, which reduces the effectiveness of early years provision as a tool to reduce social inequalities. There is also evidence that the focus on labour market outcomes has deterred some families because it leads some to conclude that childcare is not in their child's developmental interests, and low-incomeparents are less likely to feel that affordable and appropriate childcare is available locally (Speight *et al* 2009, Waldfogel and Garnham 2008, Roberts 2008).

Although take-up of the free entitlement is very high in each of the four nations (nearing 95 per cent), there is evidence that low-income families are most likely to be among those who are not accessing their entitlement (Sinclair and McKendrick 2009, Daycare Trust 2009). Parents need to have the final say on how they care for their children, but they also need the right information to enable them to make an informed decision. The UK and devolved governments have various initiatives designed to boost uptake among low-income families, such as the London Childcare Affordability Pilots, but uptake and affordability will continue to pose a problem across the UK.

Conclusion
The analysis has highlighted that the differences in policies of the devolved nations do not necessarily impact on outcomes on child poverty. Child poverty fell across the UK for almost a decade. The concern now is that the numbers are rising and how to reverse that trend. As 2010 will be the year that a key child poverty target will be missed across the UK, it provides an opportunity to reconsider what has worked and

the scale of the challenge ahead. We know what it will take to tackle child poverty: political commitment; personalised employment support and advice; flexible, affordable and high quality childcare; simplification of the tax and benefits system, and specific programmes that effectively target those areas with high levels of deprivation (Harker 2006). It requires better coordination between different levels of government and across departments. And it requires the more effective and efficient use of resources. The vision for early years education should be to pursue better outcomes for children's educational development as well as enabling parents to (re)-enter the labour market.

The child poverty targets set by the UK government in 1999 have created the impetus to eradicate child poverty. Together with the administrations of the devolved nations, more needs to be done to make it happen.

References

Bivand P, Bell L, Vaid L, Whitehurst D and Wan K (2010) *The Impact of Child Poverty: Employment and employability* York: Joseph Rowntree Foundation

Blair T (1999) *Beveridge Lecture,* 18 March 1999, Bristol University

Bradshaw P and Wasoff F (2009) *Multiple Childcare Provision and its Effect on Child Outcomes* Edinburgh: Scottish Government, available at www.scotland.gov.uk/Resource/Doc/263884/0079032.pdf

Brewer M, Browne J, Joyce R and Sutherland H (2009) *Micro-simulating Child Poverty in 2010 and 2020* London: Institute for Fiscal Studies

Brown G (2009) Speech to the 2009 *Labour Party Annual Conference,* Brighton, 29 September: www.labour.org.uk/gordon-brown-speech-conference

Children, Schools and Families Select Committee (2009) *Uncorrected Transcript of Oral Evidence,* 2 November 2009, to published as HC 799-i

Committee for the Office of the First Minister and Deputy First Minister (2008) *Final Report on the Committee's Inquiry into Child Poverty in Northern Ireland* Belfast: Northern Ireland Assembly

Cooke G and Lawton K (2008a) *Working Out of Poverty: A study of the low-paid and the 'working poor'* London: ippr: www.ippr.org.uk/publicationsandreports/publication.asp?id=581

Cooke G and Lawton K (2008b) *For Love or Money: Pay, progression and professionalisation in the 'early years' workforce* London: ippr: www.ippr.org.uk/publicationsandreports/publication.asp?id=598

Daycare Trust (2010) *Childcare Costs Survey: 2010* London: Daycare Trust: www.daycaretrust.org.uk/pages/childcare-costs-surveys.html

Department for Children, Schools and Families (DCSF) (2008) *The Sure Start Journey: A summary of evidence* London: DCSF

Department for Children, Schools and Families (DCSF) (2007) *The Children's Plan: Building brighter futures* London: HMSO

Department for Education and Employment (1998) *Meeting the Childcare Challenge: A framework and consultation document* London: DfEE

Department of Health, Social Services and Public Safety (DHSSPS) (1999) *Children First: The Northern Ireland childcare strategy* Belfast: DHSSPS

Department of Health, Social Services and Public Safety (DHSSPS) (2005) *Review of Children First: Final report* Belfast: DHSSPS

Department for Work and Pensions (DWP) (2003) *Measuring Child Poverty* London: DWP

Department for Work and Pensions (DWP) (2009) *Households Below Average Income (HBAI) 1994/95 - 2007/08* London: DWP: research.dwp.gov.uk/asd/hbai/hbai2008/contents.asp

Esping-Andersen G (2005) 'Social inheritance and equal opportunities policies' in Delorenzi S, Reed J and Robinson P (eds) *Maintaining Momentum: Promoting social mobility and life chances from early years to adulthood* London: ippr: www.ippr.org.uk/publicationsandreports/publication.asp?id=247

Harker L (2006) *Delivering on Child Poverty: What would it take? A report for the Department of Work and Pensions* Norwich: TSO

Horgan G and Monteith M (2009) *What Can We Do to Tackle Child Poverty in Northern Ireland?* York: Joseph Rowntree Foundation

HM Government (2009) *New Opportunities: Fair chances for the future* London: HMSO

HM Treasury, Department for Education and Skills, Department for Work and Pensions and Department for Trade and Industry (2004) *Choice for Parents, the Best Start for Children: A ten year strategy for childcare* London: HMSO

ippr (2009) 'ippr calls for more help for low-income families hit by recession', press release, 28 January: www.ippr.org.uk/pressreleases/archive.asp?id=3367&fID=260

Lawton K (2009) *Nice Work If You Can Get It: Achieving a sustainable solution to low pay and in-work poverty* London: ippr: www.ippr.org.uk/publicationsandreports/publication.asp?id=641

McCormick J and Harrop A (2010) *Devolution's Impact on Low-Income People and Places* York: Joseph Rowntree Foundation

Melhuish E, Quinn L, Hanna K, Sylva K, Sammons P, Siraj-Blatchford and Taggart B (2006) *Effective Pre-school Provision in Northern Ireland (EPPNI) Summary Report* Belfast: Department of Education: www.deni.gov.uk/researchreport41-2.pdf

Office for National Statistics (2009) *Work and Worklessness Among Households 2009* Newport: ONS

Office of the First Minister and Deputy First Minister (2006) *Lifetime Opportunities: Government's anti-poverty and social inclusion strategy for Northern Ireland* Belfast: Office of the First Minister and Deputy First Minister. www.ofmdfmni.gov.uk/antipovertynov06.pdf

Roberts K (2008) *Understanding Attitudes to Childcare and Childcare Language Among Low-Income Parents, DCSF Research Report RW059* London: DCSF

Save the Children and the Bevan Foundation (2008) *Children in Severe Poverty in Wales: An agenda for action* Cardiff: Save the Children

Scottish Executive (2003) *Integrated Strategy for the Early Years* Edinburgh: Scottish Executive

Scottish Executive (2001) *For Scotland's Children: Better integrated children's services* Edinburgh: Stationery Office

Scottish Executive (1999) *Social Justice: A Scotland where everyone matters* Edinburgh: Scottish Executive: www.scotland.gov.uk/Publications/1999/11/4174/File-1

Scottish Government (2008a) *Achieving Our Potential: A framework to tackle poverty and income inequality in Scotland* Edinburgh: Scottish Government: www.scotland.gov.uk/Resource/Doc/246055/0069426.pdf

Scottish Government (2008b) *The Early Years Framework* Edinburgh: Scottish Government

Sinclair S and McKendrick J H (2009) *Child Poverty in Scotland: Taking the next steps* York: Joseph Rowntree Foundation

Smith R, Purdon S, Schneider V, La Valle I, Wollny I, Owen R, Bryson C, Mathers S, Sylva K and Lloyd E (2009) *How Early Education for Two-Year-Olds Benefits Children and Their Families* London: NatCen

Smith T, Smith G, Coxon K and Sigala M (2007) *National Evaluation of the Neighbourhood Nurseries Initiative: Summary* London: Department for Children, Schools and Families

SNP (2009) 'Labour lambasted over child poverty figures', press release, 29 May: www.snp.org/node/15339

Sodha S and Margo J (2008) *Thursday's Child* London: ippr

Speight S, Smith R, La Valle I, Schneider V and Perry J (2009) *How Parents Are Tackling the Childcare Challenge* London: NatCen

Stanley K, Bellamy K and Cooke G (2006) *Equal Access? Appropriate and affordable childcare for every child* London: ippr: www.ippr.org.uk/publicationsandreports/publication.asp?id=468

Swaine J (2009) Families to keep £2,400 in childcare vouchers after Gordon Brown's u-turn' *Telegraph,* 3 December: www.telegraph.co.uk/family/6721324/Families-to-keep-2400-in-childcare-vouchers-after-Gordon-Browns-U-turn.html

Sylva K (2004) *The Effective Provision of Pre-School Education (EPPE) Project: Final report* London: Institute of Education University of London

Unicef (2008) *The Childcare Transition: A league table of early childhood education and care in economically advanced countries, Innocenti Report Card 8* Florence: Unicef Innocenti Research Centre

Unicef (2007) *Child Poverty in Perspective: An overview of child well-being in rich countries, Innocenti Report Card 7* Florence: Unicef Innocenti Research Centre

Waldfogel J (2005) 'Social mobility, life chances and early years' in Delorenzi S, Reed J and Robinson P (eds) *Maintaining Momentum: Promoting social mobility and life chances from early years to adulthood* London: ippr: www.ippr.org.uk/publicationsandreports/publication.asp?id=247

Waldfogel J and Garnham A (2008) *Childcare and Child poverty: Eradicating child poverty - the role of key policy areas* York: Joseph Rowntree Foundation

Welsh Assembly Government (2007) *One Wales: A progressive agenda for Wales* Cardiff: Welsh Assembly Government: wales.gov.uk/strategy/strategies/onewales/onewalese.pdf?lang=en

Welsh Assembly Government (2005a) *A Fair Future for Our Children: The strategy of the Welsh Assembly Government for tackling child poverty* Cardiff: Welsh Assembly Government: wales.gov.uk/dsjlg/publications/childrenyoung/ fairfuture/summarye?lang=en

Welsh Assembly Government (2005b) *Flying Start: Consultation Document* Cardiff: Welsh Assembly Government: wales.gov.uk/dcells/publications/policy_ strategy_and_planning/early-wales/flyingstart/flyingstart.pdf?lang=en

Welsh Assembly Government (2002) *Childcare Action Plan* Cardiff: Welsh Assembly Government

Winckler V (2009) *What is needed to end child poverty in Wales?* York: JRF

Wincott D (2004) 'Learning from devolution: making childcare Labour's 'big idea'' *Devolution Briefings ESRC Briefing 4,* February

Wincott D (2006) 'Devolution, social democracy and policy diversity in Britain: the case of early-childhood education and care', in Adams J and Schmuecker K (eds) *Devolution in Practice: Public policy differences within the UK* Newcastle Upon Tyne: ippr

Woolfson L and King J (2008) *Evaluation of the extended pre-school provision for vulnerable two year old pilot programme,* Edinburgh, Scottish Government Social Research: www.scotland.gov.uk/Resource/Doc/255044/0075576.pdf

13. Policies for peace of mind? Devolution and older age in the UK

James McCormick and Eleanor McDowell

This chapter considers the changing landscape of policy and practice for older people[1] over the last decade and how this varies across the four countries of the United Kingdom[2].

Policies for older people are shaped by a mix of reserved and devolved powers. The key reserved powers are those relating to pensions, pension credit and carers' benefits, which have been an important means of combating pensioner poverty. Reserved powers have also been used to introduce some universal entitlements, such as the winter fuel payment for the over-60s and free TV licences for the over-75s. A further important area of reserved policy with regard to older people is equalities and discrimination law, which in recent years has been extended to outlaw age discrimination and harassment at work.

Nonetheless, there remain a number of key policy areas that are devolved, most notably social care, healthcare and lifelong learning. These policy areas all have a significant impact on the well-being of older people, which is the main focus of this chapter. Not living in poverty is clearly an important prerequisite for well-being; however well-being is a broader concept than just income poverty, and encompasses concepts such as quality of life and emotional well-being. Evidence shows that well-being can be eroded by inactivity and loneliness. The 'cliff-edge' effects associated with age can be particularly damaging, such as where people lapse from activity as they grow older when many would prefer to combine some paid work with care roles or voluntary activity. Preventative health measures and assisting people to live independently are also recognised as having a significant impact on the well-being of older people.

This chapter considers some of these issues, and focuses particularly on the extent to which policy has sought to improve well-being for all older people or for some, for example targeted on need, resources or stage within older age. We include short

---

1. It is worth noting that there is no consistent definition of who 'older people' are. Some strategies apply to all aged over 50, while specific policies are aimed at the over-60s, are based on state pension age or target the 'older old', aged over 75 or 80.
2. For a more detailed account of issues in this chapter, see McCormick *et al* (2009)

Table 13.1. Share of people of state pension age in total population (projected, %)

Year	England	Scotland	Wales	Northern Ireland
2007	16.0	19.2	21.0	13.7
2011	16.6	20.1	21.9	14.7
2021	18.9	20.9	22.2	17.6
2031	21.7	24.0	24.4	21.6
Change	+35.6	+25.0	+16.2	+57.6

Source: Stats Wales (www.statswales.wales.gov.uk), UK National Statistics (www.statistics.gov.uk), General Register Office for Scotland (www.gros-scotland.gov.uk) and Northern Ireland Statistics and Research Agency (NISRA – www.nisra.gov.uk)

country-specific sections in the chapter involving a selective review of key policy initiatives, before going on to draw out some of the key areas of policy divergence and convergence. But first we provide some context to the UK's ageing population.

The UK's ageing society

It is well known that the population of the UK – and indeed the Western world – is ageing. While this general trend is true of all parts of the UK, there are some differences that can be discerned. Table 13.1 shows the share of the population of state pension age has grown in the four countries of the UK. Northern Ireland stands out for having a significantly younger population: fewer than one in seven of the population was of state pension age in 2007, one-third less than in Wales.

Looking ahead, demographic projections indicate an increased rate of ageing. By 2031 all four countries are projected to have more than 21 per cent of the population above the state pension age threshold: the rank order is expected to remain the same but convergence is likely to occur as Northern Ireland is set to age the fastest. In all cases, the rate of increase among the older old (aged 80-plus) is most marked. A corresponding increase in the number of people with dementia is anticipated throughout the UK; for example, a rise of 30 per cent is projected in Wales by 2021.

In the English regions, the South West has the largest proportion of people aged 65 and over (18.8 per cent) while London has the smallest (11.6 per cent). By 2031, all regions except London are projected to have more than 21 per cent in this category with the largest increases expected in the North East, East Midlands and South East.

One driver of our ageing society has been the progress made on premature mortality, which fell in every part of the UK from 1997–2007 (Palmer 2010). But despite this progress, geographical inequalities in the risk of dying before 65 remain striking, and the gap between lowest and highest risk areas is growing. In 2007, the rate in Scotland was 1.5 times higher than in the East of England, and higher than the rate recorded in all but two parts of the UK 10 years previously. The rank order of some parts of the UK has changed as well, with the North East now ranked eighth best (from eleventh in 1997) and London improving to fifth (from ninth in 1997). Even the regions with the lowest mortality rates a decade earlier saw a marked fall – down 18 per cent in the South East and 15 per cent in the East of England. These regions fared better than Scotland and Wales (both down 13 per cent) which had among the worst figures in 1997 (ibid). So the years of devolution so far have seen improvement on this measure, but this improvement has not been quicker than in comparable regions in northern England.

Until recently, old age was also strongly associated with poverty. The declining value of the Basic State Pension over recent decades allied with limited second pension coverage for older pensioners (especially women), plus the failure of benefit payments to keep pace with living costs and a higher rate of consumer price inflation for older people, led to around one-third of older people living in poverty by the mid-1990s. Since 1997, policies to tackle pensioner poverty, such as the means-tested Pension Credit, have contributed to a considerable fall in pensioner poverty rates, although progress has stalled in recent years, in line with trends in child poverty (see Ben Galim et al in this volume).

Poverty in older age fell in every part of the UK between 1997–8 and 2007–8 (measured after housing costs) (Palmer 2010). The reduction was largest in Scotland, where the proportion on a low income fell from 31 per cent in the period 1995–8 to 16 per cent in 2005–8. Scotland thus ended this period with the lowest rate of poverty in older age alongside the South East and East of England. The next largest falls were in the North East and Yorkshire and the Humber, two of the three English regions that started with the highest poverty rates. The smallest reductions were in the East Midlands and Wales.

Pension Credit was introduced by the UK government to cut poverty among older people. The Guaranteed element of Pension Credit is intended to serve as a minimum income below which no one should fall. Despite this, pensioner poverty remains an issue as Table 13.2 shows. Maintaining progress in cutting poverty among older people depends on increasing the rate of Pension Credit take-up, continuing to uprate the Pension Credit Guarantee (or any successor) and the Basic State Pension (from 2012) in line with average earnings.

But comparing Pension Credit receipt with poverty figures (as we do below) is not straightforward. Looking at uptake figures as a proportion of those eligible would in fact provide a better measure of need. Nevertheless, it appears that a higher rate of receipt in North East England and Scotland may be associated with quickening reduction in pensioner poverty, while the lower rate of receipt in the East Midlands has left the region with one of the highest poverty rates for that group.

Unfortunately, reliable figures on take-up of Pension Credit by older people who are eligible are difficult to find. In 2006–07 it was estimated that only 59 to 67 per cent

Table 13.2. Proportions of older people receiving Pension Credit and those living in poverty

Region	Proportion of people aged 60-plus in receipt of Pension Credit, Feb 2008 (%)	Proportion of pensioners in low-income, 2005–7* (%)
Northern Ireland	41.0	20
North East	22.9	19
Wales	22.2	19
Scotland	20.8	16
North West	20.4	18
London	18.7	22
Yorks & The Humber	18.1	18
West Midlands	17.0	18
East Midlands	15.9	21
South West	14.7	18
East of England	14.2	16
South East	12.6	16
Total	**17.6**	**18**

*Measured after housing costs

Source: Department for Work and Pensions data (February 2008) accessed via www.npi.org.uk

of eligible people in the UK were claiming[3]. Therefore between one-third and two-fifths of people who are entitled are not claiming – up to 1.8 million households. This indicates that the bulk of poverty among older people, at least at present, reflects entitlements not being claimed.

The influence of devolution, at least on this poverty measure, is unclear judging by the variable rates of progress seen in Scotland and Wales, as well as the large differences between rates of reduction in the English regions. This does not necessarily mean that devolution has not made a difference to the older poor. It might simply be that, since the major policy powers remain reserved to Westminster, the devolved administrations have not yet forged distinctive programmes on a scale that is big enough to show up at the national level. There may be one important exception: in Northern Ireland, the Social Development Minister reported a survey-based estimate from February 2008 of 83 per cent of people eligible for Pension Credit receiving it, up from 67 per cent in 2003–5. This is apparently the result of a Benefit Uptake Programme (2007–8) run by Northern Ireland's Social Security Agency, which contacted more than half of the province's older people. This shows that impact can be felt by more effectively administering the existing system even without significantly greater powers being devolved (NICVA 2009).

---

3. See www.poverty.org.uk for data on take-up of Pension Credit.

The next four sections selectively review some of the ways in which different parts of the UK have used their powers to address well-being among older people.

Policy approaches in England

Since devolution, the UK Government has acted for England in policy areas that are now matters for the devolved administrations. A raft of policy reforms have been made in this period, many of them under the government strategy Opportunity Age. A number of policy entitlements available to all older people have been introduced, for example free prescriptions, sight tests and off-peak bus travel for over-60s. There are also some more targeted entitlements, such as help with central heating/insulation targeted to Pension Credit recipients and free energy efficiency measures/insulation introduced for the over-70s.

England has also seen a shift in the approach to the delivery of services, with a greater emphasis than in the rest of the UK on personalisation in social care services. There has been a marked growth in the number of clients receiving Direct Payments in England in the last decade. Despite growing support for such an approach in the devolved countries, take-up has been slower at about half the rate in England (Riddell et al 2006). Individual Budgets have also been introduced under the English framework for adult social care services, Putting People First (Department of Health 2007). Piloting in 13 English councils in 2006–7 gained a generally positive response, but older people supported by adult services were more likely to report not wanting what many described as the 'additional burden' of planning and managing their own care (Individual Budgets Evaluation Network [IBSEN] 2008).

In 2009 UK Government released a new ageing strategy, which sets out its vision of 'Building a Society For All Ages'. The strategy seeks to challenge 'out-dated stereotypes about later life as a time of dependency and decline' and create a society where 'people are no longer defined by age' (HM Government 2009). The bulk of this strategy is about early intervention to enable more people to stay well for longer, focusing on well being; family and care roles, local prevention, and advocacy, scrutiny and involvement.

England has experimented with preventative, multi-agency approaches, trying to shift activity and spending away from crisis care. LinkAge Plus (LAP) is a programme being rolled out across England to ensure that services such as housing, transport, employment support and health are delivered by agencies working in partnership with each other. It is an experiment in joined-up services where central government, local government, charities and community groups work together to achieve a local, common goal. It focuses on services that provide 'a little bit of help' on a day-to-day basis to promote well-being and independence and reduce the need for more intensive support. By focusing on the 'little things,' it is expected that much bigger problems can be delayed or avoided. An evaluation published in 2007 identified considerable preventative savings (Watt et al 2007). Daly (2009) found other benefits including: enhanced safety and peace of mind (achieved, for example, through handyman services); physical and mental health benefits arising from schemes to address the inactivity and isolation that accelerate premature and preventable ill health and dependency (for example, walking groups, befriending, peer volunteering); financial security through increased benefit uptake; and mobility, through community transport initiatives which recognise older women are much more reliant on public transport and more likely to report difficulties accessing local services. LAP has been adapted by most local authorities in Wales but not in Scotland.

The Partnership for Older People's Projects (POPP) are also designed to shift resources away from crisis care towards preventative work in people's own homes and community settings (PSSRU 2008). POPP approaches range from falls prevention services to telephone advice services and befriending schemes. An impact of initial assessment of POPP projects found it was cost-effective, made long-term savings and improved quality of life (PSSRU 2008).

These policy innovations demonstrate that when agencies work in partnership with each other at the local level outcomes can be improved. In spite of this, such 'partnership' approaches do not seem be able to shift resources permanently towards preventative action in the community. These tend to be seen as 'one-off' projects and the vast bulk of resources are still held for big institutions and crisis care. A bolder conclusion is that integration of health and care services into a single agency is required if resource decision-making is to become truly responsive in an ageing society.

Advocacy, scrutiny and involvement
The establishment of a UK Advisory Forum on Ageing was announced by DWP in February 2009 (HM Government 2009). It will work with the UK Government to identify additional steps to improve well-being and independence in later life. The Forum will include devolved nation Ministers, officials from the English regions and third sector stakeholders. The UK Government will report on progress towards achieving the vision set out in its recent ageing strategy to a Cabinet Committee on Ageing and to this new Forum (HM Government 2009). At this stage it is not clear how far the new Forum will play a scrutiny or accountability role as distinct from an advisory role. It does, however, have the potential to serve as a valuable means of learning policy and practice lessons between the four countries of the UK.

In terms of advocacy, the UK Government appointed an independent Voice of Older People, Dame Joan Bakewell, in November 2008, to serve as an informed advocate on issues that affect older people's lives in England as well as on reserved issues across the UK.[4] One aim is to raise the profile of age equality issues and encourage public debate, particularly as the Equality Bill progresses through Parliament, as well as giving views on other key policies. The role is described as unique within Government.

---

4. Dame Joan's role is to advocate on behalf of older people both on English matters (especially health and care) but also on age discrimination and consumer protection issues (for the UK as a whole).

It may be useful in terms of raising awareness and influencing debate, but represents a different approach from the Commissioner and Advocate roles established in Wales and Northern Ireland respectively (discussed below). The Welsh role, in particular, appears to offer more scope to hold government and public service providers to account.

Devolution and older people's policy: Scotland

Since 1999 Scottish administrations have diverged from the UK Government on a range of policies. Generally, this has reflected the different philosophies north of the border, rather than different demands. At the same time, there has been a high degree of continuity between English and Scottish policies on health, reflecting the shared roots of the NHS, and on welfare due to benefits and employment policy being reserved to the UK level. It is notable, therefore, that the clearest point of divergence in the first decade of devolution lay at the intersection of health and welfare policy: free personal and nursing care for older people.

Among the final acts of the previous Labour-Liberal Democrat coalition was the publication in March 2007 of All Our Futures: Planning for a Scotland with an Ageing Population (Scottish Executive 2007). This strategy has by and large been continued by the SNP Government, elected in 2007. It seeks to address the role of older people in policy formation, face up to continuing ageism and develop a governance structure to ensure older people's views are central to future decision-making.

Action has focused on quality of life for older people, through a new entitlement to free personal and nursing care for everyone assessed as being in need, improved central heating and insulation packages, and free, unrestricted bus travel for over-60s throughout Scotland.

Free personal and nursing care

The decision to proceed with the free personal and nursing care policy created a significant and ongoing commitment to the well-being of older people, regardless of their ability to pay and showed that the Scottish Parliament was willing to diverge from English policy. The decision involved difficult negotiations, not only with the UK Government over the future of the Attendance Allowance, but also with local government in Scotland around the anticipated costs of care. While the policy reflected a commitment to universalism, some local variations in its delivery may be serving to maintain or open up new inequalities between different parts of Scotland. For example, some local authorities use higher need thresholds to manage demand for services, while others make use of waiting lists both for assessment of need and to access the full range of services.

Nevertheless, reviews by Lord Sutherland (Scottish Government 2008) and Audit Scotland (2008) found that overall the policy has been implemented successfully. Costs remain relatively stable at around 0.2 per cent of Scottish GDP, although this is expected to rise from 2013 due to higher rates of ageing. Currently the policy benefits around 50,000 people per year while the number of residents in care homes fell by 2 per cent from 2000–5, despite the increasing older population. However, the reviews also identified a funding gap which resulted in an additional £40 million being allocated by the Scottish Government in 2008. In addition, the Sutherland Review recommended that around £30 million per year of Attendance Allowance withdrawn by the DWP from Scottish claimants living in care homes and in receipt of personal care funding should be restored. This is not an issue on which Holyrood and Westminster are likely to agree.

Warm and safe housing
Scotland has also demonstrated a strong commitment to warm housing, partially as a result of the colder climate, which seems to be having results. The first key housing measure aimed at older people after devolution, the Central Heating Programme (2001), was aimed specifically at households with one member aged over 60 and either without central heating or with central heating in need of replacement. A review in 2004 found that the programme had taken three-quarters of clients out of fuel poverty and reduced household spending to achieve an acceptable heating standard by almost half. This was replaced in April 2009 by an Energy Assistance Package, including the same benefits but taking a more holistic approach intended to end fuel poverty by 2016 and ensure warm, dry housing for older people.

Despite the Central Heating Programme's achievements, 32 per cent of households headed by a person over 75 remained in fuel poverty in 2007. A greater proportion of older owner-occupiers experience fuel poverty than their peers in other forms of tenancy, a cause for concern as owner-occupation among older people rose by 11 per cent between 1999 and 2005. For the future, the Scottish Government plans to prioritise better uptake of existing assistance packages and benefits for older people and to offer advice to ensure older people's money goes further.

The Scottish Government is also considering provision of a loans scheme, based on partial equity release, to enable older people to fund home repairs and adaptations to allow them to remain at home in a safe living environment. New investment has also been pledged for 'telecare' services to enable older people to remain at home for longer, extended on the basis of a successful small-scale pilot in West Lothian. While telecare services are important in a country with a sparse population like Scotland's, other parts of the UK will be able to adapt their own practices from this approach.

Scrutiny and advocacy
In Scotland, responsibility for issues of ageing is split between the Communities Minister and the Minister for Public Health (who 'owns' All Our Futures-associated work). A National Forum on Ageing (All Our Futures Implementation Group) and an Older People's Consultative Forum were set up to ensure stakeholder involvement, but an independent champion for older people in Scotland has not been appointed, in contrast to the other devolved administrations. This is not for want of trying. A Private Members Bill to create a new Commissioner for Older People was first introduced to

the Scottish Parliament in 2004 (Neil 2004) but encountered a mood strongly in favour of streamlining the number of Commissioners, Ombudsmen and scrutiny bodies at work in Scotland. The creation of a new 'umbrella' Commissioner for Equalities and Human Rights means this will be the most likely home for older people's issues in future.

Ultimately, it makes sense for equalities issues to be 'mainstreamed' – in this case, for the diversity of older people's experiences to be written into the design and delivery of policies in future. An integrated Equalities and Human Rights Commission marks a step in that direction, but age remains some distance from being a mainstream consideration. So, while the case for separate strategies for ageing and older people ought to diminish over time, to reduce the focus now risks neglecting a number of critically important issues. We cannot assume we are ready yet, as a society, to make age a 'normal' element of our policy and practice, and Scotland may risk being left behind the other devolved countries in this respect.

Devolution and older people's policy: Wales

The Welsh Government Assembly (WAG)'s Strategy for Older People in Wales provides a 10-year commitment to improving the position of older people, in what appears to be the most cohesive approach to older people in the UK. The WAG is distinct for building the Madrid Declaration into national policy, and by drawing on the United Nations' Principles for Older People: independence, participation, care, self-fulfilment and dignity. Assuming the task is complex and long-term, to address discriminatory attitudes as well as barriers arising from service design and delivery, the Welsh strategy is positive in tone and comprehensive in scope, seeking to integrate many areas of devolved policy as well as taking a pragmatic approach to working with the UK Government on reserved matters.

First phase of the Strategy for Older People (2003–8)

The strategy has placed a heavy emphasis on the engagement and participation of older people, and promoted various policies to improve health, well-being and independence and to recognise older people's economic contribution. It also sought to challenge negative views associated with ageing. The WAG appointed a Minister for Older People and a National Partnership Forum for Older People to advise on policy and act as a communication channel with older people and their representatives. An independent Commissioner for Older People was also introduced – thought to be the first of its kind in Europe. Local government has played a key role in taking the strategy forward in partnership with the NHS, the voluntary and community sectors and with older people. During this phase, Local 50+ Forums were established, and each authority was expected to appoint a Champion for Older People from among its councillors – often a cabinet member.

This first phase was independently and positively evaluated, with key strengths identified as the LinkAge Wales programme, which builds on the work done in England; the development of 'telecare' services; free access to local authority swimming pools and leisure centres and continued support for agencies that nurture local networks of older people and provide avenues for two-way communication on the issues affecting them.

Overall, the evaluation concluded that the Welsh Strategy offers a case for change founded on a moral position that sees older people as equal citizens in a society that frequently leads to them being overlooked and that – because of ageist attitudes or the ways that services are configured – is prone to bring about the exclusion of many.

Second phase of the Strategy for Older People (2008–13)

The strategy's second phase was published in March 2008 and focuses on addressing older people's needs across all policy areas – so-called 'mainstreaming' (Welsh Assembly Government 2008a). The strategy is underpinned by a budget of £12 million up to April 2011, which marks the end of the current Assembly. The strategy has four core themes:

- Valuing older people: countering discrimination, developing engagement and social inclusion
- Changing society: enhancing the economic status and contribution of older people
- Well-being and independence: enhancing participation of older people in society and all levels of government
- Making it happen: implementation of the second phase.

A dozen indicators have been selected in order to monitor progress, focusing on participation (economic and social), health and social care. This represents a broader set of indicators than those in England or Scotland. It is notable that Wales has prioritised a material well-being indicator that emphasises employment and training rather than increasing rates of benefit and Pension Credit take-up for example, particularly as it is hard for the devolved administration to influence employment (a largely reserved area). The numbers benefiting from the support available through New Deal 50 Plus in Wales were relatively small even during the years of economic growth, suggesting this might be a difficult target to meet. In contrast, there is significant scope to increase uptake of welfare benefits through smarter administration of the UK system.

Improving access to public services is seen as a route to ensuring participation for all older people. A single smartcard for older people to cover use of services such as libraries, leisure centres and local buses is being considered and a business case review of the costs and benefits is underway. Another commitment in the coalition agreement between Labour and Plaid Cymru *One Wales: A progressive agenda for the government of Wales* is to extend free entry to national museums and galleries and give Welsh pensioners free entry to Assembly Government-funded heritage sites (Welsh Assembly Government 2007).

The strategy has also influenced the Welsh approach to transport, with the devolved Transport Strategy, *One Wales: Connecting Wales* recognising that accessibility is about more than making sure transport is available and free for older people. It is also about the timing, reliability and convenience of public transport, the location of key facilities, whether or not people live close to them, and whether or not a facility can be accessed by those with mobility restrictions. It includes measures to remove regulations that have slowed the growth of the community transport sector (Welsh Assembly Government 2008b). In this vein, Wales also piloted free concessionary rail travel for over-60s on two routes in Wales in 2007 (Conwy Valley and Heart of Wales). A review in 2008 extended the scheme to two other lines, but identified some problems arising from subsidising these less busy routes in summer while urban commuter routes were in need of greater capacity. The scheme was restricted on some routes to journeys in autumn and winter (Welsh Assembly Government 2008c).

The big issue of who should pay for social care remains to be addressed. As stated in One Wales, the Welsh Assembly Government has applied for a Legislative Competence Order which specifies the measures it wishes to introduce to achieve greater consistency in charging for home care services. It undertook a comprehensive review of funding required for social care in 2009. For the moment, the Welsh approach is marked by a pragmatic commitment to raising the income thresholds at which people have to start paying for their own care, allowing a greater number people on relatively low incomes to keep more of their income before care charges are payable (Bell 2010).

Scrutiny role: The Commissioner for Older People
Perhaps the most significant innovation in Wales has been the appointment of a Commissioner for Older People, currently Ruth Marks, following a process that involved older people themselves. The Commissioner, who is independent, seeks to:

- Promote awareness of the interests of older people in Wales
- Promote provision of opportunities for, and the elimination of discrimination against, older people in Wales
- Encourage good practice in the treatment of older people in Wales
- Keep under review the adequacy and effectiveness of the law affecting the interests of older people in Wales.

The Commissioner role will account for 40 per cent of the total strategy budget to 2011 (£5 million), signalling a considerable financial commitment. During 2009–10, the Commissioner's office is undertaking thematic reviews of policy areas based on extensive consultation with older people across Wales (see www.olderpeoplewales. com). Ultimately the role of the commissioner is to hold the Welsh Assembly Government, local government and the NHS to account, a role that will be increasingly important as older people's needs are mainstreamed.

In its second phase, the Welsh model seeks to achieve gradual mainstreaming via the dedicated focus of a Commissioner rather than assuming a high degree of readiness to embed older people's issues in other areas of policy and practice. It stands in contrast to the Scottish approach.

Devolution and older people's policy: Northern Ireland

During the years of direct rule in the province, UK Ministers published two strategies of direct relevance to older people, *Ageing in an Inclusive Society* (Office of the First Minister and Deputy First Minister 2005) and *Lifetime Opportunities*, the anti-poverty and social inclusion strategy (ibid 2006a). Inevitably, they reflect a mix of the prevailing views in Whitehall and conventions among Northern Ireland Office civil servants used to getting on with policymaking without a set of local legislators and scrutineers. The consultation processes underpinning the documents, as well as some of the proposals, were considered unsatisfactory by a sizeable proportion of voluntary sector stakeholders who responded. In retrospect, the strategies can be seen as draft statements of intent. They did inform action, but they were always going to be dependent on the views of incoming Ministers when devolution resumed.

Aims and actions of Northern Ireland's ageing strategy

The core aim of the ageing strategy is: 'To ensure that age related policies and practices create an enabling environment, which offers everyone the opportunity to make informed choices so that they may pursue healthy, active and positive ageing' (OFMDFM 2005). An Annual Report on assessing progress in the first year identified six priority objectives, including access to financial resources, access to integrated services, decent and secure life in their homes and communities, and equal opportunities for civic participation.

Proposed actions include:

- Addressing isolation among older people living in remote and rural areas, who face the highest rates of poverty among older people in Northern Ireland, 2.5 times the level in Belfast. 'Socially necessary transport services' would be provided through rural community transport partnerships.

- Preventing unnecessary hospital admissions, promoting timely discharge and independent living and increasing the proportion of people who have their care met in their own homes.

- Continuing the Northern Ireland Concessionary Fares Scheme which provides free public transport services to those aged 65 and over, expanding the door-to-door transport programme for people with disabilities in urban areas and addressing barriers that discourage older people from using transport services available to them.

- Supporting regular visits, book exchanges and a mobile library service in residential and nursing homes and hospitals. (This seemingly modest proposal is a sign of innovative thinking: such activity takes place in some health and care settings, but is often an after-thought.)

- Citizenship education in the Northern Ireland curriculum including a focus on inter-generational learning.

Since the Northern Ireland Assembly was elected in 2007, the voluntary sector has expressed frustration at the slow rate of progress on tackling poverty compared with other areas of policy. It appears this is now being addressed. However, a significant opportunity cost may have been paid, since the prospects for tackling poverty among older people appear much tougher for the next five years than they were in the last. On the other hand, Northern Ireland may have considerable potential for making progress on policy for older people. Although the role of local government in Northern Ireland is set to become more prominent, it has traditionally been weaker than in Great Britain. As a consequence, a thriving voluntary and community sector could make a big impact in Northern Ireland if the devolved government made a clearer commitment to implement Ageing in an Inclusive Society. The risk is that engagement around the strategy gets stuck at the level of representative involvement, rather than 'drilling down' to reach older people whose diverse experiences might otherwise be lost.

Anti-poverty and social inclusion strategy: older citizens

In 2006 an anti-poverty and social inclusion strategy was published by the UK Secretary of State, Lifetime Opportunities. The Northern Ireland Executive agreed to adopt this as policy in November 2008, although it remains too early to gauge which policy priorities will emerge. The strategy takes a life-course approach familiar in UK Government social inclusion reports in the last decade, including a section on older citizens. The primary goal of the strategy as it affects older people is: 'To ensure older people are valued and respected, remain independent, participate as active citizens and enjoy a good quality of life in a safe and shared community' (OFMDFM 2006).

The anti-poverty strategy set seven objectives (mostly to 2020–25) towards this goal for older people, including: reducing the life expectancy gap between the one-fifth most deprived areas and the average; maximum uptake of eligibility to pensions and benefits; decent, warm and secure housing for all pensioners; access to a range of support services, social networks, cultural and sporting activities; and improved access to rural transport. Among the actions applying to older people in particular were:

- A benefit uptake programme led by the Social Security Agency in partnership with the independent advice sector: four benefit uptake exercises were primarily aimed at around 20,000 older people (two-thirds of them women) targeted for assessment and help with claiming. This has resulted in a considerable increase in the uptake of Pension Credit.
- An enabling power in legislation to allow pensioners to choose to defer rate payments over their lifetime. The strategy stated it is left to a future Executive to use the power if it wishes.
- Plans for an All Ireland Free Travel Scheme, extending eligibility to travel in the Republic of Ireland.

Junior Minister Jeffrey Donaldson announced in January 2009 that a Minister-led Anti Poverty & Social Inclusion Forum would be established to oversee the process and monitor progress with stakeholders (Northern Ireland Council for Voluntary Action 2009). This adds up to an agenda that would be familiar elsewhere in the UK, not surprising since it was prepared before the devolved Executive and Assembly were restored. However, it is worth noting that Northern Ireland has a modest power to vary social security laws prior to devolution, which allows for some divergence from Great Britain. No plans have been put forward by Ministers to use them to date.

From advocate to commissioner
Northern Ireland has established an independent champion for older people's issues, drawing heavily on the Welsh experience. Currently the Older People's Advocate offers a feedback and transmission route into government for older people's concerns, rather than a means of increasing scrutiny. In that sense, the Northern Ireland focus on advocacy appears closer to the English and UK 'Voice for Older People' than to the Welsh Commissioner. Even with this quite limited role an independent focus adds significant value to the older people's agenda beyond giving responsibility solely to a Northern Ireland Executive Minister – or the status quo ante of a UK Minister and senior civil servant as in-house 'champions'.

A draft bill and consultation paper will be published in 2010 on establishing a fully-fledged Commissioner for Older People in Northern Ireland with investigative powers. This would bring Northern Ireland closely into line with Wales, leaving Scotland as the only part of the UK without a dedicated role for older people's issues.

Conclusion: What difference has devolution made?
In the last decade sustained progress has been made in reducing poverty in older age, although this has stalled since 2005 and has even reversed in some parts of the UK. Policies to tackle poverty have been led primarily by the UK Government, spanning targeted measures to boost low incomes such as Pension Credit as well as universal payments to address the impact of higher fuel costs for the over-60s and universal measures for the older old (for example, free TV licences for the over-75s and a higher Winter Fuel Allowance for the over-80s). The devolved administrations have few powers to act directly in this area, but they have taken steps to reduce costs associated with public transport and warm housing.

Apart from extending entitlement to free personal and nursing care in Scotland, most variations in policies have been modest: the age of entitlement to a free bus pass is 65 in Northern Ireland and currently 60 in the rest of the UK. Travel on any route at any time is permitted in Scotland, but restricted to off-peak journeys elsewhere. Concessionary rail travel has been piloted in parts of Wales and concessionary travel into the Republic of Ireland has been proposed in Northern Ireland. Free swimming for the over-60s (England and Wales) and access to cultural facilities (Wales) have been introduced more recently. Local authorities may also decide to reduce or remove costs for older people. Finally, despite speculation about tighter eligibility rules within central heating programmes, the basis of entitlement has remained the same or become relatively more generous in the case of Scotland. The impending squeeze on public spending is likely to throw some of these policy commitments into doubt.

It is important to note that although policy variations are mostly minor, implementation may vary substantially, especially given the different strategies and methods for scrutiny. This means that it is still too early to assess what difference devolution has made to outcomes for older people as a whole. We know quite a lot about the objectives of various policies but not enough about their impact. Nonetheless, strengths can be identified in each country of the UK.

Some genuinely innovative partnerships around preventative work at the health/care interface in the community have developed in various pilot locations across England. Approaches to preventative working discussed in this chapter appear relatively modest in scope yet interim evaluations show some initiatives having broken new ground in service commissioning, engagement with older people and capacity-building. The Treasury as well as the Department for Work and Pensions and Department of Health will want to retain a long-term interest in such approaches. But it is less clear how to make positive changes stick in the longer term – notably, how to capture budget savings in the NHS for investment in community services. No amount of good partnership work looks likely to deliver the kind of integrated planning and resource flexibility needed. It is hard to escape the conclusion that a single agency model spanning health and care services is more likely to achieve this.

Wales has developed a comprehensive Strategy for Older People spanning 10 years, rooted in a clear statement of citizenship. This seems to offer the most coherent long-term commitment to improving the position of older people of any UK administration in the last decade. A bolder policy on social care may have been enacted in Scotland, reflecting its greater legislative powers, but the Welsh Strategy appears the most likely to ensure a continuing high profile for older people's issues across many policy areas and at a local level. Its strength lies in its future potential rather than having delivered clear outcomes to date.

Scotland has more extensive powers to legislate and made the boldest move of all in extending free personal and nursing care to all older people assessed as being in need. This is seen to remove problems sometimes associated with means-testing like inefficiency, low uptake, perverse incentives and, for some, indignity, while extending benefits to those who would previously have been required to pay. Yet there is now less sense of momentum for older people's issues in Scotland.

Northern Ireland is, in many ways, just getting started but even here a clear focus on increasing the uptake of Pension Credit has led to impressive results. More significantly, the rapidly changing environment for public finances creates considerable uncertainty about future pledges. Budgets for 2010–11 signal the start of a process of cutting public expenditure which is expected to last for years.

Different approaches to advocacy and scrutiny on behalf of older people have been taken. The Commissioner for Older People in Wales represents the most advanced 'independent champion' model in the UK. Northern Ireland has established an interim Older People's Advocate who currently has no statutory powers, but will be followed by a fully-fledged Commissioner role by 2011. The UK Government has appointed an independent Voice of Older People who will raise issues of concern for England as well as UK-wide issues. Scotland is alone in having no such dedicated role.

In terms of structures for participation, various consultative forums and advisory panels have been established, usually involving older people's representatives alongside statutory and voluntary service providers. The emphasis is on stakeholder inclusion and dialogue. However, without greater clarity on their scrutiny and accountability roles, it is unclear how their impact will be demonstrated.

Overall, the bulk of policies has either put more money into the pockets of older people or reduced the cost of using services. This is likely to have some clear benefits in terms of inclusion, independence and well-being. But it is doubtful that we will see much more along these lines in the next decade, and quite likely that current eligibility will come under scrutiny within an ultra-tight public spending environment. If ages of entitlement are to change, or some element of co-payment introduced in place of free access, it is essential that this is done on the basis of rigorous impact assessment. The first priority should be to ensure that the oldest, poorest and most vulnerable of older people are not disadvantaged.

Finally, comparative analysis could be helped by greater collaboration between the four governments of the UK and between researchers who more often look internationally rather than cross-country within the UK. The establishment of a UK Advisory Forum on Ageing, involving the devolved administrations as well as the English Regions, presents an opportunity to improve our knowledge. Further divergence in policies for older people is likely in response to common challenges, but greater cross-country sharing of policy and practice lessons combined with similar budget pressures might also result in examples of re-convergence as one country's experience influences another.

References

Audit Scotland (2008) *A review of free personal and nursing care*, Edinburgh: Audit Scotland.

Bell D (2009, forthcoming) *How has devolution affected the provision of long-term care in the UK?* York: Joseph Rowntree Foundation

Daly G (2009) *LinkAge Plus: Benefits for older people, Research Report 554*, London: Department for Work and Pensions

Department of Health (DH) (2007) *Putting People First: A shared vision and commitment to the transformation of adult social care*, London: Department of Health

HM Government (2009) *Building a society for all ages*, Cm 7655, Department for Work and Pensions, London: The Stationery Office

Individual Budgets Evaluation Network (IBSEN) (2008) *Evaluation of the Individual Budgets Pilot Programme: Summary Report,* York: Social Policy Research Unit, University of York

Neil A (2004) *Commissioner for Older People (Scotland) Bill Consultation Paper,* Edinburgh: Scottish Parliament

Northern Ireland Council for Voluntary Action (2009) 'Anti-Poverty strategy adopted', news release, 29 January, available at www.nicva.org/index.cfm/section/News/key/290109-anti-poverty-strategy

Office of the First Minister and Deputy First Minister (OFMDFM) (2005) *Ageing in an Inclusive Society: Promoting the inclusion of older people strategy,* Belfast: OFMDFM

Office of the First Minister and Deputy First Minister (OFMDFM) (2006) *Lifetime Opportunities: Government's anti-poverty and social inclusion strategy for Northern Ireland,* Belfast: OFMDFM

Palmer G (2009) *Indicators of poverty and social exclusion: some cross-country comparisons,* York: Joseph Rowntree Foundation (unpublished)

Personal Social Services Research Unit (PSSRU) (2008) *National Evaluation of Partnerships for Older People's Projects: Interim Report of Progress,* Canterbury: PSSRU, University of Kent

Riddell S, Priestly M, Pearson C, Mercer G, Barnes C, Jolly D and Williams V (2006) *Disabled People and Direct Payments: A UK Comparative Study,* Leeds: ESRC/Leeds University

Scottish Executive (2007) *All Our Futures: Planning for a Scotland with an Ageing Population,* Edinburgh: Scottish Executive

Scottish Government (2008) *Independent Review of Free Personal and Nursing Care in Scotland: A report by Lord Sutherland,* Edinburgh: Scottish Government

Watt P and Blair I with Davis H and Ritters K (2007) *Towards a business case for LinkAge Plus, Department for Work and Pensions Working Paper No 42* London: DWP

Welsh Assembly Government (2007) *One Wales: A progressive agenda for the government of Wales* Cardiff: Welsh Assembly Government

Welsh Assembly Government (2008a) *The Strategy for Older People in Wales 2008-2013: Living Longer, Living Better* Cardiff: Welsh Assembly Government

Welsh Assembly Government (2008b) *One Wales: Connecting the Nation* Cardiff: Welsh Assembly Government

Welsh Assembly Government (2008c) *Review of the Concessionary Fares Rail Pilot Scheme 2007-2008, announced 23 April 2008* Cardiff: Welsh Assembly Government

14. Reshaping structures of government across the UK

Richard Parry

Devolution within the United Kingdom provides the opportunity for differentiation in both the practices and the outputs of government. Much attention has been given to the scope for policy variation, with particular emphasis on charging practices (prescription charges, means-tested charging for personal care, bridge tolls, student fees and grants). These are essentially about the political will to depart from previous UK norms that were set for a mixture of economic rationing and revenue-raising reasons. Bolder compromises of the 'social union' within the UK (the welfare state analogue of the economic market) have not been evident because of the present lack of any conceptual challenge to it and the integrative force of Labour as the dominant party in UK administrations, at least until 2007 (Trench 2007, Greer 2009).

Changes in the architecture of government – the basis of public administration and the distribution of the tasks of government – are less visible and raise different questions. Positions on them are not necessarily shaped by political parties or ideologies, and many of the decisions in this field are about whether or not to accept inherited structures. The matters involved – the civil service, central–local relations, the governance of public bodies – have generally been of low political salience compared with policy change. These facts explain why a ten-year history of the devolved administrations does not show dramatic movements in these fields; but the changes that have occurred are of interest and warrant the further, comparative examination attempted in this chapter.

The public administration of devolution

Potentially, the devolved administrations can shape the state in their jurisdictions – the way that public business is done, the horizontal and vertical architecture of government, and the financial transfers within devolved government. But their state-shaping role is limited by their responsibilities: they can join up or remodel government only within the devolved sphere. The objectives of the devolved administrations are typically conceived in broad aspirations for social and economic improvement, but this depends on the external environment or reserved powers. The administrations cannot reshape non-devolved public bodies – which continue to exercise a normative influence on the way that public business is done – within their nations and so will never have the power to achieve their most ambitious objectives for the public sector.

There is also an important issue of scale. England is so much larger than the other nations that it must be organised on a more systematic and formal basis. The hundreds of local authorities and health trusts cannot be known individually to the centre. Central government remains organised in departmental 'silos'. In contrast, Scotland and Wales can run something close to an integrated administrative machine. Scotland does not have central departments at all. Wales uses the term 'department' but these are administrative conveniences de-aligned from the committee structure of the National Assembly. Northern Ireland has statutory departments as part of the power-share of ministerial jobs but some of them are too small to sustain a personnel and finance capability and all are being drawn into Executive-wide systems. In all three nations, local and health authorities are clearly subordinate delivery mechanisms for national priorities, known and controlled individually. Local political issues quickly become national and structures respond. It is hard to detach system change from substantive political issues. And it is with the political context of each nation that discussion should begin.

Political contexts

Scotland

For the first time in any nation under devolution, in Scotland from May 2007 there was a triple play of *single-party, minority* and *nationalist* administration. The third of these attracted the most attention, but the former two were also significant for public administration. Wales had a single-party Labour administration in its second session (2003–7) and now has some nationalist ministers, but it has had nothing like the threefold change of gear. Northern Ireland by statute can never have any of the three. The three variables have had distinctive and mutually reinforcing implications in Scotland.

Single-party government replaced the Labour–Liberal Democrat coalitions of 1999–2007 that required special provisions in the Scottish Ministerial Code and the Guide to Collective Decision-Making for Cabinet behaviour and civil service briefing. More important, however, was that from the start they operated under programmes for government drafted with civil service advice. The SNP government allowed a reversion to Westminster norms, assisted by three factors: the clear drafting of the SNP manifesto, including proposals for the machinery of government; the ability of leading SNP politicians to relate well to officials, for whom a single-party government is something of a liberation; and the economics-based objectives that have been adopted. Single-party government also gives a more stable role to special advisers, and they have become notably prominent, taking part in official briefings alongside the First Minister's official spokesman.

Minority government was an unexpected outcome of an electoral system designed to produce coalitions. As Wales showed after its elections in 2007, the strangest kinds of rainbows of party combinations may be considered (a process also evident in German coalition formation after the 2005 elections). Instead of the German model that inspired its electoral system, Scotland has now followed the Canadian model where the leading party forms the government and, if a minority, manoeuvres itself through until it calls an election. This technique was also used in the UK in 1974, but, like Germany, Scotland lacks a non-contrived way to call an early election. The result is that the current Scottish Government in Parliament has a weak legislative capacity. But this weakness is not carried forward into the executive branch, where the government has at its disposal an administrative machine focused on its clear objectives and has many choices about how it conducts public business.

Nationalist government was supposed to be destabilising to the devolved political system and traumatic for the civil service. After three years, the reality has been different. From the start, the civil service has offered advice on constitutional change as well as policy areas. Once the hurdle of the precise drafting of the first independence White Paper *Choosing Scotland's Future* (August 2007) was overcome, by suggesting that a referendum on the opening of negotiations for independence would be compatible with the reservation of the Act of Union at Westminster, constitutional matters were moved into the 'national conversation' and substantive policy development in devolved areas became much more prominent (Scottish Government 2009a).

SNP ministers have proved to be effective actors within the UK-derived administrative system they occupy and at the higher end of performance of devolved ministers. The party entered office wishing to establish its credentials in government by managing its relations with a range of actors in the political system and civil society that had no great history of sympathy with nationalism. Elite economic actors were brought on board in the Council of Economic Advisers, and medical and educational leaders were spared extreme versions of the reform agenda such as the use of private contractors to provide NHS services. The civil service has been managed non-contentiously. Both the ministerial and the top civil service team have remained unusually stable: Sir John Elvidge continues as Permanent Secretary and the first departures among the six Directors-General occurred only in 2009 (Philip Rycroft's move to the Department of Business, Innovation and Skills being a notable reinstatement of the tradition of giving top officials Whitehall experience).

Wales

The model of Welsh devolution on offer initially was based on the traditional local government practice of committees of the elected body holding elected power. But this potentially innovative approach to central government responsibilities was not pursued. Even during the passage of the proposals this was modified towards a greater separation of executive and legislature. This continued through the unofficial denomination of 'ministers' and a 'Welsh Assembly Government' into a full separation on the Westminster and Scotland model in the Government of Wales Act 2006 following a full review by the Richard Commission in 2004. Further provisions in that Act, favoured by the Assembly Government, will allow a move to primary legislative powers on the Scottish model by referendum. This has been taken forward cautiously since 2008 through the 'All Wales Convention' (which reported in 2009) in search of a political context that would make the risk of a referendum worth taking, which was achieved in February 2010 when all parties in the Assembly voted for it.

After administrations formed by the Labour Party with a bare majority or none at all, interspersed by a period of Labour–Liberal Democrat coalition, the weakening of Labour's position in the 2007 elections led to an extraordinary political interlude. During this period an abortive coalition of the other parties and a temporary Labour minority administration preceded a historical compromise between Labour and Plaid Cymru (Trench 2008). The two parties, both left of centre but divided by the national issue, agreed to campaign for more Assembly powers and – as set out in their document *One Wales* – to govern in coalition on the basis of a traditional 'old Labour' type of welfare state.

Parallel to this, the Welsh devolved bureaucracy had been forming itself into a government machine. From the start, they were keener than their Scottish counterparts to develop separate personnel systems, recruiting through open advertisement and not taking new entrants through the civil service-wide Fast Stream Competition. The personal role of Sir Jon Shortridge, Permanent Secretary from 1999 to 2008, was of influence on this strategy. The response to perceived deficiencies in some public bodies – such as Education and Learning Wales – was to absorb them into the Assembly Government. This approach of 'growth by acquisition' increased its size, presence and distinctiveness.

Northern Ireland

The legal structuring of public administration issues has always been an important component of Northern Ireland devolution. The basis of the 1998 Belfast Agreement was that government ministries would form blocks of political resources to be distributed among the political parties. The departments – and even their names – were given statutory force and an Office of First Minister and Deputy First Minister was set up to supply cohesion.

In the first attempt at devolution from 1999 to 2002 Democratic Unionist and Sinn Fein ministers were not talking to one another. An interval of direct rule followed during which these two parties became the largest in their communities, displacing the Ulster Unionists and Social and Democratic Labour parties. Once the deal was done to restart the Executive in 2007 the basis of communication between ministers was achieved, but the immobility of the structure of public administration persisted. Decisions about the ministerial handling of the justice and policing portfolio were one element of the protracted disputes between the parties over this issue that began in 2009. This was finally resolved in February 2010 when the parties finally agreed to devolve powers over policing (see Muir, this volume).

A Review of Public Administration was launched in 2002 to address the congestion of the institutional landscape (Knox and Carmichael 2006). It became a vehicle for civil service reform and the reduction in the number of authorities. One implementation plan was announced by the direct rule administration in 2005 but was never implemented. The final outcome of 11 rather than 26 local authorities and a single education authority was a political compromise within the new Executive, but the debate was about numbers of authorities rather than the structure of provision. The one important Northern Ireland innovation – the unity of health and personal social services – was preserved.

Drivers of difference: the common elements

Within these political contexts, common variables apply. These involve the differentiation of public functions wither vertically (between agencies) and horizontally (between levels of government); relations between parts of the system, including reorganisations; and the role of the various types of public employees, including civil servants. The drivers of differences in public administration are different from those in policy. In policy fields, the devolved nations have somewhat different approaches to social rights, the sharing of the costs of the welfare state between users and the government, and the character of service delivery. There is some learning – or at least observation – between parts of the UK, especially on relief from charging for services.

In public administration the processes are much more hidden inside government. There are various formal constraints on differentiation of which policy actors are aware. They include the unified civil service in England, Scotland and Wales, whose rules insist on a uniform structure of pay and contracts for the Senior Civil Service, limitations on the numbers of special advisers, approval of the most senior appointments by the Prime Ministers, and the filling of vacancies in accordance with civil service codes as monitored by the Civil Service Commissioners.

While the concept of a block budget gives the devolved administrations discretion over how to spend the money transferred to them, the Treasury remains the ultimate manager of all UK public expenditure and the setter of rules on government accounting, managing the technicalities of the Barnett formula and annually managed expenditure. Questions are always arising about the handling of technical accounting matters that constrain the formal division of powers (a classic case being the Treasury's write-off of the debt of Scottish local authority housing departments if tenants voted to transfer ownership to a housing association).

There is constant traffic between finance staff in the devolved administrations and the Treasury about the protocols of conformity with the UK public finance framework. Matters covered include the treatment of debt and capital expenditure, and the way that housing benefit and council tax benefit are run by devolved local authorities on British-wide rules. Attempts by the SNP administration to develop novel means of mobilising private finance on big projects like the new Forth Road Bridge have proved difficult to implement. The Scottish Futures Trust, set up in 2008, is more of a think tank on good practice than a source of extra money. All the administrations enter into conversations – in which they are essentially supplicants to the Treasury – on matters like the use of unspent balances and the re-phasing of capital expenditure between years. The SNP has been unable to take forward its plans to replace council tax by a local income tax partly because it would lose the revenue stream from council tax benefit. It is also difficult to run 'one place' approaches to local social policy of the kind being introduced in England in 2009 under Comprehensive Area Assessments because of the mix of devolved and reserved powers involved.

As well as these formal constraints, there are others that are informal or self-imposed – and these are probably the dominant variables. The British tradition of non-partisan public officials at central and local level is of enduring influence. The architecture of public authorities (executive agencies, non-departmental public bodies, public corporations and so on) tends to be accepted, partly because of Treasury rules but also to ensure central control through direction (known as 'sponsorship') and board appointments. The efficiency strategy introduced at UK level in 2004 has been accepted as a source of money for service growth. The organisation of the welfare state, and especially the separation of health from local government, has been accepted with minor innovations such as the piloting of direct election of some health board members in Scotland. Unitary local government is the norm in the devolved administrations and is becoming increasingly so in England, with new authorities created in 2009 (ironically including Northumberland, whose preservation as a two-tier authority was a reason for voting 'No' in the referendum on devolution to the North East in 2004).

By some mixture of formal and self-imposed constraints, we are left with a rearrangement of deckchairs rather than the construction of a new ship of state. Institutional forms of public authorities are accepted; basic aspects of the organisation of the welfare state such as the separation of the health service from local government and the autonomy of universities are accepted, as is unitary, and so territorially fragmented, local government. The professions and trade unions, typically organised on a Britain-wide basis, are powerful cross-administration forces in direct contact with government, and business and the media promote UK-wide priorities.

The pattern of public administration

Even in their short lives, the policy and administrative systems of the devolved administrations have come under review for contrasting political reasons. Of the formal external reviews, Northern Ireland's Review of Public Administration, mostly carried forward under direct rule, was based on system congestion; the number of authorities was perceived as too large, given the size of the population. Wales's Richard Commission, reporting in 2004, was based on a sense of incomplete powers and laid out a direction of movement towards a Scottish level of responsibilities. It led to Westminster legislation (the Government of Wales Act 2006) that formalised the distinction between Assembly and Government and introduced a midway legislative category of Assembly Measure.

Table 14.1. Patterns of public administration in UK nations

	Scotland	Wales	N. Ireland	England
Central government	Integrated Scottish Government, no departments	Essentially integrated Welsh Assembly Government, with non-statutory 'departments'	Statutory departments, some common services	Non-statutory departments (generally) with single office of Secretary of State allowing instant reorganisation
Local government	Single-tier (32 councils)	Single-tier (22 councils)	From May 2011 11 single-tier; education and housing	56 unitary authorities, 27 counties, 268 boroughs and districts
Civil service – Senior Civil Service	Integrated with rest of Home Civil Service	Integrated with rest of Home Civil Service	Separate, but follows Home Civil Service arrangements	Central contracts and arrangements
Civil service – other grades	Part of Home Civil Service, autonomy over pay and grading	Part of Home Civil Service, autonomy over pay and grading	Separate Northern Ireland Civil Service	Departments and agencies have autonomy over pay and grading within running costs total
Health service	14 (area) Health Boards, other special boards, no trusts	7 Health Boards (from October 2009)	Health and Social Care Board (from April 2009), 5 Health and Social Care Trusts	10 Strategic Health Authorities, 152 Primary Care Trusts, 122 Foundation Trusts, 252 other Trusts
Quangos	Some public corporations (e.g. Scottish Water)	Largest public corporations and non-departmental public bodies absorbed into Welsh Assembly Government	Some public corporations (e.g. Northern Ireland Railways)	Public corporations, state-owned businesses and non-departmental public bodies

In Scotland, Westminster legislation conferred powers over railway policy on the Scottish Parliament and maintained its size (otherwise facing reduction when the number of Scottish Westminster MPs was cut in order to align their constituency size with the average). But the main impetus to change came from constitutional aspirations. The SNP's 'National Conversation' – a device to prepare the ground for an independence referendum, including civil service planning work on what independence would involve – was countered by the Calman Commission, an initiative of the unionist parties in the Scottish Parliament but serviced by the UK Government, which reported in 2009 (Commission on Scottish Devolution 2009).

At the level of nuts-and-bolts change, the pattern of both structure and change in structure is unsystematic (Table 14.1). The devolved nations have shown a preference for unitary, single-tier authorities. The major reorganisations have been in health: in Scotland in 2004, abolishing Trusts, in Wales in 2003, making health authorities smaller and coterminous with local authorities and then in 2009 when area boards on the Scottish model were introduced, and in Northern Ireland in 2009 – to a single purchasing board with multiple trusts. Wales, like Scotland, has ended commissioning/providing distinctions in favour of local boards, but Northern Ireland has not. Northern Ireland is the only nation to have reorganised local government, which in 2011 will see a reduction in the number of authorities but will increase their powers only slightly.

Current issues
As examples of the ways that devolved administrations can reappraise and change their public administration arrangements, the rest of this chapter looks at four issues – attacks on quangos (or assorted public bodies with boards appointed by ministers but without being ministerial or local authority departments); new overarching relations with local government; separate civil services; integrated public services; and the enhancing of democratic participation.

Quango-bashing
All the devolved administrations were rooted in the concept of bringing functions under democratic control and, in the imagery usually used, de-cluttering the landscape of public bodies. The test has been whether the desire for rationalisation outweighs the political convenience of having special-purpose agencies whose existence will advertise attention to a policy issue.

The most interesting action has come in Wales. In 2004 the Government decided to grow through acquisition by absorbing several quangos, including the Welsh Development Agency and the training body Education and Learning Wales. It adopted the principle, also influential in Scotland, that when a task was being performed with funding and policy direction by ministers, and where there were not arguments for arm's length control of funding as in universities and the arts, the function should be absorbed. Transitional issues around terms and pensions were difficult, but the result was that the Welsh Assembly Government became larger, more orientated to service delivery, and a greater counterweight to local government, able to run its own local offices now that it had absorbed the quangos and their local networks (Prosser *et al* 2006).

In Scotland the Labour–Liberal Democrat administration took the important decision (implemented in 2004) to eliminate NHS Trusts altogether. It also set out plans in 2001 to shed 43 of the 113 bodies studied, with arguments on accountability weighing more than those on efficiency (Parry 2009). The SNP policy in government was set out in *Simplifying Public Services*: on 30 January 2008 Alex Salmond announced a reduction of 52 in the 199 previously-identified national organisations. The arguments presented for this were over the desirability of a 'leaner, more strategic' landscape able to promote value for money and user focus. Accountability issues, traditionally the most prominent considerations in justifying particular organisational forms, were much less prominent and were presented in the context of 'effective sponsorship arrangements', which sounds reasonable but is really about giving government the means of control it seeks. This policy has been pursued since and its results can be seen on the Scottish Government website under the title 'Simplification News'[1]. Progress in cutting the quangos is charted on a 'simplification tracker' on the same website[2].

The concept of 'simplification' poses many analytical problems. If simpler means fewer, a numbers game can ensue. Counting public organisations large and small in an aggregate total is a crude approach that does not aid the discernment of the best arrangements for each service. If simpler means a more coherent conceptual pattern of public authorities it is not taken very far in the present exercise – and indeed the various forms (public corporation, executive agency, company limited by guarantee and so on) are inherited from before devolution.

In order to persevere with this process the SNP government brought forward the Public Services Reform (Scotland) Bill 2009, which would rationalise quangos in some areas and give the full rights to intervene, in the name of efficiency, in the business of those that remain. Sections of the Bill take Scotland in the direction of a single care agency (Social Care and Social Work Improvement Scotland), single health quality agency (Healthcare Improvement Scotland) and single arts funder (Creative Scotland).

The Bill would give the Scottish Government major catch-all powers to create, modify or abolish quangos by secondary legislation. It breaches the principle that if a body is set up, usually for a political purpose, by primary legislation – and with full parliamentary accountability – it should only be changed by primary legislation. Section 10 (3) (b) allows quangos (as listed in schedule 3) to be abolished by order. The great majority of bodies in the baseline of 199 bodies are covered by this – the main exceptions being National Parks Authorities, NHS Bodies, Executive Agencies

1. www.scotland.gov.uk/Topics/Government/public-bodies/simplification-programme/News
2. www.scotland.gov.uk/Topics/Government/public-bodies/Simplification-Tracker

and fire, prisons and police inspectorates. Ombudsmen appointed by Parliament are included, but not the Parliamentary Standards Commissioner. Ministers, in respect of bodies listed in schedule 3, may 'by order make any provisions which they consider would improve the exercise of public functions', having regard to efficiency, effectiveness and economy (however that might be tested). Safeguards, including that the use of powers must be 'proportionate to the policy objective', would be hard to evaluate and apply.

The previous administration's line was to favour direct accountability of ministers to Parliament without any arm's length organisational form. The present Scottish Government went down this route when Communities Scotland was taken within the Government as an executive agency and then lost that status also, a move replicated for some fisheries and fire functions. This kind of 'simplifying' may actually be very complex as terms and conditions of staff and the business systems of the organisations have to be reconciled and integrated.

The present Scottish Government's policy seems somewhat different from its predecessor's. It is based less on democratic theory than on a pragmatic search for delivery mechanisms that are 'fit for purpose' in particular contexts, within a framework of the Government having its way when it needs to. The mechanisms used are essentially derived from a jumble of legal and political forms of 'Scottish public authority' inherited from the UK system. The 'simplification' strategy claims to do this, but in practice the overall result is to reduce the number of bodies occupying the landscape. The present strategy may or may not be simplifying government, but the Bill would certainly simplify the task of the executive branch when it wishes to reconstruct or direct public bodies.

Concordats with local government
Devolved administrations have not been immune to two general tendencies in the history of central-local relations worldwide:

i) Grant consolidation in which the autonomy and managerial capability of local government is emphasised and the centre reduces the demands on itself; in this case the interest of the centre is in ensuring that local government is strong enough to meet the demands upon it.

ii) Central policy initiatives tied to specific 'ring-fenced' funding and manipulation of the grant in order to control local actions; in this case central–local relations become a political tool with unequal power resources between the two levels.

Scotland and Wales saw consolidation in the 1960s and 70s and then a movement the other way. The key political process was that the Conservatives – who legislated both reorganisations of local government – started off the 1975 two-tier system with reasonable aspirations to control some regions or counties but by the 1980s resumed interest in single-tier authorities, some of which would offer them political prospects. Promoting this required tight boundaries and resulted in 32 authorities in Scotland and 22 in Wales in 1996 (numerically at the high end of the options offered). It has become a common view to suggest that there are too many authorities and that money could be saved by rationalising them. Until 2007 the movement was in a pro-central direction, long feared in Scotland as a consequence of a Scottish Parliament but resisted better in Wales because of the strength of local interests. But Scotland, as a part of Labour–Liberal Democrat coalition deals, first aligned local and Holyrood elections in 2003. Then in 2007 it introduced the single transferable vote (STV) system for local elections (but in rather small wards of three or four councillors, which prevented full proportionality). Elections have subsequently been de-aligned following major malfunctions of the voting system in 2007, with the terms of present councils extended to 2012.

The result of STV was a clearout of the old Labour fiefdoms (it retained overall majorities in only two councils) and a chance for the minority SNP government to establish its credentials with local government by offering a new relationship. The Concordat negotiated in November 2007 was a complex deal involving increased grants to enable authorities to freeze council tax; an end to many specific grants; an undertaking that efficiency savings assumed by the centre would be retained by local authorities and not deducted from the grant; an undertaking by the centre not to pursue structural reorganisation; and the rapid production of 'Single Outcome Agreements' (in 2008 and 2009) that would relate local actions to national priorities and performance frameworks.

After years of centralisation expressed by the concept of the ring-fenced grant as the mechanism for making progress on 'wicked issues', the Concordat offered a way back for local government to the implicitly pro-local spirit of the 1970s. Although concordat-type documents have been produced in England and Wales, the Scottish one is the first to offer a radical change in financial arrangements.

Although promoted as a breakthrough in central–local relations, the Single Outcome Agreements are best seen as part of the protocol of central–local relations under the new system. They are neither single, nor outcome-based, nor an agreement. They do not help to rationalise what local authorities are doing, they express inputs and outputs as well as outcomes (and many of the outcomes are outside the control of local government), and they are more in the tradition of giving the centre what it wants in the way it wants rather than being negotiated or agreed. Their relation to the previous big idea – Community Planning Partnerships – is still being worked through. They are interesting as new ways of presenting information and they have been accompanied by the linking of Directors in the Scottish Government with a couple of local authorities to the mutual education of both levels. They are soft contracts resembling the Open Method of Coordination of the European Union and may amount to little more than a convenient device to get the Concordat underway (Community Care Providers Scotland 2008).

Separate civil services

An aspect of the devolution settlement that seemed unstable and unlikely to survive was the continued inclusion of Scottish and Welsh officials in the Home Civil Service. At present the SNP's call in its 2007 election manifesto for a 'wholly devolved Scottish civil service on the same model and basis as the Northern Irish civil service' awaits primary legislation at Westminster. A Labour bill that puts the civil service on a statutory footing might have been a vehicle for this, but the Scottish Government's view is that it is: 'committed to the establishment of a separate Scottish Civil Service; but has concluded that the Constitutional Reform and Governance Bill is not the best vehicle for promoting such proposals. Substantive change in this area is a complex and long-term project, which the Government continues to pursue separately with the UK Government' (Scottish Government 2009b: para 8.2). Never can a kick into the long grass have been more clearly signalled.

The limitations of the approach have become clear, for the Northern Ireland experience is of a service run on traditional British norms (as indeed in many ways the civil service of the Republic of Ireland is). The Northern Irish civil service (NICS) is organisationally distinct from the Home Civil Service, and so sets up an additional barrier to staff movement not faced in Scotland and Wales, but it is not distinct in character. The NICS's adoption of the pay and grading arrangements of the Senior Civil Service is telling. If the hallmark of a 'real' civil service is the shadowing of the Whitehall progenitor, there is little point in being separate.

Northern Ireland has some local services delivered by civil service departments. Because of power-sharing, its civil service has a more rigid departmental structure than in Wales and particularly Scotland (where departments within the Scottish Government no longer exist). It also has a dual centre, the Department of Finance and Personnel and the Office of First Minister and Deputy First Minister. It has its own Civil Service Commissioners, who are non-devolved and so could impede any move to new types of recruitment. Because of these singularities the NICS does not offer a very useful model to Scotland, and the UK government has become increasingly confident in arguing against the Northern Ireland model that an administration should organise its own civil service.

The civil service lacks statutory definition and so it 'is what it is' – historically crown service (so creating the illusion of not working for politicians), and latterly working in a ministerial department. The uncertain boundary between the civil service and the rest of central government makes it difficult to be categorical about what civil servants do, and so in practice being a civil servant is a personal status (this is particularly apparent in the high managerial level of the National Heath Service). Offering a statutory civil service gives the impression of a guarantee of standards and consistency that was previously exercisable by prerogative but if it is unaccompanied by any fresh thinking on the service it might be an empty shell.

The Brown Government's Constitutional Reform and Governance Bill introduced in July 2009 gives an operational definition of the civil service that excludes the Security Service, the Secret Intelligence Service, Government Communications Headquarters, the Northern Ireland Civil Service and the Northern Ireland Court Service (a tiny separate service set to become an executive agency when justice is devolved to the Northern Ireland Executive). It would be technically easy in terms of primary legislation to add the Scottish and Welsh administrations to the excluded group and so detach them managerially while maintaining the normative basis of their job, but this has not been proposed. The one point of substance in the bills for the Scottish and Welsh administrations was to free them from formal Whitehall approval and numerical constraints on special advisers on the grounds that this could be left to local political accountability.

The legislative entrenchment of civil service values has been offered as an advantage of a statutory basis, and the Bill shows that the narrative that the virtues of the civil service having to be secured at UK level has survived unscathed from the decade of devolution. It would require (Section 5) a civil service code of conduct and (section 7) a requirement to carry out duties for the assistance of the administration (UK or devolved) as it is duly constituted for the time being, whatever its political complexion – and would require officials to carry out their duties with integrity and honesty and (except for special advisers) with objectivity and impartiality. For appointments, except for special advisers, the iconic phrase 'a person's selection must be on merit on the basis of fair and open competition' would be enshrined in statute (section 10 [2]).

The UK government could issue separate codes for the Scottish and Welsh administrations (as it does cosmetically for the present Civil Service Code), and their First Ministers, alongside leaders of the two largest UK opposition parties, would be consulted about the appointment of First Civil Service Commissioner. But the Bill amounts to a more explicit restriction on the devolved administrations than the present discretionary arrangements; the Minister for the Civil Service (the UK Prime Minister) has the power to manage the civil service without qualification (section 3 [1]).

Between its interim and final reports, Kenneth Calman's Commission on Scottish Devolution (2009) defined a somewhat bolder 'devolution plus' but it did not offer any ingenious approaches to the civil service issue in the same way as it did for taxation. It suggested that the UK Prime Minister's appointment rights for the most senior officials should be delegated to the Head of the Home Civil Service acting on the advice of the Civil Service Commissioners (Para 4.202). The latter qualification is important as it is the First Minister who in practice – and rightly – exercises the ministerial involvement allowed by the commissioners. While identifying an anomaly and a problem of perception (that present arrangements might be seen as allowing the UK Prime Minister to impose senior officials) it substitutes something that might be worse (that UK senior officials would make top devolved appointments). This has been accepted by the UK Government.

Calman's statement that 'the unified civil service ensures that there are common standards of professionalism, and the same relationship between devolved Ministers and officials as in the UK Government' (para 4.39) sets out the received, but unconvincing, UK position. Whatever 'professionalism' may mean – presumably the characteristics set out in the Civil Service Code – it is unlikely to be a product of the unified service rather than of the intrinsic socialised norms of Scottish administration. And the minister–official relationships cannot be precisely the same because they operate under the principles of the Scottish Parliament. The Commission quotes evidence given to it that the present system is desirable, but fails to provide a cogent, UK-orientated defence of the unified Home Civil Service or suggest measures to differentiate the devolved administrations from UK government departments in their managerial responsibilities and delegations. Meanwhile, staff movements between Scotland and Whitehall have dried up. Between 1999 and 2007 a total of 318 civil servants were transferred from UK government departments to the Executive (59 of them in the start-up year of 1999) against 155 in the opposite direction; but from May to November 2007 there were only one in, five out and two loans each way (Scottish Parliament written answers S3W-5909 12.11.07 and S3W-6325 27.11.07).

Integrated public services

Traditionally, British public administration has been stratified horizontally according to categories of employment relationship. Civil servants had skills in high-level political management which, in the devolved system, are typified by intergovernmental dealings. But it is now very difficult to see how these are particularly facilitated, let alone guaranteed, by a common status in a unified service. Scotland and Wales emphasise joined-up delivery and are pulling their systems in the direction of a common public service leadership echelon in their nations with movement between public bodies. Outside the health departments, however, movement has been slow, not least because of pay and pension complications about moving between employers. The ideal senior official with extensive outside experience but the right skills has proved elusive.

Joined-up services centred on the citizen and the locality has been a major theme in Wales, but the concept has assigned the leadership role to the Welsh Assembly Government. This was the emphasis of its policy paper *Making the Connections* (2004), of the report of the committee led by English local government leader Jeremy Beecham, *Beyond Boundaries* (2006) and of the Labour-Plaid Cymru *One Wales* document. The Beecham report suggested:

> *The role of the Assembly Government should be to design and lead a delivery system which enables and supports this vision. This means moving from the traditional, detached central government role of issuing strategies, regulations and targets to far more engaged leadership of the delivery process.… The scale of Wales makes this possible, through direct communication between the Assembly Government and local organisations.* (Beecham report 2006: 56)

Wales has gone furthest in the direction of a unified public service through the organisation Public Service Management Wales and its Human Resources Steering Group. Officials from all parts of the public sector meet at summer schools and do some joint training. In itself, this does not break down barriers to movement. The key mechanism for transfer is the open advertisement of civil service posts in which existing officials compete with outsiders for promotion, a strategy initially pursued by the Equality of Opportunity Committee of the Assembly. The needs of particular posts and absorption of former quango staff have somewhat compromised the principle, but it stands in contrast to the traditional promotion boards in the Scottish Government. An important symbol was the appointment of a non-civil servant, Dame Gill Morgan from the NHS Confederation (who had served on the Beecham committee), as Permanent Secretary in 2008.

Scotland has attempted to integrate its public services through a common focus on its national objectives and targets as defined by the SNP government, with Cabinet Secretaries having broad portfolios. In all systems direct external advertising have become common, and precise job specifications undermine the old idea of competitive merit recruitment into a status rather than a particular post.

Enhancing democratic participation
Democracy and participation were at the heart of the devolution project. The Scottish Parliament adopted 'sharing the power' as one of its guiding principles. The public petition system in the Scottish Parliament, which can lead to investigation of even the problem of a single individual by a parliamentary committee, typifies the approach. Throughout the devolved administrations the volume of democratic control and investigation has reached levels unattainable in Westminster.

One of the most interesting innovations is the SNP's decisions to pilot direct elections to Health Boards, to give a statutory basis to local authority representation on the boards, and move to a position where elected and local authority representatives had a majority on the boards. This was enacted in the Health Boards (Membership and Elections) (Scotland) Act 2009 and piloted (in postal, single transferable vote ballots) in Fife and Dumfries and Galloway in 2010. Primary Care Trusts in England have strong membership links and working links with local authorities, but this is the boldest attempt in the UK to overcome the democratic deficits in health since it was removed from local authority control in two stages in 1948 and 1974.

The present initiative is only a pilot one, and questions remain about the size and operation of health boards as a real forum for decision-making, and about the relationship between executive and non-executive members. There is also a sense that this policy has been subject to implementation constraints that did not prevent its enactment but that will slow down its general application.

Elsewhere, the move has been to larger units (especially in health in Wales and Northern Ireland), which might be seen as a move from democratic to managerial control. In Wales, the alignment of health with local authorities has been reversed. Both Wales and Northern Ireland have a history of resistance to extending local authority powers and have ended up with centrally-run mechanisms for local involvement (such as community consultation by the new Police Service of Northern Ireland). The SNP's Concordat with local government gives more spending discretion to the local level, but the council tax freeze removes command over revenue. Taken as a whole, the record on democratisation in the devolved systems has been mixed and shows evidence of the lack of trust in elected local government evident in UK debate about the best way to secure choice and accountability.

Conclusion: transferable innovations?

What might the devolved administrations learn from one other, or from England and other jurisdictions, in the public administration field? In terms of international literature on policy transfer, the UK is well placed to facilitate compatible borrowing of practice, because of its common language and administrative traditions. In policy areas, we can distinguish gradations of value (charging more or less, spending more or less) from conservative non-innovation (deciding not to do what the UK did) and genuinely innovative policy (a new approach or instrument). All raise points of real interest for the UK system as a whole.

In the structures of government, political salience is less and the financial variable is much weaker, and so the changes are less significant. Health Service organisation is the clearest case of a distinctive path from England; the role of local government has not changed much; quangos have been cut back, but the basic model is still used; the civil service has not changed formally – left by Whitehall to go its own way, the way has not been radical. Wales, as the newest system, has shown the greatest capacity for adaptation.

The impact of the developments described in this chapter has been attenuated by their absorption into the normal processes of political power and resource bargaining. Policy on quangos, civil services, central–local relations and integrated public services has taken characteristic UK themes somewhat further than in England, but the effect has been far from radical – even in Northern Ireland, where a large-scale Review of Public Administration was attempted. As might be expected, the political sociology of UK administration, fused by political parties, professions and trade unions, remains common and familiar. Debates and initiatives have been welcome, but the general picture is of a faith in the 'British way of doing things', which is somewhat surprising in the context of worries about the policy performance of government and the capacity of devolved administrations to do something about it.

References

Beecham Report (2006) *Beyond Boundaries: Citizen-Centred Local Services for Wales* Cardiff: Welsh Assembly Government

Commission on Scottish Devolution (2009) *Serving Scotland Better: Scotland and the United Kingdom in the 21st Century (The Calman Report)* Edinburgh: Commission on Scottish Devolution

Community Care Providers Scotland (2008) *Single Outcome Agreements 2008–09.* www.ccpscotland.org/assets/files/ccps/pubilcations/research%20reports/singleoutcomereport.pdf, Edinburgh: Community Care Providers Scotland

Greer S (ed) (2009) *Devolution and Social Citizenship in the UK* Bristol: Policy Press

Knox C and Carmichael P (2006) 'Bureau Shuffling? The Review of Public Administration in Northern Ireland', *Public Administration* 84:4 941-965

Parry R (2009) 'Quangos. Agencies and the Scottish Parliament' in Jeffery C and Mitchell J (eds) *The Scottish Parliament 1999-2009: the First Decade* Edinburgh: Luath Press

Prosser S, Connolly M, Hough R and Potter K (2006) 'Making it Happen' in *Public Service: Devolution in Wales as Case-Study* Exeter: Imprint Academic

Scottish Government (2009a) *Your Scotland, Your Voice: A National Conversation* Edinburgh: Scottish Government

Scottish Government (2009b) *Constitutional Reform and Governance Bill Legislative Consent Memorandum:* www.scottish.parliament.uk/business/legConMem/LCM-2009-2010/CRGBill.htm

Trench A (ed) (2007) D*evolution and Power in the United Kingdom* Manchester: Manchester University Press

Trench A (ed) (2008) *The State of the Nations 2008* Exeter: Imprint Academic

15. Devolution or divergence? UK third sector policy since 2000

Pete Alcock

This chapter explores the extent to which devolution has led to a divergence in policy development and delivery in relation to third sector organisations across the UK.

In common with many other policy areas policy divergence in the field of third sector activity and organisation already existed before the arrival of political devolution in 1999. The major sector umbrella organisations have long had a separate national structure. The leading sector body, the National Council for Voluntary Organisations (NCVO), in fact operates in England only, and has collaborative contact with separate national umbrellas: the Scottish Council for Voluntary Organisations (SCVO), the Wales Council for Voluntary Action (WCVA) and the Northern Ireland Council for Voluntary Action (NICVA). All of these are membership organisations supporting and promoting the activities of voluntary and community organisations in each nation.

There are a range of other national agencies operating within the third sector. Indeed, there is some competition and contestation over who speaks for which parts of what are in practice wide and diverse social spaces. This is particularly true of the social enterprise sub-sector, where there are also separate national bodies: the Social Enterprise Coalition (SEC, England), the Scottish Social Enterprise Coalition (SSEC), Community Enterprise Wales (CEW) and the Social Economy Network (SEN, Northern Ireland). But there are other national bodies too, with slightly different splits. For instance, the Association of Chief Executives of Voluntary Organisations (ACEVO) operates in England and Wales and welcomes members from across the UK, but collaborates with the separate Association of Chief Officers of Scottish Voluntary Organisations (ACOSVO) and Chief Officers 3rd Sector (CO3) in Northern Ireland.

The different organisational structure for the third sector across the four nations had already contributed to some important differences in policy and practice before devolution, and to variation in the availability of data about the sector; and we will return to discuss these themes briefly below. Ironically, though, while devolution has opened up the space for policy divergence and experimentation, there has been a tendency for the devolved administrations to follow the policy lead set by the UK New Labour government, which has proved the dominant policy influence in third sector debates. In Northern Ireland this has been a consequence of the re-imposition of direct rule from 2002 to 2007, while in Scotland and Wales Labour has been in power or in coalition government for much of the century so far. The result of this has been, in part, to blunt the previous distinctiveness of the third sectors in each.

However, this policy convergence has been challenged more recently by the re-establishment of the Northern Ireland Executive and the success of the Scottish National Party in taking office in the Scottish Government. There is some emerging evidence of greater policy diversity which may flow from this, and of course this could be accentuated much more if this year's general election brings about a change of administration at Westminster. Policy devolution therefore remains a moving game.

What defines the 'third sector' and how big is it?

Analysing third sector policy is difficult because the notion of a 'third sector' is itself a problematic and contested one. The idea is based on distinction between this and the other two sectors – the state and the market. Third sector organisations are thus those that are neither public bodies nor commercial enterprises. This is a negative rather than a positive notion, however, and it is not always welcomed by third sector practitioners who, with some justification, point out that organised voluntary action in practice preceded both the state and the market. Neither is the concept consistently used either within the UK or internationally. Hence talk of the non-profit sector, the non-statutory sector, the non-government sector, and the voluntary and community sector.

It is also far from clear that all organisations within the third sector can be readily distinguished from the public and commercial worlds. Some commentators have talked about the relationships between the sectors as being characterised by overlapping landscapes rather than distinct fields (Evers and Laville 2004; see also Alcock and Scott 2007).

The third sector is sometimes referred to more generally as civil society – the space between formal government and individual action (Deakin 2001). Within this space there is in practice a wide and diverse range of activities and organisational forms, ranging from small community groups to international aid agencies (such as Oxfam) and including charities, cooperatives, mutual associations, sports and leisure clubs and social enterprises. In a sense there is as much separating these different organisations and activities as there is uniting them. Certainly many third sector organisations perceive – and organise – themselves as part of distinct sub-sectors (such as the cooperative movement) rather than any broader third sector.

Despite there existing a long and complex history between the sector and the state (see Lewis 1999), the notion of a third sector is a relatively new one in UK policy debates. It has been vigorously promoted by the Labour governments in their pursuit of a new approach to social policy reform: a third way, between state and market. This has entailed a process of modernisation and marketisation that has opened up a mixed economy of welfare to a wider range of service providers, of which third sector organisations are increasingly key players. And it has received formal government status through the establishment in 2006 of the Office of the Third Sector (OTS) within the Cabinet Office as a new site for the development and promotion of third sector policy action. However, its remit extends only to England.

One of the reasons for establishing the OTS was to bring together political and policy responsibility for the wide range of organisations in civil society into one government place. The politicians and policymakers were aware that departmental restructuring would not in itself create a homogenous third sector, however. Indeed, the definition of the third sector given on the OTS website recognises the extent to which it is operating within a field of diversity and difference, but it also seeks to identify some common characteristics that can be used to delineate the boundaries of the sector:

> *Organisations in the [third] sector share common characteristics. [They are]: non-governmental, value-driven, [and] principally reinvest any financial surpluses to further social, environmental or cultural objectives. The term encompasses voluntary and community organisations, charities, social enterprises, cooperatives and mutuals both large and small.* (www.cabinetoffice.gov.uk/third_sector/about_us.aspx)

Kendall (2003) discusses recent developments in the policy environment, in particular distinguishing between vertical policy intervention (focused on particular fields of activity such as social care, advice, or housing) and horizontal intervention (support and regulation for the sector as a whole). The latter is a more recent development and has been the dominant feature of Labour Government intervention over the last decade. Third sector policy is in a sense therefore merely the latest manifestation of relations between the state and the third sector, and this in part explains the consistency that in practice informs and underlies recent moves to policy devolution.

There are limitations in empirical knowledge and understanding of the sector. There is no consistent and undisputed data source on the size and shape of the sector, in part because of disputes about what it is that is being measured. The NCVO produces an annual Almanac[1] on the voluntary sector in the UK, now expanded and retitled to cover civil society more generally and a wider range of organisations, including universities and trade unions (Kane *et al* 2009). For 2006/7 it claims the total number of civil society organisations was 870,000 (although this includes 600,000 informal community organisations, for which NCVO admits that the data sources are poor).

Of this there were:

• 170,900 general charities

---

1. Much of the data relied on by the NCVO to construct its Almanac comes from a database developed by Guidestar (itself a social enterprise), drawn from Charity Commission and Industrial and Provident Society registers. This data, and that available from other regulators and national surveys, is now being collated and analysed by the Third Sector Research Centre (TSRC), and more detailed quantitative analysis of sector structure and trends will be available from the Centre in due course. The information included in this chapter can therefore only provide a broad overview.

- 8,500 registered industrial and provident societies
- 13,300 faith groups
- 900 community interest companies (a new legal form for social enterprises).

These are UK figures, aggregated from some of the separate country datasets discussed below. For charities the number for England and Wales was 145,000, after certain subsidiary organisations were excluded (Kane *et al* 2009). For these general charities total income for 2006/7 was £33.2 billion, an increase of 3.3 per cent on the previous year, and expenditure £31.2 billion, a similar increase. Of this income 31 per cent came from government sources, a slight decrease on the previous year but more generally this proportion has been growing in recent years. The major source of income remains voluntary contributions from individuals (52.5 per cent), with the rest coming from the private sector (4.9 per cent) or other voluntary sector sources (11.7 per cent) (ibid). The voluntary and community sector workforce in the UK in 2006 (based on those describing their employment in this way in the Labour Force Survey) was 634,000, an increase of 24 per cent since 1997 and comprising 2.2 per cent of all UK employees (ibid).

The UK policy context

The UK policy context has a long history. Lewis (1999) discusses three major shifts in this relationship over the twentieth century – from independence, to extension of public services, to a mixed economy and contracting for services. Kendall (2009) identifies three phases of post-war relations, each leading to greater degrees of engagement between the third sector and the state, and culminating in a climate of 'hyperactive mainstreaming' since 1997. There is some consensus that this has resulted in a 'sea change' (Craig *et al* 2004) in relations between the sector and the state in the last decade, which has been characterised by policymakers and commentators as a move to a new paradigm of partnership (see Lewis 2005), perhaps a fourth phase in Lewis's grand schema.

Certainly Labour's third way approach has included a more central role for the third sector in public service policy development and delivery and a new commitment from government to support the sector in delivering on this, as evidenced most recently in the Treasury report *Putting the Frontline First: Smarter government* (HM Treasury 2009). The approach has led to a higher profile for the sector in policy planning, resulting in a stream of key policy documents from the Home Office (1998, 2003, 2004), from the Treasury, which has taken a leading role in supporting funding for third sector activity (HM Treasury 2002, 2004) and from the Cabinet Office (2007a). All of these outline the importance of partnership between the sector and the state and the responsibility of government to support this proactively, as a result of which, in the early 2000s, overall UK government spending on third sector support increased significantly (see Cabinet Office 2007b).

By and large this is a partnership that has also been embraced by the third sector itself, certainly by some of the major sector agencies such as the NCVO and ACEVO, and by the large charities heavily involved in delivering public services such as MIND, the RNIB and Age Concern/Help the Aged. Indeed to some extent the initiative for an improved, and more proactive, engagement between the third sector and the state came initially from the sector itself, and in particular from the work of an independent commission (chaired by Nicholas Deakin) established by the NCVO to review the role of the sector for the new century. The commission concluded that relations with the state were now of critical importance to the development and operation of the sector and contractual funding for service provision was an important and growing feature of this. In such a context, therefore, it suggested both parties would benefit from some formalisation and regularisation of relations – preferably through the establishment of a negotiated 'concordat' which could underpin all future contracts and other funding arrangements (Deakin Commission 1996).

Despite this high profile endorsement of partnership, embracement of this new form of relations is far from universal. This is especially so among the smaller third sector organisations – such as those in England discussed below – that receive little or no direct funding from government and that are less likely to benefit from some of the new support services (see Craig *et al* 2004). There are concerns in some quarters that partnership may also lead to incorporation, with organisations increasingly dependent on public funding and support; isomorphism, with those delivering public services all looking just like the public providers they have replaced, and exclusion, with some organisations no longer able to compete for public funding or support. So while the heightening profile that the third sector has enjoyed in policy planning over the last decade has been welcomed by many both within and outside the sector, it is not without its challenges and problems.

The new policy environment, and the problems that have flowed from it, have influenced the development and implementation of third sector policy across the UK. The broad policy framework continues to be set by Westminster. However, devolution of policymaking has resulted in some significant differences in interpretation and initiative in Scotland, Wales and Northern Ireland, which have combined with the distinct histories of voluntary action and enterprise in these countries to create four separate policy regimes – albeit with common features.

England
Third sector policy in England has been a continuation of the trends identified for UK policy above, and in particular has seen a step change in policy engagement by government in order to forge a new partnership relationship between the sector and the state. The organisational, regulatory and financial terms of this new partnership build on previous policy and practice but since 2000 these policies and practices applied to England only. They can be identified as a distinctly English regime for third sector policy.

Of most importance here perhaps have been the organisational changes within government. When it came to power in 1997 Labour inherited a structure for support for voluntary and community action led primarily by the Voluntary Services Unit based in the Home Office. In 1999, as an early example of the new commitments to extend relations, this was expanded and relaunched as the Active Communities Unit with a much enhanced budget, and was later rebranded and extended again as the Active Communities Directorate.

In the same year social enterprise was identified as a distinct feature of the social economy which could contribute to the combating of social exclusion (HM Treasury 1999), and in 2001 a new Social Enterprise Unit was established within the then Department of Trade and Industry (DTI). Here, too, the idea was that, through the unit, government would provide support and policy direction for social enterprises as a new (third way) vehicle for achieving social change through independent organised activity (DTI 2002). In this case it was based on a loosely conceived model of businesses with a social purpose that reinvested its surplus in social or environmental purposes, rather than paying dividends to shareholders.

In 2006 these two strands of support were brought together as part of a broader strategic move to establish engagement with a wider conceptualisation of the third sector, embracing voluntary action, social enterprise and much more (as discussed above). The Active Communities Directorate and the Social Enterprise Unit were merged to form the new Office of the Third Sector and were relocated into the Cabinet Office, but with a focus on policy development and delivery for England only. There was concern in some quarters about the ability of a single office to cover the range of organisations and interests included within its new brief. This was accentuated for some when Campbell Robb was appointed as its first Director. Robb had previously worked in the NCVO and was seen by some as too closely associated with the voluntary organisations world – although in practice the OTS has been careful to ensure that it does engage with its broader constituency, for instance by identifying strategic partners recruited from agencies across the sector and by establishing an Advisory Body with wide-ranging representation.

The creation of the OTS has been symbolically important in raising the profile of third sector policy in England. However, its role remains one of coordination and development, rather than significant policy delivery. In practice, detailed aspects of relations between government and the third sector continue to be implemented by service Departments such as Communities and Local Government or Health, and indeed often by local rather than national government. The task for the OTS is to provide strategic guidance and organisational coordination (or 'joining up', to use the jargon). Some new vehicles now exist to support this, as discussed below, but this is still a challenging agenda within an overall government structure that remains heavily Department driven.

What has been most significant within these Departmental relations has been the greater involvement of the Treasury in leading, and supporting increasing funding of, third sector policy. The Treasury has always, of course, been a dominating influence over policy development because of its control of the purse strings of public finance. During the period of Gordon Brown's Chancellorship it became more politically powerful, too. A Charity and Third Sector Finance Unit was established within the Treasury, and third sector policy was the focus of a distinct cross-cutting review within the 2002 Comprehensive Spending Review (HM Treasury 2002).

One of the key themes of Treasury interest in third sector policy was to increase the scope for third sector organisations to play a role in the delivery of public services as part of the broader modernisation of service delivery towards choice and competition between providers within a mixed economy of welfare. Support for third sector organisations to increase their involvement in this has been a feature of some of the new horizontal policy initiatives in England. But it is not the only theme. Both the OTS and the Treasury have also embraced the support for social enterprise (Cabinet Office 2006) and both now emphasise the importance of the sector in promoting civic engagement and social renewal (Cabinet Office 2007a).

These policy themes have resulted in a range of new policy programmes in England to provide horizontal support to the sector, and to the third sector organisations operating within it. To some extent these new policy initiatives were a product of the recommendations made by the Deakin Commission (1996), and its Concordat idea was implemented in 1998 in the form of the compact, a national framework for government and sector relations (Home Office 1998). This was later followed by the establishment of local compacts at local authority level (Craig *et al* 2002), and also by codes of practice covering an increasingly wide range of relations, such as commissioning and procurement. The compact is not a legally enforceable document, and both nationally and locally there have been problems in ensuring that the guidance it provides is understood and operationalised by all. This led in 2007 to the establishment of a Commission for the Compact under the auspices of the OTS to promote its use and to oversee its implementation, and in 2009 to a formal review. The compact has not been without its problems, therefore, but is has provided a model that was replicated in the devolved administrations, and indeed has been widely copied internationally (Casey *et al* 2010).

The Deakin Commission had also recommended that the law on the definition and regulation of charities should be reviewed and updated, not least because it dated back to the seventeenth century. In 2006 this was implemented by the Charities Act, which simplified the definition of charities and more closely defined the need for all to demonstrate 'public benefit' in order to register with the Charity Commission and enjoy the benefits of tax relief. However, much of the practical implementation of this new definition was left to the Charity Commission to develop.

The Treasury's cross-cutting review of the sector in 2002 argued that increased funding for the sector was needed, 'to build capacity... and increase community participation' (HM Treasury 2002: ch.30). This led first to a £125m three-year programme of support for third sector organisations to invest in their capacity to engage with public agencies and deliver a wider range of services, called Futurebuilders, offering both small grants and investment loans to third sector organisations alongside advice and support on business planning and investment. Now called the Social Investment Business this programme has been extended with a further £215m from 2008 to 2011, and is administered by an independent agency called the Adventure Capital Fund, which also provides other sources of funding and support to the sector.

Futurebuilders was followed in 2004 by another funding initiative called ChangeUp. This provided another £150m initially over two years for support for the work of infrastructure agencies who would provide advice and guidance to third sector organisations either nationally or locally, followed by a further £88m to 2011. In 2007 administration of this initiative was handed to a non-departmental body called Capacitybuilders. Both the Futurebuilders and ChangeUp programmes are now formally the responsibility of the OTS. In 2009 the OTS and the Department for Communities and Local Government (CLG) announced a further programme, called Communitybuilders, with another £70m to invest in support for small community organisations. This is also to be administered by the Adventure Capital Fund.

These different 'building programmes' constitute a significant investment by government in horizontal support for the third sector. What is more, they have not replaced the 'vertical' support provided for third sector organisations operating within particular service fields. Indeed, there has been significant expansion here too, for instance in the £100m Social Enterprise Investment Fund provided by the Department of Health to support investment in social enterprises engaged in the delivery of health and social care services.

This new support for the sector has been welcomed by most both inside and outside government. In effect a new policy elite has been created here, comprised of the OTS officers and politicians, the independent agencies working in partnership with them and the leading sector infrastructure agencies who are both funded by these programmes and involved in implementing them. This is a policy environment within which partnership takes the form of personal networks as well as policy programmes. But it is one that is now exclusively English, for different programmes and different networks now operate within the devolved administrations.

Scotland

Information about the third sector in Scotland is provided by the SCVO, to some extent mirroring the data provided about England and the UK by the NCVO Almanac. The most recent data reveals that there were 44,000 third sector organisations in Scotland in 2006/7, of which 20,000 were registered as charities, housing associations or credit unions. Total income to the sector was £4.1bn, of which 39 per cent was public funding, higher than the UK average. The sector employed 129,000 staff, around 5 per cent of the country's workforce, again higher than the UK average. As in

England, though, most third sector organisations are small (65 per cent with annual turnover under £25k) and most funding is concentrated in a few large organisations (62 per cent going to the biggest 5 per cent) (SVCO 2009).

The third sector in Scotland has for some time been to a large extent separately organised and represented to the sector in England. As well as the separate SCVO and ACOSVO, mentioned earlier, there is the separate Scottish Social Enterprise Coalition (SSEC), set up in 2005, and a volunteering agency, Voluntary Development Scotland, which was established in 1984. At the organisational and political levels, therefore, the Scottish third sector is distinct from that in England, but closely related to it.

The third sector in Scotland is more extensively funded by government than the sector in England, with per capita public funding at £44 in 2005–6, compared to £40 in England (Cabinet Office 2007b). This is perhaps particularly significant given that the modernisation agenda of contracted-out public services and mixed economy providers has been less enthusiastically embraced north of the border. Much public support for the sector in Scotland is in practice provided by local government: 28 per cent of all funding comes from local authorities (SCVO 2009). This is supported by a Concordat with the Confederation of Scottish Local Authorities (COSLA) under which grants and other funding for third sector organisations were largely transferred to local authorities, and supported by new funding under a 'Fairer Scotland Fund'. It is also linked to a political emphasis on community-based voluntary action, which is of particular importance in the more remote rural areas of the Highlands where public sector infrastructure is sparse and third sector organisations sometimes provide a major focus for social relations.

There is thus a history of a more devolved third sector in Scotland, with more of a local focus for funding and activity, although this has led to a greater perceived dependence on public support (Vincent and Harrow 2005). The devolved structures of the Scottish Government have operated within and extended this context since 2000, developing a distinctly Scottish policy environment but one that compares closely in many respects with that which has been evolving in England. This is in part the result of a similar embracement of the need for broader changes in state and sector relations by policymakers and practitioners in Scotland following recommendations from a report by the Kemp Commission (Kemp 1997), commissioned by SCVO, which, despite some different structural elements, largely mirrored the work of the Deakin Commission in England.

A Third Sector Division has been created in Scotland, within the Directorate for Public Services Reform, with teams based in Edinburgh and Glasgow. This is smaller and potentially less influential than the English OTS but it has a similar remit. In particular, as in England, it now includes responsibility for promoting and supporting social enterprise. This broader approach is captured in the Action Plan for the sector published in 2008 (Scottish Government 2008), which talks about the need to promote an enterprising and thriving third sector in Scotland. But there is less emphasis than in England on the role of third sector organisations in delivering public services. The ministerial foreword to the Plan outlines three key roles for the sector in contributing to solidarity (social equity), cohesion (regional equity) and sustainability (inter-generational equity).

New horizontal programmes of financial support have also been developed in Scotland. In 2004 an £18m Futurebuilders Scotland programme was introduced by the then Scottish Executive, administered by a separate Social Economy Unit. Since then a number of other programmes have been introduced, linked to the new Action Plan, including a Scottish Investment Fund providing £30m for both grants and loans over 2008 to 2011, a £12m Third Sector Enterprise Fund and a £1m Social Entrepreneurs Fund, operating over much the same period. Charity law was also changed in Scotland along similar lines to England and Wales in the Charities and Trustee Investment (Scotland) Act 2005, and for the first time registration and regulation were introduced under a new body, the Office of the Scottish Charity Regulator (OSCR). There is also a Scottish Compact, modelled on the English one, introduced in 1999 and revised in 2003 (Scottish Government 2003).

Scotland thus has similar organisational forms and policy vehicles for third sector horizontal policy intervention to England – but set alongside a distinct and separate history and a greater focus on local support and community activity. It is too early to judge the effectiveness of these new vehicles. Evaluations have been commissioned but they have not yet reported (see Fyfe et al 2006). As in England, however, there is evidence of some problems. For instance, an early review of the compact found that 65 per cent of sector respondents found no change in relations and 50 per cent were unaware of its existence (Scottish Executive 2002).

Wales
Data on the third sector in Wales is less reliable than that in Scotland as quite a lot of information is gathered on an England and Wales basis as the same regulatory regime covers both. However, the WCVA does provide some data, partly grossed up from sample surveys. This puts the number of organisations at about 30,000, although the WCVA database itself comprised 26,000 organisations in 2007 (WCVA 2007).

Employment in the sector in Wales represents around 2.2 per cent of the total workforce, as in the UK more generally. Public funding provides around 43 per cent of income for the sector, a much higher proportion than the UK average, although overall per capita spending is similar to that in England (£41, compared to £40, in 2005–5 [Cabinet Office 2007b]). The evidence also suggests that a larger proportion of the Welsh third sector is made up of small local organisations relying heavily on a volunteer labour force, with fewer large national organisations, as these are perhaps more likely to be located in England (Day 2009).

There is to some extent a separate infrastructural framework for the sector in Wales, with the WCVA representing voluntary organisations and Community Enterprise Wales the social enterprise field. But other agencies, such as ACEVO, operate across England and Wales. The extent of devolution of policy and practice is also different in Wales to that in Scotland and Northern Ireland. The 1998 Government of Wales Act placed a statutory duty on the Welsh Assembly Government (WAG) to promote the interest of voluntary organisations in the exercise of all its functions. This is a clearer and broader provision than in the other devolution settlements, and requires the WAG to promote third sector activity across all its functions. However, this broad spread of responsibility has militated against the development of strong central policy steer (and funding) as in the other administrations, with third sector policy and practice being more defused across the policy landscape, and much activity focused on key policy areas such as equalities and civic engagement.

Much policy delivery in Wales is therefore channelled through service Departments, with horizontal policy initiatives relatively under-developed. In some areas, too, policy and practice remain located in England, as separate regulatory powers have not been delegated. In particular, for instance, charity regulation and the work of the Charity Commission operate across England and Wales. And although there is a separate compact for Wales, latterly known as the Voluntary Sector Scheme, it was first introduced by the UK government in 1999, modelled on the one introduced at the same time in England, and later enshrined in the 2006 Government of Wales Act as part of a restructuring of relations between the sector and the WAG.

Nevertheless, there have been some moves to develop distinct Welsh vehicles for the promotion and support of third sector activity in the country. There is a small Third Sector Unit based in the Communities Directorate in the Department for Social Justice and Local Government, and formed, as in England, by the merger in 2009 of the former voluntary sector unit with a social economy unit. Third sector policy therefore embraces promotion of social enterprise, and a strategy for social enterprise in Wales was published in 2005 (WAG 2005). There is also a Third Sector Partnership Council (formerly the Voluntary Sector Partnership Council), chaired by the Minister and with 25 third sector representatives to advise on policy development and implementation. In particular the focus of the Partnership is on the implementation of a 'Strategic Action Plan' for the sector published by the WAG in 2008. This plan outlines the elements of a horizontal policy agenda for the third sector in Wales to implement the Voluntary Sector Scheme, based on measures to empower people and communities and the establishment of frameworks to implement these (WAG 2008), with a series of targets over the period up to 2011.

However, there are not the same horizontal funding programmes in Wales that can be found in England and Scotland, with much responsibility for delivery and funding resting in the hands of service Departments and in the established links with key sector agencies such as WCVA, which recently had a five year partnership agreement with the WAG extended. And the statutory duty to promote equality in Wales has led to a more active role for third sector organisations in campaigning and representation on issues such as gender, race, faith and disability (Chaney 2009).

Northern Ireland

The political and organisational history of Northern Ireland is distinct from the rest of the UK's and, at times of course, a troubled one. For these political and cultural (and to some extent geographical) reasons, the third sector in the province has always been relatively separate from that in the rest of the UK. The sector has been represented since the 1930s by NICVA, which now collects and publishes data about the size and structure of voluntary action, the most recent version being the 2009 almanac, *State of the Sector V* (NICVA 2009). This reveals that in 2008 there were 4,700 voluntary and community organisations in the province, with a total income of £570m. This was a decline in income from 2005 and is evidence of some critical financial pressures on the sector in Northern Ireland. 46 per cent of this funding was from government, again much higher than in England, and matched by the much higher proportion of public expenditure as a proportion of economic activity in the province more generally. As a result, per capita spending on the sector is also much higher, at £67 in 2005–6 (Cabinet Office 2007b). The sector employed around 27,000 people in 2008, 3.9 per cent of the total Northern Ireland workforce, again a higher proportion than in the rest of the UK.

One of the reasons for the decline in funding for the third sector in Northern Ireland has been the severe reduction in funding from the European Union Special Peace and Reconciliation Programme, down from £82m in 1997 to £58m in 2005 and to £10.6m in 2008 (NICVA 2009). This funding was largely tied to support for the peace process in the province following the end of sectarian conflict in the mid 1990s and the Good Friday agreement of 1998. Much of the focus of EU funding was on third sector organisations and the role that they could play in (re)building community links and civil society relations in Northern Ireland, including cross border relations with the Republic of Ireland. This was also the focus of much UK Government policy planning and support in the province, accentuated by the limited role of local government in Northern Ireland and the weak and divided nature of much local democracy.

This support for voluntary action in the building of a new civil society in Northern Ireland has been a central feature of its recent history, and provides a distinct and different context to that in the rest of the UK (see Birrell and Williamson 2001). Much more has been expected of the sector by government there, and much more support has been provided, including to infrastructure agencies such as NICVA. This support has also been more closely tied to policy intervention to combat discrimination. This applies in particular to discrimination across sectarian lines but has had a more general impact in foregrounding anti-discrimination practice in the aims and structures of many voluntary and community organisations.

This history has also meant that horizontal support for a strategic role for the sector was developed early in the province, with a strategic policy approach towards the voluntary and community sector commencing in the mid 1990s, and influencing the work of the Deakin Commission in England. But as this support has reduced, in particular the EU funding streams, the strength and sustainability of the sector have been challenged. As a result the sector faces cuts in public funding sources in the near future.

Public policy towards the sector is itself also in large part a product of the peace settlement and the, somewhat fitful, process of devolution within the province. Despite its distinct history and culture, Northern Ireland was governed by direct rule from Westminster until the end of the 1990s – a process referred to in the province as 'helicopter rule' (Acheson 2009). Following the Good Friday Agreement legislation was passed to introduce devolved government from 2000, through the Northern Ireland Assembly and the Office of the First Minister and Deputy First Minister. The structure of the devolved administration was based on a complex political settlement and a parcelling out of roles and responsibilities between the leading political parties in the province.

Despite this complex politics, however, devolved rule collapsed in political conflict in 2002 and direct rule was reinstated until agreement between the two leading parties was again reached in 2007 and devolution of powers restored. One of the consequences of this was the imposition on Northern Ireland of English or UK policy initiatives, including a Northern Ireland compact, *Building Real Partnership* (DHSS 1998), implemented in 2001 and almost identical to the English compact. Charity law reform is still to be implemented in the province, although following a consultation led by the Department for Social Development (DSD) and the passing of the Charities Act (Northern Ireland) in 2008, an Order in Council was implemented in 2009 to permit registration and regulation and the establishment of a Charity Commission for Northern Ireland.

Another consequence of the Good Friday settlement has been to create vested interests among politicians in the governance and departmental structures established by devolution. Within this there remains a separation of responsibility for the voluntary and community sector, which is overseen by the Voluntary and Community Unit within DSD, and social enterprise, which is referred to as the social economy and is the responsibility of a small Social Economy Unit within the Department of Enterprise, Trade and Development (DETI). This separation of third sector policy practice has resulted in a distinct but fragmented policy environment for the sector in Northern Ireland. However, it is unlikely to be challenged because the sclerosis in governance structures created by the Good Friday agreement means that any transfer of departmental responsibilities is likely to be resisted as a threat to the influence of those politicians (and senior officers) affected.

Broad-based horizontal policy programmes are thus less well developed in Northern Ireland. The Voluntary and Community Unit (VCU), which was first established in 1993 and transferred to DSD in 1998, has responsibility for traditional voluntary and community action, including the administration of the EU peace initiative funding. The VCU has worked closely with the key sector agencies in the province, in particular

NICVA and CO3, which are funded by the unit to promote the sector and deliver public funding. Within this there has been a significant focus on combating discrimination, for instance through high levels of support for women's organisations. However, with the decline in EU funding and other pressures on budgets within DSD, there is likely to be a decline in public funding for the sector in the near future and this is likely to be accompanied by a shift towards a greater focus on a public service delivery agenda (DSD 2005).

Support for the social economy is delivered by the Social Economy Unit in DETI, working through a Social Economy Policy Group of representatives from the other major service departments, and engaging with the sector via a Social Economy Forum. This includes funding, currently until 2011, for the Social Economy Network (SEN), the umbrella body for social enterprises in Northern Ireland established in 2006.

Despite these different governance structures, however, much of the policy development for the third sector in Northern Ireland has been a rolling out of policy initiatives developed in England. This was particularly the case during the re-imposition of direct rule from 2002 to 2007. Since 2007 policy development by the new Assembly has been slow and in some cases, such as charity regulation, still dominated by UK agendas. Whether or not a new and distinct policy environment will flow from the greater devolution of power since 2007 remains to be seen therefore, but, unfortunately perhaps, it may be dominated by potential reductions in public funding and withdrawal of resources for some of the horizontal support provided through infrastructure agencies. There is fear in some third sector quarters that this may accentuate differences between 'insider' organisations, with strong policy networks and records of relatively high public funding, and 'outsiders', smaller organisations operating on the margins of core policy concerns (Acheson 2009). Given the central role accorded in the past to voluntary action in community empowerment and the building of peace and democracy in Northern Ireland, this could be potentially damaging for coordinated development of the sector in the future.

Conclusions

Devolution of policy to promote and support third sector activity has been a significant, if not widely explored, aspect of the devolved and diverging policy landscape to be found in the UK since the creation of separate government structures in Scotland, Wales and Northern Ireland. As can be seen from the analysis developed in this chapter, this has resulted in the creation of four separate policy regimes for the third sector across the four countries of the UK. What is more, these governance and policy differences have been developed for, and with, third sector practice communities that already had distinct histories, structures and cultures within the four nations. So national distinction in third sector policy and practice is not simply a product of twenty-first century devolution.

The devolution of policymaking has led to largely separate governance structures within the four nations. Each now has its own offices, units or divisions providing support and guidance for third sector activity, based on different models in each: a central, and relatively powerful, Cabinet Office department in England, a third sector division in Scotland, a small coordinating group in Wales, and a separation between support for voluntary and community activity and social enterprise in Northern Ireland. Flowing from this are significant differences in policy regimes, too – in England promotion of third sector organisations as providers within a mixed economy has been central, in Scotland much support for organisations is provided through local government, in Wales policy responsibility and delivery largely lies with service departments, and in Northern Ireland there has been direct engagement with third sector umbrella agencies which may in the future be under threat.

However, these divergences in policy regimes have not necessarily resulted in differences in policy discourse. Despite the different governance and delivery structures the broad direction of third sector policy has been remarkably similar, and builds on the longer history of state and third sector relations within the UK discussed earlier. In all countries there has been a significant shift in the new century towards a discourse of partnership between the state and the third sector, together with an embracement of the larger and more inclusive model of the sector itself. This has resulted in particular in a commitment by government to the development of strategic policy intervention, including for instance the introduction of compacts to provide a framework for state and sector relations. And linked to these strategies has been the provision of horizontal support for third sector organisations to help to build their capacity to meet the new opportunities and relationships now on offer – although the extent and delivery of these does vary across the four nations. Regulatory changes have also been introduced in all, in particular new requirements for achievement of charitable status and procedures for formal monitoring of charity registration.

It is still rather early to judge how significant the impact of these new policy regimes will be on the structure and operation of third sector activity across the four nations. However, the overwhelming impact of devolution within the three new administrations has been the requirement (and opportunity) that this has presented for the sector to engage with the new devolved policy agencies and practices. This is especially noticeable in Scotland and Wales, as separate government agencies have existed in some form for longer in Northern Ireland; in Wales it has been further accentuated by the restructuring following the Government of Wales Act in 2006. Devolution has created a new politics focused on the need to engage with changed government, and in effect has accentuated the national distinctiveness of the third sector itself, especially in Scotland and Wales.

In addition, however, some common themes are also emerging in all four countries. First, partnership is a two-way relationship and the capacity of all third sector organisations to engage in active partnership with the state, and to shape and benefit from it, varies significantly. Many practitioners in the sector are worried about the potential accentuation of distinctions between insider and outsider organisations, with only the former able to engage actively with the new governance and policy environment – the problem of exclusion. Linked to this are concerns about the independence, and distinctive ethos, of any organisations that engage closely with, and in particular are largely funded by and accountable to, the state – the problems of incorporation and isomorphism. The challenge to third sector independence was explored in a collection of papers sponsored by the Baring Foundation, which compared the different experiences of the four UK nations with a small number of other western industrial countries (Smerdon 2009). All concluded that independence could be threatened by extensive engagement with the state.

Conversely, however, the new UK policy regimes have provided a higher political profile for the third sector than it has enjoyed for at least a century. The levels of support provided by all four governments are unprecedented and have made real differences to the capacity and effectiveness of many organisations. What is more, the engagement between policymakers and sector leaders in the development and delivery of these programmes of support has created new and active political links and networks – indeed, it has led to the creation of new policy elites, which now exercise considerable power and influence over the sector in each of the four countries. Here too, of course, there are fears about insider status in, and outsider exclusion from, these new political networks, but in itself this provides opportunities and challenges for sector practitioners. Making partnership work is now on the agenda for most third sector actors.

Perhaps the final question to be posed is: to what extent has devolution led to new and significant differences in policy and practice for the third sector across the four countries of the UK? Or, to put this more bluntly, is it still Westminster and Whitehall that set the policy agenda? The answer must be a cautious one, not least because the picture is ever changing. However, on current assessment, although there is evidence of significant structural change in the forums for engagement flowing from devolution, there has been less to suggest significant policy divergence within these, with English policy initiatives still pervading across the new national borders.

The author gratefully acknowledges the support of the Economic and Social Research Council (ESRC), the Office of the Third Sector (OTS) and the Barrow Cadbury UK Trust in preparing this chapter, which was done as part of the programme of the joint ESRC, OTS Barrow Cadbury Third Sector Research Centre.

References

Acheson N (2009) 'Northern Ireland and the independence of the voluntary sector', in Smerdon M (ed.) *The First Principle of Voluntary Action: Essays on the independence of the voluntary sector in Canada, England, Germany, Northern Ireland, Scotland, United States of America and Wales*, London: The Baring Foundation

Alcock P and Scott D (2007) 'Voluntary and community sector welfare', in Powell M (ed.) *Understanding the Mixed Economy of Welfare*, Bristol: The Policy Press

Birrell D and Williamson A (2001) 'The Voluntary–Community Sector and Political Development in Northern Ireland, since 1972', *Voluntas*, 12.3, pp.205-20

Blair T (1998) *The Third Way*, London, Fabian Society

Brown G (2004) Speech to NCVO Annual Conference

Cabinet Office (2006) *Social Exclusion Action Plan: Scaling New Heights*, London: The Stationery Office

Cabinet Office (2007a) *The future role of the third sector in social and economic regeneration: final report July 2007*, London: The Stationery Office

Cabinet Office (2007b) *Estimates of Central Government Expenditure on Voluntary and Community Organisations, 2004-05 to 2005-06*, London: The Stationery Office

Casey J, Dalton B, Melville R and Onxy J (2010) 'Strengthening Government-Nonprofit Relations: International Experiences with Compacts', *Voluntary Sector Review*, 1.1, forthcoming

Chaney P (2009) 'Devolved Governance and the Political Participation of Equalities Organisations in Public Policy Making in Wales', Paper to VSSN Day Conference, Belfast, May 2009

Craig G, Taylor M and Parkes T (2004) 'Protest or Partnership? The Voluntary and Community Sectors in the Policy Process', *Social Policy and Administration*, 38.3, pp.221-39

Craig G, Taylor M, Wilkinson M and Monro S (2002) *Contract or Trust? The role of compacts in local governance*, Bristol: The Policy Press

Day G (2009) 'The independence of the voluntary sector in Wales', in Smerdon M (ed.) *The First Principle of Voluntary Action: essays on the independence of the voluntary sector in Canada, England, Germany, Northern Ireland, Scotland, United States of America and Wales*, London: The Baring Foundation

Deakin N (2001) *In Search of Civil Society*, Basingstoke: Palgrave

Deakin Commission (1996) *Meeting the Challenge of Change: Voluntary Action into the 21st Century, Report of the Commission on the Future of the Voluntary Sector in England*, London: NCVO

Department for Social Development (DSD) (2005) *Partners for Change: Government's Strategy for Support of the Voluntary and community Sector*, Belfast: DSD

Department for Trade and Industry (DTI) (2002) *Social Enterprise: a Strategy for Success*, London: DTI

Department of Health and Social Services (DHSS) (1998) *Building Real Partnership: Compact between Government and the Voluntary and Community Sector in Northern Ireland*, Belfast: DHSS

Evers A and Laville J-L (Eds.) (2004) *The Third Sector in Europe*, Cheltenham: Edward Elgar

Fyfe N, Timbrell H and Smith F (2006) 'The third sector in a devolved Scotland: from policy to evidence', *Critical Social Policy*, 26.3, pp.630-41

HM Treasury (1999) *Enterprise and Social Exclusion: National Strategy for Neighbourhood Renewal, Policy Action Team 3*, London: HM Treasury

HM Treasury (2002) *The Role of the Voluntary and Community Sector in Service Delivery: A Cross Cutting Review*, London: HM Treasury

HM Treasury (2004) *Voluntary and Community Sector Review 2004: Working Together, Better Together,* London: HM Treasury

HM Treasury (2009) *Putting the Frontline First: Smarter government* London: HM Treasury

Home Office (1998) *Compact on Relations between Government and the Voluntary and Community Sector in England, Cm. 4100,* London: The Stationery Office

Home Office (2003) *Building Civil Renewal: Government support for community capacity building and proposals for change,* London: Home Office

Home Office (2004) *ChangeUp: Capacity Building and Infrastructure Framework for the Voluntary and Community Sector,* London: Home Office

Kane D et al (2009) *The UK Civil Society Almanac 2009,* London: NCVO

Keating M (2002) 'Devolution and public policy in the United Kingdom: divergence of convergence?', in Adams J and Robinson P (eds.) *Devolution in Practice: Public Policy difference within the UK,* London: ippr